O SECURE

THE LIBERTY

OF THE

PEOPLE

O SECURE THE

Liberty

OF THE PEOPLE

James Madison's

Bill of Rights and

the Supreme Court's

Interpretation

ERIC T. KASPER

Northern Illinois University Press / DeKalb

© 2010 by Northern Illinois University Press

Published by the Northern Illinois University Press, DeKalb, Illinois 60115

Manufactured in the United States using postconsumer-recycled, acid-free paper.

All Rights Reserved

Design by Julia Fauci

Frontispiece: "James Madison" by Catherine A. Drinker, after Gilbert Stuart, 1875. Courtesy of Independence National Historical Park

Library of Congress Cataloging-in-Publication Data

Kasper, Eric T.

To secure the liberty of the people : James Madison's Bill of Rights and the Supreme Court's interpretation / Eric T. Kasper.

　　p.　　cm.

Includes bibliographical references and index.

ISBN 978-0-87580-421-7 (clothbound : alk. paper)

1. United States. Constitution. 1st–10th Amendments—History. 2. Constitutional history—United States. 3. Civil rights—United States—History. 4. Madison, James, 1751–1836—Influence. 5. United States. Supreme Court. I. Title.

KF4749.K365 2010

342.7302'9—dc22

2010001725

Dedicated to Julie

Contents

ACKNOWLEDGMENTS

As in the successful completion of any major work, I have been privileged to have the financial, intellectual, and emotional support of many people while writing this manuscript. First, I must express my gratitude to Northern Illinois University Press for agreeing to publish this book and for working with me to improve it for publication. In particular, I would like to thank my editor, Sara Hoerdeman, with whom it has been a pleasure to work, and the rest of the staff at NIU Press, most notably Susan Bean and Julia Fauci. Financially, I am indebted to the Lynde and Harry Bradley Foundation, which provided me with a generous fellowship when I was writing an early draft of this work as my doctoral dissertation.

The intellectual support I have received has been vast. All members of my dissertation committee provided valuable advice: Leonard Kaplan, Herbert M. Kritzer, Richard Boyd, Howard Schweber, and Donald Downs. Don is responsible more than anyone else for helping me turn vague ideas about James Madison, the Bill of Rights, and the Supreme Court into a legible manuscript. I would also like to thank the peer reviewers who gave me thoughtful insights to improve the work: John Vile, James Read, and David Siemers.

I cannot begin to express my thanks and appreciation to my family. My in-laws, Dick and Carol Wegner, have always been supportive. My father, Clint, instilled a work ethic in me at a very young age, something that was quite important as I was finishing this publication. My mother, Sharon, has always encouraged my love of learning, and I know she will be eager to read this text. My daughter, Maddie, at a young age has shown that she has developed patience, tolerating me constantly telling her, "Just wait one more minute while I type up this sentence." Most importantly, none of this would have been possible without the love and support from my wife, Julie. She has left an indelible mark of her own on this manuscript, from reading through the first draft to providing me with the emotional support to finish writing it. She has always helped me pursue my dreams, and I could not imagine life without her.

Finally, I must acknowledge James Madison, who inspired not just this work but also its title, *To Secure the Liberty of the People*. The words are derived from the speech Madison gave when he introduced the Bill of Rights in Congress. When describing the different types of freedoms he was proposing to become a bill of rights, Madison stated, "Trial by jury cannot be considered as a natural right, but a right resulting from a social compact which regulates the action of the community, but is as essential *to secure the liberty of the people* as any one of the pre-existent rights of nature." These lines tie together three major elements of this book: Madison's multifaceted liberal political theory, the Bill of Rights, and the courts. As is often the case throughout this book, I could not write it better than Madison, so I borrowed his words here.

O SECURE

THE LIBERTY

OF THE

PEOPLE

PART I

James Madison

One

THE SUPREME COURT, THE BILL OF RIGHTS, AND JAMES MADISON

The Bill of Rights is perhaps the most revered document in the pantheon of American governing texts, having an almost mythical quality about it. For more than two hundred years it has been cited by a multitude of groups to defend their various rights, including civil rights leaders and the Ku Klux Klan, neo-Nazis and socialists, pacifists and gun owners, major newspapers and street preachers, homeowners and renters, women seeking abortions and abortion protesters, and the innocent and the guilty alike.

Given the high regard many have for the liberties protected in the Bill of Rights, one could easily imagine that it was handed down from Mount Olympus by Zeus or perhaps that God decreed it to Moses on Mount Sinai. One could envision President George Washington, the general who had won the Revolution and who towered over most of his contemporaries at six feet two inches tall, going in front of Congress and announcing the rights that should be protected in the Constitution. Or one could even picture Thomas Jefferson, the six-feet-three-inches-tall, red-locked, world-traveling "Sage of Monticello" penning the Bill of Rights much like he drafted the eloquent language of the Declaration of Independence. Indeed, any of these stories would be fitting for a document that has been cited by so many as protecting some of the liberties that we hold so dear.

However, none of the above stories is true. Instead, James Madison introduced the Bill of Rights in Congress and was instrumental in ushering the document through that legislative body. Physically, Madison was not a godlike Zeus or even a demigod like Jefferson. Instead, he stood five feet three inches tall and weighed barely one hundred pounds.[1] Madison was not a god who created the heavens, nor did he lead the new nation to victory in the Revolutionary War like Washington. Rather, Madison had his minute service in the Revolutionary Army cut short by ailments, and he suffered from serious health problems throughout his life.[2] Unlike

Jefferson, Benjamin Franklin, and Patrick Henry, Madison was not a flamboyant man, nor was he known for giving captivating or eloquent speeches. To the contrary, Madison almost always wore black clothing in public, and his speeches were frequently heavy on logic, low on inspiration, and at times barely audible.[3]

Although Madison was not a classically mythical figure like so many others of the Founding generation, he was one of the most important Founders. This is especially true with freedoms protected by the Bill of Rights, where no name is mentioned as often as Madison's. This should come as no surprise, as Madison concentrated on protecting liberty throughout his political career: Madison offered a major amendment to the 1776 Virginia Provincial Constitution in support of the equal rights of conscience; he wrote a "Memorial and Remonstrance against Religious Assessments" arguing against the use of tax dollars for the funding of religion in Virginia; he wrote how he believed the Constitution would harness the ill effects of factions based on property; he gave speeches in Congress to defend the rights of Democratic-Republican Societies that spoke out in support of France and the Whiskey Rebellion in the 1790s; he wrote newspaper articles in defense of strong property rights; he championed the freedoms of speech and press during the Alien and Sedition Acts controversy; and as president he vetoed congressional grants to religious institutions on the grounds that the acts violated the separation of church and state. Indeed, Madison spent a great deal of time in his political career trying to promote and protect freedoms now enshrined in the Bill of Rights. Madison was the driving force behind the Bill during the first Congress, and without Madison's leadership we may not have the Bill of Rights at all. At the very least, without Madison our Bill of Rights would have been drastically different and perhaps much less protective of many of the freedoms we value so highly.

MADISON'S USE BY THE UNITED STATES SUPREME COURT

Since Madison wrote and spoke about the freedoms protected in the Bill of Rights so often, it is easy to find things said by him that support different versions of what the Bill protects. The U.S. Supreme Court, the highest court in the United States and the final expositor of the Constitution, cannot make up its collective mind as to what Madison wanted to protect when he introduced the Bill of Rights in Congress. Instead, the history of the Court is replete with justices invoking Madison to support various interpretations of provisions of the Bill of Rights. Even today, the justices frequently make use of Madison in disputes over the First Amendment, property rights, and the rights of the criminally accused. The subjects where the justices use Madison to support their different interpretations include some of the most provocative and controversial constitutional topics today: government postings of the Ten Commandments, campaign finance reform, eminent domain, and the suppression of evidence. The justices have vigorously disputed what Madison believed and what his vision was for these freedoms.

For example, Madison drafted the Establishment Clause in 1789, and it was ratified as part of the First Amendment in 1791, reading, "Congress shall make no law respecting an establishment of religion." When interpreting the Establishment Clause, the justices on the Supreme Court generally fall into two categories. Some claim that Madison wanted a great deal of separation between church and state; others, that Madison wanted government only to refrain from giving one religion preference over others. This disagreement was squarely faced by the justices in *Rosenberger v. Rector* (1995), a case that involved the disbursement of student activity fees to organizations at the University of Virginia. The university had a policy in which it used student fees to reimburse student organizations for costs they incurred in extracurricular activities. At issue in *Rosenberger* was the request of student funds by a group called Wide Awake Publications (WAP) for its Christian-perspective journal, *Wide Awake*. WAP was denied university funds by the student government on the grounds that *Wide Awake* was a religious activity, and funding such activity would violate the Establishment Clause. WAP then sued the University of Virginia, claiming discrimination. In *Rosenberger,* the Court held that the university's denial of funds to a religious organization, when it funded other campus groups, violated the free speech rights of WAP. Furthermore, the majority found no Establishment Clause violation if the group were allowed to use funds from the university.[4]

Justice Clarence Thomas wrote a concurring opinion in *Rosenberger,* agreeing with the Court majority's conclusions but not all of the majority's reasoning. Thomas began by citing Madison's opposition to the Virginia Assessment Bill. The assessment was introduced in the Virginia Assembly in 1784 by Patrick Henry. If passed, the assessment would have provided for the collection of a tax to be given to churches in Virginia for educational purposes. However, the Assessment Bill was defeated, in part owing to the influence of petitions such as Madison's 1785 "Memorial and Remonstrance against Religious Assessments" (hereafter "Memorial and Remonstrance"). Thomas claimed that Madison did not oppose the tax in principle but only because it "violated that equality which ought to be the basis of every law."[5] Thomas seized upon the following line from the "Memorial and Remonstrance": "Who does not see that the same authority which can establish Christianity, in exclusion of all other Religions, may establish with the same ease any particular sect of Christians, in exclusion of all other Sects."[6] For Thomas, the tenor of Madison's "Memorial and Remonstrance" was very clear: the chief flaw of the religious "tax" was its unequal application among different religious sects.

However, Thomas also had to deal with language in the "Memorial and Remonstrance" that was more sweeping and indicated more of a "separation of church and state" approach by Madison. For instance, Madison stated in his "Memorial and Remonstrance," "It is the duty of every man to render to the Creator such homage, and such only, as he believes to be acceptable to him. This duty is precedent both in order of time and degree of obligation, to the claims of Civil Society."[7] Likewise, Madison opposed the religious assessment in his "Memorial and Remonstrance," in part, because such assessments and establishments have led to, "more or less in all places, pride and indolence in the Clergy; ignorance and servility in the laity; in both, superstition, bigotry and persecution."[8] These passages suggest that Madison opposed *all* religious assessments, whether they were based on the principle of equality or not. Thomas dismissed the relevance of these points by stating,

> Even if more extreme notions of the separation of church and state can be attributed to Madison, many of them clearly stem from arguments reflecting the concepts of natural law, natural rights, and the social contract between government and a civil society, rather than the principle of nonestablishment in the Constitution. In any event, the views of one man do not establish the original understanding of the First Amendment.[9]

Although this passage seems to make Thomas's earlier discussion of Madison moot, Thomas had a clear point: since the "Memorial and Remonstrance" was written before the Establishment Clause, any appeal that Madison made to the Virginia assessment violating natural law was irrelevant after the ratification of the First Amendment. Furthermore, even if Madison wanted more separation, Madison was only one of the framers of the Establishment Clause, so his views were far from dispositive on its meaning. According to Thomas,

> Even if Madison believed that the principle of nonestablishment of religion precluded government financial support for religion per se (in the sense of government benefits specifically targeting religion), there is no indication that at the time of the framing [of the Bill of Rights] he took the dissent's extreme view that the government must discriminate against religious adherents by excluding them from more generally available financial subsidies.[10]

Thomas negated any of Madison's statements contrary to his understanding of establishment by claiming that Madison made many of those statements in 1785 when discussing the Virginia assessment, not in 1789 when proposing the Establishment Clause. Thus, Thomas believed that Madison would have supported the constitutionality of the program in

Rosenberger. To the extent that Madison said otherwise, it is irrelevant.

Justice David Souter wrote a dissenting opinion in *Rosenberger.* Souter directly challenged Thomas's interpretation of Madison, maintaining that Madison was a stronger advocate of the separation of church and state than Thomas had allowed. Souter began with the following Madison quote: "Who does not see that . . . the same authority which can force a citizen to contribute three pence only of his property for the support of any one establishment, may force him to conform to any other establishment in all cases whatsoever?"[11] For Souter, Madison was fearful of tyrannical, runaway public spending for religious purposes, because a small crack in the wall of separation between church and state could eventually cause the whole wall to crumble. Souter then alleged that "Madison's Remonstrance captured the colonists' 'conviction that individual religious liberty could be achieved best under a government which was stripped of all power to tax, to support, or otherwise to assist any or all religions, or to interfere with the beliefs of any religious individual or group,'" and that this vision of religious liberty was responsible for the defeat of the assessment and the enactment of the subsequent Virginia Bill for Establishing Religious Freedom (two events for which Madison was heavily responsible).[12] Justice Souter, in a footnote, then attacked Thomas's view of Madison: "Madison strongly inveighed against the proposed aid for religion for a host of reasons . . . many of those reasons would have applied whether or not the state aid was being distributed equally among sects, and whether or not the aid was going to those sects in the context of an evenhanded government program."[13] Thus, Souter understood Madison as supporting a view of the Establishment Clause that would have denied funding to WAP in *Rosenberger.*

Note how stark the contrast is between the competing visions of Madison in *Rosenberger.* Although Thomas and Souter examine the same piece of writing by Madison, their interpretations are radically different and lead to opposite conclusions. Has one or both of these two justices committed a serious error in interpreting Madison's "Memorial and Remonstrance"? Are they each using the piece to support some type of ideological agenda? At the very least, there are some rather disturbing inconsistencies in the interpretation of Madison by these two justices.

Another example of the justices disagreeing over Madison involved the rights of the accused in *United States v. Verdugo-Urquidez* (1990). Rene Martin Verdugo-Urquidez was a Mexican citizen believed by the Drug Enforcement Agency (DEA) to be the head of a violent organization that smuggled drugs from Mexico into the United States. The DEA obtained an arrest warrant for Verdugo-Urquidez and went into Mexico to arrest him. After arresting Verdugo-Urquidez, DEA agents conducted a search of his houses in Mexico. Since the DEA agents searched without a warrant, Verdugo-Urquidez moved to suppress the seized evidence, based on the Fourth Amendment: "The right of the people to be secure in their persons, houses, papers, and effects, against unreasonable searches and seizures, shall not be violated, and no warrants shall issue, but upon probable cause, supported by oath or affirmation, and particularly describing the place to be searched, and the persons or things to be seized." In *Verdugo-Urquidez* the Court ruled that the Fourth Amendment protection of "people" from unreasonable searches and seizures did not apply to the search and seizure by U.S. agents of property that was owned by a nonresident alien and located in a foreign country.[14]

Writing for the majority, Chief Justice William Rehnquist stated that the Fourth Amendment's purpose "was to restrict searches and seizures which might be conducted by the United States in domestic matters."[15] Accordingly, "[t]he Framers originally decided not to include a provision like the Fourth Amendment, because they believed the National Government lacked power to conduct searches and seizures. *See* . . . 1 Annals of Cong. 437 (1789) (statement of J. Madison)."[16] Rehnquist then explained how Madison was fearful that Congress would abuse citizens' rights by passing laws under the Constitution's Necessary and Proper Clause: "Madison . . . argued that 'there is a clause granting to Congress the power to make all laws which shall be necessary and proper for carrying into execution all of the powers vested in the Government of the United States,' and that general warrants might be considered 'necessary' for the purpose of collecting revenue."[17] Based on this, Rehnquist concluded that

> The driving force behind the adoption of the Amendment, as suggested by Madison's advocacy, was widespread hostility among the former colonists to the issuance of writs of assistance empowering revenue officers to search suspected places for smuggled goods, and general search warrants permitting the search of private houses, often to uncover papers that might be used to convict persons of libel. The available historical data show, therefore, that the purpose of the Fourth Amendment was to protect the people of the United States against arbitrary action by their own Government; it was never suggested that the provision was intended to restrain the actions of the Federal Government against aliens outside of the United States territory.[18]

Thus, Rehnquist invoked Madison's statements in defense of a narrow, "citizen-only" interpretation of the Fourth Amendment. He did not focus on Verdugo-Urquidez as a rights-bearing individual but, rather, on the needs of American citizens to be protected against actions by their own government.

Justice William Brennan dissented in *Verdugo-Urquidez,* and concluded that Verdugo-Urquidez in this case was one of "the people" for Fourth Amendment purposes. According to Brennan, an alien is "entitled to the protections of the Fourth Amendment because our Government, by investigating him and attempting to hold him accountable under United States criminal laws, has treated him as a member of our community for purposes of enforcing our laws. He has become, quite literally, one of the governed."[19] Brennan claimed that this position of mutuality, where the government is to respect aliens' Fourth Amendment rights if we expect aliens to obey our laws, is one that Madison supported:

> James Madison, universally recognized as the primary architect of the Bill of Rights, emphasized the importance of mutuality when he spoke out against the Alien and Sedition Acts less than a decade after the adoption of the Fourth Amendment: "It does not follow, because aliens are not parties to the Constitution, as citizens are parties to it, that, whilst they actually conform to it, they have no right to its protection. Aliens are not more parties to the laws than they are parties to the Constitution; yet it will not be disputed that, as they owe, on one hand, a temporary obedience, they are entitled, in return, to their protection and advantage."[20]

For Brennan, this statement was evidence that Madison wanted an expansive view of Fourth Amendment rights, including the application of those rights to individual aliens.

The *Verdugo-Urquidez* case involved disagreement between the justices over whether Madison was a strong proponent of the rights of the accused or a believer in stronger powers for law enforcement. Rehnquist and Brennan used Madison to justify vastly different interpretations of criminal procedural rights. Much like the example from *Rosenberger,* this raises the question, why?

It would not matter much if *Rosenberger* and *Verdugo-Urquidez* were isolated cases, rare instances in which the justices differed over Madison. But justices on the Supreme Court have used Madison's words to validate their reasoning in Bill of Rights cases many times over its history. In total, Madison has been cited in 230 opinions (majority, plurality, concurrence, or dissent) written by 38 different justices between 1869 and 2009. The Supreme Court's use of Madison has been a constant in recent years, as 12 of the 16 justices serving on the Court during the Rehnquist and Roberts Courts (1986–2009) have utilized Madison in 65 different opinions and in a variety of areas in Bill of Rights cases.

Take, for example, the Establishment Clause of the First Amendment: "Congress shall make no law respecting an establishment of religion." One prominent theory of interpreting this amendment is called separationism, which states that the Establishment Clause placed a high wall of separation between religion and government in order to sever relations as much as possible between the two. This was the theory espoused by Justice Souter above. The other major Establishment Clause theory is nonpreferentialism, which simply advocates for government to treat all religions in an equal and neutral manner, as Justice Thomas argued.

There have been 56 Establishment Clause opinions over the Supreme Court's history that reference Madison, some claiming him as a separationist and others as a nonpreferentialist. Since the beginning of the Rehnquist Court in 1986, there have been 24 opinions in Establishment Clause cases referring to Madison. Madison has been cited by the justices when discussing this clause more than for any other passage in the Bill of Rights. Furthermore, Madison's view of the Establishment Clause has been interpreted inconsistently well beyond the hallowed halls of the U.S. Supreme Court building. Madison is misunderstood throughout academia as well. Much like the Court, most scholars fall into one of two camps: those who see Madison as a separationist and those who believe he was a nonpreferentialist.[21]

Disagreements regarding Madison and religion do not end with the Establishment Clause. The justices of the Supreme Court also split into two groups in how they interpret Madison's vision behind the Free Exercise Clause. The Free Exercise Clause, when read together with the Establishment Clause, states: "Congress shall make no law respecting an establishment of religion, or prohibiting the free exercise thereof." One major interpretation of this clause is called accommodationism. Accommodationists claim that government should assist persons, especially those of minority religions, in alleviating burdens on their religious worship. Under an accommodationist theory of free exercise, the clause "requir[es] the government to justify any substantial burden on religiously motivated conduct by a compelling state interest and by means narrowly tailored to achieve that interest."[22] The other major theory of free exercise advocates a strict form of neutrality, whereby government is required by the Free Exercise Clause only to make laws that are neutral to all religions. Under a neutrality-based interpretation of free exercise, which was first advanced by a majority of the Court in *Employment Division v. Smith* (1990), "the right of free exercise does not relieve an individual of the obligation to comply with a valid and neutral law of general applicability on the ground that the law proscribes (or prescribes) conduct that his religion prescribes (or proscribes)."[23]

Madison has been cited by the justices to support both of these positions. During the Rehnquist and Roberts Courts, Madison has been invoked in free exercise opinions eight times, and over the Court's history Madison has been used as authority in 19 free exercise opinions. Much like the Court, scholars who have tried to identify Madison's views regarding the free exercise of religion are divided into two groups: those who see Madison accommodating a broad, liberal right to free exercise (especially the rights of minority religions), and those believing Madison supported a neutrality-based approach.[24]

Supreme Court justices have also discussed Madison in cases dealing with the expressive freedoms of speech, press, and association. The relevant First Amendment language for these debates is "Congress shall make no law . . . abridging the freedom of speech, or of the press; or the right of the people peaceably to assemble, and to petition the government for a redress of grievances." Here, the debate can best be characterized as between justices who see Madison supporting the protection of individual liberal rights and those who see him supporting the protection of a more democracy-centered understanding of freedom. A classically liberal theory of Madison states that these expressive freedoms are rights that belong to the individual—that they are essentially a type of personal "property" that government can regulate only in the rarest of circumstances. If Madison advocated a democracy-centered understanding of the First Amendment, on the other hand, he wanted these rights protected only when they facilitate a representative form of government; for instance, when they are essential for citizens to find information about, and communicate with, their elected representatives.

In many ways, the difference between these two positions is only one of degree—one puts its emphasis on individual rights, and the other places emphasis on democracy. However, much like the differences between separationism and nonpreferentialism, or between accommodationism and neutrality, whichever theory one adopts today has consequences for what types of speech, press, and association one believes ought to be protected. For example, from a democracy-centered standpoint, it would be easier to make the argument that hate speech should be regulated on the grounds that it causes harm to the community and that it serves no democratic function. But when one uses a more liberal, natural-rights approach, it becomes much more difficult to make an argument supporting the regulation of hate speech because such expression is the property of the person speaking. This leads to very different conclusions, depending on the position one takes on Madison's works.

Supreme Court justices have repeatedly referred to Madison when interpreting the freedoms of speech, press, and association. Since the beginning of the Rehnquist Court, the justices have cited Madison in 14 opinions on these clauses or on First Amendment rights generally. Over the Court's history Madison has been used as authority in 79 opinions in these types of cases. Scholars also disagree over Madison's meaning when he discussed what constituted the freedom of speech, press, and association. Much like the Court, scholarship differs over whether Madison held a more liberal or democracy-centered position regarding these freedoms.[25]

Although scholars and justices on the Supreme Court have primarily focused on using Madison in First Amendment cases, they have also employed Madison to support their interpretations of other portions of the

Bill of Rights. One example is the Takings Clause, the last clause of the Fifth Amendment, which states: "nor shall private property be taken for public use, without just compensation." Here, all justices who have written about Madison generally agree on his intent: Madison wanted to protect a liberally understood right to private property from being physically seized by the government for anything but a public use. The corollary to this, upon which all the justices who invoke Madison also agree, is that Madison did not think compensation was necessary for regulatory takings. A body of academic literature also exists on the issue of what Madison favored regarding property rights. One position is that Madison was a staunch defender of a classically liberal position on property rights; the other major position sees Madison as more of a classical republican.[26]

Defining these terms can be tricky. Classical republicanism generally holds that government should be focused on the common good of society. It promotes the idea of civic virtue and moral education, and it typically requires people to live in small, relatively uniform communities, where they can get to know their fellow citizens and live frugal lives. A virtuous republican citizen has a greater desire to engage in public service than in private pursuits. The emphasis is on positive liberty, whereby government tries to promote the full potential of all citizens from interference from others. In other words, liberty is not just freedom from government interference; it is also government promoting the participation of all citizens. Freedom is only extended to things that are in the best interests of the community, with individual concerns seen as less important. In addition to allowing more regulation of property, a democracy-centered vision of expressive rights would also be in line with classical republican theory.[27]

Classical liberalism, on the other hand, begins with the proposition that the government is instituted to protect private property and allow people to pursue their private interests. For the classical liberal, the good of the community is not the immediate goal; rather, the rights of individuals, including rights to pursue economic self-interest in a free market, are more important. Thus, unlike classical republicanism, classical liberalism allows the individual more freedom to pursue his or her passions.[28]

Under a natural-rights-based classical liberalism, a law is valid only if it conforms to the law of nature. In the state of nature (prior to political society and government), all humans began as equals, but this led to each person being vulnerable to everyone else. This vulnerability led humans to leave the state of nature and enter into a compact to form civil society. In this theory, espoused most prominently by English philosopher John Locke, government's purpose is to protect liberty. Liberty here is defined as being "free from restraint and violence from others," which includes for all persons a "liberty to dispose, and order as he lists, his persons, actions, and his whole property."[29]

Even though there are differences between the types of rights that proponents of republicanism and of liberalism claim to protect, the differences are a question of degree. It is not simply the case that every advocate of liberalism demands a soulless type of laissez-faire capitalism or that every proponent of republicanism requires citizens to give in to whatever a majority believes to be virtuous and for the public good. Liberalism can also include obedience to the law, honesty, tolerance, respect, and generosity. Likewise, liberalism needs people to have a focus on the community, not just themselves as individuals. And republicanism also finds room to protect individual freedoms. Although there are important differences between classical republicanism and classical liberalism, the Framers, including Madison, might not have seen the two philosophies as inconsistent.[30]

Finally, examining the Court's interpretation of the constitutional rights of the criminally accused also demonstrates diverging views among the justices on James Madison. The rights at stake for the accused range from the right against unreasonable searches and seizures to the right to remain silent to the right to an attorney, among many others listed in the Fourth, Fifth, Sixth, and Eighth Amendments. Much like other areas in the Bill of Rights, the opinions fall into two classifications—those who invoke Madison to defend a strong protection of rights of the accused and those who cite Madison to support more of a pro-prosecution position. Of course, the differences here are once again more ones of degree than rigid, separate categories. Even the most ardent defender of liberal, individual rights of the accused would agree that there are limits on those rights, and even the staunchest protector of prosecutorial authority would admit some limitations on that power. Nevertheless, the general categories can be used to pinpoint differences that could lead one down very different paths when interpreting Madison's objectives. Since the beginning of the Rehnquist Court, 8 opinions have invoked Madison in cases involving constitutional rights of the accused, and 50 opinions have done so over the Court's history.

There is also disagreement among scholars over whether Madison intended a broad or narrow protection for his drafts of what eventually became these amendments. This debate has raged in several areas, including the Compelled Self-Incrimination Clause[31] and the Due Process Clause.[32] There is also disagreement among scholars on whether Madison advocated a liberal or more limited view of the Fourth Amendment.[33] That Madison said very little directly on criminal procedures has not stopped scholars from commenting on Madison's intent with these amendments.

Thus, Madison's ideas have been extensively utilized by the justices through the Court's history. Members of the current Court are still using Madison in Bill of Rights cases, but they are using his ideas in divergent ways to justify opposing conclusions. The differences that justices have over Madison are a microcosm of disputes over Madison among academics. Scholarly books and journal articles, written by historians, political scientists, and law professors, have the same high level of disagreement. There are real world consequences to these academic disagreements. They can contribute to the disputes on the Court by packaging evidence and arguments that justices can easily cite in their opinions.[34]

UNDERSTANDING MADISON

On the Supreme Court and in academia, there are great disputes over what constitutes a Madisonian interpretation of the various provisions of the Bill of Rights. What can cause such strong disagreements? Justices (and some scholars) often focus on a limited number of works by Madison to reach their conclusions about him on a particular provision of the Bill of Rights.[35] This method essentially ignores Madison's larger body of political theory and statements about politics generally. By focusing on select statements by Madison, and neglecting to look at his more comprehensive ideas on politics, it becomes easier to "cram" Madison into one theory or another, neglecting the subtleties and complexities of his thinking. The fact that Madison wrote and spoke about liberty across multiple decades also makes it easier for one to single out a few statements during one period while ignoring the context of those statements and how they relate to what Madison said at other times.

For instance, in all the debates about Madison's theories on the establishment and free exercise of religion, rarely do the justices cite anything beyond Madison's "Memorial and Remonstrance," Madison's speech when he introduced the Bill of Rights, his two vetoes as president, and a few letters from Madison to friends and acquaintances. Likewise, when interpreting a Madisonian view of the freedoms of speech, press, and association, there is little quoted beyond his Bill of Rights speeches, his *Report on the Alien and Sedition Acts*, and a few essays later in Madison's life. When discussing Madison's intent behind the Takings Clause, few refer to anything beyond *Federalist* 10, Madison's speech introducing the Bill of Rights, and his "Property" essay. Finally, when arguing Madison's intent regarding the rights of the accused, little is ever cited beyond Madison's scant comments when introducing those amendments in Congress and perhaps a few smatterings from Madison's contributions to *The Federalist*. Granted, these are all necessary documents to be examined when determining what Madison envisioned regarding each of these freedoms. However, these works alone are not sufficient, as the great disputes over his ideas demonstrate.

Madison made many statements that touch directly on freedoms articulated in the Bill of Rights, such as the need to protect "the diversity in the faculties of men [which] is the first object of government";[36] that "in matters of Religion, no man[']s right is abridged by the institution of Civil

Society, and that Religion is wholly exempt from its cognizance";[37] that "the censorial power is in the people over the government, and not in the government over the people";[38] that the freedom of the press is "one of the great bulwarks of liberty" and should be "inviolable";[39] that "the people" have "the right of acquiring and using property";[40] that no person shall "be obliged to relinquish his property, where it may be necessary for public use, without a just compensation";[41] and that "the trial by jury" is one of "the great rights."[42] Nevertheless, each statement is quite abstract, offering little detail about what such freedoms specifically meant to Madison. To better understand Madison's intent, one needs to look beyond the ambiguous quotes that are traditionally examined in Bill of Rights cases, articles, and books. Instead, one must study Madison's overall theory of government and politics, placing the Bill of Rights within this context. This begins a framework to harmonize Madison's writings and speeches. But even looking solely to political theory does not completely answer the question of what Madison thought. Indeed, there have been spirited debates over Madison's political theory—whether he was a classical republican, a classical liberal, or something in between.[43]

The best way to harmonize these differences is to ground Madison's statements about politics in his theory of human nature. Grasping Madison's ideas about human nature is the key to unlocking both Madison's political theory and his thoughts on the Bill of Rights. Chapter 2 provides historical and documentary evidence that Madison had a complex understanding of human nature. Madison's views were shaped during his study before, during, and after his time at Princeton University with John Witherspoon. Largely owing to Witherspoon's tutelage, Madison gained a healthy appreciation for the idea that humans are prone to corruption and vice. However, Madison also came to believe that the human race is capable of moral advancement and improvement. Perhaps the most influential of the authorities Madison read was David Hume, under whom Witherspoon had studied at Edinburgh. Hume's outlook on human nature was a mix of both hope and despair. This left Madison with a "realistic" understanding of human nature, whereby no one could be completely trusted but some would be capable of achieving virtue. Because Madison saw human nature as heterogeneous, he believed that some of us can attain virtue and some of us cannot. Madison even came to believe that at certain times a given person could be capable of virtue and at other times that person would not. Therefore, Madison wanted to construct a political regime in which those who could attain sufficient virtue could rise to the top while protecting against granting too much power to anyone, power that could be used by those who lacked virtue.

Chapter 3 explores how Madison's views on human nature helped lead him to believe in a political theory that is best characterized as classical liberalism. Madison believed that we are endowed with certain natural rights that government is instituted to protect. Thus, those in government should act virtuously to protect those rights. This came, in part, from a germ planted in Madison's mind by Witherspoon, but also independently from the study of John Locke's theories on natural rights, the state of nature, and the social contract. Madison understood human beings as rights-bearing individuals, with each human being having a right by nature to his or her personal autonomy. Government must protect those rights.

Still, Madison's views on human nature brought him beyond natural-rights liberalism. Madison also advocated a liberal understanding of rights because he saw that there would be generous secondary benefits to society. He thought liberal freedoms were the best way to achieve virtue *and* to achieve the most good for those persons not capable of sufficient virtue. Madison wanted the maximum amount of freedom possible, so that those who were truly virtuous could utilize that freedom for the betterment of society. In this way, Madison made use of the liberal themes espoused by Adam Smith and Thomas Jefferson. Madison believed that virtue could coexist with liberalism and even be cultivated by people exercising their rights. People need to be free to act virtuously and to learn how to be more virtuous. Madison believed that by exercising our rights we could learn from our successes and mistakes and would feel more empathy and tolerance for others in the community, given that the community as a whole respects our independence. This would make a self-interested majority less likely to abuse the rights of the minority. Madison thought that this path to virtue could only be realized if we were given the autonomy to have such life experiences. However, Madison also went beyond the theories of Smith and Jefferson, as he understood that many people would be largely incapable of attaining virtue. Again, for Madison, liberalism was the answer, as he thought that the hard work, productivity, and economic growth caused by those who are solely self-interested could still create the public good of better products and more opportunities when left relatively unrestrained. In other words, Madison believed that protecting liberal rights would be the best way for society to achieve virtue *and* the common good. This theory fits perfectly with Madison's understanding of human nature, as it recognizes and tries to harness both our virtue and our self-interest.

Chapter 4 examines what at first seems like a perplexing question: if Madison was so committed to protecting liberal rights, why did he originally reject adding a bill of rights to the Constitution? Piecing together this puzzle requires demonstrating how Madison's understanding of human nature initially led him to oppose a bill of rights. Immediately following the 1787 Constitutional Convention, Madison thought that a bill of rights was nothing more than a "paper barrier" that would have no effect in restraining a self-interested majority or small cabal of powerful interests.

Instead, Madison thought that the best way to protect essential rights was through structural constraints such as an extended republic, federalism, and the separation of powers. For a time, Madison even believed that a bill of rights could be at best ineffective and at worst detrimental to rights, if the bill were written by the wrong hand, if it were not written comprehensively enough, or if it were written in such absolute terms that it was essentially ignored by those in power during emergencies. Chapter 4 also depicts Madison's move to supporting a bill of rights for strategic reasons unrelated to the protection of liberty. Indeed, Madison was a consummate politician. He recognized that a bill of rights would ground Anti-Federalist attempts at a second constitutional convention, it would be useful politically to help forge a consensus in the new union, and it would fulfill a campaign promise that Madison made to his constituents while running for a House seat in the First Congress.

Although Madison never abandoned his belief that structural constraints were an effective way of protecting liberty, chapter 5 explores how he eventually became convinced that a bill of rights could also protect human freedom. Madison thought that a bill of rights could serve as another check (beyond the separation of powers and federalism) that restrained government from harming our rights, that it could help prevent transgressions of enumerated powers, and that it could be a useful guide for courts to protect rights. Madison also came to think that a bill of rights written by him could protect against both minority and majority tyrannies. A bill of rights became a more pressing concern for Madison after the Constitutional Convention, where he lost two battles to create structural constraints that he believed would protect freedoms, a Council of Revision and a congressional veto of state laws. Above all, Madison's correspondence with his good friend Thomas Jefferson helped convince him that only a bill of rights would fully protect the liberal freedoms he cherished.

The focus of chapter 6 is on Madison's idea of a *system* of liberal rights that would also promote virtue and the common good. When Madison proposed the Bill of Rights to Congress, he envisioned a system of rights consisting of the freedoms of and from religion, the freedoms of speech and press, property rights, and the rights of the criminally accused. These rights came up often, and often together, in Madison's speeches and writings. Madison believed that when these rights, both natural and civil, were protected, it would best achieve his vision of the good society. Madison thought that protecting any one of these rights would, in turn, help to protect others. For instance, properly constructed criminal procedures would curb the ability of the government to unfairly prosecute religious or political dissenters. Likewise, Madison thought that protecting property, especially real estate, would safeguard other rights, as it would allow people to have a protected "castle" where they could think and work free from government interference. He proposed these rights to work in conjunction with structural protections of liberty in the original Constitution, including the separation of powers, federalism, and enumerated powers. Indeed, an examination of Madison's proposed amendments reveals that these structural themes were still on his mind when he proposed the Bill of Rights in 1789 as productive ways to protect liberty.

In trying to create an organically whole system of rights, Madison also wanted to protect specific rights, a topic investigated in chapter 7. Madison advocated a separationist idea of disestablishment of religion because he feared that vice and tyranny would result from any fusing of government power with religion. Madison believed that separating religion and government would promote the growth of religion naturally, which would result in the attainment of virtue in addition to protecting free exercise rights. For free exercise, Madison wanted to protect a natural right to religious freedom. He believed that religion was prior to, and wholly exempt from, the cognizance of civil government. Madison thought that an accommodationist stance allowed people to attain virtue via the exercise of their freedom, something that would benefit the whole community. Madison was most concerned that a self-interested majority would attempt to take away the rights of a religious minority. To allow people to fully exercise this right, he saw the need for government to accommodate religion, especially minority religious groups.

Madison had a liberal vision of other First Amendment rights, as he understood them to be gifts from nature to the human individual. Madison also thought that protecting these liberal rights would best lead to virtue and the achievement of the common good. There were numerous times, including when he introduced the Bill of Rights in Congress, that Madison proclaimed these rights to be natural ones that should not be taken by government. However, Madison also noted that protecting these freedoms would help representative government function properly. Madison tried to reconcile this and the natural-rights tradition, and saw a near absolute protection of these rights as a way to protect individual autonomy *and* to achieve virtue and to serve the public interest. For example, Madison thought that protecting a liberal freedom of the press would allow members of the media to learn how best to serve the needs of the public while also allowing for all information, good or bad, to be printed about the government.

Madison's understanding of the freedom of association followed his attempt to find a compromise between the republican and liberal traditions. Madison protected the freedom of association both as an end in itself (as a natural right giving people the opportunity to come together to collectively express themselves) and as a means to the greater end of promoting a competitive, deliberative democracy. Thus, much like the freedoms of speech and press, Madison tried to reconcile individual rights and the common good. In doing so, he reached the conclusion that a strong, liberal protection of the right of association would serve both ends.

Madison had a liberal vision of property rights, too. He thought that protecting this natural, individual right would be proper in itself and that it would lead to more virtue through the exercise of freedom as well as the common good of more productivity in a free market. In other words, Madison saw property as an individual right worthy of protection for its own sake, and he also thought that protecting property would have worthy secondary benefits. Madison thought that protecting a classically liberal right to property was a way to lead people, most notably farmers, toward working the land and engaging in hard work to make themselves into more virtuous citizens. Madison also believed that fully protecting this right would allow society to be more productive, serving the general welfare.

Finally, chapter 7 is an explanation of how Madison wanted the rights of the accused to be strongly protected as another way to secure our natural liberties and to protect our ability to attain virtue and the common good. Madison comprehended the rights of defendants as one method to effectually safeguard other liberal rights, such as First Amendment freedoms and property rights. In this way, Madison understood the rights of the accused to be another check on the government from trying to use the courts to take away other freedoms, much like federalism and the separation of powers. At the same time, Madison believed that protecting broadly defined rights of the accused would enable citizens on juries to learn more about the precious procedural guarantees and the importance of juries in our system, thus making them more educated and more virtuous citizens after their jury service.

Chapter 8 is a study of Madison's integral role in shaping the Bill of Rights. What becomes truly remarkable and what makes Madison all the more relevant to us is how our Bill of Rights was largely the brainchild of Madison alone. He had to push other members of Congress tremendously hard just to get the Bill considered. Most Federalists in the First Federal Congress did not think a bill of rights was important compared to other matters facing the new government, and most Anti-Federalists were more concerned about weakening the new national government than protecting rights. In spite of this, Madison continually brought up the issue of amendments, and he was finally successful in proposing a draft to the House of Representatives. Additionally, Madison sat on the influential House committees that amended his initial draft, he was heavily involved during the House floor debate, and he chaired the House-Senate conference committee. Due to his heavy involvement throughout this process, the final version of the Bill of Rights is substantially similar to Madison's original proposal. In many cases, the language of the amendments is identical to

Madison's draft, or the differences are minute. Although this does not mean that Madison's views should be our only star and compass when interpreting the Bill of Rights, it does mean that Madison should not be ignored when we interpret the document.

After demonstrating Madison's comprehensive intent behind the Bill of Rights, part II revisits the Supreme Court and the justices who have invoked Madison to support their opinions. This begins in chapter 9 with a broad overview of how the Court has come to protect freedoms in the Bill against both the federal and state governments. Chapters 10–13 each examine four different types of justices when it comes to Madison and the Bill of Rights: those who fully comprehend Madison (devotees), those who gradually come to understand Madison (learners), those who express Madison's theory sometimes but not always (inconsistents), and those who routinely fail to give a proper expression of Madison's theory when citing him (name droppers). Undoubtedly, there is a wide range in the amount of influence Madison has had among current and past Supreme Court justices. Finally, chapter 14 has some concluding remarks.

Justices on the Supreme Court have cited Madison when interpreting each clause of the First Amendment, as well as the Second Amendment, the Fourth Amendment, the Grand Jury Clause, the Double Jeopardy Clause, the Compelled Self-Incrimination Clause, the Due Process Clause, the speedy and public criminal trial requirement, the Criminal Jury Trial Clause, the Assistance of Counsel Clause, the Seventh Amendment, the Eighth Amendment, and the Ninth Amendment. Appendix A is a comprehensive list of these cases. For reference, appendices B and C contain, respectively, Madison's draft bill of rights and the final version of the Bill of Rights ratified by the states.

two

MADISON'S CONCEPTION OF
HUMAN NATURE

A STUDENT OF JOHN WITHERSPOON

Madison held a complex and realistic view of human nature, in which he saw people as capable of acting out of both virtue and self-interest. This understanding of human nature helped to shape Madison's liberalism as well as his ideas behind the Bill of Rights. In addition to believing in natural rights, Madison defended those rights for their secondary benefits to society, including the cultivation of virtue and the promotion of the public good.

Madison's conception of human nature was informed by his philosophical studies. Perhaps no American politician before or since was as well read in moral philosophy as Madison. He alluded in his writings and speeches to thinkers as ancient as Socrates and Thucydides while also citing authors as contemporary as Jean-Jacques Rousseau, David Hume, and Adam Smith.[1] There is evidence that when he studied as a boy with Donald Robertson in King and Queen County, Virginia, he read many of the classics, such as Cicero, Virgil, Horace, Justinian, and Ovid.[2] While at Robertson's school, Madison also studied more modern thinkers such as Locke, Montaigne, and Montesquieu.[3] As a student at the College of New Jersey (now Princeton), Madison studied Horace, Virgil, Cicero, Lucian, Xenophon, the Bible, Hobbes, and Locke, among others.[4] After graduating from Princeton, Madison stayed at the university for an additional six months, studying authors such as Thomas Hobbes, Niccolò Machiavelli, Locke, James Harrington, Hume, Adam Ferguson, Plato, and Aristotle in greater depth.[5] Madison's knowledge of a wide variety of past and contemporary political philosophers can be garnered from a list of books he recommended that Congress purchase for a national library in 1783. Among the 550 titles in about 1,300 volumes, Madison suggested that Congress have on hand the political and legal theories penned by

Ferguson, Hume, Plato, Aristotle, Thomas More, Hobbes, Locke, Adam Smith, John Millar, Montesquieu, William Blackstone, and Edward Coke.[6] In many ways, Madison was a true bibliophile.

However, the most powerful influence on Madison in his college years and his postgraduate work was not an author but his teacher, John Witherspoon. Witherspoon left his native Scotland for America in 1768 when he accepted the presidency of the College of New Jersey. Madison arrived at the college one year later. Before departing Scotland, Witherspoon studied with some of the intellectual giants of the Scottish Enlightenment, including David Hume and Adam Smith. Upon arriving in America, Witherspoon remade the curriculum at Princeton to emphasize the Scottish Enlightenment. In the courses that Witherspoon taught, he put on his reading lists and highlighted the works of Hume, Smith, Ferguson, and Francis Hutcheson. Madison's postgraduate work was at the direction of Witherspoon, and it is clear that Madison's formative thinking clearly began to take shape under Witherspoon's guidance.[7]

Witherspoon taught the Scottish Enlightenment to his students. This included the ability of humans to achieve virtue, which has "its own intrinsic evidence," and gives to us "a hope of future happiness."[8] Indeed, Witherspoon believed that we were given a natural ability to discern right from wrong: "I think it must be admitted that a sense of moral good and evil is as real a principle of our nature as either the gross external or reflex senses."[9] Madison learned about the Scottish Enlightenment from Witherspoon, with an emphasis on the resilient ability of human nature to achieve progressive ends. Most notably, records exist that Madison took a class from Witherspoon entitled "Moral Philosophy," which was divided into sections on ethics and politics.[10] The reading list included some notable thinkers of the Scottish Enlightenment, including "Ferguson's History of Civil Society," "David Hume's Essays," and "Hutchinson's [sic] System."[11] Madison appears to have retained this education years later: when he compiled his list of books for Congress in 1783, the influence of Witherspoon and the Scots was readily apparent, as it included many works by Scottish Enlightenment thinkers.[12]

However, Witherspoon also brought another intellectual tradition to Princeton, one with a very different perception of human nature. Before coming to America, Witherspoon worked as a Calvinist minister in Scotland. One of the key characteristics of John Calvin's theology was that we as humans are "vitiated and perverted in every part of our nature."[13] According to Calvin, "all parts of the soul were possessed by sin after Adam deserted the fountain of righteousness" in the Garden of Eden.[14] It was Calvin's belief that, after the Fall, Adam's sinful nature was transgressed from one generation to the next throughout the course of human history: "rotten branches come forth from a rotten root, which transmitted their rottenness to the other twigs sprouting from them. For thus were the children corrupted in the parent, so that they brought disease upon their children's children."[15]

Calvinism was an integral part of Witherspoon's thinking, and it made him ever skeptical of people's motives, even when he embraced the "sunnier" views of the Scottish Enlightenment. For Witherspoon, "the history of the world [was] little else than the history of human guilt."[16] For the Calvinist Witherspoon, "Nothing can be more absolutely necessary to true religion than a clear and full conviction of the sinfulness of our nature and state."[17] At times, Witherspoon was quite pessimistic regarding human nature: "Others may, if they please, treat the corruption of our nature as a chimera; for my part, I see it everywhere, and I feel it everyday."[18] Witherspoon even went so far as to decry the "depravity" of human nature.[19]

Overall, a balanced and realistic view of human nature ran throughout Witherspoon's writings and speeches. Even when sermonizing to his listeners that he wished "to impress on your minds . . . the depravity of our nature," Witherspoon would go on to praise "the happy influence of renewing grace each for ourselves."[20] Similarly, Witherspoon told his listeners that, although we are prone to sin, "[t]here are times when the mind may be expected to be more awake to divine truth, and the conscience more open to the arrows of conviction."[21] Although there is no direct evidence that Madison took on Witherspoon's Calvinist beliefs, such sermonizing may have worked to temper the more positive view of human nature espoused by Scottish Enlightenment thinkers. In order to guard properly against the depravity of human nature but to harness also its potential goodness, Witherspoon inculcated in Madison the need to divide political power. According to Witherspoon, "[E]very good form of government must be complex so that one principle may check the other. It is of consequence to have as much virtue among the particular members of a community as possible, but it is folly to expect that a state should be upheld by integrity in all who have a share in managing it."[22] Thus, Witherspoon taught Madison the progressive tradition of the Scottish Enlightenment whereby people were capable of virtue. But he also inculcated in Madison a healthy respect for the sinful nature of humanity.

THE INFLUENCE OF DAVID HUME

More than any thinker that Madison read or that Witherspoon taught to Madison, David Hume (one of Witherspoon's teachers) best exemplified a "realistic" conception of human nature. The influence of Hume on Madison, both directly through reading and indirectly through Witherspoon, has been well documented.[23]

Hume stated in *A Treatise of Human Nature* that both "vice and virtue must be part of our character."[24] Hume explained in more detail that none of us are capable of virtue all of the time: "What we call strength of mind, implies the prevalence of the calm passions above the violent; tho' we may easily observe, there is no man so constantly possess'd of this virtue, as never on any occasion to yield to the sollicitations of passion and desire."[25] Hume believed that humanity was capable of exercising reason to achieve virtue, but that we could also fall prey to our own base desires and follow the path of self-interest. In this regard, Hume gave an ominous caution: "Reason is, and ought only to be the slave of the passions, and can never pretend to any other office than to serve and obey them."[26] In Hume's view, as much as we may want to be virtuous, our violent passions continue to pull us toward self-interest.

Hume believed that it was quite reasonable to expect humans to act both virtuously for the public good and also out of self-interest. When explaining humans' decisions to submit to the rules of society, Hume stated that "After men have found by experience, that their selfishness and confin'd generosity, acting at their liberty, totally incapacitate them for society; and at the same time have observ'd, that society is necessary to the satisfaction of those very passions, they are naturally induc'd to lay themselves under the restraint of such rules, as may render their commerce more safe and commodious."[27] Hume concluded: "self-interest is the original motive to the establishment of justice: but a sympathy with public interest is the source of the moral approbation, which attends that virtue. This latter principle of sympathy is too weak to controul our passions; but has sufficient force to influence our taste."[28] In other words, Hume thought we acted both out of self-interest and for the public interest, out of both vice and virtue. And even when we acted out of self-interest (such as submitting to the rules of society for our own economic benefit), the public good could result. Madison thought highly of Hume in general, as he recommended several of Hume's works to Congress for purchase.[29] Madison also adopted several of Hume's arguments regarding politics, most notably the analysis of factions and the theory of the extended republic.[30]

MADISON'S REALISM

Witherspoon and Hume had a great influence on the young James Madison's views of human nature. With their guidance, Madison developed a philosophy in which humanity had the capacity for great achievements and great wrongs. Madison came to believe that individuals could be virtuous, self-interested, both, or that they could vacillate between the two. Madison cannot be read as having full faith in the civic virtue of the citizenry or as a proponent of all humans being solely self-interested. Instead, Madison blended these traditions to conclude that humans are a diverse species, and that all of us can be both virtuous and self-interested. It is this understanding of human nature that one sees throughout Madison's works, as he tried to structure a government that will take advantage of the possible virtues of humanity while also safeguarding against humanity's dark side.[31]

From one of his earliest political writings, the 1787 "Vices of the Political System of the United States," Madison was clear that the "most prevalent" motivations of legislators are "ambition" and "personal interest."[32] Madison's understanding of humanity here is one of both virtue and vice: the *most prevalent* motives of legislators are ambition and personal interest. But Madison noted in the same essay that another motivation is "the public good,"[33] thus demonstrating his belief that some politicians are capable of acting in the public interest. In the same piece, Madison discussed how the public generally *may* fall to vice: "a prudent regard to their [the majority's] own good as involved in the general and permanent good of the Community . . . is found by experience to be too often unheeded."[34] Madison continued to state regarding "respect for character," that "[h]owever strong this motive may be in individuals, it is considered as very insufficient to restrain them from injustice."[35] In his "Vices" essay Madison repeatedly affirmed that humans are capable of acting for the good of the community and having a virtuous character, but he also cautioned that this is often not the case.

Madison took a similar position on human nature in a 1787 letter to Thomas Jefferson. Madison mocked the idea that everyone has "precisely the same interests, and the same feelings in every respect."[36] Instead, Madison maintained, "We know however that no Society ever did or can consist of so homogeneous a mass of Citizens."[37] Madison went on to tell Jefferson that "[t]hree motives only" can restrain a self-interested majority.[38] First, Madison claimed people may be restrained by "a prudent regard to private or partial good, as essentially involved in the general and permanent good of the whole."[39] Madison warned that "[e]xperience however shews that it has little effect on individuals, and least of all on a majority."[40] Madison next stated that a majority may be restrained by "respect for character," but "[t]his motive is not found sufficient to restrain individuals from injustice, and loses its efficacy in proportion to the number which is to divide the praise or blame."[41] Finally, Madison avowed that religion may restrain the majority, but on this point he cautioned that "[t]he inefficacy of this restraint on individuals is well known. The conduct of every popular Assembly, acting on oath, the strongest of religious ties, shews that individuals join without remorse in acts agst. which their consciences would revolt, if proposed to them separately in their closets."[42] Although the main thrust of Madison's argument here is that we can trust individuals more than a mob of people engaged in "group-think," Madison's realistic view on human nature is also apparent. He stated that a regard for the good may have an effect on individuals, but that it often has *little* effect. Note too that Madison understood individuals as capable of acting virtuously, but that often in groups we stop thinking for ourselves, again confirming his realistic view of human nature.

Madison's understanding of human nature was consistent with this when he wrote *Federalist* 10. Madison asserted that it is "impracticable" to give "every citizen the same opinions, the same passions, and the same interests."[43] This was true according to Madison because

> As long as the reason of man continues fallible, and he is at liberty to exercise it, different opinions will be formed. As long as the connection subsists between his reason and his self-love, his opinions and his passions will have a reciprocal influence on each other; and the former will be objects to which the latter will attach themselves . . . The latent causes of faction are thus sown in the nature of man.[44]

Madison once more discussed how human nature is corruptible—we are susceptible to falling prey to our "self-love" and not acting virtuously for the public good. But note as well that Madison said here only that we are *fallible* to such things, not that it is a *certainty* all will act against the public good. Later in *Federalist* 10, Madison discussed public officials. He noted that one proposed remedy to the problems of self-interested factions is having enlightened statesmen. However, Madison continued: "It is in vain to say that enlightened statesmen will be able to adjust these clashing interests, and render them all subservient to the public good. Enlightened statesmen will not always be at the helm."[45] Note the use of the modifier "not always"—Madison believed that sometimes enlightened statesmen *will* be at the helm, but this is not a certainty. Once more, Madison was concerned about fallible human nature and safeguarding against it, but he also left open the possibility that there would be virtuous persons to guide the ship of state.

In *Federalist* 37, Madison discussed the problems faced by the Constitutional Convention. In the course of doing this he explained that "The history of almost all the great councils and consultations held among mankind for reconciling their discordant opinions, assuaging their mutual jealousies, and adjusting their respective interests, is a history of factions, contentions, and disappointments, and may be classed among the most dark and degraded pictures which display the infirmities and depravities of the human character."[46] Madison espoused another realistic understanding of human nature in this passage. He classified *almost all* great counsels as having factions and being dark and degraded. He even went so far as to claim that in most cases "the human character" is infirm and depraved. But he did not say this was true in all cases. Indeed, a few sentences later Madison praised the 1787 Constitutional Convention as one where the delegates held an uncharacteristically "deep conviction of sacrificing private opinions and partial interests, to the public good."[47] Again, Madison chose his words carefully and qualified his discussion of human abilities.

This theme continued for Madison when he penned *Federalist* 51. In this essay he discussed the necessity of the separation of powers. Madison claimed that we can prevent the concentration of power in the same department of government by "giving to those the constitutional means, and personal motives, to resist encroachments of others."[48] This relies on the belief that "[a]mbition must be made to counteract ambition. The interest of the man must be connected with the constitutional rights of the place."[49] Madison continued:

> It may be a reflection on human nature, that such devices should be necessary to control the abuses of government. But what is government itself, but the greatest of all reflections on human nature? If men were angels, no government would be necessary. If angels were to govern men, neither external nor internal controls on government would be necessary. In framing a government which is to be administered by men over men, the great difficulty lies in this: you must first enable the government to control the governed; and in the next place oblige it to control itself. A dependence on the people is, no doubt, the primary control on the government; but experience has taught mankind the necessity of auxiliary precautions.[50]

Madison had a simple message in this passage. Since we are not angels, we need to empower government to act on behalf of the community. But we must also prevent government from running away with its power because those in the government may not be virtuous either. Madison also reaffirmed his conviction that there will be those who act for the public good when he stated that a "dependence on the people" is "the primary control on the government." Madison was convinced that the people will sometimes make the right decisions, act virtuously, and elect leaders who will promote the public good. Yet Madison also believed "auxiliary precautions" would be necessary to stop those with less than virtuous motives, thus hampering the ability of a factious majority or a corrupt leader to act against the public good.

Madison continued his realism when he wrote *Federalist* 55. Madison, in defending the ratio of electors to the number of representatives in the House of Representatives, claimed that a relatively small ratio would not be dangerous. He noted:

> As there is a degree of depravity in mankind which requires a certain degree of circumspection and distrust, so there are other qualities in human nature which justify a certain portion of esteem and confidence. . . . Were the pictures which have been drawn by the political jealousy of some among us faithful likenesses of the human character, the inference would be, that there is not sufficient virtue among men for self-government; and

that nothing less than the chains of despotism can restrain them from destroying and devouring one another.[51]

Madison believed that there is "a certain depravity in mankind" which we should "distrust." However, Madison also maintained that there is "sufficient virtue" to continue representative government. Although there are bad elements in society, there are enough of us acting virtuously enough of the time to ensure that a government of the people can work. Madison was saying that republican (representative) government *can* work if properly cultivated, given the variable nature of humanity.

A final selection from *The Federalist* helps confirm Madison's heterogeneous view on human nature. In *Federalist* 57 Madison defended the method of selecting members of the House of Representatives, and in doing so he stated that the elected would act on behalf of the public.

> [T]hey will enter into the public service under circumstances which cannot fail to produce a temporary affection at least to their constituents. There is in every breast a sensibility to marks of honor, of favor, of esteem, and of confidence, which, apart from all considerations of interest, is some pledge for grateful and benevolent returns. Ingratitude is a common topic of declamation against human nature; and it must be confessed that instances of it are but too frequent and flagrant, both in public and in private life. But the universal and extreme indignation which it inspires is itself a proof of the energy and prevalence of the contrary sentiment.[52]

Madison remained a realist regarding human nature. Ungratefulness is possible, but so are the revered traits of honor, esteem, and confidence. Our nature requires a government that can take advantage of people who are good and guard against the motives of those who are not.

Madison's "realistic" view of human nature ran throughout his career, and it can be found in his public writings and speeches as well as his private letters. For instance, at the Constitutional Convention in 1787 Madison stated, "The truth was that all men having power ought to be distrusted to a *certain* degree."[53] This is not the statement of one who has great trust or mistrust in humanity; rather, it is the statement of one who is cautiously optimistic. Likewise, in a 1788 letter to Thomas Jefferson, Madison maintained that "[w]herever there is an interest and power to do wrong, wrong will *generally* be done."[54] Madison again voiced his view that there is a danger of human nature being corrupted, but it is not an absolute certainty. Similarly, in *Helvidius No. 5*, published anonymously in 1793, Madison stated that "*some* sacrifices of interest will be made to other motives; by nations as well as by individuals."[55] Finally, when speaking at the 1829 Virginia Constitutional Convention, Madison noted that the "essence of Government is power; and power, lodged as it must be in human hands, will ever be liable to abuse . . . man is known to be a selfish, as well as a social being. Respect for character, though often a salutary restraint, is but too often overruled by other motives."[56] In this comment, made relatively late in his life, Madison confirmed his belief that human nature is diverse, capable of both good and wrong. Government is *liable* to abuse, and humans will *often* act selfishly, but neither is a certainty. Thus, Madison consistently qualified his view on people's motives, and he held a complex understanding of human nature throughout his political life, both publicly and privately.

Given that Madison understood human nature as diverse—with some capable of being virtuous, and others not—how did he incorporate this belief into his political theory? The key to unlocking this riddle is to understand that Madison advocated liberalism as an end *and* as a means to other ends. Madison wanted to achieve a virtuous society. Indeed, as he stated at the Virginia Ratifying Convention, "the people will have virtue and intelligence to select men of virtue and wisdom [to govern]. Is there no virtue among us? If there be not, we are in a wretched situation."[57] Madison wanted to achieve an end typically ascribed to classical republicanism, that of virtue: "To suppose that any form of government will secure liberty or happiness without any virtue in the people, is a chimerical idea."[58] Based only on these statements and others like them, it would appear that Madison was a classical republican who emphasized virtue, and that no harmonization is needed. However, Madison believed that humans are prone to acting selfishly, not just virtuously. How could we achieve the most virtue then? For Madison, the answer was in liberalism.

Madison believed that government had a duty to protect natural, liberal rights. In this sense, Madison thought that those in government should act virtuously to protect such natural rights. This was driven in part by Madison's debt to Witherspoon, who had instilled in Madison the belief that we have retained natural liberties. Madison also took to the theories of John Locke, another prominent author he studied at Princeton.

However, Madison also believed there was a need to justify these natural rights for the secondary benefits that he believed would result from their protection; these secondary goods came in two forms. First, a government that protects liberal rights would coexist with and even cultivate virtue when citizens *learn* how to be virtuous by exercising their rights. This is closest to the model of liberalism advocated by Adam Smith and Thomas Jefferson. Yet even for those selfish persons with such a vicious nature that no amount of cultivation could make them virtuous, liberalism still provided the best cure for this disease. Madison believed that persons, through hard work and industry, would help create a more productive society that would benefit all. For Madison, the protection of natural liberty would achieve those results.

What throws off Supreme Court justices and many academics is the rich complexity of Madison's thought. Those who see Madison as a classical republican often focus too much on his statements regarding the attainment of virtue. This group of scholars neglects Madison's views on natural rights and on the ability of a liberal system to lead people to the achievement of virtue. On the other hand, those who see Madison solely as a natural-rights liberal often neglect Madison's statements on virtue. Grasping Madison's ideas on human nature—which directed Madison to fear our vices and find hope in our virtues—allows one to draw together a coherent set of ideas about Madison's political theory.

three

MADISON'S MULTIFACETED LIBERALISM

NATURAL RIGHTS AND LOCKEAN LIBERALISM

Throughout his career, Madison was passionate about protecting natural rights, which was partly attributable to his studies under Witherspoon. When Witherspoon came to America, he brought with him not only a complex view of human nature but also a political theory that included natural rights. According to Witherspoon in his "Lectures on Moral Philosophy," at least some rights are the gift of nature: "Rights may be . . . natural or acquired."[1] Witherspoon also believed that "[r]eason teaches natural liberty, and common utility recommends it."[2] Indeed, for Witherspoon, "Liberty either cannot or ought not to be given up in the social state: the end of the union should be the protection of liberty, as far as it is a blessing."[3]

Madison held similar beliefs. Madison first articulated his thoughts on natural rights when discussing the freedom of religion. In his proposed religious freedom amendment at the 1776 Virginia Provincial Convention, Madison recommended that "all men are equally entitled to enjoy the free exercise of religion, according to the dictates of conscience, unpunished and unrestrained by the magistrate, Unless the preservation of equal liberty and the existence of the State are manifestly endangered."[4] Madison defined the free exercise of religion as an almost unlimited right, except when it infringes on the equal rights of others *and* threatens the existence of the state itself. Additionally, it is something to be exercised "according to the dictates of conscience," implying that it is a pre-societal right that is to be exercised however the person owning the right desires. This is a very broad and liberal protection of this right—the focus is on individual autonomy, not the collective needs of the community.

Likewise, Madison in his "Memorial and Remonstrance" took a liberal stance on rights. He began by stating, "The Religion then of every man must be left to the conviction and conscience of every man; and it is the right of every man to exercise it as these may dictate."[5] Madison continued: "It is unalienable. . . . This duty is precedent, both in order of time and in degree of obligation, to the claims of Civil Society."[6] Calling something an unalienable right that is more important than the claims of civil society certainly classifies it as a natural right. Madison went on to state, "We maintain therefore that in matters of Religion, no man[']s right is abridged by the institution of Civil Society and that Religion is wholly exempt from its cognizance."[7] This theme runs throughout the "Memorial and Remonstrance." Madison expanded his liberal statements beyond that of religion later in the "Memorial and Remonstrance" when he emphasized the liberal understanding of equality and natural rights by stating that "all men are to be considered as entering into Society on equal conditions; as relinquishing no more and therefore no less, one than another, of their natural rights."[8] Later Madison reaffirmed his view that religion "is held by the same tenure with all our other rights. If we recur to its origin, it is equally the gift of nature."[9] It is quite evident again that Madison was focusing on protecting a liberal, natural right to freedom of religion, *and* he stated that there are other rights that are gifts of nature too.

When composing his contributions to *The Federalist,* Madison also used the tools of liberal, natural rights discourse. In *Federalist* 43, Madison defended the requirement that the Constitution would be established once nine states had ratified it. Madison stated that this question is "answered at once by recurring . . . to the great principle of self preservation; to the transcendent law of nature and of nature's God, which declares that the safety and happiness of society are the objects at which all political institutions aim, and to which all such institutions must be sacrificed."[10] The emphasis on a liberal understanding of rights is once again clear. Madison defended the "great principle" of self-preservation of life itself. Madison referenced the law of nature and of nature's God. Madison allowed for the "sacrifice" of political institutions that do not adhere to the natural law.

Madison's liberal sentiments continued in *Federalist* 44, when he proclaimed that "[b]ills of attainder, *ex post facto* laws, and laws impairing the obligation of contracts, are contrary to the first principles of the social compact."[11] Madison defended those protections because allowing such laws would run contrary to the reasons why we entered into the social compact in the first place. This echoed Locke's liberal statements on the social compact in *The Second Treatise of Government:* "Despotical power is an absolute, arbitrary power one man has over another. . . . This is a power, which neither nature gives . . . nor compact can convey: for man not having such an arbitrary power over his own life, cannot give another man such a power over it."[12] In other words, according to Locke, "whoever has the legislative or supreme power of any common-wealth, is bound to govern by established standing laws, promulgated and known to the people, and not by extemporary decrees."[13] Madison espoused a similar theory in *The Federalist.* John Witherspoon had held much the same position: "From this view of society as a voluntary compact results this principle, that men are originally and by nature equal, and consequently free."[14]

When Madison was proposing the Bill of Rights, he also used liberal language to describe at least some of the rights he wanted protected from government infringement. This was manifested most clearly in Madison's suggestion to add the following prefix at the beginning of the Constitution:

> That all power is originally vested in, and consequently derived from, the people.

> That Government is instituted and ought to be exercised for the benefit of the people; which consists in the enjoyment of life and liberty, with the right of acquiring and using property, and generally of pursuing and obtaining happiness and safety.

> That the people have an indubitable, unalienable, and indefeasible right to reform or change their Government, whenever it be found adverse or inadequate to the purposes of its institution.[15]

Madison's prefixed declaration closely follows the pattern of two other liberal documents—the Declaration of Independence and Locke's political theory in *The Second Treatise of Government*. First, consider the second paragraph of the Declaration of Independence, primarily drafted by Thomas Jefferson:

> WE hold these Truths to be self-evident, that all Men are created equal, that they are endowed by their Creator with certain unalienable Rights, that among these are Life, Liberty and the Pursuit of Happiness—That to secure these Rights, Governments are instituted among Men, deriving their just Powers from the Consent of the Governed, that whenever any Form of Government becomes destructive of these Ends, it is the Right of the People to alter or to abolish it, and to institute new Government, laying its Foundation on such Principles, and organizing its Powers in such Form, as to them shall seem most likely to effect their Safety and Happiness.

Now, consider the following passages from Locke's *Second Treatise of Government:*

> Man being born, as has been proved, with a title to perfect freedom, and an uncontrouled enjoyment of all the rights and privileges of the law of nature, equally with any other man, or number of men in the world, hath by nature a power, not only to preserve his property, that is, his life, liberty and estate, against the injuries and attempts of other men; but to judge of, and punish the breaches of that law in others.[16]

> Where-ever therefore any number of men are so united into one society, as to quit every one his executive power of the law of nature, and to resign it to

the public, there and there only is a political, or civil society. And this is done, where-ever any number of men, in the state of nature, enter into society to make one people, one body politic, under one supreme government.[17]

THE great end of men's entering into society, being the enjoyment of their properties in peace and safety.[18]

[W]hen by the miscarriages of those in authority, [government power] is forfeited; upon the forfeiture, or at the determination of the time set, it reverts to the society, and the people have a right to act as supreme, and continue the legislative in themselves; or erect a new form, or under the old form place it in new hands, as they think good.[19]

Note the similarity of Madison's proposed prefix to the other two works. Madison, the Declaration, and Locke all claim the people have unalienable rights of nature. Government power is originally derived from the people. The people give away some of this power in order to institute a government for the ends of protecting their lives, liberty, property (or happiness). However, the people retain a right to reform that government or to institute a new government if these natural ends are not attained.

Locke's and Jefferson's theories were particularly appealing to Madison. Indeed, reading Locke's idea of natural rights under the direction of Witherspoon struck a chord with a young James Madison. There is no doubt that this happened, as Locke was on the reading list for Witherspoon's moral philosophy class that Madison took as an undergraduate.[20] Witherspoon's lectures emphasized many arguments drawn from Locke's *Second Treatise,* and the Princeton library at the time of Madison's attendance had more books by Locke than any other political philosopher.[21] As will be examined in more detail below, Madison also had a strong friendship with Jefferson throughout his life, and the two of them profoundly influenced each other's respective political theories and ideas on liberty.

When Madison drafted what would eventually be edited into the Ninth Amendment, he proposed to Congress that the "exceptions here or elsewhere in the constitution, made in favor of particular rights, shall not be so construed as to diminish the just importance of other rights retained by the people."[22] Presumably, Madison stated "other rights retained" to imply that certain natural rights are kept by the people after the formation of government. Madison's liberal understanding of rights continued later in this same speech, when he described the liberties he proposed in the Bill of Rights. Madison stated that

In some instances they assert those rights which are exercised by the people in forming and establishing a plan of government. In other instances, they specify *those rights which are retained when particular powers are given up to be exercised by the legislature.* In other instances, they specify positive rights, which may seem to result from the nature of the compact. Trial by jury cannot be considered as *a natural right* . . . but is as essential to secure the liberty of the people as any one of *the pre-existent rights of nature.*[23]

Madison classified the different types of freedoms he was trying to protect in his proposed Bill of Rights. Some of the rights he submitted were natural ones retained by the people when power was given away to government. Conversely, some rights were positive, simply created by the social compact. His discussion of rights in his speech proposing the Bill of Rights included rights that must be considered liberal—individual, unalienable, natural rights that are always kept by the people and which should not be violated by any legitimate government.

In a 1790 letter to Thomas Jefferson, Madison continued debating within a liberal framework of natural rights. In a discussion with Jefferson regarding how long a current majority may bind future generations, Madison stated:

Prior then to the establishment of this principle [of majority rule], unanimity was necessary; and strict Theory at all times presupposes the assent of every member to the establishment of the rule itself. If this assent cannot be given tacitly, or be not implied where no positive evidence forbids, persons born in Society would not on attaining ripe age be bound by acts of the Majority; and either a unanimous repetition of every law would be necessary on the accession of new members, or an express assent must be obtained from these to the rule by which the voice of the Majority is made the voice of the whole.[24]

Madison took as given in his debate with Jefferson that we make a unanimous decision whether to enter civil society, presumably because each of us retains the natural right whether to keep all of our liberties in the state of nature or to join civil society. Once in civil society, we make decisions based on the principle of majority rule, and by living in a country we are giving "tacit assent" to abide by its laws. This political theory again sounds very much like Locke's *Second Treatise of Government,* where he used similar reasoning regarding the rules of unanimity and majority: "For when any number of men have, by the consent of every individual, made a community, they have thereby made that community one body, with a power to act as one body, which is only by the will and determination of the majority."[25] Likewise, Madison employed the idea of tacit consent in a manner similar to Locke: "every man, that hath any possessions, or enjoyment, of any part of the dominions of any government, doth thereby give his *tacit consent,* and is as far forth obliged to obedience to the laws of that government, during such enjoyment."[26] In *Federalist* 43,

Madison also made use of the term "law of nature,"[27] a phrase employed by Locke 43 times in the *Second Treatise*.[28]

Madison directly mentioned John Locke's name on one occasion in his *National Gazette* essays. In "Spirit of Governments" in 1792, Madison spoke of Isaac Newton and Locke as having "established immortal systems, the one in matter, the other in mind."[29] Although it is likely here that Madison was referencing Locke's philosophical empiricism, not his liberalism, it is strong evidence that Locke, a champion of classical liberalism, was held in high regard by Madison. This reading is confirmed when Madison resorted to Locke in his *Helvidius No. 1* essay. Approvingly, Madison observed that Locke "discussed . . . particularly the principles of liberty."[30]

Madison's advocacy of classically liberal natural rights was very apparent in another of his *National Gazette* essays, "Property." In this essay Madison explained that property "in its particular application means 'that dominion which one man claims and exercises over the external things of the world, in exclusion of every other individual.'"[31] Madison continued: "In its larger and juster meaning, it embraces everything to which a man may attach a value and have a right; and *which leaves to everyone else the like advantage*."[32] There is a distinctive liberal flavor to this statement, as it defined "property" more broadly than simply physical things. It also followed Locke's equality requirement of leaving to everyone else the like advantage in matters of property. Compare Madison's statement above with the following from Locke regarding property usage: "Nothing was made by God for man to spoil or destroy . . . there was never the less left for others because of his enclosure for himself: for he that leaves as much as another can make use of, does as good as take nothing at all."[33] Furthermore, Madison clarified in "Property" that he defined property as broadly as Locke:

> In the former sense, a man's land, or merchandize, or money is called his property. In the latter sense, a man has a property in his opinions and the free communication of them. He has a property of peculiar value in his religious opinions, and in the profession and practice dictated by them. He has a property very dear to him in the safety and liberty of his person. He has an equal property in the free use of his faculties and free choice of the objects on which to employ them. In a word, as a man is said to have a right to his property, he may be equally said to have a property in his rights.[34]

This was similar to Locke in *The Second Treatise of Government*: "every man has a property in his own person: this nobody has any right to but himself. The labour of his body, and the work of his hands, we may say, are properly his."[35] Locke would further broaden the word "property" to include one's "life, liberty and estate,"[36] and "property which men have in their persons as well as goods."[37] Thus, there is a liberal, Lockean definition that Madison had when he spoke generally of the word property. For both men, property included not only tangible items, but also liberties such as the freedoms of religion and speech that we possessed as human beings. Both men ultimately focused on protecting the autonomy of the individual to dispose of property and exercise rights as he or she saw fit.

Madison concluded his "Property" essay with a liberal, natural-rights understanding of the subject. He stated that "Government is instituted to protect property of every sort; as well that which lies in the various rights of individuals, as that which the term particularly expresses. This being the end of government, that alone is a *just* government, which *impartially* secures to every man, whatever is his *own*."[38] Madison also then implied that government should maintain "the inviolability of property."[39] Compare how similar Madison is to Locke when claiming that government's central purpose is to protect property. According to Locke, "The great and chief end . . . of men's uniting into commonwealths, and putting themselves under government, is the preservation of their property."[40] Overall, Madison defended the idea of natural rights within a liberal framework, and like Locke he emphasized that a government is legitimate *only* if it protects everyone's individual property rights on an equal basis. Since Madison defined "property" as including one's life and liberty, Madison placed a large emphasis on the protection of freedom, akin to that of a contemporary libertarian.

For Madison, the idea of natural, liberal rights was in perfect conformity with his realistic belief in human nature. Madison believed that a government made of virtuous leaders would act justly and protect these natural rights. He also knew that there would be governments of tyrants, who would take away those rights. Furthermore, the principles of natural rights and a realistic view of human nature acted in harmony for Madison. Indeed, Madison thought that protecting natural rights would have valuable secondary benefits to society, given all the strengths and weaknesses he saw in human nature.

PROTECTING NATURAL RIGHTS TO CULTIVATE VIRTUE

In addition to believing in natural rights, Madison also saw liberalism as necessary because, realistically, some will be virtuous and some will not. According to Madison, we need freedom but at the same time we cannot trust one another or the government. Thus, Madison did not see liberalism as simply an end in itself, but also as a means to the dual ends of achieving virtue and the common good. In the first sense, Madison believed that protecting liberal rights would cultivate virtue among people. Since Madison thought that some people were capable of virtue, he wanted to provide them with a broad set of liberties to allow them to cultivate and use their virtue, a view similar to that expressed in the political theories of Adam Smith and Thomas Jefferson.

Adam Smith is perhaps best known for his theory of free trade and self-interest in *The Wealth of Nations*. Take, for instance, the following passage from Smith's influential work: "It is not from the benevolence of the butcher, the brewer, or the baker, that we expect our dinner, but from their regard to their own interest. We address ourselves, not to their humanity but to their self-love."[41] Adam Smith's economic system was built not only upon the realization of humans' self-interest, but also upon the idea that the invisible hand will best regulate the market:

> As every individual, therefore, endeavours as much as he can both to employ his capital in the support of domestic industry, and so to direct that industry that its produce may be of the greatest value; every individual necessarily labours to render the annual revenue of the society as great as he can. He generally, indeed, neither intends to promote the public interest, nor knows how much he is promoting it . . . by directing that industry in such a manner as its produce may be of the greatest value, he intends only his own gain, and he is in this, as in many other cases, led by an *invisible hand* to promote an end which was no part of his intention. Nor is it always the worse for the society that it was no part of it. By pursuing his own interest he frequently promotes that of the society more effectually than when he really intends to promote it.[42]

Thus, an important part of Smith's philosophy is the economic need of individuals having the freedom to pursue their rational self-interest.

However, there was much more to Smith's philosophy. He also stated in *The Wealth of Nations*, "All for ourselves and nothing for other people, seems, in every age of the world, to have been the vile maxim of the masters of mankind."[43] Smith was quite adamant that we should strive toward more than blind self-interest. Smith's belief that humans are capable of virtue was evident in his other major work, *The Theory of Moral Sentiments:* "How selfish soever man may be supposed, there are evidently some principles in his nature, which interest him in the fortune of others, and render their happiness necessary to him, though he derives nothing from it, except the pleasure of seeing it."[44] According to Smith, self-interest is not *necessarily* bad, but some types of self-interest may be harmful. Therefore, Smith believed that we should still strive toward being virtuous, and he believed we are all quite capable of virtue. For Smith, humanity could be virtuous even when we have the liberal freedom to act selfishly.[45] But Madison went a step further than this, also believing that protecting liberal rights, particularly land ownership, would *lead* people to become more virtuous.[46] According to this theory, working the land (particularly as a farmer) made one appreciate the fruit of one's labor, and one who owned property was also more likely to see his or her interests tied up with the good of the community.

One of the most prominent American proponents of this political philosophy was Madison's close friend Thomas Jefferson. Although Jefferson and Madison did not have identical political philosophies, they shared the idea of property ownership leading to virtue. Indeed, Jefferson focused heavily on the need to protect the rights of farmers as a class (which included protecting their property rights) as a way to achieve virtue. According to Jefferson, "Those who labour in the earth are the chosen people of God, if ever He had a chosen people, whose breasts he has made his peculiar deposits for substantial and genuine virtue."[47] Indeed, for Jefferson, protecting property ownership was important because those who own their own land and work that land had the opportunity to become virtuous: "It is the mark set on those, who not looking up to heaven, to their own soil and industry, as does the husbandman, for their subsistence, depend for it on the casualties and caprice of customers. Dependence begets subservience and venality, suffocates the germ of virtue, and prepares fit tools for the designs of ambition."[48] Jefferson believed that owning one's own farm and working the land would lead to the cultivation of virtue through hard work. On the other hand, relying on others for money and food would lead to dependence and would lessen one's concern with virtue and liberty. As Jefferson later clarified in a letter to John Jay, "Cultivators of the earth are the most valuable citizens. They are the most vigorous, the most independent, the most virtuous, and they are tied to their country, and wedded to its liberty and interests, by the most lasting bonds."[49] Conversely, Jefferson understood those who were not property owners to be "the panders of vice, and the instruments by which the liberties of a country are generally overturned."[50] Thus, it was imperative for Jefferson that property rights be protected, so people could learn to become virtuous through the valuable experience of independently working and living off of the land.

But how much of this theory did Madison, Jefferson's lifelong friend and supporter, advocate? Based on his writings and speeches, it is evident that from very early on in his life Madison did subscribe to this theory.[51] Madison thought that having autonomy was essential to one's ability to attain virtue. Indeed, for Madison, protecting liberal freedoms would allow us to learn from our successes and our mistakes when exercising our freedoms. Protecting these freedoms would place us in a community that respects our individual rights, thus giving us a mutual respect for our community and toleration for others who exercise their freedoms. Finally, Madison believed that protecting liberal rights would allow the majority the chance to learn the importance of those rights and then restrain themselves from acting out of self-interest against the minority.

As early as 1774 Madison stated in a letter to William Bradford that without religious freedom a society will have "Pride, ignorance and Knavery among the Priesthood and Vice and Wickedness among the Laity."[52] However, Madison went on in the same letter to state that a society which protects "religious as well as Civil Liberty" will be one in which "Industry and Virtue have been promoted."[53] Madison thus espoused very early on that the protection of civil liberty could lead one to be virtuous, but the absence of such rights could lead to the opposite result. Over a decade later Madison reaffirmed this belief in his "Memorial and Remonstrance": "During almost fifteen centuries has the legal establishment of Christianity been on trial. What have been its fruits? More or less in all places, pride and indolence in the Clergy, ignorance and servility in the laity, in both, superstition, bigotry and persecution."[54] Madison also characterized religious establishments of any kind (where religious freedom is obviously lacking) as promoting "intolerance."[55] Thus, even early on in his life Madison clearly believed that, at least for religious liberty, protecting liberal rights was a good way to achieve virtue.

This belief continued throughout Madison's career. For instance, Madison's Smithian/Jeffersonian liberalism was on full display in a 1785 letter to James Monroe when he spoke about potential congressional regulation of trade. "Much indeed is it to be wished, as I conceive, that no regulations of trade, that is to say, no restrictions or imposts whatever, were necessary," wrote Madison. "A perfect freedom is the System which would be my choice."[56] Madison publicly maintained this attitude when in Congress: "commerce ought to be free, and labor and industry left at large to find its proper object."[57] There is substantial evidence that Madison consistently supported a philosophical position in favor of free trade.[58] Madison took this stance because it gave people the opportunity to become more virtuous, as a later speech in Congress on commercial policy reveals: "Universal freedom presents the most noble spectacle, unites all nations—makes (every man) a citizen of the whole society of mankind—and perfects the good aimed at by Social union & Civil Govt."[59] Again, Madison confirmed his belief that providing more freedom will make us more virtuous, and it will remind us that we as individuals are part of a moral community and should work for the betterment of our fellow human beings living in that community.

When Madison proposed the Bill of Rights in Congress he stated that "I am inclined to believe, if once bills of rights are established in all the states as well as the federal constitution, we shall find that altho' some of them are rather unimportant, yet, upon the whole, they will have a salutary tendency."[60] What "tendency" is Madison speaking of? Later in that speech he explained that bills of rights, while they at their core are only "paper barriers" that the majority could disregard, also "have a tendency to impress some degree of respect for them, to establish the public opinion in their favor, and rouse the attention of the whole community, [so] it may be one mean to controul the majority from those acts to which they might otherwise be inclined."[61] Madison believed that the protection of liberty could have a positive effect on people and nurture them to become more virtuous. By exercising the liberties in the Bill of Rights and realizing their value, Madison believed an otherwise self-interested majority would eventually learn to restrain itself from taking away the rights of the minority.

Madison continued making statements such as these in his 1792 *National Gazette* essays. For instance, in "Republican Distribution of Citizens" Madison stated, "The class of citizens who provide at once their own food and their own raiment, may be viewed as the most truly independent and happy. They are more: they are the best basis of public liberty, and the strongest bulwark of public safety. It follows, that the greater the proportion of this class to the whole society, the more free, the more independent, and the more happy must be the society itself."[62] Here, Madison quite pointedly stated the Jeffersonian position. Because farmers produce their own food and clothing, it educates them and makes them more independent. Madison believed that this would then lead to the "best basis of public liberty," which ultimately means acting virtuously in the name of the community. All of this must be precipitated by the protection of liberal rights, such as property ownership, that allow the farmer a free hand to work the land and decide which crops to plant and which livestock to raise.

Madison continued this sentiment in another one of his *National Gazette* essays, "Fashion." Here, Madison praised "the independent situation and manly sentiments of American citizens, who live on their own soil, or whose labour is necessary to its cultivation, or who were occupied in supplying wants, which being founded in solid utility, in comfortable accommodation, or in settled habits, produce a reciprocity of dependence, at once ensuring subsistence, and inspiring a dignified sense of social rights."[63] Madison claimed that farmers would be more independent and happy, and they are the best basis of liberty and public safety. By making use of the right of property ownership and choosing one's occupation freely, it will inspire a "dignified sense of social rights" and the awareness that it is better to act for the public that protects these rights than solely out of self-interest. For this reason, Madison believed that more than any other group farmers were concerned with the good of society, and they constituted the "commanding part of society."[64] This is another strong stance in favor of protecting liberally understood property rights so that people can freely farm the land and become virtuous citizens in the process.

Finally, Madison repeatedly and publicly expressed his praise for Smith's theories and works. Madison used Smith's seminal phrase "the invisible hand" when he gave the House of Representatives response to Washington's

First Inaugural Address.[65] Madison also demonstrated his respect for Smith by recommending that Congress acquire Smith's *The Wealth of Nations*[66] and by referring to Smith in a congressional speech as one of "the most enlightened patrons of banks."[67] According to fellow House member Fisher Ames, during the First Congress Madison was nearly obsessed with Smith's theory, and Madison's speeches were littered with quotes from *The Wealth of Nations*. Speaking of Madison in a May 1789 letter, Ames observed that "he is too much attached to his theories, for a politician. He is well versed in public life, was bred to it, and has no other profession. Yet, may I say it, it is rather a science, than a business, with him. He adopts his maxims as he finds them in books, and with too little regard to the actual state of things. One of his first speeches in regard to protecting commerce, was taken out of Smith's *Wealth of Nations*."[68] At least in the minds of his contemporaries, Madison was under the influence of Smith in spring 1789, the same time he penned his draft of the Bill of Rights. However, the next section will demonstrate that Madison also went beyond Smith's theories when configuring the bounds of civil liberties.

PROTECTING NATURAL RIGHTS FOR THE COMMON GOOD

Adam Smith influenced Madison, but the Father of the Constitution did not completely share Smith's more optimistic view of human nature and moral progress. For Madison, only some were capable of virtue, and even virtuous persons might stray from time to time. So, what of those humans with a nature that could not be made more virtuous? In such cases Madison still thought that protecting liberal, natural rights could be used to a greater end. Madison believed that through protecting liberal rights, the actions of those who were primarily self-interested could be harnessed for the greater good. Indeed, Madison thought that if we selfishly and jealously guarded our own rights, it would result in the public good.

Madison still wanted to promote virtue in his liberal republic. However, Madison also believed that his liberal system of rights would be beneficial to society, even for those who acted out of self-interest. Indeed, Madison's understanding of human nature and his statements make clear that he believed self-interest could result in some good for the community.

Early in his career in the "Memorial and Remonstrance" Madison remarked that "it is proper to take alarm at the first experiment on our liberties. We hold this prudent jealousy to be the first duty of Citizens."[69] This was a prescription by Madison to jealously and selfishly guard our own freedoms; by doing so, it will make society overall better off by fortifying these rights for all.

Madison continued this line of thought in *Federalist* 10, where he explained why the Constitution would be a good vehicle to "break and control the violence of faction."[70] First, Madison defined a "faction" as "a number of citizens, whether amounting to a majority or a minority of the whole, who are united and actuated by some common impulse of passion, or of interest, adverse to the rights of other citizens, or to the permanent and aggregate interests of the community."[71] Madison was speaking of persons exercising their liberties and acting out of self-interest. Madison saw that a powerful faction might act contrary to the common good. Madison then explained how *not* to solve this problem:

> There are two methods of curing the mischiefs of faction: the one, by removing its causes; the other, by controlling its effects. There are again two methods of removing the causes of faction: the one, by destroying the liberty which is essential to its existence; the other, by giving to every citizen the same opinions, the same passions, and the same interests. It could never be more truly said than of the first remedy, that it was worse than the disease. Liberty is to faction what air is to fire, an aliment without which it instantly expires. But it could not be less folly to abolish liberty, which is essential to political life, because it nourishes faction, than it would be to wish the annihilation of air, which is essential to animal life, because it imparts to fire its destructive agency.[72]

Madison was adamantly opposed to taking away the liberties that allow people to form factions, even dangerous factions. And keep in mind that these are liberties Madison knew would eventually lead a faction to commit violence. Presumably, the most relevant liberties of which Madison spoke were freedom of religion, freedoms of speech and association, and property rights, as Madison noted that

> A zeal for different opinions concerning religion, concerning government, and many other points, as well of speculation as of practice; an attachment to different leaders ambitiously contending for pre-eminence and power; or to persons of other descriptions whose fortunes have been interesting to the human passions, have, in turn, divided mankind into parties, inflamed them with mutual animosity, and rendered them much more disposed to vex and oppress each other than to co-operate for their common good. So strong is this propensity of mankind to fall into mutual animosities, that where no substantial occasion presents itself, the most frivolous and fanciful distinctions have been sufficient to kindle their unfriendly passions and excite their most violent conflicts. But the most common and durable source of factions has been the various and unequal distribution of property.[73]

Madison reaffirmed that protecting these liberties will inevitably lead to grave problems, as they have created vexation and oppression in the past. Yet, Madison's solution was not to ban these factions from forming. Rather, he suggested that we harness their potentially destructive power and focus it toward the public good. This is done, according to Madison in *Federalist* 10, in two ways. First, we adhere to "the republican principle, which enables the majority to defeat its sinister views by regular vote," and we elect legislators "whose wisdom may best discern the true interest of their country, and whose patriotism and love of justice will be least likely to sacrifice it to temporary or partial considerations."[74] Second, we should extend the size of the republic so that "as each representative will be chosen by a greater number of citizens in the large than in the small republic, it will be more difficult for unworthy candidates to practice with success the vicious arts by which elections are too often carried."[75] Thus, Madison believed that the vice that results from allowing people to exercise their liberal, natural rights can still be limited and be used for good because it can lead to the election of more virtuous leaders. Protecting liberties, even when some people will exercise them solely for their self-interest, ultimately leads to the common good. Madison's theory about rights again conforms to his realistic views on human nature.

In *Federalist* 51, Madison claimed that part of the genius of the Constitution is that it employs the separation of powers to prevent the "gradual concentration of the several powers in the same department."[76] Madison stated that the Constitution prevents this evil because the Framers understood that "[a]mbition must be made to counteract ambition. The interest of the man must be connected with the constitutional rights of the place."[77] He subsequently asserted that we need a "policy of supplying, by opposite and rival interests, the defect of better motives."[78] As discussed earlier, Madison was conceding that there are many who are incapable of virtue. For Madison, the best way to prevent a self-interested person from taking too much power is to allow for multiple self-interested power seekers to compete with one another. Since it is likely that each branch of government will have at least some such persons in it, we should allow them to compete with one another. This competition will prevent any one person from becoming an all-powerful, tyrannical despot. Madison summed this up in the following statement: "the constant aim is to divide and arrange the several offices in such a manner as that each may be a check on the other; that the private interest of every individual may be a sentinel over the public rights."[79] Thus, if we can properly channel the self-interest that naturally exists in humans, we can turn it into something which will promote the public good.

Madison continued to express this position throughout his works. In *Federalist* 43, he defended the Copyright Clause's grant of exclusive rights to authors and inventors for their writings and discoveries, respectively. Madison noted that the "utility of this power will scarcely be questioned" because the "copyright of authors has been solemnly adjudged, in Great Britain, to be a right of common law. The right to useful inventions seems with equal reason to belong to the inventors. The public good fully coincides in both cases with the claims of individuals."[80] Madison described how protecting individual freedoms, even if their use is motivated by self-interest, will lead to the common good. He stated that it is good for authors and inventors to be able to exercise selfishly their right to exclusive rights over their creations. This "fully coincides" with the "public good" because it provides an incentive for authors and inventors to toil away at their work, knowing that if they create something useful they will have exclusive rights to it and the opportunity to become wealthy from it. This greed will enhance the lives of those of us who will be employed by such authors and inventors as well as those of us who will be the readers of their writings and the consumers of their inventions. Thus, Madison's beliefs regarding self-interest being engrained in so many people's nature again led him to the belief that by protecting liberal rights we could channel this self-interest toward something better for all of society.

In his *Report on the Alien and Sedition Acts,* written in 1800, Madison defended a libertarian understanding of the freedom of the press. In doing so, Madison claimed that a free press even with elements of self-interest is still good for society: "Some degree of abuse is inseparable from the proper use of everything; and in no instance is this more true, than in that of the press. It has accordingly been decided by the practice of the states, that it is better to leave a few of its noxious branches to their luxuriant growth, than by pruning them away, to injure the vigour of those yielding the proper fruits."[81] For Madison it was better to protect a classically liberal understanding of the press because limiting the freedom of the press would harm the press's ability to keep the public informed. Even though there will be some in the press who will lack virtue and will publish items that lack journalistic integrity just to make a buck, we are still all better off by allowing the press as a whole to have the freedom to report on public issues. Once again, the liberal freedom should be protected because the cure of ending liberty would be worse than the disease of self-interested journalism. Of course, another benefit discussed by Madison in this passage is that some members of the press will maintain and even develop virtue through the exercise of their freedom—they will yield "the proper fruits."

Madison also believed that allowing people selfish economic pursuits would leave all of society better off. In a 1789 speech in Congress, Madison gave his reasoning for this belief as follows: "I own myself the friend to a very free system of commerce, and hold it as a truth, that commercial shackles are generally unjust, oppressive and impolitic—it is also a truth, that if industry and labor are left to their own course, they will generally be directed toward those objects which are the most productive."[82] Madison's message again is that allowing for economic freedoms, even if people are selfish, can lead to more productivity, which benefits us all.

Finally, there is evidence that Madison maintained this position into his later years. Indeed, in 1821 he commented that "[i]n civilized communities, property as well as personal rights is an essential object of the laws, which encourage industry by securing the enjoyment of its fruits."[83] Once more, Madison proclaimed that we should protect liberties and property rights because, by allowing people to make good use of these rights, their natural inclination will be to use them to acquire wealth and increase the overall "fruits" of society.

Madison was a multifaceted liberal who found it paramount that we protect natural liberal rights both for their own sake and as a means to the best possible ends. Madison believed this was the most viable political theory because of his views on human nature. As Madison understood it, we retained certain liberties from nature, and any legitimate government must protect these natural, liberal rights. Madison also advocated a political theory that could take advantage of the potential virtue in humanity as well as the more common self-interest. He thought that protecting liberal rights would promote virtue and the common good. In this regard, Madison's primary influences were Witherspoon, Hume, Locke, Smith, and Jefferson.

Now, before demonstrating what rights Madison wanted to see protected in the Bill of Rights, an important question needs to be answered: if Madison consistently defended and advocated the protection of liberal rights, why did Madison *not* initially advocate a Bill of Rights in the Constitution? In other words, if Madison really did want to protect liberal rights, why did he not propose doing this at the Constitutional Convention, instead of waiting almost two years later to do it in the First Congress? This is an important question to answer because, if Madison was not committed to protecting liberty, then all of his statements about freedom are disingenuous, and it is pointless to cite what he said about the Bill of Rights. As the next two chapters demonstrate, Madison was at first opposed to a bill of rights; then he favored one for strategic reasons; and, ultimately, he supported a bill of rights for its own sake. Thus, Madison's statements were not disingenuous, and his initial reservations toward a bill of rights were because of his love of liberty, not in spite of it.

MADISON OPPOSES A BILL OF RIGHTS,
THEN SEES ITS STRATEGIC VALUE

A BILL OF RIGHTS AS SUPERFLUOUS

Madison did not originally think that a bill of rights could fully safeguard the liberal freedoms he thought were natural rights, necessary to the cultivation of virtue, and important to promoting the public good. Instead, Madison initially believed that the separation of powers, federalism, and ambition checking ambition would be the most effective safeguards of liberal rights against a runaway majority or against a small group of self-serving aristocrats. At the outset, Madison believed that a bill of rights would not sufficiently protect liberties for three reasons: he feared it would be superfluous, dangerous, and ineffective.

At first, Madison opposed a bill of rights because he believed that in a best case scenario a bill of rights would be superfluous to protecting liberty. This was due to Madison's belief that power to infringe on rights was never given to the federal government. In *Federalist* 38, Madison rhetorically asked, "Is a bill of rights essential to liberty? The confederation has no bill of rights."[1] In other words, the lack of a bill of rights in the proposed Constitution was no reason to oppose it when the existing Articles of Confederation also had no bill of rights. However, Madison's larger point was that a bill of rights was not essential to liberty. But why? Madison believed that the federal government did not possess adequate power to make a bill of rights necessary: "There cannot be a more positive and unequivocal declaration of the principle of the adoption—that every thing not granted is reserved. This is obviously and self-evidently the case, without the declaration [of rights]."[2] Instead, Madison thought that the state governments were more in need of limitations than the new, relatively weak, federal government: "The powers delegated by the proposed Constitution to the federal government are few and defined. Those which are to remain in the State governments are numerous and indefinite."[3] At this point, Madison was concerned with ensuring that the new national government had sufficient powers to accomplish national goals. It was partially the fear of state power run amuck that precipitated the Constitutional Convention.[4] Madison had many more reasons to fear abuses by the relatively strong, well-established state governments than to fear the nascent federal government with its limited list of enumerated powers. In the year after the adjournment of the 1787 Constitutional Convention, Madison repeatedly stated that there was no need to fear the federal government harming rights because it was given such little power.

For instance, in January 1788, Madison averred in *Federalist* 41 that it was a "misconception" to believe that a "power to destroy the freedom of the press, the trial by jury, or even to regulate the course of descents, or the forms of conveyances, must be very singularly expressed by the terms 'to raise money for the general welfare.'"[5] In June of that same year at the Virginia Ratifying Convention, Madison noted that "I have no reason to conclude that uniformity of government will produce that of religion. This subject is, for the honor of America, perfectly free and unshackled. The [federal] government has no jurisdiction over it: the least reflection will convince us there is no danger to be feared on this ground."[6] In a subsequent speech that same month in the Virginia Ratifying Convention, Madison stated that "[t]here is not a shadow of right in the general government to intermeddle with religion. Its least interference with it would be a most flagrant usurpation."[7] Finally, in a letter to Thomas Jefferson in October 1788, Madison wrote that "the rights in question are reserved by the manner in which the federal powers are granted."[8]

Indeed, after the Constitutional Convention Madison believed that the original Constitution *was* a bill of rights through its limited, enumerated powers delegated to the federal government. Madison also saw a bill of rights as superfluous because of mechanisms such as representation in a large republic, checks and balances produced by a separation of powers, and federalism. For instance, Madison stated that a republican form of government under the Constitution would protect liberty because "[i]f a faction consists of less than a majority, relief is supplied by the republican principle, which enables the majority to defeat its sinister views by regular vote."[9] Madison believed in a strong link between representative government and the protection of liberty: "As it is essential to liberty that the government in general should have a common interest with the people, so it is particularly essential that the branch of it under consideration should have an immediate dependence on, and an intimate sympathy with, the people. Frequent elections are unquestionably the only policy by which this dependence and sympathy can be effectually secured."[10] Likewise, Madison had confidence that enlarging the size of a republic would protect freedoms adequately because if you "[e]xtend the sphere," "you take in a greater variety of parties and interests," which will "make it less probable that a majority of the whole will have a common motive to invade the rights of other citizens; or if such a common motive exists, it will be more difficult for all who feel it to discover their own strength, and to act in unison."[11] In this way, Madison believed that the parameters of a properly constructed system of electing representatives are one of the best guarantees of liberty.

In addition to the republican form of government under the Constitution, Madison felt confident that no bill of rights was necessary: federalism would protect liberty. He stated in *Federalist* 51 that in "the compound republic of America, the power surrendered by the people is first divided between two distinct governments, and then the portion allotted to each subdivided among distinct and separate departments. Hence a double security arises to the rights of the people. The different governments will control each other."[12] In *Federalist* 46 Madison predicted that any time the federal government might try to infringe upon fundamental liberties, state governments would be able to put a stop to such tyranny:

> [S]hould an unwarrantable measure of the federal government be unpopular in particular States . . . the means of opposition to it are powerful and at hand. The disquietude of the people; their repugnance and, perhaps, refusal to co-operate with the officers of the Union; the frowns of the executive magistracy of the State; the embarrassments created by legislative devices, which would often be added on such occasions, would oppose, in any State, difficulties not to be despised; would form, in a large State, very serious impediments; and where the sentiments of several adjoining States happened to be in unison, would present obstructions which the federal government would hardly be willing to encounter.[13]

Again, Madison stated that federalism protected rights. If the federal government were to transgress our rights, the states have many options to thwart such an endeavor.

Likewise, the other major structural control on government in the Constitution, the separation of powers, was Madison's other chief protection of liberty. Indeed, Madison found it "essential to the preservation of liberty that the Legislative, Executive, and Judiciary powers be separate."[14] Madison believed that dividing up power would be a safe way to protect liberty, and that, conversely, "[t]he accumulation of all powers, legislative, executive, and judiciary, in the same hands, whether of one, a few, or many, and whether hereditary, self appointed, or elective, may justly be pronounced the very definition of tyranny."[15] Indeed, as Madison put it, "No political truth is certainly of greater intrinsic value or is stamped with the authority of more enlightened patrons of liberty" than the separation of powers.[16] Adding up all of these points led Madison to the logical conclusion that a bill of rights was simply unnecessary.

A BILL OF RIGHTS AS DANGEROUS

One may still wonder though—even if Madison believed a bill of rights could be superfluous, why would a champion of natural, liberal rights initially take a stance against it? Madison's initial belief was also that a bill of rights could be dangerous to liberties if placed in the Constitution incorrectly. Accordingly, in an October 1788 letter to Jefferson, Madison expressed his trepidation: "there is great reason to fear that a positive declaration of some of the most essential rights could not be obtained in the requisite latitude. I am sure that the rights of Conscience in particular, if submitted to public definition would be narrowed much more than they are ever likely to be by an assumed power."[17] Madison had great concern that a bill of rights could not be written that would be as protective of rights as possible. Whether because of bad motives by the drafters or because Madison feared that many people did not want to protect rights as much as he did, this was a major worry for him. And even if people with the best intentions drafted a bill of rights, Madison's fear was that inadvertent drafting errors would lead to people disregarding the law. For instance, Madison was afraid that if unconditional language were placed in a bill of rights, it would lose all meaning: "Supposing a bill of rights to be proper . . . I am inclined to think that *absolute* restrictions in cases that are doubtful, or where emergencies may overrule them, ought to be avoided."[18] Madison's ultimate fear in this regard was that "after repeated violations in extraordinary cases they will lose even their ordinary efficacy."[19] Madison gave an absolute prohibition on the suspension of the writ of habeas corpus as an example: "The extension of the Habs. Corps. to the cases in which it has been usually suspended, merits consideration at least. If there be emergences which call for such a suspension, it can have no effect to prohibit it, because the prohibition will assuredly give way to the impulse of the moment; or rather it will have the bad effect of facilitating other violations that may be less necessary."[20] For Madison, a bill of rights can be dangerous because, if any provision in it is drafted incorrectly, people will simply ignore it and violate the right that should be protected. This would become a precedent for the government to violate other parts of a bill of rights in the future. That Madison believed this is no surprise, given his confidence that many times people will act without virtue and simply take advantage of a situation for their own personal gain.

At the other end of the spectrum, Madison feared a bill of "rights" that was not really a bill of rights at all but an attack on powers allocated to the federal government in the new Constitution. In Madison's view, this wolf-in-sheep's-clothing bill of "rights" would be as dangerous to liberty as a bill of rights that meant well but was improperly drafted. Madison thought that the Constitution's increased grant of powers to the national government was important to the protection of rights because "[e]nergy in government is essential to that security against external and internal danger."[21] Put more forthrightly, Madison believed that the power of "the union" was "essential to guard them [the people] against those violent and oppressive factions which imbitter the blessing of liberty."[22] Madison's anxiety was that state governments were not adequately protecting the people's rights, so a more vigorous federal government with more powers was a necessary remedy. This point can be seen in Madison's derision that "the tendency of federal bodies" is more prone to "anarchy among the members than to tyranny in the head."[23] This was why Madison feared bills of rights that included provisions weakening federal power—because ultimately that would make the states more powerful, more capable of infringing on rights. For example, at the Virginia Ratifying Convention a proposed bill of rights was drafted to be recommended to Congress. Although there were many rights proposed (including various First Amendment freedoms, property rights, criminal procedures, voting rights, and a right to bear arms), this was only the first half of the suggested amendments.[24] The rest of the proposal suggested that Congress be stripped of its constitutional power over elections and direct taxation, that congressional power over the raising of armies and approving treaties be restricted, and that federal court jurisdiction be limited.[25] Madison wrote to Hamilton that these structural amendments were "highly objectionable,"[26] no doubt because he saw this bill of "rights" as a thinly veiled attempt to shred federal powers. Madison thought this was dangerous to liberty because it would upset the balance of powers in a separated system, it would take away the ability of federal courts to protect rights, and it would limit federal ability to check state abuses of rights.

A BILL OF RIGHTS AS INEFFECTIVE

Madison had one more reason to initially oppose a bill of rights to protect the liberal rights he found so essential. A bill of rights could be a false safeguard of freedom because "experience proves the inefficacy of a bill of rights on those occasions when its controul is most needed."[27] Madison originally believed that, while even a perfectly drafted bill of rights looks nice on paper, when a true emergency strikes that flowery language will simply be ignored by those in power: "Should a Rebellion or insurrection alarm the people as well as the Government, and a suspension of the Hab. Corp. be dictated by the alarm, no written prohibitions on earth would prevent the measure."[28] Likewise, when a majority simply wants to oppress a minority, a bill of rights will be worthless to those being tyrannized: "Repeated violations of these parchment barriers have been committed by overbearing majorities in every State. In Virginia I have seen the bill of rights violated in every instance where it has been opposed to a popular current."[29] Or, as Madison stated on another occasion regarding religious liberty, "If there were a majority of one sect, a bill of rights would be a poor protection for liberty."[30] Madison thus saw a bill of rights as less effective than such checks as a large republic, the separation of powers, and federalism, which could stymie the potential power of an overbearing majority. This stance is consistent with Madison's views on human nature, as Madison did not believe a "parchment barrier" could be an effective safeguard of liberty against a majority lacking virtue. Instead, Madison understood structural constraints to be much more useful.

Later in 1788 Madison noted that a bill of rights would be less effective in a republic than in a monarchy because in a "monarchy the latent force of the nation is superior to that of the Sovereign, and a solemn charter of popular rights must have a great effect, as a standard for trying the validity of public acts, and a signal for rousing & uniting the superior force of the community."[31] Conversely, in a republic "the political and physical power may be considered as vested in the same hands, that is in a majority of the people, and, consequently the tyrannical will of the Sovereign is not to be controuled by the dread of an appeal to any other force within the community."[32] This notwithstanding, Madison eventually did change his mind and find that there were better reasons to have a bill of rights than not. The next section examines how Madison made this transition to believing that a bill of rights could be a strategic way to protect the liberal rights that he believed the Constitution's structural constraints also served to defend.

A BILL OF RIGHTS AS A PRACTICAL WAY
TO SAVE THE CONSTITUTION

As time progressed after the Constitutional Convention, Madison began to warm to the idea of a bill of rights. Initially, however, he did this as a tactical measure. Madison was still not convinced that a bill of rights would substantively protect rights, but supporting a bill of rights could be an effective way to convince those skeptical of the Constitution to throw their support behind ratification. Or, as one writer stated, when Madison proposed the Bill of Rights, he "tossed a tub to the whale."[33] There has been significant scholarly debate over Madison's intent in this regard—whether he proposed the Bill of Rights for tactical reasons, or if he really wanted to protect those liberties.[34] This question is easily settled by understanding that Madison advocated for the Bill of Rights because of *both* considerations.

First, it is important to explore the strategic and political reasons that Madison initially came to support a bill of rights; unless one understands this, one cannot have a full understanding of Madison's intent with the Bill of Rights. Madison was concerned about supporting a bill of rights for strategic reasons because of his realistic understanding of human nature.

Madison believed that there were many people who wanted to sabotage the Constitution that he had worked so hard to help build. Madison feared that this might unravel the union itself, and that attacks on the Constitution's separation of powers and federalism would harm the ability of those structural constraints to protect rights. Thus, believing that there were many people working for selfish or provincial motives, Madison undertook to save the Constitution and the country itself via amendments.

First, Madison thought that a bill of rights would serve to take away the fuel for the Anti-Federalist fire—that the Constitution had no bill of rights. Madison's greatest fear was that the Anti-Federalists would campaign on that issue for a second constitutional convention, which they would use, not to propose a bill of rights, but to initiate a series of structural amendments that would severely weaken the new federal government. If Madison could propose a bill of rights first, it would prevent the Anti-Federalists from achieving their true objective of crippling the young federal government.

Between the Constitutional Convention and the First Congress of 1789, Madison expressed his fear of the Anti-Federalists' holding a second convention on dozens of occasions. In a letter to Edmond Randolph, he noted, "I must own that I differ still more from your opinion, that a prosecution of the experiment of a second Convention will be favorable . . . It appears also that the ground taken by the opponents in different quarters, forbids any hope of concord among them."[35] Madison thought that a second convention would end without the consensus of the first one. He then described to Randolph that the Constitution's opponents had some potentially dangerous goals:

> In this State the party adverse to the Constitution, notoriously meditate either a dissolution of the Union, or protracting it by patching up the Articles of Confederation. In Connecticut & Massachussetts, the opposition proceeds from that part of the people who have a repugnancy in general to good government, to any substantial abridgment of State powers, and a part of whom in Massts. are known to aim at confusion, and are suspected of wishing a reversal of the Revolution. The Minority in Pennsylva. as far as they are governed by any other views than an habitual & factious opposition, to their rivals, are manifestly averse to some essential ingredients in a national Government. You are better acquainted with Mr. [Patrick] Henry's politics that [sic] I can be, but I have for some time considered him as driving at a Southern Confederacy, and as not farther concurring in the plan of amendments than as he hopes to render it subservient to his real designs.[36]

Regardless of whether Madison was accurate in his description of Anti-Federalist motives, the possibility of adverse action was on his mind. Based on Madison's survey of Anti-Federalist plans around the new nation he reached the following conclusion:

Viewing the matter in this light, the inference with me is unavoidable that were a second trial to be made, the friends of a good constitution for the Union would not only find themselves not a little differing from each other as to the proper amendments, but perplexed & frustrated by men who had objects totally different. A second Convention would of course be formed under the influence, and composed in great measure of the members of opposition in the several States. But were the first difficulties overcome, and the Constitution re-edited with amendments, the event would still be infinitely precarious.[37]

One cannot help but sympathize a little with Madison in this regard. After he worked so hard to set in motion the Constitutional Convention, spent four months hammering out a new government at that Convention, and then worked diligently for several months in both New York and Virginia to help secure ratification of the Constitution, Madison certainly did *not* want to see the entire process reopened by his political foes, who could possibly undo all of his efforts. Madison had already been fighting the ratification battle since right after the Constitutional Convention adjourned—in September 1787 there was an attempt by Richard Henry Lee to amend the proposed Constitution in the Confederation Congress before it was passed to the states for ratification. Madison weathered that storm and made sure that the Constitution was offered to the states without being amended by Congress, but after fighting so many long conflicts over ratification he surely did not want to lose the new government so late in the game.[38]

Madison privately stated his fear of a second convention to other colleagues as well. In a letter to George Eve, Madison stated that "I have intimated that the amendments ought to be proposed by the first Congress. I prefer this mode to that of a General Convention."[39] Madison maintained the following as one of his reasons why he was apprehensive toward a second convention: "A convention . . . meeting in the present ferment of parties, and containing perhaps insidious characters from different parts of America, would at least spread a general alarm, and be but too likely to turn everything into confusion and uncertainty."[40] Even if a second convention were unsuccessful at making any changes to the new Constitution, at the very least it could call into question the legitimacy of the document and prohibit the new government from functioning effectively. However, if amendments were proposed in Congress, Madison thought these potential pitfalls could be avoided.

In many letters that Madison wrote between the Constitutional Convention and the First Federal Congress, he tried to persuade colleagues that a second convention would result in disaster. Madison wrote to George Nicolas that selfish motives would likely reign during such a venture:

Conditional amendments or a second general Convention, would be fatal. . . . The circumstances under which a second Convention composed of even wiser individuals, would meet, must extinguish every hope of an equal spirit of accommodation; and if it should happen to contain men who secretly aim at disunion, (and such I believe would be found from more than one State) the game would be as easy as it would be obvious, to insist on points popular in some parts, but known to be impermissible in other parts of the Union.[41]

In a letter to Edmund Randolph, Madison wrote that a "conditional ratification or a second convention appears to me utterly irreconcilable in the present state of things with the dictates of prudence and safety."[42] In a letter to Thomas Jefferson in April 1788, Madison wrote that, "if a second Convention should be formed, it is as little to be expected that the same spirit of compromise will prevail in it as produced an amicable result to the first."[43] Madison reiterated his concerns to Jefferson in another letter less than four months later: "if another Convention should be soon assembled, it would terminate in discord, or in alterations of the federal system which would throw back *essential* powers into the State Legislatures."[44] Less than two weeks after that, Madison wrote to Jefferson again, claiming that a second convention would be "composed of men who will essentially mutilate the system," and "is in every view to be dreaded."[45] Then again in December 1788, Madison wrote to Jefferson, expressing his fear of "the hazardous experiment of a second Convention."[46] Even George Washington could not escape hearing of Madison's fears: "If an Early General Convention cannot be parried, it is seriously to be feared that the system which has resisted so many direct attacks may at last be successfully undermined by its enemies."[47] Madison also expressed his fright to George Lee Turberville, explaining that a second convention would include "the most violent partizans on both sides," who "under the mask of seeking alterations popular in some parts of the Union might have a dangerous opportunity of sapping the very foundations of the fabric" of the Union, which "would be viewed by all Europe as a dark and threatening Cloud hanging over the Constitution just established, and perhaps over the Union itself."[48] And to Phillip Mazzei, Madison wrote that the "object of the antifederalists is to bring another General Convention, which would either agree on nothing as would be agreeable to some, and throw away everything into confusion; or expunge from the Constitution parts which are held by its friends to be essential to it."[49] Madison's fear of the Anti-Federalists holding a second convention was reaching near paranoia!

Madison also expressed his concern publicly. In *Federalist* 37 Madison proclaimed serious fears regarding a second constitutional convention. First, he noted what a special occurrence the Constitutional Convention was in the history of such assemblies: "the convention must have enjoyed, in a very singular degree, an exemption from the pestilential influence of party animosities; the disease most incident to deliberative bodies, and most apt to contaminate their proceedings."[50] Madison continued, "All the deputations composing the convention were satisfactorily accommodated by the final act, or were induced to accede to it by a deep conviction of the necessity of sacrificing private opinions and partial interests to the public good, and by a despair of seeing this necessity diminished by delays or by new experiments."[51]

Since something so special occurred at the Constitutional Convention, we should be suspicious of a second convention, or any other "new experiment," that may undo all of the work that was completed at the first one. Madison continued to express his concern that a second convention would be detrimental when he penned *Federalist 38:*

> As it can give no umbrage to the writers against the plan of the federal Constitution, let us suppose, that as they are the most zealous, so they are also the most sagacious, of those who think the late convention were unequal to the task assigned them, and that a wiser and better plan might and ought to be substituted. Let us further suppose that their country should concur, both in this favorable opinion of their merits, and in their unfavorable opinion of the convention; and should accordingly proceed to form them into a second convention, with full powers, and for the express purpose of revising and remoulding the work of the first. Were the experiment to be seriously made, though it required some effort to view it seriously even in fiction, I leave it to be decided . . . whether, with all their enmity to their predecessors, they would, in any one point, depart so widely from their example, as in the discord and ferment that would mark their own deliberations.[52]

Finally, when Madison proposed his amendments to Congress in 1789, he expressed his belief that it was necessary to initiate amendments in that body rather than wait for a second convention to form. Madison stated that "I should be unwilling to see a door opened for a re-consideration of the whole structure of the government, for a re-consideration of the principles and the substance of the powers given," because "I doubt, if such a door was opened, if we should be very likely to stop at that point which would be safe to the government itself."[53] Regardless of the factual accuracy of Madison's predictions regarding a second convention, his fears were consistent with his realistic views on human nature: Madison thought that a second convention would be made up primarily of self-interested partisans who would be motivated more by the desire to horde power at the state level for their own benefit than by a love of liberty.

A second strategic reason Madison had to support a bill of rights was to win over the support of those who were skeptical of the new Constitution. Madison realized that not everyone was a zealous opponent of the Constitution who would do anything to sabotage it like some of the Anti-Federalists he wrote about in his various letters. On the contrary, he knew that some people had only a healthy skepticism of what transpired at the Constitutional Convention and therefore simply needed more convincing before they could trust the new national government. By passing and ratifying a bill of rights, people in this group would be assured that the federal government would protect freedom. Indeed, the absence of a bill of rights was certainly a very common and probably the most persuasive criticism of the Constitution.[54] No one was more abreast of this fact than Madison.

During his speeches in Congress urging that body to consider a bill of rights Madison noted this point quite frequently. When he was struggling to get the House to take up his proposed amendments, Madison noted that "if we continue to postpone . . . it may occasion suspicions, which, though not well founded, may tend to inflame or prejudice the public mind, against our decisions."[55] Madison continued: "they may think we are not sincere in our desire to incorporate such amendments in the constitution as will secure those rights, which they consider as not sufficiently guarded."[56] Madison stated in Congress that a bill of rights "would stifle the voice of complaint, and make friends of many who doubted its merits. Our future measures would then have been more universally agreeable and better supported."[57] Indeed, Madison wanted his colleagues in the House to be aware that "if congress will devote but one day to this subject, so far as to satisfy the public that we do not disregard their wishes, it will have a salutary influence on the public councils, and prepare the way for a favorable reception of our future measures."[58] And Madison wanted to point out in Congress that "notwithstanding the ratification of this system of government by eleven of the thirteen United States . . . yet still there is a great number of our constituents who are dissatisfied with it."[59] Thus, Madison was quite clear that amendments were a useful way to coax skeptics into supporting the Constitution.

Of particular importance to Madison was the need to convince those averse to the Constitution in the two states that had not yet ratified the document: North Carolina and Rhode Island. On this point, Madison noted during his Bill of Rights introductory speech that

> perhaps there is a stronger motive . . . for our going into a consideration of the subject [of amendments]. . . . I allude in a particular manner to those two States who have not thought fit to throw themselves into the bosom of the Confederacy: it is a desirable thing, on our part as well as theirs, that a reunion should take place as soon as possible. I have no doubt, if we proceed to take those steps which would be prudent and requisite at this juncture,

that in a short time we should see that disposition prevailing in those states that are not come in, that we have seen prevailing in those States which have embraced the constitution.[60]

Madison would reiterate the importance of making concessions toward states that had not yet ratified when he wrote to Richard Peters two months later that "Some amendts. are necssy for N. Carola."[61] Clearly, then, Madison thought that a bill of rights would be one useful way of convincing North Carolina and Rhode Island to ratify the Constitution.

After Madison made his proposal on the floor of Congress, he continued to make the argument in the House that his amendments should be ratified because they would win over skeptics of the Constitution. Madison asserted that "it will be proper in itself, and highly politic, for the tranquility of the public mind, and the stability of the government, that we should offer something, in the form I have proposed, to be incorporated in the system of government, as a declaration of the rights of the people."[62] For Madison to state that amendments would be "highly politic" is good evidence indeed that he had strategic reasons for his involvement therein. Likewise, Madison privately remarked of the Bill of Rights that "*[i]t will kill the opposition everywhere,* and by putting an end to the disaffection to the Govt. itself, enable the administration to venture on measures not otherwise safe."[63] It would be difficult to find a statement that suggests a more strategic reason for proposing the Bill of Rights than this one.

A third strategic reason why Madison supported the Bill of Rights was to give the people who truly supported a bill of rights what they wanted. In this regard, Madison wanted to make sure that the people of the United States received from their elected representatives the changes in the law that they desired. Madison was straightforwardly honest that this was another of his strategic motivations: "The applications for amendments come from a very respectable number of our constituents, and it is certainly proper for congress to consider the subject."[64] Madison was clear that Congress should give the people what they want in a representative republic, as he stated that "this house is bound by every motive of prudence, not to let the first session pass over without proposing to the state legislatures some things to be incorporated into the constitution, as will render it as acceptable to the whole people of the United States."[65] According to Madison, "We ought not to disregard their inclination, but, on principles of amity and moderation, conform to their wishes," and propose a bill of rights.[66] Madison had gauged public opinion, and he had found that many people wanted a bill of rights, so that was precisely what he intended to give them. Thus, Madison stated that "the great mass of the people who opposed [ratification of the Constitution], disliked it because it did not contain effectual provisions against encroachments on particular rights."[67] By proposing a bill of rights,

Madison claimed that "our constituents may see we pay a proper attention to a subject they have much at heart."[68] Madison and other members of Congress gave the people of the United States what they wanted in this respect when he proposed the Bill of Rights.

A final strategic reason why Madison supported a bill of rights was that it fulfilled a campaign promise he had made while running for his seat in the first Congress. Madison believed it necessary to promise amendments in order to get elected, and once he won election Madison was obligated to his district to propose a bill of rights. Madison wrote a letter to George Eve, a Baptist pastor in Madison's home county, in January 1789 so that Eve could show it to parishioners and others to prove that Madison was a friend of religious liberty.[69] Madison stated in the letter to Eve that

> whilst it remained unratified, and it was necessary to unite the States in some one plan, I opposed all previous alterations as calculated to throw the States into dangerous contentions, and to furnish the secret enemies of the Union with an opportunity of promoting its dissolution. Circumstances are now changed: The Constitution is established on the ratifications of eleven States and a very great majority of the people of America. . . . Under this change of circumstances, it is my sincere opinion that the Constitution ought to be revised, and that the first Congress meeting under it, ought to prepare and recommend to the States for ratification, the most satisfactory provisions for all essential rights.[70]

Madison felt the need to explain himself so that Anti-Federalists could not claim he was opposed to protecting liberty. Madison subsequently won election to his House seat on February 2, 1789, by a margin of 1,308 to 972.[71]

There is evidence in his speech proposing amendments in Congress that this campaign pledge was still on Madison's mind during the summer of 1789. While the House was debating whether to take up the subject of amendments, Madison announced, "I wish then to commence the consideration at the present moment; I hold it to be my duty to unfold my ideas, and explain myself to the house in some form or other without delay."[72] Madison's "duty" here was the fulfillment of his campaign pledge, which he confirmed later during that debate: "If I thought I could fulfil the duty which I owe to myself and my constituents, to let the subject pass over in silence, I most certainly should not trespass upon the indulgence of this house. But I cannot do this."[73] According to Madison, proposing amendments was a duty he owed, in part, to his constituents. Finally, after Madison proposed the Bill of Rights, he concluded his speech by stating that he had "done what I conceived was my duty, in bringing before this house the subject of amendments."[74] Thus, Madison had kept his promise to his constituents.

Madison had several strategic reasons for supporting and subsequently introducing the Bill of Rights to Congress. One could read the section above and easily conclude that Madison proposed the Bill of Rights solely for strategic purposes. Indeed, one could argue that Madison was playing a brilliant game of chess against the Anti-Federalists; by proposing a bill of rights, Madison made a brilliant sacrifice that ultimately led him to checkmate the opposition.

As simple and logical as that version of the story seems, it is incomplete. The foregoing reasons were "strategic" ones for a bill of rights. But bear in mind that anything Madison did to save the Constitution he ultimately did to protect liberty. Indeed, if Madison's only reasons for proposing a bill of rights were related to settling down the opposition and protecting the original Constitution from being rewritten, that alone would be guaranteeing the liberty that Madison thought the original Constitution already protected. Furthermore, as the next chapter demonstrates, Madison eventually did change his mind on a bill of rights, coming to see it not just as a strategic measure but also as having substantive value in its own right to protect freedom.

MADISON SEES THAT A BILL OF RIGHTS CAN PROTECT LIBERAL FREEDOMS

A Bill of Rights Was on Madison's Agenda

Just as Madison had a multifaceted understanding of human nature, a complex political philosophy, and various reasons for thinking it important to protect liberal rights, Madison also believed that there were multiple justifications for proposing and ratifying a bill of rights. One of those reasons was that a bill of rights could be an effective safeguard for liberty.

This notwithstanding, there are several statements by Madison during the period of ratification that can be marshaled as evidence that his support for a bill of rights was lukewarm at best. During the ratification struggle in late 1788, Madison stated, "I have never thought the omission [of a bill of rights] a material defect. . . . I have not viewed it in an important light."[1] Madison's cautious optimism was evident when he remarked that "amendments, if pursued with a proper moderation and in a proper mode, will be . . . safe."[2] These statements do not appear to be ringing endorsements for a bill of rights.

One could even argue that Madison lacked enthusiasm for a bill of rights when he introduced his proposed amendments in Congress. Indeed, on June 8, 1789, Madison remarked at one point during his speech that "The first of these amendments, relates to what may be called a bill of rights; I will own that I never considered this provision so essential to the federal constitution, as to make it improper to ratify it, until such an amendment was added; at the same time, I always conceived, that in a certain form and to a certain extent, such a provision was neither improper nor altogether useless."[3] If one states that something is "neither improper nor altogether useless," one probably does not hold that "something" in a very high regard. Furthermore, when Madison concluded his introduction of the Bill of Rights, he made this statement: "nothing is in contemplation, so far as I have mentioned, that can endanger the beauty of the government in any one important feature."[4] Again, it does not seem that Madison gave much support to his own proposal.

However, there is much more evidence that supports the proposition that Madison *did* advocate a bill of rights for its own sake. First, consider that a bill of rights was on Madison's agenda for quite some time before he proposed it in Congress. In April 1789 Madison complained that the "subject of amendments has not yet been touched."[5] When Madison wrote Washington's First Inaugural Address that same month, he had Washington say that it was within Congress's judgment to "decide, how far an exercise of the occasional power delegated by the Fifth article of the Constitution is rendered expedient at the present Juncture by the nature of the objections which have been urged against the System, or by the degree of inquietude which has given birth to them."[6] In the official House reply to the president, Madison affirmed the following: "The question arising out of the fifth article of the Constitution, will receive all the attention demanded by its importance; and will, we trust be decided, under the influence of all the considerations to which you allude."[7] If Madison were proposing a bill of rights solely for strategic reasons, he could have left it out of his speech and Washington's speech, as there was already a large public clamor for a bill of rights. However, if Madison really was committed to a bill of rights for substantive reasons and wanted to ensure that he could protect the most rights possible, it would make sense for him to bring up the subject continually as a way to prod his congressional colleagues into action.

Indeed, Madison brought up the subject of amendments at every opportunity. Again and again from late 1788 and throughout 1789 Madison kept his friends and colleagues abreast of his quest to amend the Constitution. He mentioned it in letters to Thomas Jefferson, Edmund Randolph, Samuel Johnston, Edmund Pendleton, Tench Coxe, James Madison Sr. (Madison's father), George Nicholas, Wilson Cary Nicholas, Richard Peters, and George Washington.[8] Of course, this *could* have been for strategic reasons, in the way that Madison wanted some amendments to pass in order to placate Anti-Federalists. But this theory neglects two important points. First, many of these letters were written to Madison's friends for their eyes only. Thus, there would not have been a need strategically to obsess over a bill of rights if Madison was corresponding solely with his closest colleagues. Second, even his private letters that may have been intended to be exposed to the public were not written with an attitude toward duping his political opponents. Rather, during this period Madison's primary focus was ensuring the protection of substantive liberties and preventing others' strategic amendments that might instead alter the structure of the federal government. Take, for instance, the following statement by Madison in a letter to Jefferson: "The friends of the Constitution . . . wish the revisal to be carried no farther than to supply additional guards for liberty, without abridging the sum of power transferred from the States to the general Government."[9] Certainly, Madison would have considered himself a "friend" of the Constitution, and he wanted to provide more safeguards for freedom as well.

At various points during his speech in Congress introducing his amendments, Madison referred to the freedoms to be protected in his proposed bill of rights in strongly supportive terms. Indeed, Madison described these rights (or subsets of them) as "the great work," an "important subject," "the great rights of mankind," "the great rights," "those choicest privileges of the people," and "these great and important rights."[10] This is sounding more like the Madison described above, a man who was a guardian of strong, broad, liberal rights. Indeed, knowing that Madison described these rights in such glowing terms, his statement of the need to "fulfil the duty which I owe to myself and my constituents"[11] takes on a new meaning—not only was he fulfilling a campaign pledge, but he was also being true to his *own* beliefs by protecting rights which he believed were important. Madison's speech was dotted with examples of his opinion that the Bill of Rights was not just a strategic ploy: "I will not propose a single alteration which I do not wish to see take place, as intrinsically proper in itself"; "it will be proper in itself"; "I have proposed nothing that does not appear to me as proper in itself."[12] Madison's use of the word "proper" multiple times to describe the Bill of Rights suggests that he believed it was a fitting corollary to the original Constitution, a document which he certainly held in high regard.

At later dates during the debate on the Bill of Rights in Congress, Madison reaffirmed his commitment to the substance of the first ten amendments. In August 1789 Madison asserted, "It was wished that some security should be given for those great and essential rights which they had been taught to believe were in danger. I concurred, in the convention of Virginia, with those gentlemen, so far as to agree to a declaration of those rights . . . which I had the honor to bring forward before the present congress."[13] If Madison was not committed to the substance of the Bill of Rights, it would not be necessary for him to refer to them as "great and essential rights," or to characterize his involvement therein as an "honor."

Madison's strong support for the substance of the Bill of Rights continued through the summer of 1789. In a congressional speech on August 17, Madison referred to the freedoms of religion, speech, press, and the right to a trial by jury as "essential rights."[14] In a letter to Richard Peters, Madison stated that "a constitutional provision in favr. of essential rights is a thing not improper in itself and was always viewed in that light by myself."[15] Thus, there is ample evidence not only that from late 1788 through the summer of 1789 Madison supported the Bill of Rights as a brilliant political ploy to checkmate his Anti-Federalist opposition, but also that Madison found independent significance in passing those amendments and having those rights enshrined in the Constitution.

By August 1789 the passage of *a* bill of rights in some form was virtually guaranteed, as the House had debated it for months and was about to send it to the Senate. There was no longer a need for Madison to push for amendments only for strategic reasons. Yet Madison continued to worry about the passage and ratification of the Bill of Rights, and he often did so in *private* letters. In these largely confidential writings cited above there would have been little need for Madison to emphasize the importance of specifics of the Bill of Rights if he only wanted them ratified for the strategic reason of saving the Constitution.

Another explanation of some scholars who understand Madison to have supported the Bill of Rights only for strategic reasons is that Madison seemingly changed his position on the issue of a bill of rights, first denying the need or efficacy of them and later stating that they could be useful. However, given Madison's concerns regarding a bill of rights, particularly Madison's fear that the important work done at the Constitutional Convention could be undone, Madison's positions are not that inconsistent. Take, for instance, a statement that Madison made to Alexander Hamilton in the summer of 1788:

> My opinion is that a reservation of a right to withdraw if amendments be not decided on under the form of the Constitution within a certain time, is a *conditional* ratification, that it does not make N. York a member of the New Union, and consequently that she could not be received on that plan. Compacts must be reciprocal, this principle would not in such a case be preserved. The Constitution requires an adoption *in toto*, and *forever*. It has been so adopted by the other States. An adoption for a limited time would be as defective as an adoption of some of the articles only. In short any *condition* whatever must viciate the ratification.[16]

Madison opposed a bill of rights during the ratification process because he did not want states conditionally ratifying the Constitution if they were promised certain concessions. For Madison, this would be promising to add certain amendments before the new government was in operation. Who would be charged with fulfilling this promise, and how would we know if the right amendments were proposed to sufficiently fulfill the conditions? Accordingly, Madison noted the following in a letter to George Washington: "It is a little singular that three of the most distinguished Advocates for amendments; and who expect to unite the thirteen States in their project, appear to be pointedly at variance with each other. . . . It is pretty certain that some others who make a common cause with them in the general attempt to bring about alterations differ still more from them, than they do from each other."[17] Madison reiterated his aversion to conditional ratification several times during 1787–1789.[18]

For Madison, amendments were something to be discussed later in Congress, by the states that had ratified the Constitution. Madison staked out this position in a letter to Jefferson when he remarked, "My own opinion has always been in favor of a bill of rights; provided that it be so framed as not to imply powers not meant to be included in the enumeration."[19] Similarly, Madison wrote to Henry Lee that "if alterations of a reasonable sort are really in view, they are much more attainable from Congress than from attempts to bring about another Convention."[20] As Madison wrote to Edmund Pendleton, "Let the enemies to the System wait untill some experience shall have taken place, and the business will be conducted with more light as well as with less heat."[21] By late 1788 enough dust had settled regarding ratification that Madison stated, "I trust the Constitution is too firmly established to be now materially vulnerable."[22] In his legendary letter to George Eve in January 1789, Madison commented that

whilst it remained unratified, and it was necessary to unite the States in some one plan, I opposed all previous alterations as calculated to throw the States into dangerous contentions, and to furnish the secret enemies of the Union with an opportunity of promoting its dissolution. Circumstances are now changed: The Constitution is established on the ratifications of eleven States and a very great majority of the people of America; and amendments, if pursued with a proper moderation and in a proper mode, will be not only safe, but may serve the double purpose of satisfying the minds of well meaning opponents, and of providing additional guards in favour of liberty. Under this change of circumstances, it is my sincere opinion that the Constitution ought to be revised, and that the first Congress meeting under it, ought to prepare and recommend to the States for ratification, the most satisfactory provisions for all essential rights.[23]

Madison would express this view in very similar language less than two weeks later in a letter to Thomas Mann Randolph.[24] Madison restated this reason for his change in position throughout this period of ratification and during the debate over the Bill of Rights, including in a letter published in the *Fredericksburg Herald:* "With regard to the mode of obtaining amendments, I have not withheld my opinion that they ought to be recommended by the first Congress, rather than be pursued by way of a General Convention."[25] Seen in this light, his change of position cannot be attributed just to seeing a political opportunity to "kill the opposition everywhere," but also as being consistent with Madison's fear that the new government's structure would be tinkered with even before it began operation. Once the Constitution was ratified, Madison found amendments as an important way to provide additional safeguards in favor of liberty.

Thus, Madison was largely consistent in his support of a bill of rights, as he had no desire to see *any* amendments proposed before the Constitution was ratified; only after ratification did Madison advocate amendments for either strategic or substantive reasons. By doing anything else, Madison thought he may be endangering ratification. This is one important reason why Madison and a majority of participants at the Constitutional Convention did not support George Mason's motion to draft a bill of rights at *that* time—the motion was made just five days before adjournment after four long months of hammering out compromises that Madison and others did not wish to jeopardize.[26] Although Madison did have some concerns about a bill of rights, he eventually came to believe it was a good idea in its own right. In this way, Madison never fundamentally changed his mind regarding the need to protect liberal freedoms, as he thought the nation only needed to wait until the appropriate moment for a bill of rights to be proposed.

SUBSTANTIVE REASONS FOR A BILL OF RIGHTS

It should be no surprise that Madison rethought his position and began to see the efficacy of a bill of rights. As time passed after the Constitutional Convention, Madison eventually altered his thinking on the subject of how best to protect liberty. This section examines how Madison was influenced by the political realities of the time, and how he became convinced that his earlier beliefs on a bill of rights needed to be reevaluated.

First, although Madison firmly believed that federalism and the separation of powers would be the most effective ways to curb abuses of government power, Madison also came to realize that a bill of rights could serve as a backup if these structural measures failed. Madison did not simply develop this reasoning after he saw it would be politically advantageous to support a bill of rights. Rather, it was a form of reasoning he began using early on when writing *The Federalist*. In *Federalist* 44, Madison was defending the prohibitions on congressional power in Article I, Section 9:

> Bills of attainder, *ex post facto* laws, and laws impairing the obligation of contracts, are contrary to the first principles of the social compact, and to every principle of sound legislation. The two former are expressly prohibited by the declarations prefixed to some of the State constitutions, and all of them are prohibited by the spirit and scope of these fundamental charters. Our own experience has taught us, nevertheless, that additional fences against these dangers ought not to be omitted. Very properly, therefore, have the convention added this constitutional bulwark in favor of personal security and private rights.[27]

Thus, even though the states protect many of these rights, it also made sense to specifically prevent the national government from violating them. Likewise, in *Federalist* 48 Madison claimed that the separation of powers was not a foolproof way of protecting freedom: "a mere demarcation on parchment of the constitutional limits of the several departments, is not a sufficient guard against those encroachments which lead to a tyrannical concentration of all the powers of government in the same hands."[28] Madison continued to use this reasoning when he introduced the Bill of Rights: "if all power is subject to abuse . . . then it is possible the abuse of the powers of the General Government may be guarded against in a more secure manner than is now done."[29] Even more to the point, later in his introduction Madison claimed that "I know in some of the state constitutions the power of the government is controuled by such a declaration [of rights], but others are not. I cannot see any reason against obtaining even a double security on those points."[30] And when discussing his proposal that was the forerunner of the Tenth Amendment, Madison commented that "[p]erhaps words which may define this more precisely, than the whole of the instrument now does, may be considered as superfluous. I admit they may be deemed unnecessary; but there can be no harm in making such a declaration."[31] Thus, Madison unmistakably believed that a bill of rights could serve as one more check on government to help protect liberties.

Second, Madison realized that even though he and the other Framers worked hard to construct a limited, enumerated set of powers for the federal government, those limits might eventually be transgressed. Given Madison's beliefs on human nature, he knew that there would always be some members of Congress who would attempt to exceed their enumerated powers. A bill of rights could serve as another way to limit those transgressions. Madison advocated this argument several times when ushering the Bill of Rights through Congress. Initially, Madison explained that, as to a bill of rights, "It has been said that in the Federal Government they are unnecessary, because the powers are enumerated, and it follows that all that are not granted by the constitution are retained; that the constitution is a bill of powers, the great residuum being the rights of the people; and therefore a bill of rights cannot be so necessary as if the residuum was thrown into the hands of the Government."[32] Madison continued on to explain why that argument against a bill of rights was not sufficient:

> It is true the powers of the General Government are circumscribed; they are directed to particular objects; but even if Government keeps within those limits, it has certain discretionary powers with respect to the means, which may admit of abuse to a certain extent . . . because in the constitution of the United States there is a clause granting to Congress the power to make all laws which shall be necessary and proper for carrying into execution all the powers

vested in the government of the United States. . . . Now, may not laws be considered necessary and proper by Congress, for it is them who are to judge of the necessity and propriety to accomplish those special purposes which they may have in contemplation, which laws in themselves are neither necessary or proper; as well as improper laws could be enacted by the state legislatures, for fulfilling the more extended objects of those Governments.[33]

Since it is possible for power-seekers in Congress to abuse the Necessary and Proper Clause, the enumerated powers of the federal government might not always be adhered to. Thus, a bill of rights could be added as a list of negative limitations on federal power and serve as a corollary to the list of affirmative limitations on Congress's power in Article I, Section 8, of the Constitution.

Later that summer, Madison would comment that the Establishment Clause was necessitated by the possible abuse of the Necessary and Proper Clause. Madison observed that it

had been required by some of the state conventions, who seemed to entertain an opinion that under the clause of the constitution, which gave power to congress to make all laws necessary and proper to carry into execution the constitution, and the laws made under it, enabled them to make laws of such a nature as might infringe the rights of conscience, or establish a national religion. To prevent these effects he presumed the amendment was intended, and he thought it as well expressed as the nature of the language would admit.[34]

For Madison the enumeration of power could be subject to abuse, and so negative limitations on federal power in a bill of rights could help prevent the creation of constitutional loopholes.

Third, Madison believed that the Bill of Rights would be a useful way for courts and the states to check the powers of Congress and the president. By writing down limitations on congressional and executive power, Madison thought it could serve as a source of authority for courts and states to claim they are in the right when Congress or the president has acted unconstitutionally. Regarding the ability of courts to protect people's liberty under the Bill of Rights, Madison stated, "If they are incorporated into the constitution, independent tribunals of justice will consider themselves in a peculiar manner the guardians of those rights; they will be an impenetrable bulwark against every assumption of power in the legislative or executive; they will be naturally led to resist every encroachment upon rights expressly stipulated for in the constitution by the declaration of rights."[35] Madison hypothesized that courts would understand themselves as protectors of liberties that are enshrined in a bill of rights. He understood that a bill of rights would provide an opportunity to the courts that might not otherwise be present under the original Constitution.

In addition to providing authority for courts, Madison thought that the Bill of Rights would empower the states to combat a potentially overzealous federal government. "There is a great probability," Madison commented, "that such a declaration in the federal system would be enforced; because the State Legislatures will jealously and closely watch the operations of this Government, and be able to resist with more effect every assumption of power than any other power on earth can do; and the greatest opponents to a Federal Government admit the State Legislatures to be sure guardians of the people's liberty."[36] Madison conjectured that a bill of rights could serve as a point of reference for states to battle the national government if it began violating liberties. Madison would put this theory into practice during the Alien and Sedition Act controversy nearly a decade later, when he acted through the Virginia legislature to criticize Congress's usurpation of unauthorized power. In the "Virginia Resolutions against the Alien and Sedition Acts" Madison reaffirmed his understanding of the Bill of Rights as arming the states with authority to combat excessive use of power by Congress. Madison stated of the Virginia General Assembly that "it is their duty, to watch over and oppose every infraction of those principles, which constitute the only basis of that union, because a faithful observance of them, can alone secure its existence, and the public happiness."[37] Madison went on to claim that "the states who are parties thereto [of the Constitution] have the right, and are in duty bound, to interpose for arresting the progress of the evil, and for maintaining within their respective limits, the authorities, rights and liberties appertaining to them."[38] For Madison, a bill of rights gives state legislatures a shield to protect rights from federal infringement.

Fourth, it eventually became unbearable for Madison to see the Constitution go unamended after Madison lost some of his most important battles at the Constitutional Convention. One of Madison's chief priorities at the Convention was a proposal that the president and several members of the national judiciary compose a "Council of Revision" that would have examined every act of Congress. This Council of Revision would have had the power to review and reject federal laws before they took effect.[39] This was consistent with Madison's views on human nature, as Congress (which Madison viewed as the most powerful branch) could be checked by a self-interested body comprising the other two branches. Madison found this check over Congress to be an effective way of stopping unconstitutional or unreasonable legislation before it could be enacted. Losing this battle at the Constitutional Convention was another factor that persuaded Madison of the value of a bill of rights.

How important was the Council of Revision to Madison? Before the Constitutional Convention Madison wrote to Edmund Randolph that a "Council of Revision may be superadded, including the great ministerial officers."[40] Madison restated this proposition in a letter to Washington: "As a further check, a council of revision including the great ministerial officers might be superadded."[41] One of the proposals in the Virginia Plan, which Madison helped draft, proposed a Council of Revision.[42] At the Constitutional Convention he seconded a motion on two different days to insert the Council in the Constitution, and he introduced the motion himself on another occasion.[43] Madison commented during the Convention debates that the Council of Revision would "be useful to the Community at large as an additional check against a pursuit of those unwise & unjust measures which constitute so great a portion of our calamities," including that of "a powerful tendency in the Legislature to absorb all power into its vortex."[44] Losing this additional check on congressional power tormented Madison, eventually leading him to find some solace to the problem in the Bill of Rights.

Besides losing the Council of Revision, Madison had other major defeats at the Constitutional Convention. Most notably, Madison wanted Congress to have the power to "veto" state laws. Madison partially advocated a Constitutional Convention as a way to empower the national government while also limiting the potentially dangerous powers of the states. Many of the abridgments of rights and economic problems in the 1780s were being caused by overzealous state governments, so having a congressional power to nullify laws that were detrimental to rights would be an effective way of dealing with this problem.[45] This position is consistent with Madison's views on human nature, whereby he believed that power-hungry state officials could be checked by Congress. After losing this battle at the Constitutional Convention, a bill of rights became another way to rein in state power.[46]

Madison's own words bear out the importance to him of having a congressional veto, and how losing that battle made him reconsider the need for a bill of rights. In a March 1787 letter to Thomas Jefferson he penned the following: "In order to render the exercise of such a negative prerogative convenient, an emanation of it must be vested in some set of men within the several States so far as to enable them to give a temporary sanction to laws of immediate necessity."[47] In a letter to Randolph, Madison wrote of Congress that "perhaps the negative on the State laws may be most conveniently lodged in this branch."[48] Madison was even more adamant in the importance of this power when he wrote to Washington that "a negative *in all cases whatsoever* on the legislative acts of the States . . . appears to me to be absolutely necessary, and to be the least possible encroachment on the State jurisdictions."[49] Thus, when Charles Pinckney moved at the Constitutional Convention "that the National Legislature shd have authority to negative all laws which they shd judge to be improper," Madison seconded the motion.[50] Madison then stated that he could not but regard an indefinite power to negative legislative acts of the States as absolutely necessary to a perfect system. Experience had evinced a constant tendency in the States to encroach on the federal authority; to violate national Treaties; to infringe the rights & interests of each other; to oppress the weaker party within their respective jurisdictions. A negative was the mildest expedient that could be devised for preventing these mischiefs.[51]

Later in the Convention Madison remarked once again that he "considered the negative on the laws of the States as essential to the efficacy & security of the General Government."[52] These statements at the Convention demonstrate Madison's commitment to ensure that state governments could not cause damage to liberty or to the functioning of the federal government.

After the Constitutional Convention, Madison maintained that losing the battle over a congressional veto power was very difficult to stomach. In a letter to Thomas Jefferson, Madison noted why the congressional veto would have been so useful:

A constitutional negative on the laws of the States seems equally necessary to secure individuals agst. encroachments on their rights. The mutability of the laws of the States is found to be a serious evil. The injustice of them has been so frequent and so flagrant as to alarm the most stedfast friends of Republicanism. I am persuaded I do not err in saying that the evils issuing from these sources contributed more to that uneasiness which produced the Convention, and prepared the public mind for a general reform, than those which accrued to our national character and interest from the inadequacy of the Confederation to its immediate objects.[53]

The loss of this congressional power at the Constitutional Convention continued to nag Madison until he finally devised another way to protect liberty from such potential abuses, in the language of the Bill of Rights. Thus, when Madison proposed the Bill of Rights, he put in the following provision: "No state shall violate the equal rights of conscience, or the freedom of the press, or the trial by jury in criminal cases."[54] Later that summer, when Thomas Tucker moved to strike this amendment, Madison spoke out in Congress that this was "the most valuable amendment on the whole list," because if "there was any reason to restrain the Government of the United States from infringing upon these essential rights, it was equally necessary that they should be secured against the State Governments."[55] Indeed, for Madison it was important to protect liberty from state infringement in the Constitution because "some States have no bills of rights, there are others provided with very defective ones, and there are others whose bills of rights are not only defective, but absolutely improper; instead of securing some in the full extent which republican principles would require, they limit them too much to agree with the common ideas of liberty."[56] This is more evidence that Madison supported the Bill of Rights for its own sake, in order to protect those freedoms.

Fifth, Madison saw that incorporating statements protective of liberty into the Bill of Rights could educate people and make the majority less likely to oppress people's liberties in the future. Madison believed that if some people are capable of virtue, enshrining these freedoms in the Bill of Rights might be one way of trying to inculcate that virtue in the people. Indeed, Madison stated that this was a reason in favor of a bill of rights when he introduced his amendments before Congress: "It may be thought all paper barriers against the power of the community, are too weak to be worthy of attention . . . yet, as they have a tendency to impress some degree of respect for them, to establish the public opinion in their favor, and rouse the attention of the whole community, it may be one mean to controul the majority from those acts to which they might be otherwise inclined."[57] Madison believed that the process of writing down amendments and ratifying them would serve as a reminder to the people that these are the liberties which our community has said are valuable. This would create veneration over time among the people, making tyranny of the majority less likely in the future. Madison did not simply adopt this reasoning for his introduction of the Bill of Rights. In a letter to Thomas Jefferson nearly eight months before he introduced the Bill, Madison noted that a bill of rights could be useful because the "political truths declared in that solemn manner acquire by degrees the character of fundamental maxims of free Government, and as they become incorporated with the national sentiment, counteract the impulses of interest and passion."[58] Thus, Madison saw the usefulness of a bill of rights as a way to educate people about the value of liberty and virtue, which certainly was not a strategic or political reason for introducing amendments.

Sixth, Madison understood that sometimes the majority will not be the oppressor, but the oppressed. Although Madison always feared the tyranny of the majority, he also recognized that sometimes the problem is *not* "enabl[ing] the government to control the governed," but rather "oblig[ing] it to control itself."[59] It was for this reason that Madison remarked to Jefferson that a bill of rights could be useful because

> Altho' it be generally true as above stated that the danger of oppression lies in the interested majorities of the people rather than in usurped acts of the Government, yet there may be occasions on which the evil may spring from the latter sources; and on such, a bill of rights will be a good ground for an appeal to the sense of the community. Perhaps too there may be a certain

degree of danger, that a succession of artful and ambitious rulers, may by gradual & well-timed advances, finally erect an independent Government on the subversion of liberty. Should this danger exist at all, it is prudent to guard agst. it, especially when the precaution can do no injury.[60]

For Madison a bill of rights could protect the community if a tyrant seizes power, much like it could protect the minority from the majority becoming tyrannical. Madison understood a bill of rights to serve yet another valuable purpose of protecting rights.

Seventh, Madison became convinced that there was a proper way to draft a bill of rights that would safeguard all important rights. Indeed, one of the most common Federalist arguments against a bill of rights was that even the best-drafted bill of rights might inadvertently leave out some rights, thereby implying that rights not listed in a bill of rights are not protected.[61] Although Madison feared that an improperly drafted bill of rights could be dangerous to liberty, he also realized that a runaway federal government could transgress its enumerated powers by using the Necessary and Proper Clause. This problem began to weigh heavily on Madison. His solution to this quandary was to draft a comprehensive bill of rights *and* include a provision that eventually became the Ninth Amendment. Madison's original formulation of this amendment was, "The exceptions here or elsewhere in the constitution, made in favor of particular rights, shall not be so construed as to diminish the just importance of other rights retained by the people; or as to enlarge the powers delegated by the constitution; but either as actual limitations of such powers, or as inserted merely for greater caution."[62]

When introducing his amendments before Congress, Madison explained what this clause was designed to protect against: "It has been objected also against a bill of rights" that, "by enumerating particular exceptions to the grant of power, it would disparage those rights which were not placed in that enumeration, and it might follow by implication, that those rights which were not singled out, were intended to be assigned into the hands of the General Government, and were consequently insecure."[63] Madison then admitted that this "is one of the most plausible arguments I have ever heard urged against the admission of a bill of rights into this system."[64] Madison subsequently stated, "that may be guarded against. I have attempted it, as gentlemen may see by turning to the last clause of the fourth resolution," which is the amendment cited above. [65] Madison had undercut a strong argument against a bill of rights, proving again that he truly believed in the substantive need for a bill of rights. Indeed, if Madison wanted a bill of rights for strategic reasons only, it would make little sense for him to spend time constructing a catch-all amendment to protect unenumerated liberties.

CORRESPONDENCE WITH THOMAS JEFFERSON

Thomas Jefferson played a prominent role in convincing his good friend James Madison that a bill of rights really could serve to protect liberty. Madison's change of heart regarding the usefulness of a bill of rights was due in large part to the correspondence he had with Jefferson from 1787 to 1789. Indeed, on several different occasions between the Constitutional Convention and Madison's introduction of the Bill of Rights in Congress, Jefferson urged Madison in multiple letters that not only was a bill of rights a good idea but that it was essential for the new nation.

On December 20, 1787, Jefferson wrote his thoughts on the newly proposed Constitution. After describing what he found admirable in the document, Jefferson turned to some problems he had with it: "I will now tell you what I do not like. First, the omission of a bill of rights, providing clearly, and without the aid of sophism, for freedom of religion, freedom of the press, protection against standing armies, restriction of monopolies, the eternal and unremitting force of the habeas corpus laws, and trials by jury in all matters of fact triable by the laws of the land, and not by the laws of nations."[66]

Madison eventually proposed amendments that protected four of the items in Jefferson's list: freedom of religion, freedom of the press, a partial protection against standing armies, and jury trials.[67] In this same letter Jefferson also dealt with a Federalist counterargument against a bill of rights, commenting that even though one *could* argue that a bill of rights is not necessary because Congress was given limited, enumerated powers, it could just as easily be argued that a bill of rights is necessary because such powers could be violated.[68] As noted above, Madison eventually adopted this argument as his own when he proposed the Bill of Rights to Congress.[69] Finally, Jefferson concluded his letter by stating that a "bill of rights is what the people are entitled to against every government on earth, general or particular; and what no just government should refuse, or rest on inference."[70] It is unlikely that this unequivocally bold statement by Jefferson could have been read by Madison without having an effect on him.

Seven months later in July 1788, Jefferson wrote another letter to Madison, again urging Madison to support a bill of rights. Jefferson claimed that there was a "general voice, from north to south, which calls for a bill of rights. It seems pretty generally understood, that this should go to juries, habeas corpus, standing armies, printing, religion and monopolies."[71] Jefferson then alleged that although "there may be difficulty in finding general modifications of these suited to the habits of all the States," the "few cases wherein these things may do evil, cannot be weighed against the multitude wherein the want of them will do evil."[72] After giving some specific examples of how a bill of rights could be useful, Jefferson concluded that "I hope therefore a bill of rights will be formed to guard the people against the federal government, as they are already guarded against their state governments in most instances."[73] Jefferson subsequently wrote a letter to Madison in November 1788, again reiterating that "[a]s to the bill of rights, however, I still think it should be added."[74] Jefferson was relentless in his pursuit of a bill of rights during his correspondence with Madison.

Finally, on March 15, 1789, Jefferson wrote what was probably the most important letter to Madison in their discussion over the need for a bill of rights. In this letter, Jefferson responded to a series of arguments for and against the usefulness of a bill of rights that Madison wrote in an October 17, 1788, letter to Jefferson. Jefferson began by adding to the favorable arguments Madison had noted for a bill of rights: "In the arguments in favor of a declaration of rights, you omit one which has great weight with me, the legal check which it puts into the hands of the judiciary. This is a body, which if rendered independent, and kept strictly to their own department merits great confidence for their learning and integrity."[75] This was one of the arguments Madison used in his speech introducing the Bill of Rights— a bill of rights would create a legal mechanism for the federal courts to protect liberty. Jefferson next commented, "I am happy to find that on the whole you are a friend to this amendment," and that the "Declaration of rights is like all other human blessings alloyed with some inconveniences, and not accomplishing fully it's object. But the good in this instance vastly overweighs the evil."[76] Jefferson then announced to Madison, "I cannot refrain from making short answers to the objections which your letter states to have been raised."[77]

Madison's first reservation regarding a bill of rights that he expressed in his October 1788 letter to Jefferson was that "I conceive that in a certain degree . . . the rights in question are reserved by the manner in which the federal powers are granted."[78] In other words, Madison claimed that since federal powers were specifically enumerated, this placed an affirmative limitation on federal power, making a bill of rights unnecessary. Jefferson's response in March 1789 was as follows: "A constitutive act may certainly be so formed as to need no declaration of rights. The act itself has the force of a declaration as far as it goes: and if it goes to all material points nothing more is wanting . . . in a constitutive act which leaves some precious articles unnoticed, and raises implications against others, a declaration of rights becomes necessary, by way of supplement. This is the case of our new federal Constitution."[79] Jefferson claimed that simply because federal powers are enumerated, this does not necessarily prohibit the government in the future from acting outside the scope of this power. Creating negative proscriptions on power as a corollary to affirmative prescriptions for the exercise of power was, as noted above, another reason given by Madison in favor of a bill of rights when he introduced his amendments in Congress.

Madison's next reservation regarding a bill of rights was that "there is great reason to fear that a positive declaration of some of the most essential rights could not be obtained in the requisite latitude."[80] Jefferson had a poetic response: "Half a loaf is better than no bread. If we cannot secure all our rights, let us secure what we can."[81] Madison eventually came to agree with Jefferson, and he put in place the provision that matured into the Ninth Amendment as a way to prevent the potential harms he had initially expressed to Jefferson.

Madison's third reservation to a bill of rights was that "the limited powers of the federal Government and the jealousy of the subordinate Governments, afford a security which has not existed in the case of the State Governments, and exists in no other."[82] Jefferson's response: "The jealousy of the subordinate governments is a precious reliance. But observe that those governments are only agents. They must have principles furnished them, whereon to found their opposition. The declaration of rights will be the text whereby they will try all the acts of the federal government. In this view it is necessary to the federal government also: as by the same text they may try the opposition of the subordinate governments."[83]

Jefferson here averred that a bill of rights can be something that state governments turn to for support when trying to halt the federal government from transgressing rights. As noted earlier, Madison would eventually adopt this line of reasoning when he proposed the Bill of Rights. Jefferson posited that a bill of rights can be a useful way for the federal government to prevent the states from violating rights. Madison agreed, as he proposed his "most valuable amendment" to limit state powers over certain liberties.

Finally, Madison complained to Jefferson that "experience proves the inefficacy of a bill of rights on those occasions when its controul is most needed. Repeated violations of these parchment barriers have been committed by overbearing majorities in every State."[84] Jefferson had a reply for this too:

> True. But though it is not absolutely efficacious under all circumstances, it is of great potency always, and rarely inefficacious. A brace the more will often keep up the building which would have fallen with that brace the less. There is a remarkable difference between the characters of the Inconveniencies which attend a Declaration of rights, and those which attend the want of it. The inconveniences of the Declaration are that it may cramp government in its useful exertions. But the evil of this is short-lived, moderate, and reparable. The inconveniencies of the want of a Declaration are permanent, afflicting and irreparable. They are in constant progression from bad to worse.[85]

Jefferson admitted that bills of rights may not always be effective; however, Jefferson also pointed out to Madison that over the long term a bill of rights offers many more benefits when compared to the costs of not having a bill of rights. Madison made a similar point when he proposed the Bill of Rights: "[I]f all power is subject to abuse, that then it is possible the abuse of the powers of the general government may be guarded against in a more secure manner than is now done, while no one advantage, arising from the exercise of that power, shall be damaged or endangered by it. We have in this way something to gain, and, if we proceed with caution, nothing to lose."[86] Once again, Madison was persuaded by Jefferson that the reasons in favor of a bill of rights far outweigh the reasons against them.

Whatever reservations Madison may have had regarding a bill of rights, his friend Thomas Jefferson convinced him otherwise. Madison used all of Jefferson's arguments in support of his amendments when he proposed them in Congress. Given that all of Jefferson's stated reasons in favor of a bill of rights were substantive in nature, the case for Madison coming to support a bill of rights for substantive reasons (in addition to strategic reasons) is bolstered by his correspondence with Jefferson.

There are several compelling reasons why Madison supported the Bill of Rights for its own sake as a protection of liberty. With a better understanding of Madison's motivations for the Bill of Rights, it is easier to put into context some of his statements on specific freedoms. The next chapter examines what Madison thought about individual freedoms as well as how he proposed freedoms in the Bill of Rights to reinforce each other and work with the original Constitution to protect liberty, promote virtue, and enhance the common good.

MADISON'S SYSTEM OF RIGHTS

A SYSTEM OF LIBERTIES THAT MUTUALLY
REINFORCE EACH OTHER

The Bill of Rights is nearly always studied on a clause-bound basis, whereby each right is considered and interpreted in isolation from the others. This is certainly the case with most Supreme Court justices. Conversely, a comprehensive view of the Bill of Rights would understand how each right relates to the others and to the original Constitution. A key to understanding Madison's thoughts on the Bill of Rights is that it must be analyzed holistically. Madison did not propose the Bill of Rights in such a way that each freedom would be simply an isolated right, having a meaning independent from the other rights and the Constitution. Instead, Madison wanted each of the rights he proposed to be part of a larger system of liberal rights that would work together to promote virtue and the common good. Moreover, these rights were not meant to be something siphoned off from the rest of the Constitution, but they were meant to work with the structural safeguards that were originally ratified, including the separation of powers, federalism, and the enumeration of powers. When looking at the Bill of Rights in the context of Madison's political theory, First Amendment rights, property rights, and the rights of the accused were of paramount importance to him, and he tried to construct a system whereby these core rights would reinforce each other.

Madison was clear during his speech introducing the Bill of Rights that he was trying to promote the Bill as part of a larger system to achieve the goals he believed were important. Madison asserted that, "if once bills of rights are established in all the states as well as the federal constitution, we shall find that although some of them are rather unimportant, yet, upon the whole, they will have a salutary tendency."[1] Madison claimed that some of the rights he proposed were "rather unimportant." So, why put such "unimportant" freedoms in the Bill of Rights? According to Madison, they would work with other rights enshrined in the Bill, as well as with other rights protected by the states, to have a greater effect. For Madison, the "whole" of the Bill of Rights was worth more than the sum of its parts.

Madison stated that there were several different types of rights that he proposed: (1) those that "do nothing more than state the perfect equality of mankind"; (2) those "exercised by the people in forming and establishing a plan of Government"; (3) those that specify "rights which are retained when particular powers are given up to be exercised by the Legislature"; and (4) those which are "positive rights, which seem to result from the nature of the compact," including "Trial by jury."[2] This classification demonstrates that Madison was trying to combine a series of different types of rights, which together formed a system of liberal rights to achieve the good society.[3] How did Madison believe these liberties reinforced each other to promote virtue and the common good?

First, Madison understood First Amendment rights as reinforcing each other—protecting a given First Amendment right, such as the freedom of the press, would lead to a protection of another First Amendment right, such as the freedom of religion. For instance, Madison claimed during the Alien and Sedition Act controversy that both "the liberty of conscience and of the press, rest equally on the original ground of not being delegated by the Constitution, and consequently withheld from the government. Any construction, therefore, that would attack this original security for the one, must have the like effect on the other."[4] In this way, Madison believed that since Congress was not empowered to take away one of these rights, protecting the one right will also protect the other. Madison continued regarding the freedoms of press and religion: "They are both equally secured by the supplement to the Constitution; being both included in the same amendment, made at the same time, and by the same authority. Any construction or argument, then, which would turn the amendment into a grant or acknowledgment of power with respect to the press, might be equally applied to the freedom of religion."[5]

For Madison, each of these rights helps to protect the other. He further explained that all of the rights in the First Amendment were meant to be protected to the same degree: "If the words and phrases in the amendment, are to be considered as chosen with a studied discrimination, which yields an argument for a power over the press, under the limitation that its freedom be not abridged, the same argument results from the same consideration, for a power over the exercise of religion, under the limitation that its freedom be not prohibited."[6] The fact that all of these freedoms are protected in the same amendment serves as reinforcement for them all. Consider also Madison shepherding Jefferson's Act for Establishing Religious Freedom through the Virginia Legislature in 1786. When Madison had managed to secure passage of the law, he wrote to Jefferson of his happiness that "this country" has "extinguished forever the ambitious hope of making laws for the human mind."[7] In this statement, Madison expressed a tie between religious freedom and the freedom of thought generally.

By analogy, these First Amendment rights are like the NATO pact—an attack on one is an attack on them all. Under this theory, the coupling of the freedoms of speech and press with religion in the First Amendment helps protect religious speech more than if the freedoms of speech and press had never been listed in the Bill of Rights. Although Madison did not originally propose these freedoms together in one amendment, Madison did propose his clause protecting religious freedoms directly before his clause protecting other expressive freedoms. One can even find a semblance of coherence in the order in which Madison proposed these rights: religious conscience, speech, press, assembly, and petition. These rights move from protecting the right to autonomously ponder the meaning of life, to the right to express our thoughts, to the right to broadly disseminate information, to the right to gather with other like-minded individuals, to the right to act on our ideas by lobbying the government.[8] Indeed, when viewed in this way there is a coherent logic to First Amendment rights, as Madison may have intended to protect first the inner rights of dignity and defining oneself, believing that this would ultimately lead to protecting the rights to express our opinions, spread our ideas, meet with others, and achieve the society we view as ideal.

Recall also that Madison proposed his "most valuable amendment" to protect rights against state infringement. It originally stated, "No state shall violate equal rights of conscience, or the freedom of the press, or the trial by jury in criminal cases." Later, Madison was able to add "the freedom of speech" to the middle of this list. Again, Madison placed these "First Amendment" rights back-to-back. Thus, there is evidence that Madison positioned these freedoms together in the Bill of Rights in order better to protect them and have them mutually reinforce each other while also promoting virtue and the common good.[9]

A second major connection intended by Madison was that First Amendment rights collectively would strengthen and help protect all other rights, and vice versa. There are several different liberties that Madison thought were tied to First Amendment freedoms, including freedom generally. For instance, Madison claimed that "[p]ublic opinion sets bounds to every government, and is the real sovereign in every free one."[10] Madison was referencing the power of public opinion to be the "real" sovereign and thus the real power. Allowing the people freely to express their opinions would thus protect all other rights by serving as a barrier to the government from taking away other rights. More pointedly, Madison stated in his "Virginia Resolutions" that "that right of freely examining public characters and measures, and of free communication among the people thereon . . . has ever been justly deemed, the only effectual guardian of every other right."[11] Madison's ideas begin to become clearer here, as he squarely put First Amendment rights, particularly speech, press, and association, into a position of protecting all other rights. Madison's theory is simple and well known. These First Amendment rights allow us to discuss how government should function and to criticize or praise the government for how it has acted. Without the protection of these rights, there would be no ability to check the government by debating about the government. This, in turn, would put all other rights in jeopardy—if we are prohibited from discussing government seizure of property, for instance, then our property rights would not be as safe as when we are allowed to discuss the issue.

Madison also saw protection of religious freedom as beneficial to all other rights. Madison claimed that religious establishments led to "slavery and Subjection";[12] that the freedom of conscience "is one of the Characteristics of a free people";[13] and that "[r]ulers who wished to subvert . . . liberty, may have found an established Clergy convenient auxiliaries."[14] In his "Memorial and Remonstrance" Madison claimed that freedom of religion "is held by the same tenure with all our other rights."[15] Madison continued on to affirm,

> Either then, we must say, that the Will of the Legislature is the only measure of their authority; and that in the plenitude of this authority, they may sweep away all our fundamental rights; or, that they are bound to leave this particular right [free exercise of religion] untouched and sacred: Either we must say, that they may control the freedom of the press, may abolish the trial by jury, may swallow up the Executive and Judiciary Powers of the State; nay that they may despoil us of our very right of suffrage, and erect themselves into an independent and hereditary Assembly or, we must say, that they have no authority to enact into law the Bill under consideration.[16]

Thus, Madison understood First Amendment rights to be tied to all other rights—if you protect one set of rights, you will protect the other. Others have also noted this connection that Madison made in his writings and speeches between the First Amendment and all other liberties.[17]

Commerce and free trade are other areas where Madison saw a particular connection to First Amendment rights. Indirectly, this is a tie between the First Amendment and property rights, as the ability to engage freely in commercial enterprise is contingent upon the right to use one's property without undue restraint. From a very early age, Madison stated that societies that have protected religious liberty are the ones in which "Commerce and the Arts have flourished."[18] Madison believed that protecting First Amendment rights would allow people to express themselves creatively, meaning that better commercial ideas could be promoted and used to advance the common good. Madison's own words demonstrate that he thought the causal arrow pointed in the opposite direction as well—that commercial trade would enhance First Amendment rights. When defending the Constitution, Madison noted that "the increased intercourse among those of different States will contribute not a little to diffuse a mutual knowledge of their affairs."[19]

Furthermore, Madison understood commerce and First Amendment rights to work together to promote all liberty: "Whatever facilitates a general intercourse of sentiments, as good roads, domestic commerce, a free press, and particularly a circulation of newspapers through the entire body of the people, and Representatives going from, and returning among every part of them, is equivalent to a contraction of territorial limits, and is favorable to liberty, where these may be too extensive."[20] For Madison, First Amendment rights and freely flowing commerce were intricately tied together. If lines of commerce became set up between regions and among countries, it would allow people of different religions and different ways of life to become more accustomed to each other. This would make them more tolerant of each other through their interactions and friendships, as well as by the fact that it would be bad for business to discriminate against someone on the basis of religious or political beliefs. This explains why Madison, who had a long track record of emphasizing First Amendment rights, also advocated protection of property rights and free commerce throughout his life.[21] Indeed, Madison saw the link between commerce and the freedom of religion quite clearly: if a nation began to engage in commercial enterprise with other nations, it would have to be tolerant of other countries' religions, lest it risk offending them and threatening its trade lines.

Madison also saw a particular connection between First Amendment rights and the rights of the accused. Madison thought that if one were not protected, the other may also be subject to abuse. For instance, in his "Memorial and Remonstrance" Madison maintained that "ecclesiastical establishments" lead to "bigotry and persecution."[22] Madison continued: "Instead of holding forth an Asylum to the persecuted, [a religious establishment] is itself a signal of persecution. It degrades from the equal rank of Citizens all those whose opinions in Religion do not bend to those of the Legislative authority. Distant as it may be in its present form from the Inquisition, it differs from it only in degree. The one is the first step, the other the last in the career of intolerance."[23]

In Madison's theory, a failure to protect religious liberty would lead to persecutions and lesser protections of criminal procedural rights. He expressed a similar view in a 1785 letter to Edmund Randolph. When discussing his disdain for the Virginia Assessment Bill, Madison stated the difference between Virginia's status quo and Virginia under the proposed assessment: "It may be of little consequence what tribunal is to judge of Clerical misdemeanors or how firmly the incumbent may be fastened on the parish, whilst the Vestry & people may hear & pay him or not as they like. But should legal salary be annexed to the title, this phantom of power would be substantiated into a real monster of oppression."[24] So, if religion had been established, judges and juries would have been forced to determine if the clergy had violated the laws of the assessment. For Madison, this would create a "monster of oppression."

Madison also claimed a connection between the rights of the accused and other First Amendment rights, particularly the freedoms of speech, press, and association. During his crusade against the Alien and Sedition Acts, Madison asserted that "opinions, and inferences, and conjectural observations, are not only in many cases inseparable from the facts, but may often be more the objects of the prosecution than the facts themselves; or may even be altogether abstracted from particular facts; and that opinions and inferences, and conjectural observations, cannot be subjects of that kind of proof which appertains to facts, before a court of law."[25] Madison continued:

> It is manifestly impossible to punish the intent to bring those who administer the government into disrepute or contempt, without striking at the right of freely discussing public characters and measures: because those who engage in such discussions, must expect and *intend* to excite these unfavourable sentiments, so far as they may be thought to be deserved. . . . Nor can there be a doubt, if those in public trust be shielded by penal laws from such strictures of the press, as may expose them to contempt or disrepute, or hatred, where they may deserve it, in exact proportion as they may deserve to be exposed, will be the certainty and criminality of the intent to expose them, and the vigilance of prosecuting and punishing it.[26]

Madison saw that eroding First Amendment rights would often lead to biased prosecutions and erosion of the rights of the criminally accused. Madison reiterated this point after President Washington had publicly denounced the Democratic-Republican Societies in 1794:

> It must be seen that no two principles can be either more indefensible in reason, or more dangerous in practice—than that 1. arbitrary denunciations may punish what the law permits, & what the Legislature has no right, by law, to prohibit—and that 2. the Govt. may stifle all censures whatever on its misdoings; for if it be itself the Judge it will never allow any censures to be just, and if it can suppress censures flowing from one lawful source it may those flowing from any other—from the press and from individuals as well as from Societies, &c.[27]

If the government is trying to silence a religious or political dissenter, it may stop at nothing to secure a conviction, as such speech often strikes directly at the base of religious or governmental power structures, or both. In these situations, government using its power to criminally try such speech is the quintessential example of bias that Madison opposed in *Federalist* 10: "No man is allowed to be a judge in his own cause; because his interest would certainly bias his judgment, and, not improbably, corrupt his integrity."[28] Thus, government prosecution of speech that is seditious (or blasphemous in the case of a religious establishment) will often result in overzealous enforcement. Madison saw this link as a young man, as he witnessed Elijah Craig, a Baptist minister from Culpepper, Virginia, sermonizing to a small group of his flock through the bars of his prison cell; Craig had been jailed for preaching dissenting doctrine.[29] Madison understood the importance of protecting First Amendment rights to prevent the slide into another Inquisition, as well as the importance of protecting criminal procedures to put a stop to any potential First Amendment violations. It was for this reason that, in addition to introducing amendments in the Bill of Rights that prohibited the federal government from violating religious freedom, the freedoms of speech and press, and criminal procedural rights, Madison also offered his "most valuable amendment" that limited these rights from being infringed by the states. Madison initiated no other amendments to protect rights against state infringement, suggesting the paramount importance with which he held First Amendment rights and rights of the criminally accused, as well as the connection he saw between these different rights.

Blasphemy and sedition prosecutions were often some of the most flagrant violations of criminal procedural rights in English history, and Madison saw a need to protect against such prosecutions when he drafted the Bill of Rights. In England, those convicted of seditious libel or blasphemy suffered unthinkable punishments, including placement in a dungeon with no bed or food, flogging, whipping, pillorying, ear cropping, cheek branding, nose slitting, disembowelment, quartering, and beheading.[30] In fact, Madison recommended that Congress purchase books describing the history of trials, including prosecutions for seditious libel and blasphemy.[31] Thus, Madison was concerned about protecting First Amendment rights by strengthening criminal procedures, and he also thought that fortifying protections of First Amendment rights would lead to fewer violations of criminal procedures.

A third major connection that Madison saw as essential in his system of liberal freedoms was between protecting property rights and protecting all other rights. As Madison stated in his "Republican Distribution of Citizens" article, "The class of citizens who provide at once their own food and their own raiment, may be viewed as the most truly independent and happy. They are more: they are the best basis of public liberty, and the strongest bulwark of public safety. It follows, that the greater the proportion of this class to the whole society, the more free, the more independent, and the more happy must be the society itself."[32] There is no question that Madison believed it important to safeguard property. Indeed, without protecting property rights, one could not secure his or her "own food" and "own raiment," as the property to grow such food and to cultivate resources for such clothing would not be secure for such practices. Protecting one's right to real property could ensure that one was able to have personal property such as food and clothing. For Madison, this right to property followed closely from the idea of justice: "That is not a just government, nor is property secure under it, where arbitrary restrictions, exemptions, and monopolies deny to part of its citizens that free use of their faculties, and free choice of their occupations, which not only constitute their property in the general sense of the word; but are the means of acquiring property strictly so called."[33]

Madison saw a tie between protecting property rights (including the property in one's occupation) and other rights. He claimed that not giving proper protection to property rights would negatively affect us. Furthermore, Madison feared what the results would be if those without property were in control. Madison believed that property ownership allows us freedom to exercise our rights in our self-interest (which gives us a chance to succeed economically) and it promotes virtue (which encourages us to exercise our rights for the good of the community). However, if we do not own our own property, we do not have that chance to become virtuous or to protect our other rights. Instead, we are liable to be unduly influenced by others. Therefore, Madison stated that

> the freeholders of the Country would be the safest depositories of Republican liberty. In future times a great majority of the people will not only be without landed, but any other sort of, property. These will either combine under the influence of their common situation; in which case, the rights of property & the public liberty, will not be secure in their hands: or which is more probable, they will become the tools of opulence & ambition, in which case there will be equal danger on another side.[34]

Madison was mindful of the dangers to every liberty we have if the right to property ownership is not protected. For this reason, Madison thought it necessary to protect property rights (particularly ownership of real estate) as a way for us to be able to exercise our rights and not have an employer or landlord retaliate against us for exercising our rights. Indeed, according to Madison, "Of all occupations those are the least desirable in a free state, which produce the most servile dependence of one class of citizens on another class."[35] But by protecting property rights so that we have the freedom to live off the land, we are allowed to exercise our political rights such as freedom of speech and voting, without having to worry about undue influence from private actors.

Also of particular importance, Madison did not want the government to directly be able to use its power of eminent domain to attack political dissenters, which is partly why he proposed that "[n]o person shall . . . be obliged to relinquish his property, where it may be necessary for public use, without a just compensation."[36] Madison additionally proposed protections of the rights of our "houses" and "other property" to be secure from "unreasonable searches and seizures," he proposed a right against "[e]xcessive bail" and "excessive fines," and he proposed preventing the peacetime quartering of soldiers in homes.[37] Madison believed that the danger that the public sector posed to our rights was greater than the dangers posed by the private sector. For this reason, prohibiting the government from unjustly taking our lands, our possessions, and our money would take away a potential avenue of tyranny. Without such a power, our rights to First Amendment freedoms would be subject to less abuse, and there would be less of an opportunity for our criminal procedural rights to be adversely affected. In fact, Madison even noted the potential for a government to take away our liberties through abridging property rights via excessive taxation. According to Madison "A just security to property is not afforded by that government, under which unequal taxes oppress one species of property and reward another species: where arbitrary taxes invade the domestic sanctuaries of the rich, and excessive taxes grind the faces of the poor; where the keenness and competitions of want are deemed an insufficient spur to labor, and taxes are again applied, by an unfeeling policy, as another spur."[38] Madison also saw a connection specifically between protecting property rights and First Amendment rights. In *Federalist 10*, Madison stated that protection of "the diversity in the faculties of men" was "the first object of government."[39] Madison was at least implicitly referring to First Amendment rights here—that government should protect the expression of different opinions. Madison subsequently claimed, "From the protection of different and unequal faculties of acquiring property, the possession of different degrees and kinds of property immediately results."[40] This line of thought followed Madison's statement that trying to remove the liberty that causes faction is "folly," "unwise," and a remedy "worse than the disease."[41] Madison wanted these First Amendment rights protected so that people would have the freedom to use these rights to acquire property. Lastly, Madison also defined "opinions and free communication of them" as a form of "property."[42] Thus, Madison tied protecting property rights to all other liberties, and vice versa.[43]

Finally, Madison believed that properly constructed rights in court, particularly trial by jury, would help to protect all other liberties. According to Madison, "Trial by jury . . . is as essential to secure the liberty of the people as any one of the pre-existent rights of nature."[44] Madison also maintained regarding trial by jury that

I think it will be proper, with respect to the judiciary powers, to satisfy the public mind on those points which I have mentioned. Great inconvenience has been apprehended to suitors from the distance they would be dragged to obtain justice in the Supreme Court of the United States, upon an appeal on an action for a small debt. To remedy this, declare, that no appeal shall be made unless the matter in controversy amounts to a particular sum: This, with the regulations respecting jury trials in criminal cases, and suits at common law, it is to be hoped will quiet and reconcile the minds of the people.[45]

In the same speech, Madison also commented that, "If they are incorporated into the constitution, independent tribunals of justice will consider themselves in a peculiar manner the guardians of those rights."[46] Finally, during the controversy over the Alien and Sedition Acts, Madison noted that

although aliens are not parties to the Constitution, it does not follow that the Constitution has vested in Congress an absolute power over them. . . . If aliens had no rights under the Constitution, they might not only be banished, but even capitally punished, without a jury or the other incidents to a fair trial. But so far has a contrary principle been carried, in every part of the United States, that except on charges of treason, an alien has, besides all the common privileges, the special one of being tried by a jury, of which one-half may be also aliens.[47]

Madison especially tied criminal trials to the protection of liberty. Madison easily came to this conclusion during his political career and advocated protecting the rights of the criminally accused, in part, for this reason. Overall, then, Madison thought that liberal rights could protect and reinforce each other, to better achieve the greater goal of advancing virtue and the common good.

THE CORE RIGHTS

At the center of Madison's liberal system of rights were some key First Amendment rights (freedom of and from religion, freedom of speech, and freedom of the press), criminal procedures (particularly the right to trial by jury), and property rights. These rights formed the core of a liberal system of rights that Madison thought it was essential to protect. A survey of some of Madison's statements regarding these rights will bear out the truth of this proposition.

Madison was an adamant defender of religious freedom from the earliest years of his career. Madison claimed in his "Memorial and Remonstrance" that religion "must be left to the conviction and conscience of every man," that religious duty "is precedent, both in order of time and degree of obligation, to the claims of Civil Society," and that "Religion is wholly exempt from [civil society's] cognizance."[48] Madison observed in a speech in the Virginia Ratifying Convention that he "*warmly* supported religious freedom."[49] Freedom of and from religion was the first right that Madison proposed to be added to the list of freedoms that Congress could not violate, and he also proposed that "no person religiously scrupulous of bearing arms, shall be compelled to render military service in person."[50] Madison noted in a congressional speech that "it is the particular glory of this country, to have secured the rights of conscience which in other nations are least understood or most strangely violated."[51] In a newspaper article he stated that "Conscience is the most sacred of all property."[52] In his First Inaugural Address, Madison proclaimed that one of the principles of his presidency would be "to avoid the slightest interference with the rights of conscience, or the functions of religion so wisely exempted from civil jurisdiction."[53] Finally in a letter to Edward Livingston, Madison remarked, "I observe with particular pleasure the view you have taken of the immunity of Religion from civil jurisdiction [in Louisiana], in every case where it does not trespass on private rights or the public peace. This has always been a favorite principle with me."[54] Indeed, Madison maintained this strong defense of religious freedom throughout his career.[55]

Likewise, Madison held other First Amendment rights in a very high regard. In *Federalist* 10, Madison claimed that protection of the "diversity of faculties in men" is "the first object of government."[56] In *Federalist* 49, Madison stated that "all governments rest on opinion."[57] In a 1791 newspaper article Madison penned, "Public opinion sets bounds to every government, and is the real sovereign in every free one."[58] Similarly, in a later article Madison noted, "All power has been traced up to opinion. The stability of all governments and security of all rights may be traced to the same source. The most arbitrary government is controuled where the public opinion is fixed."[59] In the "Virginia Resolutions" Madison praised "that right of freely examining public characters and measures, and of free communication among the people thereon, which has ever been justly deemed, the only effectual guardian of every other right."[60] In another newspaper article Madison affirmed the importance of protecting the freedom of the press because the press is a "guardian of public rights," and an "organ of necessary truths."[61] In the *Report on the Alien and Sedition Acts*, Madison averred that protecting the freedom of the press is more of a concern in the United States than in Great Britain because

> in the United States, the great and essential rights of the people are secured against legislative, as well as against executive ambition. They are secured, not by laws paramount to prerogative, but by constitutions paramount to laws. This security of the freedom of the press requires, that it should be exempt,

not only from previous restraint by the executive, as in Great Britain, but from legislative restraint also; and this exemption, to be effectual, must be an exemption not only from the previous inspection of licensers, but from the subsequent penalty of laws.[62]

Since Madison saw a need to protect rights against *both* the legislative and executive branches of government, he understood that vital liberties such as the freedom of the press needed more protection in the United States. Finally, in his First Inaugural Address, Madison avowed that he would be committed "to preserve in their full energy, the other salutary provisions in behalf of private and personal rights, and of the freedom of the press."[63] Thus, Madison had a strong commitment to First Amendment rights beyond freedom of religion.[64] He believed that the most effective way to organize society would be to protect liberal freedoms of speech and press. According to Madison, if these rights are infringed upon, society will be disadvantaged overall because some of the best ideas might not be expressed and put to good use.

Another core part of Madison's liberal system was the rights of the criminally accused, particularly the right to a jury trial. In a speech at the Virginia Ratifying Convention, Madison asserted that the "trial by jury is held as sacred."[65] When proposing the Bill of Rights, Madison listed the right to a criminal jury trial no less than three different times: "In all criminal prosecutions, the accused shall enjoy the right to a speedy and public trial"; "No state shall violate . . . the trial by jury in criminal cases"; "The trial of all crimes . . . shall be by an impartial jury of freeholders of the vicinage."[66] During his speech introducing the Bill of Rights, Madison declared of the right to a jury trial that it "is as essential to secure the liberty of the people as any one of the pre-existent rights of nature."[67] Finally, Madison thought that this right should also be extended to noncitizens.[68]

Protection of property was the final core right in Madison's liberal system. Indeed, Madison consistently emphasized the need to protect property rights during his career. Madison stressed in *Federalist* 10 the need of government to protect the "diversity in faculties of men from which the rights of property originate."[69] Later, Madison explained in his "Property" essay that "property" has a dual meaning: "This term in its particular application means 'that dominion which one man claims and exercises over the external things of the world, in exclusion of every other individual.' In its larger and juster meaning, it embraces every thing to which a man may attach a value and have a right; and which leaves to every one else the like advantage."[70]

Madison claimed that there are two ways to understand property. In its former sense, it means "a man's land, or merchandise, or money," or what we typically think of when we use the word property. Madison also integrated the protection of other rights when he discussed the term property:

In the latter sense, a man has a property in his opinions and the free communication of them. He has a property of peculiar value in his religious opinions, and in the profession and practice dictated by them. He has a property very dear to him in the safety and liberty of his person. He has an equal property in the free use of his faculties and free choice of the objects on which to employ them. In a word, as a man is said to have a right to his property, he may be equally said to have a property in his rights.[71]

Thus, in addition to the narrower idea that our physical possessions are our property, Madison saw all rights as a form of property. And he went on in that essay to state that "Government is instituted to protect property of every sort."[72] As noted above, this was similar to Madison's proposed preamble to the Bill of Rights: "government is instituted, and ought to be exercised for the benefit of the people; which consists in the enjoyment of life and liberty, with the right of acquiring and using property, and generally of pursuing and obtaining happiness and safety."[73]

Overall, Madison wanted to protect the core rights of religious freedom, freedoms of speech and of the press, the rights of the criminally accused, and property rights, and he drew them all within his broad definition of property. A survey of Madison's writings and speeches reveals that he frequently discussed all or some of these core rights together.

Before the Constitutional Convention, Madison noted the rights that should be protected from infringement if a new national government were created:

If it were possible it would be well to define the extent of the Legislative power but the nature of it seems in many respects to be indefinite. It is very practicable however to enumerate the essential exceptions. The Constitution may expresly *restrain them from medling with religion—from abolishing Juries from taking away the Habeus corpus—from forcing a citizen to give evidence against himself, from controuling the press, from enacting retrospective laws at least in criminal cases,* from abridging the right of suffrage, *from seizing private property for public use without paying its full Value* from licensing the importation of Slaves, from infringing the Confederation &c &c.[74]

When defending Congress's taxing and spending power for the common defense and general welfare of the United States, Madison declared the following would not be possible under this power: "A power to destroy *the freedom of the press, the trial by jury,* or even to regulate the course of descents, or *the forms of conveyances.*"[75] In *Federalist* 54, Madison avowed that "Government is instituted no less for protection of the property, than of the persons, of individuals."[76]

In his well-known letter to George Eve, Madison affirmed that "it is my sincere opinion that the Constitution ought to be revised, and that the first

Congress meeting under it, ought to prepare and recommend to the States for ratification, the most satisfactory provisions for all essential rights, particularly *the rights of Conscience in the fullest latitude, the freedom of the press, trials by jury, security against general warrants* &c."[77]

In a letter to Thomas Mann Randolph, Madison reaffirmed that position: "It is particularly, my opinion, that the clearest and strongest provision ought to be made, for all those essential rights, which have been thought in danger, such as *the rights of conscience, freedom of the press, trials by jury, exemption from general warrants,* &c."[78]

In his draft bill of rights, Madison of course proposed protecting all of these core rights.[79] Of particular interest are two proposals where Madison combined these different rights. In what eventually became the Fourth Amendment, Madison seemingly proposed to protect criminal procedures, property, and First Amendment rights (through the protection of "papers") all at once: "The rights of the people to be secured in *their persons, their houses, their papers, and their other property from all unreasonable searches and seizures,* shall not be violated by warrants issued without probable cause, supported by oath or affirmation, or not particularly describing the places to be searched, or the persons or things to be seized."[80]

Even more relevant in Madison's proposed bill of rights was his "most valuable amendment" to limit state infringement of certain freedoms: "No state shall violate the equal rights of conscience, or the freedom of the press, or the trial by jury in criminal cases."[81] According to Madison when he introduced this amendment, it was important "because it is proper that every government should be disarmed of powers which trench upon those particular rights."[82] Madison was subsequently on the House Committee of Eleven that altered this amendment to protect what was apparently Madison's oversight of not mentioning the freedom of speech: "No state shall infringe the equal rights of conscience, nor the freedom of speech, or the freedom of the press, nor of the right of trial by jury in criminal cases."[83]

Madison also referred in his June 8, 1789, congressional speech to "the trial by jury, freedom of the press, [and] liberty of conscience" as "the great rights."[84] In the same paragraph Madison contended that the "freedom of the press and rights of conscience" are "those choicest privileges of the people."[85]

While defending his proposed amendments before Congress, Madison stated on August 15, 1789, that "It was wished that some security should be given for those *great and essential rights* which they had been taught to believe were in danger. I concurred, in the convention of Virginia . . . have not the people been told that *the rights of conscience, the freedom of speech, the liberty of the press, and trial by jury,* were in jeopardy; that they ought not to adopt the constitution until those *important rights* were secured to them."[86]

Years later during the congressional debate over the national bank,

Madison asserted why, in his opinion, the only proper understanding of the Constitution was one whereby "the powers not given were retained; and that those given were not to be extended by remote implications."[87] Madison explained, "On any other supposition, the power of Congress to abridge *the freedom of the press, or the rights of conscience*, &c. could not have been disproved."[88]

In his "Property" essay, Madison mentioned the rights of property, free speech, and freedom of religion together: "If there be a government then which prides itself in maintaining the inviolability of property; which provides that none shall be *taken directly even for public use without indemnification to the owner, and yet directly violates the property which individuals have in their opinions, their religion, their persons, and their faculties* . . . such a government is not a pattern for the United States."[89]

In his *Report on the Alien and Sedition Acts* Madison discussed his core liberal rights together on multiple occasions. For instance, Madison professed the following: "A bigoted or tyrannical nation might threaten us with war, unless *certain religious or political regulations* were adopted by us; yet it never could be inferred, if the regulations which would prevent war, were such as Congress had otherwise no power to make, that the power to make them would grow out of the purpose they were to answer."[90] Madison further alleged that "[t]he freedom of conscience, and of religion, are found in the same instruments which assert the freedom of the press. It will never be admitted, that the meaning of the former, in the common law of England, is to limit their meaning in the United States."[91] In Madison's view, "Words could not well express, in a fuller or more forcible manner, the understanding of the convention, that the *liberty of conscience and the freedom of the press*, were equally and completely exempted from all authority whatever of the United States."[92] Madison continued to reference these rights together:

> Under an anxiety to guard more effectually these rights against every possible danger, the convention, after ratifying the Constitution, proceeded to prefix to certain amendments proposed by them, a declaration of rights, in which are two articles providing, the one for *the liberty of conscience, the other for the freedom of speech and of the press* . . . it will remain with a candid public to decide, whether it would not mark an inconsistency and degeneracy, if an indifference were now shown to a palpable violation of one of those rights, *the freedom of the press;* and to a precedent therein, which may be fatal to the other, *the free exercise of religion.*[93]

Finally, Madison explained that "Both of these rights, *the liberty of conscience and of the press*, rest equally on the original ground of not being delegated by the Constitution, and consequently withheld from the government. Any construction, therefore, that would attack this original security for the one, must have the like effect on the other."[94] Overall, a pattern emerges when one reads Madison's words, as he continually emphasized the importance of the core liberal freedoms of religion, speech, press, and association, as well as the right to property and the rights of the accused.[95] No other set of rights came up nearly as frequently, nor did he mention any other rights together so often. Madison believed that this subset of rights was the key to his liberal system of rights, whereby protecting natural rights would lead to a cultivation of virtue and the promotion of the public good. It is for this reason that part II focuses primarily on Supreme Court opinions in these areas—these are instances where the Supreme Court has used Madison to interpret the meaning of rights that were extremely important to Madison.

WORKING WITH THE GENIUS OF THE ORIGINAL CONSTITUTION

Not only did Madison devise a liberal system of freedoms when he launched the Bill of Rights in Congress in the summer of 1789; he also proposed a set of liberties that worked in conjunction with the system of government that he helped initiate in Philadelphia two years earlier. Indeed, the true genius of Madison's bill of rights was that it conformed to the political ideas underlying the structure of the new government. The Bill of Rights worked with the separation of powers, federalism, limited government with enumerated powers, and representative government to achieve Madison's liberal vision.

The separation of powers was one of the key components of Madison's theory to make the new government work and to protect liberty. For Madison, "The accumulation of all powers, legislative, executive, and judiciary, in the same hands . . . may justly be pronounced the very definition of tyranny,"[96] and so for him it was "essential to the preservation of liberty that the Legislative, Executive, and Judiciary powers be separate."[97] How does this come into play regarding the Bill of Rights? Madison still believed so strongly in the connection between liberty and the separation of powers that he included a provision reinforcing that doctrine *in* his proposed bill of rights: "The powers delegated by this constitution, are appropriated to the departments to which they are respectively distributed: so that the legislative department shall never exercise the powers vested in the executive or judicial; nor the executive exercise the powers vested in the legislative or judicial; nor the judicial exercise the powers vested in the legislative or executive departments."[98] Madison had not abandoned his commitment to the separation of powers in 1789 as a way to protect rights. Instead, he wished to incorporate it into the Bill of Rights as an important way to protect the liberal system of rights he proposed. Madison went on to state that this amendment would "lay down dogmatic maxims with respect to the construction of the Government; declaring, that the legislative, executive, and judicial branches shall be kept separate and distinct."[99]

Madison also recognized in his introductory speech that the freedoms in the Bill of Rights can be protected by the system of separated institutions sharing powers, when he claimed that federal judges "will be an impenetrable bulwark against every assumption of power in the legislative or executive; they will be naturally led to resist every encroachment upon rights expressly stipulated for in the constitution by the declaration of rights."[100] The separation of powers would be one way to help enforce a bill of rights, for which Madison initially had lukewarm support. In fact, it was the breakdown of the separation of powers that Madison believed left First Amendment rights and criminal procedures vulnerable during the Alien and Sedition Acts controversy: "the 'alien and sedition acts,' . . . the first of which . . . by uniting legislative and judicial powers, to those of executive, subverts the general principles of free government, as well as the particular organization and positive provisions of the federal constitution."[101] One threat to liberty that Madison saw in the Alien Act was that "it unites legislative, judicial, and executive powers in the hands of the President."[102] Madison then explained, "It has become an axiom in the science of government, that separation of the legislative, executive and judicial departments, is necessary to the preservation of public liberty."[103] Thus, Madison designed the Bill of Rights to work in conjunction with the separation of powers, and it was consistent with Madison's overall theory.[104]

Madison was also consistent in his stance that federalism was an essential way to protect rights. Madison's vision of intertwining liberty and federalism began with the proposal that eventually became the Tenth Amendment: "The powers not delegated by this constitution, nor prohibited by it to the States, are reserved to the States respectively."[105] Madison was noting the limited nature of federal government power in relation to the states. However, Madison also saw that states could be a threat to liberty, so he tried to limit state powers with his "most valuable amendment." Madison also stated of this amendment in his introduction of the Bill of Rights that "I think there is more danger of those powers being abused by the state governments than by the government of the United States. The same may be said of other powers which they possess. . . . I cannot see any reason against obtaining even a double security on those points."[106] But Madison did not distrust only the governments of the states. In addition to Madison's proposal that became the Tenth Amendment, Madison claimed that under the Bill of Rights,

> there is a great probability that such a declaration in the federal system would be enforced; because the State Legislatures will jealously and closely watch the operations of this Government, and be able to resist with more effect every

assumption of power than any other power on earth can do; and the greatest opponents to a Federal Government admit the State Legislatures to be sure guardians of the people's liberty.[107]

Madison's belief that the Bill of Rights and federalism could work together to protect his liberal system of rights continued through the controversy regarding the Alien and Sedition Acts. Madison spoke the following of the Virginia Assembly: "it is their duty, to watch over and oppose every infraction of those principles, which constitute the only basis of that union, because a faithful observance of them, can alone secure its existence, and the public happiness."[108] Madison continued to explain that

> the powers of the federal government, as resulting from the compact to which the states are parties; as limited by the plain sense and intention of the instrument constituting that compact; as no farther valid than they are authorised by the grants enumerated in that compact, and that in case of a deliberate, palpable and dangerous exercise of other powers not granted by the said compact, the states who are parties thereto have the right, and are in duty bound, to interpose for arresting the progress of the evil, and for maintaining within their respective limits, the authorities, rights and liberties appertaining to them.[109]

Madison would later elucidate that position: "The states, then, being the parties to the constitutional compact, and in their sovereign capacity, it follows of necessity, that there can be no tribunal above their authority, to decide in the last resort, whether the compact made by them be violated."[110] One of the parts of the "compact" that Madison thought Congress had violated in this instance was the First Amendment—and it was the state of Virginia (along with Kentucky) that took a stand to protect these freedoms from federal encroachment.

Madison's belief in a government of enumerated powers also clearly interconnected with his proposals in the Bill of Rights to protect a liberal system of rights. Madison stated in his speech proposing the Bill of Rights that "the great object in view is to limit and qualify the powers of Government, by excepting out of the grant of power those cases in which the Government ought not to act, or to act only in a particular mode."[111] Madison also admitted that a bill of rights was necessary because "in the constitution of the United States there is a clause granting to Congress the power to make all laws which shall be necessary and proper for carrying into execution all the powers vested in the government of the United States."[112] This position of limited federal power was one Madison would always maintain: "the federal powers are derived from the Constitution, and from that alone."[113] Madison explained, "Whenever, therefore a question arises concerning the constitutionality of a particular power; the first question is, whether the power be expressed in the constitution. If it be, the question is decided. If it be not expressed; the next enquiry must be, whether it is properly an incident to an express power, and necessary to its execution. If it be, it may be exercised by Congress. If it be not; Congress cannot exercise it."[114]

So how does this relate to what Madison proposed in the Bill of Rights? The other side of the coin of enumerated powers is the protection of unenumerated rights. Madison proposed in June 1789 what eventually became the Ninth Amendment: "The exceptions here or elsewhere in the constitution, made in favor of particular rights, shall not be so construed as to diminish the just importance of other rights retained by the people; or as to enlarge the powers delegated by the constitution; but either as actual limitations of such powers, or as inserted merely for greater caution."[115]

If there is any doubt of Madison's intent in this proposal to ensure the limited powers of the federal government, read Madison's own words on the subject:

> It has been objected also against a bill of rights, that, by enumerating particular exceptions to the grant of power, it would disparage those rights which were not placed in that enumeration, and it might follow by implication, that those rights which were not singled out, were intended to be assigned into the hands of the general government, and were consequently insecure. This is one of the most plausible arguments I have ever heard urged against the admission of a bill of rights into this system; but, I conceive, that may be guarded against. I have attempted it, as gentlemen may see by turning to the last clause of the 4th resolution.[116]

Madison's proposal which eventually became the Ninth Amendment was the last clause of the fourth resolution in his proposed bill of rights. Undoubtedly, Madison still saw that the connection of enumerated powers and unenumerated rights remained important enough to reaffirm in 1789, even when Madison was cataloguing a list of enumerated rights.

Finally, Madison believed that protecting freedom, particularly liberal First Amendment rights, would be good for representative government. In defending the principles underlying the new Congress, Madison claimed that "the door of this part of the federal government is open to merit of every description . . . without regard to poverty or wealth, or to any particular profession of religious faith."[117] When supporting the amendments Madison proposed in Congress, he declared that "The right of freedom of speech is secured; the liberty of the press is expressly declared to be beyond the reach of this Government; the people may therefore publicly address their representatives; may privately advise them, or declare their sentiments by petition to the whole body; in all these ways they may communicate their will."[118] Madison was adamant in defending the following proposition, which he thought essential to representation: "If we advert to the nature of republican government, we shall find that the censorial power is in the people over the government, and not in the government over the people."[119] Madison also believed that free speech rights for members of Congress were essential to a well-functioning republic: "the house must have a right, in all cases, to ask for information, which might assist their deliberations on subjects submitted to them by the constitution."[120]

Madison's conviction that protecting liberal First Amendment rights would promote a representative form of government was evident in the debate over the Alien and Sedition Acts: "Let it be recollected, lastly, that the right of electing the members of the government, constitutes more particularly the essence of a free and responsible government. The value and efficacy of this right, depends on the knowledge of the comparative merits and demerits of the candidates for public trust; and on the equal freedom, consequently, of examining and discussing these merits and demerits of the candidates respectively."[121] Throughout his *Report on the Alien and Sedition Acts* Madison repeatedly drew a connection between First Amendment freedoms and having a successful democratic republic.[122] This is additional evidence that Madison wanted a republic where the people had a near absolute freedom to discuss public issues and candidates.[123]

Thus, the Bill of Rights was quite consistent with Madison's overall views on politics and government. For Madison, the separation of powers, federalism, the enumerated nature of the federal government, and representation all work in conjunction with the Bill of Rights to create his liberal system of freedoms. Indeed, Madison's liberalism shined through not only when he proposed a set of freedoms in the Bill of Rights but also in his reaffirmation at that time that government power must be divided in various ways and guarded in multiple ways in order to best protect the rights of the people.

Seven

MADISON'S VISION OF SPECIFIC FREEDOMS IN THE BILL OF RIGHTS

THE FREEDOM OF AND FROM RELIGION

Madison wrote and said more on the freedom of religion (including both free exercise and disestablishment) than on any other liberty in the Bill of Rights. Regarding Establishment Clause issues, Madison advocated something very close to what we today would call a strict separationist position. Madison commented of religion, "The government has no jurisdiction over it."[1] Madison's separationism was so strong that he once arguably implied that churches should be taxed:

> Ye States of America, which retain in your Constitutions or Codes, any aberration from the sacred principle of religious liberty, by giving to Caesar what belongs to God, or joining together what God has put asunder, hasten to revise & purify your systems, and make the example of your Country as pure & compleat, in what relates to the freedom of the mind and its allegiance to its maker, as in what belongs to the legitimate objects of political & civil institutions.[2]

Requiring churches to give "legitimate objects" to "political & civil institutions" just like other taxable entities would have made it more difficult for a religion to be established. Indeed, the implication here by Madison is to treat religion as though it has no special status before the law. Note below, however, that Madison's position on how to treat religious believers for free exercise purposes was very different from how he conceived of religious institutions interacting with government for Establishment Clause purposes.

Regarding the funding of religion by government, Madison believed that "it is proper to take alarm at the first experiment on our liberties."[3] Or, as he once asked rhetorically, "Who does not see . . . that the same authority which can force a citizen to contribute three pence only of his property for the support of any one establishment, may force him to conform to any other establishment in all cases whatsoever?"[4] To the contrary, Madison always wanted government power separated from that of religion.

Madison was of the opinion that uniting government and religion would not promote the public good or instill virtue in the citizenry. Examine, for instance, the following statement on requiring religious oaths:

> Is not a religious test as far as it is necessary, or would operate, involved in the oath itself? If the person swearing believes in the supreme Being who is invoked, and in the penal consequences of offending him, either in this or a future world or both, he will be under the same restraint from perjury as if he had previously subscribed a test requiring this belief. If the person in question be an unbeliever in these points and would notwithstanding take the oath, a previous test could have no effect.[5]

Madison believed religious establishments attacked human dignity, and they did nothing to make one more virtuous. Either one is a religious believer or one is not, and an establishment will do nothing to alter the situation. As stated in the Virginia Act for Establishing Religious Freedom that Madison shepherded through the Virginia Assembly: "to compel a man to furnish contributions of money for the propagation of opinions which he disbelieves, is sinful and tyrannical."[6] In this way, Madison understood religious establishments as promoting vice, not virtue. "No distinction seems to be more obvious than that between spiritual and temporal matters," wrote Madison. "Yet whenever they have been made objects of Legislation, they have clashed and contended with each other, till one or the other has gained the supremacy."[7] For Madison, the common good would be threatened by religious establishments, as he believed that such establishments would lead to the growth of an excessive amount of dangerous factions.

Madison thought that virtue and the common good could be best achieved by religion and government being separated. Thus, Madison opposed the religious assessment in his "Memorial and Remonstrance," in part, because such assessments and establishments led to, "more or less in all places, pride and indolence in the Clergy; ignorance and servility in the laity; in both, superstition, bigotry and persecution."[8] For Madison, virtue would be denied if religion and government were united. He certainly thought this was true in the controversy over the Virginia assessment:

> [T]he establishment in question is not necessary for the support of Civil Government. If it be urged as necessary for the support of Civil Government only as it is a means of supporting Religion, and it be not necessary for the latter purpose, it cannot be necessary for the former. If Religion be not within the cognizance of Civil Government, how can its legal establishment be necessary to civil Government? What influence in fact have ecclesiastical establishments

had on Civil Society? In some instances they have been seen to erect a spiritual tyranny on the ruins of Civil authority; in many instances they have been seen upholding the thrones of political tyranny: in no instance have they been seen the guardians of the liberties of the people. Rulers who wished to subvert the public liberty, may have found an established Clergy convenient auxiliaries. A just government instituted to secure & perpetuate it needs them not. Such a government will be best supported by protecting every Citizen in the enjoyment of his Religion with the same equal hand which protects his person and his property; by neither invading the equal rights of any Sect, nor suffering any Sect to invade those of another.[9]

Madison believed this because he knew that self-interest was a powerful motivator and an integral part of human nature. Establishing religion made it more possible for those with self-interested designs to achieve unvirtuous ends by taking advantage of the uniting of religious and civil power. Furthermore, according to Madison, in *no* instance have ecclesiastical establishments guarded the people's liberties. Thus, Madison took what would today be classified as a separationist stance regarding the Establishment Clause. For Madison, this was the best way to allow religion to flourish without government interference and to foster the protection of natural, liberal rights. Consider the following sentiment of Madison:

> [T]he establishment proposed by the Bill is not requisite for the support of the Christian Religion. To say that it is, is a contradiction to the Christian Religion itself; for every page of it disavows a dependence on the powers of this world: it is a contradiction to fact; for it is known that this Religion both existed and flourished, not only without the support of human laws, but in spite of every opposition from them, and not only during the period of miraculous aid, but long after it had been left to its own evidence, and the ordinary care of Providence. Nay, it is a contradiction in terms; for a Religion not invented by human policy, must have pre-existed and been supported, before it was established by human policy. It is moreover to weaken in those who profess this Religion a pious confidence in its innate excellence, and the patronage of its Author; and to foster in those who still reject it, a suspicion that its friends are too conscious of its fallacies to trust it to its own merits.[10]

Given Madison's thoughts on political theory and human nature, this quote is certainly not out of character. Madison wanted religion to thrive as a way to teach virtue and achieve the common good, but he thought the best way to do that was to protect the right from government interference as much as possible. For Madison, this liberal understanding of the Establishment Clause is one that respects the idea of inherent human dignity. Madison personally put this theory into practice on the floor of Congress in 1795.

During a congressional debate over naturalization rules that at one point began to degenerate into an attack on Catholic immigrants, Madison stated that he "did not approve the ridicule attempted to be thrown out on the Roman Catholics."[11]

Although he held a realistic view of human nature, Madison still believed that each of us is capable of virtue, and we should each be given that opportunity under the best possible set of circumstances. Preventing the government from hijacking religion was one way of accomplishing this goal. Perhaps this best explains why, after securing passage of Jefferson's Act for Establishing Religious Freedom, Madison stated, "I flatter myself have in this Country extinguished forever the ambitious hope of making laws for the human mind."[12] To have something other than a separation between church and state would have been, in Madison's opinion, making laws for the human mind—which would have limited the mind's capacity for virtue and infringed on a natural right to think and express one's thoughts.

Conversely, under a nonpreferentialist theory of the Establishment Clause, independent growth of religions would be stifled by the government's power to treat all religious groups generally in whichever way the majority sect deemed to be "nonpreferential." This is certainly not Madison's vision of the Establishment Clause, as he remarked later in his life on the successes of disestablishment in Virginia and at the federal level: "the number, the industry, and the morality of the Priesthood, & the devotion of the people have been manifestly increased by the *total separation* of the Church from the State."[13] Nor would an allowance of the majority to define neutrality be consistent with Madison's desire to limit the power of the majority, expressed most succinctly in *The Federalist*. Indeed, Madison's idea of the tyranny of the majority could easily be realized under a nonpreferentialist approach to the Establishment Clause.

For Madison, government and religion needed to be kept separate. Anything less would be implying that government has a monopoly on religious truth, or that religion is the only guide of correct public policy. Madison said as much when he stated that establishment "implies either that the Civil Magistrate is a competent Judge of Religious Truth; or that he may employ Religion as an engine of Civil policy. The first is an arrogant pretension falsified by the contradictory opinions of Rulers in all ages, and throughout the world: the second an unhallowed perversion of the means of salvation."[14] In neither of these scenarios is virtue or liberty promoted. For Madison, disestablishment was a way to promote the liberal virtues that he held dear, and it was a way to protect other liberties such as the freedom of speech. Neither of these would be safeguarded if government and religion have formed an alliance. Given Madison's view of human nature, he believed that, once such power was fused, it would be easier for self-interested individuals to take advantage of the rest of us.

As an example, consider Madison's views regarding religion and colleges. At the Constitutional Convention, Madison moved to give Congress the power "to establish an University, in which no preferences or distinctions should be allowed on account of Religion."[15] His fear of establishments was clearly on his mind in this proposed amendment, even though this congressional power was never established. Madison would later express a similar sentiment when comparing the sectarian professorships at Harvard University and the lack of such positions at the university Madison helped Jefferson found, the University of Virginia:

> A University with sectarian professorships, becomes, of course, a Sectarian Monopoly: with professorships of rival sects, it would be an Arena of Theological Gladiators. Without any such professorships, it may incur for a time at least, the imputation of irreligious tendencies, if not designs. The last difficulty was thought more manageable than either of the others. On this view of the subject, there seems to be no alternative but between a public University without a theological professorship, and sectarian Seminaries without a University.[16]

Madison believed that learning and the attainment of virtue could occur freely at a university only if it were officially detached from religion. Nor would the common good emerge in such an environment, as the religious competition would drive reason from any such college. Indeed, for Madison a campus that is officially dominated by religion would take away from the liberal autonomy that Madison thought so essential for each person to possess. It is likely that Madison would have held this conviction even more strongly for a public university, which is run by the government and limited by the requirements of the Constitution.

Given Madison's realistic understanding of human nature, it is no surprise that he feared that the mixing of religion and politics would result in dangerous factions: "A zeal for different opinions concerning religion . . . have, in turn, divided mankind into parties, inflamed them with mutual animosity, and rendered them much more disposed to vex and oppress each other than to co-operate for their common good."[17] Disestablishment was Madison's remedy for protecting our freedoms from an overzealous combination of government and religion. If that requisite separation is not in place, "it will destroy that moderation and harmony which the forbearance of our laws to intermeddle with Religion has produced amongst its several sects. Torrents of blood have been spilt in the old world, by vain attempts of the secular arm, to extinguish Religious discord."[18] In order to prevent religious wars, Madison advocated that we cut off any budding tree of establishment at its roots, before it grows into a mighty oak too difficult to saw down. In such situations, it is difficult for people to attain virtue or the common good, and if war ensues other liberties will certainly be endangered.

Madison advocated separationism because he truly believed that bad results would arise from empowering religion with the might of government. Indeed, Madison believed that "Religion itself may become a motive to persecution & oppression."[19] Since Madison thought that "equality . . . ought to be the basis of every law,"[20] it is no surprise that Madison wanted to disestablish religion in order to protect the liberties of everyone, including, in his words, "Jews Turks & infidels."[21] Thus, Madison even extended the protections of freedom to atheists and other nonbelievers. Furthermore, separationism was the proper stance for what might appear to be de minimis intrusions, or at least this was the stance Madison took regarding the Virginia assessment: "Distant as it may be in its present form, from the Inquisition it differs from it only in degree. The one is the first step, the other the last in the career of intolerance. The magnanimous sufferer under this cruel scourge in foreign Regions, must view the Bill as a Beacon on our Coast, warning him to seek some other haven, where liberty and philanthrophy [sic] in their due extent may offer a more certain repose from his Troubles."[22]

Under a Madisonian theory of religious freedom, severe trouble is created by government's support of one religion over others or of multiple religions at the expense of those who are not its adherents. And for Madison, allowing the government to take sides for religion against nonreligion in a nonpreferential manner opens the door to government eventually singling out for protection one religion, and perhaps even one denomination: "Who does not see that the same authority which can establish Christianity, in exclusion of all other Religions, may establish with the same ease any particular sect of Christians, in exclusion of all other Sects?"[23] For Madison, this could lead to the weakening of government's legitimacy, as "attempts to enforce by legal sanctions, acts obnoxious to so great a proportion of Citizens, tend to enervate the laws in general, and to slacken the bands of Society."[24] Under Madison's political theory and view of human nature, it is better to sever this connection between religion and government, keep religion in private hands, and allow our religious freedom to flourish knowing that we are all equal members of the political community. This, in turn, allows each of us to find virtue without government interference. Otherwise, religion is "armed with the sanction of law, [which] will be a dangerous abuse of power."[25]

Madison always feared government collaboration with religion, regardless of how benevolent the purported motives might be:

> When Indeed Religion is kindled into enthusiasm, its force like that of other passions is increased by the sympathy of a multitude. But enthusiasm is only a temporary state of Religion, and whilst it lasts will hardly be seen with pleasure at the helm. Even in its coolest state, it has been much oftener a motive to

oppression than a restraint from it. If then there must be different interests and parties in Society; and a majority when united by a common interest or passion cannot be restrained from oppressing the minority, what remedy can be found in a republican Government, where the majority must ultimately decide, but that of giving such an extent to its sphere, that no common interest or passion will be likely to unite a majority of the whole number in an unjust pursuit. In a large Society, the people are broken into so many interests and parties, that a common sentiment is less likely to be felt, and the requisite concert less likely to be formed, by a majority of the whole.[26]

Since Madison believed that human nature could not be trusted, we cannot rely on benevolent motives to restrain religion once the door is opened by a union between government and religion. It was for this reason that Madison remarked the following: "Is the appointment of Chaplains to the two Houses of Congress consistent with the Constitution, and with the pure principle of religious freedom? In strictness the answer on both points must be in the negative."[27] Madison thought that by asking even one member of the clergy to give a blessing in a public setting, it would trample on the rights of the minority: "The establishment of the chaplainship to Congs is a palpable violation of equal rights, as well as of Constitutional principles. The tenets of the chaplains elected shut the door of worship agst the members whose creeds & consciences forbid a participation in that of the majority."[28] Madison thought it better to protect the liberal right of the individual to practice such religious observances privately, rather than having government dictate how religion should be practiced: "If Religion consist in voluntary acts of individuals, singly, or voluntarily associated, and it be proper that public functionaries, as well as their Constituents shd discharge their religious duties, let them like their Constituents, do so at their own expence."[29] Madison's fear here was that too close of an association between religion and government, even if the primary purpose is only to offer general spiritual guidance, will produce adverse results. For this reason, Madison stated that it is "[b]etter also to disarm in the same way, the precedent of Chaplainships for the army and navy, than erect them into a political authority in matters of religion."[30] For Madison, this allows each of us privately to attain virtue in the best way we see fit, without undue influence, and it also protects other rights from infringement from an overbearing, overzealous majority.

However, the one controversy that must not be neglected in this discussion of disestablishment is Madison's issuance of religious proclamations as president. In part II, one can see how multiple justices erroneously seize on this point to demonstrate their respective views that Madison must have been a nonpreferentialist. This does raise an interesting question: could Madison have been a separationist if he was offering religious proclamations as a public official? Upon reflection later in life, Madison had a very good explanation for this contradiction:

> During the administration of Mr. Jefferson no religious proclamation was issued. It being understood that his successor [Madison] was disinclined to such interpositions of the Executive and by some supposed moreover that they might originate with more propriety with the Legislative Body, a resolution was passed requesting him to issue a proclamation. . . . It was thought not proper to refuse a compliance altogether, but a form & language were employed, which were meant to deaden as much as possible any claim of political right to enjoin religious observances by resting these expressly on the voluntary compliance of individuals, and even by limiting the recommendation to such as wished simultaneous as well as voluntary performance of a religious act on the occasion.[31]

Thus, Madison thought it unwise to issue such proclamations and only did so reluctantly when Congress pushed him into making them. Looking back years later, it was clear to Madison that making such a concession was a mistake: "Religious proclamations by the Executive recommending thanksgivings & fasts are shoots from the same root with the legislative acts reviewed. Altho' recommendations only, they imply a religious agency, making no part of the trust delegated to political rulers."[32] Madison then gave several reasons why such government-sponsored prayers are objectionable. For one, "Govts ought not to interpose in relation to those subject to their authority but in cases where they can do it with effect. An *advisory* Govt is a contradiction in terms."[33] To Madison such proclamations "seem to imply and certainly nourish the erroneous idea of a *national* religion."[34] Madison also commented of such acts that the "last & not the least objection is the liability of the practice to a subserviency to political views."[35] In other words, religion may be forced to do something it would not otherwise do. For these reasons, Madison's views on human nature and the need to protect our liberal rights led him to believe that "religion is essentially distinct from Civil Govt and exempt from its cognizance," and "that a connexion between them is injurious to both."[36]

Now for the other side of the coin of religious freedom—free exercise. The best way to explain Madison's overall stance on questions of religious freedom is that he wanted to keep government and religion as two separate institutions, but he also wanted to make sure the people had full liberty to practice (or not to practice) the religion of their choice. The way for Madison to accomplish both of these goals was to take a separationist stance on the Establishment Clause (thus making sure that government and the public sphere are independent of religion and not run by a majority sect) and then adopt an accommodationist approach on the Free Exercise Clause (thus making people, especially those adhering to minority religions, better able to practice their religion privately to the fullest extent possible). Madison thought that the freedom of religion was a natural right to be protected by the government, and he believed that by allowing us the fullest latitude to practice our religion, we would also be able to better achieve virtue. Madison's statements on free exercise bear this out.

For free exercise, Madison held a general position of accommodationism because he wanted people to be able to exercise their natural right to religion. Madison maintained that religious "duty is precedent both in order of time and degree of obligation, to the claims of Civil Society. Before any man can be considered as a member of Civil Society, he must be considered as a subject of the Governour of the Universe."[37] The free exercise of religion was a liberal, natural, and inalienable right—one in which practitioners should be able to observe their faith as they best see fit without government intrusion. In this way, Madison believed that the government should "avoid the slightest interference with the rights of conscience, or the functions of religion so wisely exempted from civil jurisdiction."[38] Madison also argued that "a man has a property . . . of peculiar value in his religious opinions, and in the profession and practice dictated by them."[39] Madison saw religion as a natural right to be accorded to the individual, something that government should be careful not to infringe upon.

In addition to seeing freedom of religion as a natural right, Madison was adamant that protecting this right would be good for promoting virtue. Taken out of context, Madison made many statements that could be interpreted to have espoused accommodationism or the other major theory of free exercise, neutrality. However, when looking at Madison's overall philosophy and understanding that he wanted to protect liberal, natural rights, it becomes much easier to understand that Madison sought out an accommodationist stance. For Madison, that position protects religious exercise in its freest, most liberal position, where all religious groups have the opportunity to exercise their religious freedom as much as possible. For instance, when Madison stated that "equality . . . ought to be the basis of every law," and one does not put this within the context of his greater political philosophy, it could easily be interpreted to support a neutral or an accommodationist approach to free exercise.[40] Furthermore, if one continues on with this statement of Madison's from the "Memorial and Remonstrance" with no other context, it might appear more likely than not that Madison was espousing a type of neutrality: "As the Bill violates equality by subjecting some to peculiar burdens; so it violates the same principle, by granting to others peculiar exemptions."[41] However, knowing that Madison was a classical liberal, a quote such as this requires closer examination. Indeed, Madison did not say he opposed *all* religious exemptions—he opposed only *peculiar* exemptions. Thus, there were at least some religious exemptions that Madison was prepared to say *should be* allowed under the notion of free exercise. So how does one know which exemptions will be the peculiar ones? Looking to Madison's second draft of his religious freedom amendment at the Virginia Constitutional Convention offers a telling clue: "That religion, or the duty which we owe to our CREATOR, and the manner of discharging it, can be directed only by reason and conviction, not by force or violence; and therefore, that all men are equally entitled to enjoy the free exercise of religion, according to the dictates of conscience, unpunished and unrestrained by the magistrate, Unless the preservation of equal liberty and the existence of the State are manifestly endangered."[42]

Madison advocated accommodation of private religious practices unless a liberty of the same importance is manifestly endangered *and* the existence of the state itself is manifestly endangered. This is strong language indeed. Presumably, not all other liberties that are threatened will be a problem here—it has to be an equally important one, probably one of the core liberties explained in the previous chapter. Also, that liberty would have to be manifestly endangered by the religious practice; thus, minor intrusions created by religious exemptions would not raise a problem for Madison. The other half of the roadblock to accommodationism—a threat to the existence of the state itself—is obviously going to be a rare occurrence. That Madison held this position was confirmed when he proposed in Congress a clause that he wanted to be part of the Second Amendment: "no person religiously scrupulous of bearing arms, shall be compelled to render military service in person."[43] Madison believed it was so important to give exemptions based on religious affiliation that he believed pacifists should be exempt from military duty. And keep in mind that, under the amendment Madison proposed at the Virginia Constitutional Convention, freedom of religion could not be infringed upon unless *both* an equal liberty *and* the state were threatened. This theory of free exercise is very broad, probably even broader than the accommodationist stance taken by Justice Sandra Day O'Connor in her *Employment Division v. Smith* (1990) concurrence—that the Free Exercise Clause "requir[es] the government to justify any substantial burden on religiously motivated conduct by a compelling state interest and by means narrowly tailored to achieve that interest."[44] For Madison, the compelling interest is a threat to equal liberty and the existence of the state, making him an accommodationist. ·

Madison rejected a neutrality approach to Free Exercise Clause cases, given his understanding of human nature and his fears of the tyranny of the majority. Consider, for example, the situation in *Smith,* where the Court held it constitutional for Oregon to deny unemployment compensation to two employees fired by a drug rehabilitation organization after ingesting peyote for sacramental purposes. The Court reasoned that the law was neutral and generally applicable, and thus the state law was not aimed at promoting or restricting religious beliefs.[45] The largest problem for Madison with any neutrality approach to free exercise would be the tyranny of the majority, or when "the public good is disregarded in the conflicts of rival parties, and that measures are too often decided, not according to the rules of justice and the rights of the minor party, but by the superior force of an interested and overbearing majority."[46] For instance, it would be easy for a majority to say that peyote is a dangerous controlled substance, and thus should be banned, without considering the religious needs of the Native American Church. However, the majority, consisting overwhelmingly of Protestant Christians, would be well aware of the religious needs of Christian churches' use of similar intoxicants such as wine. In this way, allowing peyote to be banned while wine is freely accessible *could* be a tyranny of the majority based on religious faction. Thus, a neutrality approach presented substantial problems for Madison because he saw it as a convenient way for the majority to pass laws that technically apply to all persons equally but in fact harm the religious needs of some groups disproportionately. Given how Madison thought that in the unamended Constitution "[t]here is not a shadow of right in the general government to intermeddle with religion," an accommodationist approach is much more in line with Madison's political theory and his view of human nature.[47] Note here too that Madison said government had no power to *intermeddle* with religion, not that it had no power to *accommodate* people in the exercise of their religion.

Madison's original bill of rights proposals to protect free exercise rights against the federal and state governments also support an accommodationist stance. First, the proposal limiting federal power: "The civil rights of none shall be abridged on account of religious belief or worship . . . nor shall the full and equal rights of conscience be in any manner, or on any pretext infringed."[48] Second, the proposal that would have limited state powers over free exercise rights: "No state shall violate the equal rights of conscience."[49] In both of these drafts and Madison's concomitant draft in the Virginia Declaration of Rights, Madison focused heavily on the idea of having an equal right of conscience. Madison went a step further in his draft limiting the powers of Congress, emphasizing that the "full" rights of conscience are to be protected, and noting that this right shall not in any manner or on any pretext be infringed. Once again, Madison expressed a preference for a strong protection of free exercise rights, one in which the government may need to accommodate persons practicing their faith, particularly persons from minority religions.

It is clear from his political philosophy and his legislative proposals that Madison wanted to protect the rights of all persons to express their bona fide faith legitimately. Madison believed that religious freedom was a natural right upon which the government should not infringe; thus, anytime the government came inadvertently close to intruding on this right, it should accommodate people's religion. Madison also thought that giving people the freedom to practice their religion would lead them more likely than not to virtue; thus, the government should assist religions to promote virtue. Finally, Madison believed that having many sects compete openly for adherents would lead to the emergence of the common good, as there would be something of a free market of religious ideas. Indeed, for Madison, "moderation and harmony" are the result of having "several sects" exist, with the government establishing none of them while ensuring that all of them are on an equal footing.[50]

However, this approach creates a serious problem when considered in conjunction with the Establishment Clause. If Madison was a strong separationist, he believed that government and religion needed to have a wall between them. If he was an accommodationist, he believed that government must do what is necessary to assist persons, especially those of minority religions, to practice their faith equally. The two positions have the potential to clash. Indeed, Madison thought it unjust to "force a citizen to contribute three pence only of his property for the support of any one establishment."[51] On the other hand, Madison did not want ministers treated differently from others when it came to public matters:

> Does not the exclusion of Ministers of the Gospel [from being electors or officeholders] as such violate a fundamental principle of liberty by punishing a religious profession with the privation of a civil right? Does it not violate another article of the plan itself which exempts religion from the cognizance of Civil power? Does it not violate justice by at once taking away a right and prohibiting a compensation for it. And does it not in fine violate impartiality by shutting the door agst the Ministers of one religion and leaving it open for those of every other.[52]

The greatest area here for conflict might be a financial one: the funding to religion that could be considered establishment under a separationist theory could also be accommodationist for free exercise purposes. Madison's general position on free exercise was to protect the rights of all to practice their faith as they choose. Madison placed emphasis on accommodating smaller religions as a way to protect their natural rights from a self-interested majority. When it came to government financial support, however, Madison viewed the question more as an Establishment Clause question, not a Free Exercise Clause one. Thus, for neither majority nor minority religious groups did Madison advocate direct funding by the government. His statements above on funding bear this out, as did his presidential veto of an in-kind contribution of land to a Baptist church.[53]

THE FREEDOMS OF SPEECH, PRESS, AND ASSOCIATION

Another set of liberties that were extremely important to Madison through-out his life were the expressive freedoms of speech, press, and association. Madison advocated liberal protections for these freedoms because they were natural rights and because Madison saw them as a way to achieve virtue and the common good. Madison's original draft amendment regarding the protec-tion of the freedoms of speech and of the press against the federal government was as follows: "The people shall not be deprived or abridged of their right to speak, to write, or to publish their sentiments; and the freedom of the press, as one of the great bulwarks of liberty, shall be inviolable."[54] In this proposal, Madison advocated protecting a right that sounds natural, as he stated that the people shall not be deprived or abridged their right to communicate their sentiments in any form cognizable in 1789. Madison also stated that the freedom of the press was "inviolable" because it protected other rights. He fol-lowed this with a limitation on state powers as well ("No state shall violate . . . the freedom of the press"),[55] and the committee on which Madison sat added "the freedom of speech" to this protection.[56] Finally, the seeds of the freedom of association were sown by Madison when combining these amendments with a third proposal made by him: "The people shall not be restrained from peaceably assembling and consulting for their common good."[57] Madison's statement here reaffirms his commitment to liberalism because it promotes the common good: by allowing individuals to congregate into groups, they will work with each other to achieve their vision of the good. Even if they are in error, we all benefit from hearing what these groups have to say when they advance their agenda.

With this general background on Madison's theory and his relevant pro-posals in Congress, one can apply Madison's specific statements regarding these freedoms to see that Madison truly was a classical liberal regarding these First Amendment rights. For instance, Madison noted that "a man has a property in his opinions and the free communication of them,"[58] implying that this is a natural property right that should not be regulated by the government. Madison later stated in Congress that "[o]pinions are not the objects of legislation. You animadvert on the abuse of reserved rights—how far will this go? It may extend to the liberty of speech and of the press."[59] For Madison, opinions, as expressed through speech and the press, are not to be governed by anyone but the autonomous individual. Madison also believed that vigorously protecting these natural rights would create valuable secondary benefits, as "unanimity is not to be expected in any great political question."[60] People will always have diverse opinions, but Madison thought it would be unjustifiable for a majority to silence the views of the minority. Additionally, allowing as much freedom of speech as possible would ensure that every idea from this diversity of opinion may be heard by all, giving everyone a chance to hear more virtuous opinions and learn from them. And even if some of what we hear is motivated by the speakers' self-interest, there is value in us hearing them and learning how to refute such positions—in this way, even potentially harmful speech results in the common good under Madison's political theory.

Madison felt particularly strongly about a liberal understanding of the freedom of the press, as is evident in the following analogy: "Some degree of abuse is inseparable from the proper use of everything; and in no instance is this more true, than in that of the press . . . it is better to leave a few of its noxious branches to their luxuriant growth, than by pruning them away, to injure the vigor of those yielding the proper fruits."[61] Madison believed that it is better to leave the "noxious branches" of the press to publish what might amount to tabloid trash or worse, because it is the best way to ensure that reporters committed to journalistic integrity will be able to report on public and private issues without interference from the government. As Madison once put it when speaking of newspapers, "the circulation of political intelligence thro' these vehicles being justly reckoned among the surest means of preventing the degeneracy of a free Govt.; as well as of recommending every salutary public measure to the confidence & cooperation of all virtuous Citizens."[62] Madison believed that protecting liberal freedom for the press to publish would make more citizens virtuous and it would ensure that the government was checked by an outside force:

> I am glad to find in general that everything that good sense & accurate information can supply is abundantly exhibited by the Newspapers to the view of the public. It is to be regretted that these papers are so limited in their circulation, as well as that the mixture of indiscretions in some of them should contribute to that effect. It is to [be] hoped however that any arbitrary attacks on the freedom of the Press will find virtue eno' remaining in the public mind to make them recoil on the wicked authors.[63]

Even though Madison knew a liberal freedom of the press would result in "indiscretions," he still advocated this as better than the alternatives. Madison's liberalism was so forthright regarding the press that he did not think the press should be taxed, as taxation on the press is "an insidious forerunner of something worse."[64] Considering that Madison implied that churches *should* be taxed, this was quite a statement by Madison. Madison knew that there would always be "wicked authors," but he still believed that it was better to leave the press free to its devices than to let government officials decide that some critical journalists should be silenced.

For Madison, "the people ought to be enlightened, to be awakened, to be united, that after establishing a government they should watch over it, as well as obey it."[65] Madison believed that protecting a liberal freedom of the press could achieve this, noting that, "[a]s a vehicle of influence, the press, though the last to be named, must be allowed all its importance," and referring to the press as "this guardian of public rights, this organ of necessary truths."[66] Thus, Madison believed that a liberal freedom of the press should be protected, and that a natural outgrowth of this would be a public better informed about its government.

Madison's liberal commitment to rights of association cannot be under-estimated when one reads one of his influential passages from *Federalist* 10:

> There are two methods of curing the mischiefs of faction: the one, by removing its causes. . . . There are again two methods of removing the causes of faction: the one, by destroying the liberty which is essential to its existence. . . . It could never be more truly said than of the first remedy, that it was worse than the disease. Liberty is to faction what air is to fire, an aliment without which it instantly expires. But it could not be less folly to abolish liberty, which is essential to political life, because it nourishes faction, than it would be to wish the annihilation of air, which is essential to animal life, because it imparts to fire its destructive agency.[67]

Even though Madison believed that factions had the potential to be dan-gerous and destructive, he found it much worse to take away the rights of people to join such groups than to limit associational freedoms. Even though vice may result, Madison found that the positive effects of protect-ing this right, including the virtue that one might obtain from joining a virtuous group, far outweighed any negative effects. Madison believed that by being able to freely join organizations, one would be able to learn more from those in the group, and any clashing that went on with other groups would also have the potential to teach one the other groups' ideas as well as the valuable lesson of tolerance. Madison reaffirmed his liberal commitment to the freedom of association often in his career, perhaps most notably in the 1790s when he proclaimed that the right to join a dissenting group like the Democratic-Republican Societies was "the most sacred principle of our Constitution."[68] Although Madison did not employ the term "freedom of association" in his speeches or writings, he clearly conveyed his belief that this liberal right was of paramount importance to him. Thus, for Madison government protection of natural liberal rights to speech, press, and asso-ciation was the best way to achieve virtue in political life.

For Madison, the nexus of free speech, freedom of association, and the ability to use one's property freely was an important one: "That is not a just government, nor is property secure under it, where arbitrary restrictions, exemptions, and monopolies deny to part of its citizens that free use of their faculties, and free choice of their occupations, which not only consti-tute their property in the general sense of the word; but are the means of acquiring property strictly so called."[69] Madison believed that we should be free to use our faculties and gain property from them. Allowing us to then dispense our property as we see fit would lead to the common good, to virtue, or to a combination of the two.

Madison was clear on this point in a speech in Congress regarding the controversy over Democratic-Republican Societies: "As he had confidence in the good sense and patriotism of the people, he did not anticipate any lasting evil to result from the publications of these societies; they will stand or fall by the public opinion; no line can be drawn in this case."[70] Madison believed that it was better to protect a liberal system of rights because letting the people hear all sides of an argument would give them the benefit of sifting through all of the ideas they hear and hopefully having a more informed opinion because of it. Indeed, Madison believed, "If we advert to the nature of republican government, we shall find that the censorial power is in the people over the government, and not in the government over the people."[71] As Madison put it in his crusade against the Alien and Sedition Acts, "Let it be recollected, lastly, that the right of electing the members of the government, constitutes more particularly the essence of a free and responsible government. The value and efficacy of this right, depends on the knowledge of the comparative merits and demerits of the candidates for public trust; and on the equal freedom, consequently, of examining and discussing these merits and demerits of the candidates respectively."[72]

For Madison, as long as all people's rights to speak were protected, "In a republic, light will prevail over darkness, truth over error."[73] For Madison, a government power to ban expression was "a power which more than any other ought to produce universal alarm, because it is levelled against that right of freely examining public characters and measures, and of free communication among the people thereon, which has ever been justly deemed, the only effectual guardian of every other right."[74]

Madison had a substantial fear that the tyranny of the majority was afoot whenever government censored these freedoms: "In our Governments the real power lies in the majority of the Community, and the invasion of private rights is *cheifly* to be apprehended, not from acts of Government contrary to the sense of its constituents, but from acts in which the Government is the mere instrument of the major number of the constituents."[75] Madison knew that people were prone to selfishness, and that those in the majority might exercise their power to silence critics. Because of this, he recognized that protecting the people's natural rights to freedom of speech, press, and association would be the only way for our society to function effectively. Madison wanted the people to have the ability to use their natural rights for good. Given human nature, government must be limited in its ability to infringe on these expressive rights.

PROPERTY AND THE TAKINGS CLAUSE

Property was another right that Madison believed deserved strong, liberal protection. Throughout his public life Madison advocated for the people to have a broad freedom to dispense of their real estate and their personal property. Given Madison's zeal for protecting religious freedom, the following statement should indicate how strong his beliefs were regarding property rights when he was 34 years of age (in 1785): "A just Government . . . will be best supported by protecting every Citizen in the enjoyment of his Religion with the same equal hand which protects his person and his property."[76] Madison maintained this position through the peak of his legislative career, claiming at age 41 (in 1792): "Government is instituted to protect property of every sort; as well that which lies in the various rights of individuals, as that which the term particularly expresses. This being the end of government, that alone is a *just* government, which *impartially* secures to every man, whatever is his *own*."[77] Madison's fierce advocacy for property rights continued through his retirement, as evidenced by the following statement he made at age 78 (in 1829): "It is sufficiently obvious, that persons now and property are the two great subjects on which Governments are to act; and that the rights of persons, and the rights of property, are the objects, for the protection of which Government was instituted. These rights cannot well be separated. The personal right to acquire property, which is a natural right, gives to property, when acquired, a right to protection, as a social right."[78] Madison believed that property was an individual, natural right that government was created to protect, and it was something to be respected over nearly every other value.

Madison proposed that the Bill of Rights be prefixed with a statement that "Government is instituted, and ought to be exercised for the benefit of the people; which consists in the enjoyment of life and liberty, *with the right of acquiring and using property,* and generally of pursuing and obtaining happiness and safety."[79] Madison left no doubt as to his liberal, natural, unalienable rights position on property rights.

Madison also believed that the common good and personal virtue would be inherent outgrowths of protecting these natural rights.[80] In the Articles of Confederation Congress in 1784, Madison authored a Bill Prohibiting Further Confiscation of British Property.[81] Madison's commitment to property rights was evident here, as it was only one year after the Revolutionary War had concluded, and the nation was deeply in debt. Certainly, Madison could have acquiesced and allowed these confiscations to continue; however, he wanted the property rights of all persons, including British subjects, to be protected. Since Madison believed property was a natural right, possessing it was a liberty that government should protect for anyone, whether they are a citizen of the United States or not. Madison also took this position because he believed that allowing people the free use of their property would give them the chance to be more virtuous, and at the very least it would lead to a more productive society. However, if government threatened this right for some, even for the British during and directly after the Revolution, then the door would be opened for the government to confiscate the property of anyone else.

One of the most notable amendments Madison proposed to protect property rights was the Takings Clause. Before the Constitutional Convention, the thought of government being required to compensate justly for a taking was already on Madison's mind. He noted a limit he believed should be put on legislative power: "The Constitution may expressly restrain [the legislature] from seizing private property for public use without paying its full Value."[82] The language Madison proposed in Congress in 1789 was that "[n]o person shall . . . be obliged to relinquish his property, where it may be necessary for public use, without a just compensation."[83] There are three ideas present here. First, we have a right to private property, which, given the context noted above, meant for Madison a liberal, natural right to property. Second, the government has a limited right as the sovereign to seize our property, but only if it is for a public purpose. Third, if the government does seize our property, we have a right to "just compensation" for the taking, likely meaning the full market value of the property. For Madison, this would have reimbursed the inconvenienced property owner with money equal to the property's value. This would allow the property owner at least to purchase a comparable tract of land and be in a position similar to his or her state of affairs before the government seized the land.

The liberal Madison also proposed in the Bill of Rights that '[n]o person shall . . . be deprived of life, liberty, or *property, without due process of law,*"[84] which implied that one can be deprived of one's property if due process is followed. Madison certainly did not have the unrealistic position that regulations generally require compensation, based on his signing a Constitution that granted Congress the power to impose taxes and protect copyrights and patents. In Madison's proposal, the Takings Clause only served to prevent government from seizing an entire piece of property without providing compensation. The Due Process Clause was proposed to cover every other instance where the government comes in contact with private property rights. When the government touches upon their property rights out of necessity, the Due Process Clause requires it to treat people equally: "A just security to property is not afforded by that government, under which unequal taxes oppress one species of property and reward another species."[85] Madison's emphasis on the government's equitable treatment of people's property rights becomes paramount when the threat of faction looms. Indeed, as Madison remarked in *Federalist* 10, "the most common and durable source of factions has been the various and unequal distribution of property."[86] Such factions will compete with each other to take government power and then use that power to seize property unjustly.

Madison did not have a problem with property regulations generally as long as they were universal ones that treated people equally. However, if government started dealing with people differently by taking property from one group and giving it to another, this could be unjust. One of Madison's fears was that a ruling faction would try to take the property of those outside of their faction, and Madison believed a larger union would be one method to help prevent such discrimination: "A rage for . . . an equal division of property, or for any other improper or wicked project, will be less apt to pervade the whole body of the Union than a particular member of it."[87] Thus, Madison's position on property rights was similar to that of religious freedom: Madison thought everyone had a natural, equal right to acquire property (or practice religion), which government had a duty to protect and accommodate; however, government crossed the line when it became too involved by redistributing real property from one group to another (or establishing a religion to the detriment of other religions). And just as government equally protects religious freedom by accommodating everyone's ability to practice their religion freely, government should equally protect property rights by allowing people the maximum use of their property. The one major difference between rights of religion and property is that, unless tax dollars are involved, government can accommodate religious freedom without taking away from the ability of others to practice their religion. Government cannot as easily accommodate property rights without a redistribution of property, which in Madison's thinking could quickly amount to too much government intervention in the private market and unequal treatment of people.

THE RIGHTS OF THE CRIMINALLY ACCUSED

The final major area of rights that was an integral part of Madison's liberal system was the set of rights protecting the criminally accused. Among other protections, Madison frequently advocated broad rights to habeas corpus (which was already protected in the original Constitution), to criminal jury trials, to due process, against unreasonable searches and seizures, and against cruel and unusual punishments. Although Madison said substantially less about these subjects than he had about the liberties discussed above, Madison's statements still reveal that protecting these rights in the broadest form possible was important to him. Madison saw a broad protection of the rights of the accused as essential security for other liberties in the Bill of Rights, especially First Amendment rights and property rights. Madison noted in his speech introducing his draft of the Bill of Rights that "Trial by jury . . . is as essential to secure the liberty of the people as any one of the pre-existent rights of nature."[88] With this and the discussion above describing Madison's emphasis on the importance of the trial by jury, it is interesting that the U.S. Supreme Court has not cited Madison as authority in a case litigating the criminal Jury Trial Clause since *Apodaca v. Oregon* in 1972,[89] while the justices continue to frequently cite Madison in areas like the Establishment Clause.

As noted above, Madison thought that "it is manifestly impossible to punish the intent to bring those who administer the government into disrepute or contempt, without striking at the right of freely discussing public characters and measures."[90] For Madison, it was important to protect broadly the rights of the criminally accused. This was one way of safeguarding individual human dignity, and it allowed people to maintain their freedom if they had to prove their innocence, which Madison believed would contribute to the common good. Consider Madison's proposal that eventually became the Fourth Amendment: "The rights of the people to be secured in their persons, their houses, their papers, and their other property from all unreasonable searches and seizures, shall not be violated by warrants issued without probable cause, supported by oath or affirmation, or not particularly describing the places to be searched, or the persons or things to be seized."[91] His proposal was a broad protection of the rights of persons from government intrusion, consistent with his general theory. As he had written in a 1792 newspaper article, "That is not a just government, nor is property secure under it, where the property which a man has in his personal safety and personal liberty, is violated by arbitrary seizures of one class of citizens for the service of the rest."[92] A strong protection of the rights of the accused was a paramount way for Madison to ensure that natural rights such as First Amendment freedoms and property rights would also be protected.

Also of note here was Madison's emphasis on the courts' limiting executive power. Recall that during the speech in which Madison introduced his bill of rights, he stated that, if the Bill of Rights were ratified, "independent tribunals of justice will consider themselves in a peculiar manner the guardians of those rights; they will be an impenetrable bulwark against every assumption of power in the legislative or executive."[93] Madison considered judges as another guardian of the Bill of Rights against *every* assumption of power.

Madison's liberal views on the rights of the accused can also be seen when examining his statements on the Eighth Amendment. Madison's proposal was that "[e]xcessive bail shall not be required, nor excessive fines imposed, nor cruel and unusual punishments inflicted."[94] A liberal understanding of punishments and proportionality is consistent with the only other known action by Madison regarding sentences for criminal defendants. In 1785 the Virginia Assembly was debating a Bill for Proportioning Crimes and

Punishments, which read in relevant part, "Whoever, on purpose, shall disfigure another by cutting out or disabling the tongue, slitting or cutting off a nose, lip or ear, branding, or otherwise, or shall maim him, shall be maimed or disfigured in like sort."[95] Madison moved to amend the bill as follows: "strike out remainder of the clause after 'maim him' . . . and insert 'shall be condemned to hard labour in the public works for such term not exceeding six—years."[96] This language is consistent with the liberal position that Madison took generally. Our lives and bodies are naturally our property, which the government should not take away. By doing so, the government would intrude upon the fundamental dignity that is attached to our natural right to life. In addition, by the government's punishing mayhem in kind, that person's ability to contribute to the common good may forever be lost with the loss of that person's body parts.

Finally, Madison's statements regarding the due process of law were consistent with a liberal characterization of him. Madison proposed the Due Process Clause on June 8, 1789, as follows: "No person shall . . . be deprived of life, liberty, or property without due process of law."[97] Madison used the phrase "due process of law," as opposed to the weaker and more common "law of the land," likely as a way to place a greater limit on legislative power.[98] Madison also interjected into the Due Process Clause (and many other clauses in the Bill of Rights) the prohibition "shall," as opposed to the then more common (and more permissive) "ought."[99] Madison was attempting to strengthen criminal procedures beyond what was the accepted norm at the end of the eighteenth century. Although Madison never defined "due process of law," he gave us a clue as to what he might have meant during the Alien and Sedition Act controversy:

> In the administration of preventive justice, the following principles have been held sacred: that some probable ground of suspicion be exhibited before some judicial authority; that it be supported by oath or affirmation; that the party may avoid being thrown into confinement, by finding pledges or sureties for his legal conduct sufficient in the judgment of some judicial authority; that he may have the benefit of a writ of *habeas corpus,* and thus obtain his release, if wrongfully confined; and that he may at any time be discharged from his recognizance, or his confinement, and restored to his former-liberty and rights, on the order of the proper judicial authority, if it shall see sufficient cause.[100]

Madison claimed that these criminal procedures are "held sacred," again demonstrating the importance he placed on such rights. By ensuring that these rights were honored, Madison believed that the other liberal rights he loved would also be protected.

Now, before comparing Madison's theory of the Bill of Rights to the way that Supreme Court justices have used Madison, it is necessary to demonstrate why Madison's views on the Bill of Rights are relevant. If Madison's proposal in Congress and Madison's involvement with the legislative processes regarding the Bill of Rights were minimal, there would be little reason to care about his theory of the Bill of Rights—instead, one could chastise the Supreme Court for using Madison as an authority. However, as the next chapter demonstrates, Supreme Court justices are justified in invoking Madison as an authority regarding the Bill of Rights. In fact, Madison was instrumental in securing the Bill of Rights that we have today.

THE RELATION OF MADISON'S BILL OF RIGHTS TO OUR BILL OF RIGHTS

FIGHTING FOR THE BILL OF RIGHTS

James Madison was the most important figure in producing the American Bill of Rights, and without him we might not have a bill of rights at all. Many of the Federalists elected to Congress were much more interested in creating the federal courts and finding ways to raise revenue; most Federalists in the First Congress cared relatively little about a bill of rights. Likewise, many of the former Anti-Federalists now hoped that a failure to adopt a bill of rights would lead to a second constitutional convention. With Federalists now more concerned with setting up the new government and with former Anti-Federalists unable in Congress to achieve the structural changes they desired, there was little support for a bill of rights in the House of Representatives in the spring of 1789. Almost immediately after being seated in the new House, however, Madison embarked on a campaign to amend the Constitution.[1]

On May 4, 1789, "Before the House adjourned, Mr. Madison gave notice that he intended to bring on the subject of amendments to the constitution, on the 4th Monday of this month [May 25]."[2] Although the *Annals of Congress* are silent on the subsequent wait, it was apparently agreed by the House to postpone the May 25 date by two weeks to June 8.[3] On June 8, "Mr. Madison rose, and reminded the House that this was the day that he had heretofore named for bringing forward amendments to the constitution."[4] Madison also felt compelled to note that he was "sorry to be accessory to the loss of a single moment of time by the House" by proposing the Bill of Rights.[5] In what seems incredible today, Madison's motion was opposed by other members of Congress who had no desire to address a bill of rights and thought that discussing such amendments was less important than the revenue business in which the House was then engaged.[6] For example,

Representative James Jackson stated, "I am against taking up the subject at present, and shall therefore be totally against the amendments, if the Government is not organized, that I may see whether it is grievous or not."[7] Representative Benjamin Goodhue agreed: "I believe it would be perfectly right in the gentleman who spoke last [Jackson], to move a postponement. . . . I think the present time premature."[8] Representative Alexander White voiced a similar opinion: "I hope the House will not spend much time on this subject [of amendments], till the more pressing business is dispatched."[9]

Several other representatives also spoke against taking up the subject of amendments at that time. For instance, Representative Aedanus Burke declared "amendments to the constitution necessary, but this was not the proper time to bring them forward," as he thought it more important that the Treasury Department be established first.[10] Representative Roger Sherman of Connecticut announced that, since his state and others adopted the Constitution and "desired no amendments," "it will therefore be imprudent to neglect much more important concerns for this."[11]

Madison was able to introduce his draft version of the Bill of Rights to the House of Representatives later that day. Yet, after he gave an impassioned speech describing the necessity and importance of a bill of rights, the other members of the House appeared to be more strongly *against* amendments. James Jackson was the first speaker after Madison introduced his proposal, and his speech began by stating that *"[t]he more I consider the subject of amendments, the more I am convinced it is improper. . . . If such an addition is not dangerous, or improper, it is at least unnecessary."*[12] Jackson then gave an example of the pointlessness of the House taking up discussion of a bill of rights: "The gentleman [Madison] endeavors to secure the liberty of the press; pray how is this in danger? There is no power given to Congress to regulate this subject as they can commerce, or peace, or war. Has any transaction taken place to make us suppose such an amendment necessary? . . . These are principles which will always prevail. . . . Where, then, is the necessity of taking measures to secure that neither is nor can be in danger?"[13] Jackson then maintained that it could be dangerous to adopt Madison's amendments: "That part of the constitution which is proposed to be altered, may be the most valuable part of the whole . . . notwithstanding the honorable gentleman's ingenious arguments on that point, *I am now more strongly persuaded it is wrong.*"[14] Ironically, Madison had made similar arguments against a bill of rights before finally coming to see its potential value. His words were coming back to bite him.

The next speaker, Elbridge Gerry, agreed that a bill of rights was low on his list of priorities: "I consider it improper to take up this business, when our attention is occupied by other important objects."[15] Almost every other representative who spoke was against considering amendments (at least at that time), including John Vining, who rhetorically asked Madison "whether he would be responsible for the risk the Government would run of being injured by an *interregnum?*"[16] The debate on June 8 ended with Madison's amendments being referred to the Committee of the Whole,[17] which effectively tabled the subject indefinitely.

More than six weeks passed with no action on the subject. Recall that during this time Madison wrote several letters to his friends and colleagues about his concern that the subject of amendments was being neglected by the House. Finally, on July 21 Madison "begged the House to indulge him in the further consideration of amendments to the constitution, and as there appeared, in some degree, a moment of leisure, he would move to go into a Committee of the whole on the subject, comfortably to the order of the 8th of last month."[18]

Madison once again faced stern opposition. Fisher Ames wanted the amendments referred to a select committee rather than being debated at that time by the full House. Theodore Sedgwick thought that discussing a bill of rights would take up too much time. Representative White admitted that he did not think the amendments in their present form proposed by Madison could pass both houses by the requisite two-thirds vote. Representative Sherman rhetorically asked whether the states would ratify Madison's proposal and concluded that "[i]t is hardly to be expected that they will. Consequently we shall lose our labor, and had better decline having anything further to do with it for the present."[19] Incredible as it may sound to us today, many members of the first Congress took the floor of the House to say that it would be a waste of time even to *consider* the Bill of Rights!

After significant debate among the representatives again on the issue of whether a bill of rights should even be discussed (most of it against discussing Madison's proposal), the House eventually referred Madison's amendments to a select committee with one member from each state represented in the House, known as the Committee of Eleven.[20] The Committee, of which Madison was chosen to be a member, promptly reported the amendments back to the House floor one week later on July 28.[21] However, with no recorded debate the House tabled the amendments yet again.[22]

After the House failed to consider the work of the Committee of Eleven to which the amendments had been referred, Madison made a motion on August 3 for the amendments to be made an order of business on August 12.[23] However, when August 12 arrived, the House was engrossed in a discussion of Indian treaties and failed to take up the issue of amendments.[24] Finally, on August 13, Madison asked the House to consider his proposal, noting that he "did not think it was an improper time to proceed in this business [of amendments]. . . . Already has the subject been delayed much longer than could have been wished."[25] Yet Madison still faced opposition from those who did not want to take up amendments.

Sedgwick was of the opinion that "there were several matters before them of more importance" than a bill of rights; Gerry thought "the discussion would take up much more time than the House could now spare [and] was, therefore, in favor of postponing the consideration of the subject"; and William Smith stated that he "could not conceive the necessity of going into any alterations of the Government until the Government itself was perfected."[26] However, this time with the help of other representatives who now believed that considering a bill of rights was proper, the House began debate on Madison's proposal.[27] After more than three months of Madison's prodding the chamber to action, the Bill of Rights was finally being debated on the floor of the House.

But simple discussion did not assure passage. Some of the same Anti-Federalists who had originally opposed the Constitution for lacking a bill of rights now secretly wanted to stall a bill of rights and popular amendments in order to sabotage the new national government with a second constitutional convention.[28] If such plans were not practical, at the very least Anti-Federalists in Congress wanted to ratify amendments that weakened the structure of the federal government, and they had comparatively little concern for the freedoms that Madison put in his proposal.[29] In particular, Representative Thomas Tucker proposed amendments that would have done the following: set limits to the number of terms members of Congress and the president could serve, make senators come up for annual election, limit congressional power over regulating federal elections, limit congressional taxation power, limit congressional power to create lower federal courts, limit federal court jurisdiction, and weaken the clause prohibiting religious tests.[30] Both Tucker and noted Anti-Federalist Elbridge Gerry also proposed weakening the powers of the federal government by moving to insert into what would become the Tenth Amendment the word "expressly," so that the draft of the amendment would have read "the powers not *expressly* delegated by this constitution, nor prohibited by it to the States, are reserved to the States respectively" (emphasis added).[31] Tucker's proposal would have made the Tenth Amendment almost identical to a similar clause in the Articles of Confederation: "Each state retains its sovereignty, freedom, and independence, and every power, jurisdiction, and right, which is not by this Confederation *expressly* delegated to the United States, in Congress assembled" (emphasis added). This would have handcuffed federal power, setting the country back on the course it had traveled under the Articles.

When Tucker's initial amendments failed, later that summer he proposed amendments that would have limited Congress's taxing power.[32] Madison fought these amendments, which were less a bill of rights and more of a thinly veiled attempt to bring back a confederate form of government. In particular, he objected to the amendment to add the word "expressly" to the Tenth Amendment because "it was impossible to confine a Government to the exercise of express powers; there must necessarily be admitted powers by implication, unless the Constitution descended to recount every minutia . . . the word 'expressly' had been moved in the convention of Virginia, by the opponents to the ratification, and, after full and fair discussion, was given up by them, and the system allowed to retain its present form."[33] At every attempt by Anti-Federalists to make the Bill of Rights more about protecting state power instead of individual rights, Madison was a prominent speaker, refocusing the House on protecting freedoms, not redistributing federal power back to the states.[34] Had Madison not been in Congress, these Anti-Federalist amendments might have been the only ones proposed. If that had been the case, it is unlikely that the Federalist-dominated House would have entertained their amendments as they would for Madison, a prominent statesman and fellow Federalist. It is also very likely that, had Anti-Federalists made the only proposals *and* they had succeeded in passage, they would *not* have included many of the individual liberties proposed by Madison. Furthermore, if the Anti-Federalists had been successful in stripping power from the federal government, it might very well have spelled an early death for the Union. Madison was vitally important, not just in securing a hearing for and passage of *a* bill of rights, but also in securing *our* Bill of Rights with its series of enumerated liberties.

In addition to Anti-Federalist opposition to a bill of rights and attempts to weaken the new national government, Federalists in the House did not make passage of the amendments an easy task. Madison continually stopped members of the House from watering down or eliminating amendments he thought were essential. Madison spoke out against attempts to strike and weaken his proposal to protect religious freedom.[35] Madison fought attempts to turn the freedom of petition from an ability of private individuals to lobby their government into a right of instruction that would have forced members of Congress to vote in accordance with whatever a majority of their constituents wanted.[36] Madison contested an attempt in the House to remove his "most valuable amendment" that would have limited state power over his core liberties,[37] although this amendment would eventually be dropped by the Senate.[38] Again and again, Madison pushed hard to keep the House on track to pass the Bill of Rights.

How did Madison respond to all of this? He persevered toward passage of amendments without reserve, although the strain of fighting against both apathy and open hostility by other members of Congress eventually took its toll on Madison. As Madison noted in a letter to his colleague Richard Peters: "The papers inclosed will shew that the nauseous project of amendments has not yet been either dismissed or despatched. We are so deep in them now, that right or wrong something must be done. I say this not by way of apology, for to be sincere I think no apology requisite."[39] Some have claimed this as evidence that Madison really did not wish to amend the Constitution, referring to the Bill of Rights as a "nauseous project."[40] However, when one understands that Madison faced substantial obstacles from his colleagues in Congress while attempting to introduce and pass the Bill of Rights, one can see that the process triggered Madison to become frustrated with many of his colleagues. Madison was referring to the "project" of trying to get his amendments heard as a "nauseous project"; he was not saying this of the amendments themselves. Madison was stealing an analogy from a poem Peters had written to Madison in a July 20, 1789, letter that compared the process of amending the Constitution to cooks spoiling a fine soup:

> Eleven Cooks assembled once
> To make a Treat of Soup
>
> . . .
>
> The Soup was made—delicious! good!
> Exclaim'd each *grateful* Guest,
> But some who would not taste the Food,
> Declar'd it wanted Zest.
> Among those Malcontents were found
> Some faulting each Ingredient
> While others eager search'd around
> To find some Expedient
> With which to damn the whole
>
> . . .
>
> To mend is truly always right
> But then the Way to do it
> Is not so facile to the Wight
> Who undertakes to shew it.[41]

Clearly, Madison thought that dealing with some of his fellow "cooks" in Congress was the "nauseous project," and he hoped that the "soup" that was the Bill of Rights would not be "spoiled" in the process. Thus, Madison was displeased with the amending process, *not* the amendments he had proposed. Indeed, two days after he wrote his letter to Peters, Madison spoke of this legislative process in other letters as "extremely difficult and fatiguing"[42] and the progress of the amendments as "extremely worrisome."[43] A month later Madison expressed his displeasure in other letters at changes made by the Senate that were difficult to compromise with his proposals in the House.[44] Still, Madison continued to urge Congress to consider his amendments, and, as the next section describes, Congress would approve these amendments largely as he drafted them.

A PROPOSAL APPROVED WITHOUT SUBSTANTIAL ALTERATION

When we discuss the text and intent of the Bill of Rights, it is largely the text penned by Madison and largely the intent ascribed to it by Madison. It should not be surprising that Madison had the opportunity to propose the Bill of Rights and to sit on the two influential committees that slightly refined his work. Madison was revered among many of his colleagues and well known for his extensive work at the Constitutional Convention. Additionally, he was a member of the Virginia Constitutional Convention in 1776. By 1789, Madison had impeccable credentials as a constitution builder. He also had previously worked on protecting the freedoms that he proposed in the Bill, most notably his impassioned defense of the freedom of religion at the Virginia Constitutional Convention, and his work in defeating the Virginia Assessment Bill before helping to enact the Virginia Statute for Religious Freedom. Thus, it was quite natural for members of the House to defer to Madison on issues of constitutional rights and liberties.

Madison began his project of proposing the Bill of Rights by sifting through the multitude of proposals for amendments made at state ratification conventions, winnowing out the scores he thought were improper and keeping the ones he found to have merit.[45] Once Madison proposed his draft amendment to Congress, the historical record suggests that few, if any, substantive changes were made to Madison's list. Every element of the completed bill was drawn from Madison's initial resolutions, and except for a proposed amendment concerning state infringements of rights and a measure to impose a monetary floor on appeals to federal courts, all of Madison's proposals passed both chambers of Congress.

Part of the reason the Bill of Rights so profoundly reflects Madison's intent is that he not only introduced the amendments but was also very active in shepherding them through Congress. Madison served on the Committee of Eleven, the House committee that reviewed his draft amendments.[46] The report generated by the Committee contained no major changes to Madison's proposal.[47] Once the amendments returned from the Committee of Eleven to the House agenda in August 1789, Madison was an active speaker on the amendments. Historical records from the *Annals of Congress* indicate that from August 13 to August 22 the House discussed the amendments on eight separate days, and Madison spoke on the substance of the amendments on six of those eight days.[48]

After the House passed the Bill of Rights in substantially the same form as Madison proposed it, the amendments went on to the Senate. Although little is known about the Senate debate (the Senate sat in closed session until 1794),[49] the Senate did make a few substantive changes to the House version.[50] However, Madison also served on the House-Senate conference committee on amendments that hammered out compromises between the two chambers' versions of the Bill of Rights.[51] As the chair of the three House conferees of the six-member committee, Madison was able to reinstate some of his proposals that the Senate altered, especially regarding the Religion Clauses.[52] Thus, Madison exercised influence over the Bill of Rights not just by proposing them but also by being the most involved member of Congress during the debates and committee work on the amendments. The final version of the amendments is strikingly similar to Madison's proposal.

Some illustrative examples will show just how much of Madison's proposal became the Bill of Rights without being significantly altered. For instance, note the similarity between Madison's draft religion clauses and the final wording of those clauses. The Religion Clauses merit special attention, given Madison's focus on religious freedom, and given that these clauses underwent more amendments than perhaps any other provisions in the Bill of Rights. The evolution of the Religion Clauses also demonstrates Madison's considerable influence during the amending process. Madison proposed, "The civil rights of none shall be abridged on account of religious belief or worship, nor shall any national religion be established, nor shall the full and equal rights of conscience be in any manner, or on any pretext infringed."[53] This incorporated both the idea of preventing establishment and protecting free exercise. The Committee of Eleven shortened it to "No religion shall be established by law, nor shall the equal rights of conscience be infringed,"[54] but similar wording regarding both provisions remained. The final House version that went to the Senate for debate was even more similar to Madison's original proposal, as it bolstered free exercise rights: "Congress shall make no law establishing religion or prohibiting the free exercise thereof, nor shall the rights of Conscience be infringed."[55] That these amendment are still nearly identical to Madison's proposal should not be a surprise, given that Madison sat on the committee to which they were referred, and he was actively engaged in the debate in the House. However, in the Senate these clauses were weakened: "Congress shall make no law establishing articles of faith, or a mode of worship, or prohibiting the free exercise of religion."[56] Indeed, in the Senate the Establishment Clause was changed from a prohibition on Congress establishing religion in any way to a prohibition on Congress establishing articles of faith or a mode of worship. The latter would arguably be a narrower limitation on Congress's power, as anything outside of articles of faith or a mode of worship could be considered fair game for an establishment. In a similar vein, the Senate weakened the Free Exercise Clause by completely dropping the phrase prohibiting the rights of conscience from being infringed. This phrase, with slightly different wording, had been in Madison's original proposal.

At this point, the Religion Clauses had been watered down from what Madison initially proposed. However, Madison was able to restore his language to a certain degree when he chaired the House-Senate conference committee. The language that finally emerged was "Congress shall make no law respecting an establishment of religion, or prohibiting the free exercise thereof." Madison was able to broaden out the protection of the Establishment Clause, even if he was not able to restore all of his original language in the Free Exercise Clause. Nevertheless, even after the phrasing of the clauses was changed and the language was streamlined, the basic rights protected are considerably close to Madison's first draft.

For every other freedom in the Bill of Rights, Madison's language was comparable or identical to the finished product. After the clauses protecting religious liberty, Madison's proposal on June 8, 1789, followed with protections for freedom of speech, press, assembly, and petition:

> The people shall not be deprived or abridged of their right to speak, to write, or to publish their sentiments; and the freedom of the press, as one of the great bulwarks of liberty, shall be inviolable.

> The people shall not be restrained from peaceably assembling and consulting for their common good; nor from applying to the legislature by petitions, or remonstrances for redress of their grievances.[57]

These proposals by Madison have phrasing similar to the final version of the clauses of the First Amendment that do not deal with religion: "Congress shall make no law . . . abridging the freedom of speech, or of the press; or the right of the people peaceably to assemble, and to petition the government for a redress of grievances." Madison's use of the verb "abridge" was retained, as was his prohibition on restraining the people's ability "peaceably" to assemble and his protection of the right to petition to government for "redress" of "grievances." The structure, order, and substantive rights protected also remained the same in the First Amendment as it was in Madison's proposal.

Madison's most direct protection of property rights, the Takings Clause, also remained remarkably similar from introduction on the floor of Congress through passage. Madison proposed that "No person shall . . . be obliged to relinquish his property, where it may be necessary for public use, without a just compensation."[58] This is quite akin to the final version of the Takings Clause: "nor shall private property be taken for public use, without just compensation." Indeed, notice the parallelism—a protection of private "property" that can only be taken by government with a "just compensation," and then only "for public use." The only alteration of import was the substitution of "relinquish" with "taken" (the implications of this will be discussed in part II). Although some of the wording was changed, the overall structure remains the same.

The resemblance between Madison's proposal to protect the people against unreasonable searches and seizures and what eventually became the

Fourth Amendment is truly striking. Here is Madison's proposal: "The rights of the people to be secured in their persons, their houses, their papers, and their other property from all unreasonable searches and seizures, shall not be violated by warrants issued without probable cause, supported by oath or affirmation, or not particularly describing the places to be searched, or the persons or things to be seized."[59]

The Fourth Amendment reads "The right of the people to be secure in their persons, houses, papers, and effects, against unreasonable searches and seizures, shall not be violated, and no warrants shall issue, but upon probable cause, supported by oath or affirmation, and particularly describing the place to be searched, and the persons or things to be seized." Madison's proposal protects us from unreasonable searches and seizures of persons, houses, papers, and other property; the final language only modifies this by changing "other property" to "effects." Only cosmetic changes were made to the Warrants Clause that have no noticeable effect on the substantive meaning.

The Fourth Amendment is not the only place where nearly identical language to that of Madison was adopted by Congress to protect the rights of the criminally accused. Note this paragraph from Madison's proposal: "No person shall be subject, except in cases of impeachment, to more than one punishment, or one trial for the same offence; nor shall be compelled to be a witness against himself; nor be deprived of life, liberty, or property without due process of law."[60] Now compare it to the eventual wording of the Fifth Amendment: "nor shall any person be subject for the same offense to be twice put in jeopardy of life or limb; nor shall be compelled in any criminal case to be a witness against himself, nor be deprived of life, liberty, or property, without due process of law." Madison's progression of rights—double jeopardy, compelled self-incrimination, and due process—was retained in substantially similar language.

Likewise, there is a great similarity between the Sixth Amendment and Madison's paragraph regarding the rights available to a criminal defendant. Here is Madison's proposal: "In all criminal prosecutions, the accused shall enjoy the right to a speedy and public trial, to be informed of the cause and nature of the accusation, to be confronted with his accusers, and the witnesses against him; to have a compulsory process for obtaining witnesses in his favor; and to have the assistance of counsel for his defence."[61]

This proposal is nearly identical to the eventual wording of the Sixth Amendment: "In all criminal prosecutions, the accused shall enjoy the right to a speedy and public trial, by an impartial jury of the state and district wherein the crime shall have been committed, which district shall have been previously ascertained by law, and to be informed of the nature and cause of the accusation; to be confronted with the witnesses against him; to have compulsory process for obtaining witnesses in his favor, and to have the assistance of counsel for his defense."

There is only one clause in the final version of the Sixth Amendment that was not in Madison's proposal: that the accused shall enjoy a speedy and public trial "by an impartial jury of the state and district wherein the crime shall have been committed, which district shall have been previously ascertained by law." However, Madison proposed language similar to this in a different place in his draft: "The trial of all crimes . . . shall be by an impartial jury of freeholders of the vicinage."[62] Otherwise, Madison's proposal is nearly identical to the Sixth Amendment.

In addition to the above criminal rights protections, Madison's grand jury clause is quite comparable to the one finally adopted. Madison proposed that, "in all crimes punishable with loss of life or member, presentment or indictment by a grand jury, shall be an essential preliminary."[63] Notice the similarity to our Grand Jury Clause: "No person shall be held to answer for a capital, or otherwise infamous crime, unless on a presentment or indictment of a grand jury." Finally, there is an absolute parallel of Madison's proposal ("Excessive bail shall not be required, nor excessive fines imposed, nor cruel and unusual punishments inflicted"[64]) with the Eighth Amendment ("Excessive bail shall not be required, nor excessive fines imposed, nor cruel and unusual punishments inflicted"). The two are a perfect match.

Comparing language itself is not a conclusive factor when trying to find intent behind a document. However, the strong similarities between Madison's proposals and the language eventually adopted in the Bill of Rights is so powerful that it is difficult to see how one could have a complete understanding of these amendments without learning Madison's reasons for proposing them. Madison's significance here cannot be underestimated. If it had been Tucker, not Madison, who introduced the Bill of Rights in Congress, not only would the Bill of "Rights" have looked much different, but there is a strong case that it would not even have been given a hearing by the House. The fact that Madison was successful in convincing Congress to take up and pass without substantial alteration *his* proposals is a compelling reason to consider Madison's intent when we interpret *our* Bill of Rights today.

MADISON'S INTENT SHOULD NOT BE OUR ONLY CONSIDERATION

Although Madison was the principal figure regarding the Bill of Rights for all of the reasons noted above, it is also important to remember that what Madison thought about these rights is only one part of the larger puzzle of constitutional interpretation. In other words, Madison's intent may be a *necessary* criterion for interpreting the Constitution, but it alone is not *sufficient*.

First, Madison was not the only person who was integral in giving us a Bill of Rights. Although the evidence above shows that a bill of rights would have been highly unlikely without him (or at the very least it would have looked very different), Madison certainly did have help in convincing Congress to consider his amendments. When Madison introduced his amendments on June 8, 1789, one person, Representative John Page, spoke in favor of considering Madison's proposal at that time.[65] Likewise, it was Richard Bland Lee who moved on August 13, 1789, for the House to consider the amendments that had been referred to the Committee of Eleven, and it is clear that by that time a majority of representatives had agreed it was time to consider a bill of rights in the House.[66] Thus, it is not as though Madison was the only influential member of his generation to advocate a bill of rights. Rather, he was one person (albeit the most important one) among many who advocated for a bill of rights.

Second, it is far from clear that Madison would have given us the exact Bill of Rights that we have today, were he the only decision maker in question. Madison was only one member of the six-member House-Senate conference committee, he was only one member of the Committee of Eleven, and he was only one member of all of Congress. Given the different political philosophies of his colleagues, not all of Madison's proposals survived the House and Senate. The House scrapped Madison's plan to incorporate the amendments into the body of the Constitution[67] and eliminated his proposed preamble to the Bill of Rights.[68] The Committee of Eleven also changed some of the wording of Madison's proposals regarding the freedom of speech and of the press.[69] In addition, the Senate eliminated Madison's "most valuable amendment," which would have protected the freedoms of religion, speech, press, and criminal jury trials from state infringement[70] (although, as explored in the next chapter, that failed amendment has effectively been restored by the Supreme Court). Finally, Madison's proposal regulating the number of representatives passed the House and Senate only to be defeated in the state ratification process (although the other failed amendment, which limited Congress's ability to vote itself a pay raise, was finally ratified in 1992).

The House made some minor alterations to at least some of the wording of Madison's proposed religion clauses,[71] his proposal that eventually became the Ninth Amendment,[72] and his proposal that eventually became the Tenth Amendment.[73] The Senate also altered at least some of the wording of Madison's proposed Religion Clauses,[74] and it rearranged and combined some of his other proposals.[75]

Since Madison was only one member of the Congress that passed the Bill of Rights on to the states for ratification, we should not automatically accord his intent with that of Congress as a whole or with the states that ratified the amendments. However, this does not change the fact that

Madison was the most influential member in Congress and in the nation regarding the introduction and passage of the Bill of Rights. Having an understanding of his intent will still give us some important insight into the meaning of the Bill of Rights.

Third, it may not have even been Madison's intent that we consider Madison's intent. As odd as that may sound, there is evidence that Madison did not think his views on the Constitution should be controlling. Indeed, regarding the topic of constitutional interpretation, Madison wrote late in his life that "You give me a credit to which I have no claim, in calling me *the* writer of the Constitution of the U.S.' This was not, like the fabled Goddess of Wisdom, the offspring of a single brain. It ought to be regarded as the work of many heads & many hands."[76]

Madison saw himself, not as the Father of the Constitution and the Bill of Rights, but as one member of a much larger group of persons who created those two documents. Instead, Madison gave special attention, not to the debates of the Constitutional Convention or the debates in Congress, but to the understanding of the Constitution and Bill of Rights by state ratifying conventions and state legislatures, respectively. Madison emphasized this position in an 1821 letter:

> As a guide in expounding and applying the provisions of the Constitution, the debates and incidental decisions of the Convention can have no authoritative character. However desirable it be that they should be preserved as a gratification to the laudable curiosity felt by every people to trace the origin and progress of their political institutions, . . . the legitimate meaning of the Instrument must be derived from the text itself; or if a key is to be sought elsewhere, it must be, not in the opinions or intentions of the body which planned and proposed the Constitution, but in the sense attached to it by the people in their respective State Conventions, where it received all the authority which it possesses.[77]

Thus, Madison heavily emphasized state ratification and the text of the document. Madison held this position earlier during his political career as well. Madison noted the following on constitutional interpretation in a 1796 debate on the Jay Treaty:

> But, after all, whatever veneration might be entertained for the body of men who formed our constitution, the sense of that body could never be regarded as the oracular guide in the expounding of the constitution. As the instrument came from them, it was nothing more than the draught of a plan, nothing but a dead letter, until life and validity were breathed into it, by the voice of the people, speaking through the several state conventions. If we were to look therefore, for the meaning of the instrument, beyond the

face of the instrument, we must look for it not in the general convention, which proposed, but in the state conventions, which accepted and ratified the constitution.[78]

Likewise, during a 1791 debate on the national bank, Madison cited several factors when interpreting the Constitution. Madison claimed that we should look to interpretations that protect the "very characteristics of the government," and those that consider "the consequences, whatever they may be," "the meaning of the parties to the instrument," and "contemporary and concurrent expositions."[79] Presumptively, "the meaning of the parties to the instrument" referred to the states, like it did in Madison's theory of interpretation that he expressed on the debate during the Jay Treaty. However, nowhere on this list did Madison say that "Framer intent" is something to be considered during constitutional interpretation. Thus, there is significant evidence that Madison might not want to be cited as an authority regarding the meaning of the Bill of Rights, just as he did not seek such recognition for the Constitution generally.

Madison's point about considering "consequences, whatever they may be," when interpreting the constitution merits reflection. Madison lived in a country of barely three million people scattered up and down the Atlantic coast, where long distance travel was treacherous and it took weeks to mail a letter across the country. He certainly did not live in a country of 300 million, with interstate highways, international air travel, e-mail, the Internet, 24-hour news cycles, television, radio, fax machines, and cellular phones. Therefore, the contours of the rights Madison thought were necessary in the late 1780s may not be fully applicable to life today. This point takes on added meaning when reading *Federalist* 14: "Is it not the glory of the people of America, that, whilst they have paid a decent regard to the opinions of former times and other nations, they have not suffered a blind veneration for antiquity, for custom, or for names, to overrule the suggestions of their own good sense, the knowledge of their own situation, and the lessons of their own experience?"[80] In a similar vein, at the Constitutional Convention Madison stated that, "[i]n framing a system which we wish to last for ages, we should not lose sight of the changes which ages will produce."[81] And Madison's disdain for ad hominem fallacies was confirmed by his statement in *Federalist* 40 that the "prudent enquiry in all cases, ought surely to be not so much *from whom* the advice comes, as whether the advice be *good*."[82] Thus, Madison would certainly not want us citing his name simply to bolster our arguments *because* he was a prominent Framer. Likewise, there is strong evidence that Madison would likely not want us to consider what he and other Framers thought more than two centuries ago to be completely dispositive when interpreting the Bill of Rights today.

Of course, none of this changes the importance of Madison as the Father of the Bill of Rights. Unlike the Constitution, the Bill of Rights primarily *was* the offspring of his brain. Whereas the original Constitution was debated six days per week for nearly four months, the substance of the Bill of Rights was only debated over eight days on the House floor and over seven days on the floor of the Senate. Furthermore, the original proposal of the Constitution, the Virginia Plan, was substantially revised, amended, reworked, and compromised throughout the summer of 1787 in Philadelphia; Madison's draft of the Bill of Rights was adopted almost as written by him.

Likewise, from reading Madison's writings, particularly his contributions to *The Federalist,* it is easy to see that for Madison the study of history was of paramount importance. Madison is relevant in this respect because his role in framing the Bill of Rights is one important thing to understand among many other factors, including an examination of the text, other relevant history, supervening traditions, the broader structural goals of the Constitution, Supreme Court precedent, and practical consequences. And it is certainly important to have an accurate record of the debates, intents, and understandings of the Framers, regardless of one's favored method of constitutional interpretation. Nowhere is this more relevant than in Bill of Rights cases that reach the U.S. Supreme Court. Part II will analyze some of the Supreme Court's decisions that cite Madison as an authority, and it will explore how Madison's theory of the Bill of Rights can be used to better understand the rights at issue in those cases.

PART II

The United States Supreme Court

nine

MADISON AND THE BILL OF RIGHTS IN THE U.S. SUPREME COURT

Extrapolating Madison's Theory

Madison's theory was complex and contained many nuances. This alone makes his theory difficult to be pigeonholed to support certain legal or policy positions. Nevertheless, this is exactly what some Supreme Court justices have done—they have used Madison's quotes, sometimes out of context, to claim that they have found Madison's theory behind a particular provision in the Bill of Rights. Some justices have then used Madison as support for their position on a case. Have these justices truly understood the complexity of Madison's theory, or have they simply engaged in "name dropping," plucking quotes that support their position while ignoring the vast body of Madison's writings and speeches?

The following chapters examine a sampling of U.S. Supreme Court opinions that have invoked Madison in Bill of Rights cases. The justices' "use" of Madison is compared to Madison's political theory and view of human nature. This is done to determine if these justices have been influenced by Madison, if they have used him as authority when he makes an argument that is convenient for them, or if they have fundamentally misunderstood Madison. The justices can be placed into four categories based on their treatment of Madison: Devotees, Learners, Inconsistents, and Name Droppers.

However, caution should be observed below. The discussion of court cases in chapters 10 through 13 is *not* intended to argue how Madison would have resolved any of these cases. Madison lived in a prior era, and his statements should not be twisted to come to any specific conclusion about our contemporary world. Rather, these chapters compare how the justices have characterized Madison's theory, to see whether the justices who have cited Madison have grasped the complexity and nuances of his thought. The justices have opened the door to this inquiry, as *they* are the ones who have cited a late eighteenth- and early nineteenth-century Madison to support their legal positions in the twentieth and twenty-first centuries.

Thus, the discussion below is limited to how accurately the justices have portrayed Madison's theory, not how accurately they have used Madison to achieve certain legal results.

Likewise, any attempt to puzzle together how a Supreme Court justice conceptualizes of the theory of one of the Framers is a task littered with hazards. In some instances, a given justice provides only a few lines of text to explain why he or she believes Madison would have supported his or her position. Chapters 10–13 do not try to "read the tea leaves" or psychoanalyze a justice when discerning what a justice meant when citing Madison. That would be extrapolating too much based on the available evidence. Instead, these chapters examine the cited passages in context, and they subsequently draw from the text of the justice's opinion whether he or she understood Madison's theory.

Before commenting on specific justices and amendments, it is important to reflect on two of Madison's general statements about rights and how the nineteenth and twentieth centuries led to Madison's civil liberties legacy being vindicated. First, his statement regarding courts becoming the "guardians" of rights came true. Second, his "most valuable amendment," which would have protected core rights against infringement from state governments, was effectively added to the Constitution and interpreted by the U.S. Supreme Court to do exactly what Madison had hoped would be possible.

"INDEPENDENT TRIBUNALS OF JUSTICE" AS THE "GUARDIANS" OF LIBERTY

Recall that one of Madison's largest defeats at the Constitutional Convention was his inability to create the Council of Revision. Madison had envisioned this body to be made up of the president and members of the federal judiciary; its purpose would have been to review acts of Congress. Madison believed that this measure would have contained the power of Congress, including when Congress tried to act against liberty. Losing this battle was an important reason why Madison thought it would be valuable to have a bill of rights. Even with a bill of rights, however, someone needed to protect the freedoms contained therein. Without a Council of Revision, to whom would this duty fall?

When introducing the Bill of Rights, Madison emphasized the role of courts in protecting liberty: "If they are incorporated into the constitution, independent tribunals of justice will consider themselves in a peculiar manner the guardians of those rights; they will be an impenetrable bulwark against every assumption of power in the legislative or executive; they will be naturally led to resist every encroachment upon rights expressly stipulated for in the constitution by the declaration of rights."[1] This brief statement that Madison gave in defense of the Bill of Rights would be proven true in the twentieth century. In this respect, Madison prognosticated the role that the federal courts, particularly the Supreme Court, have fulfilled as the guardians of liberty. Beginning with what appeared to be a mundane case, *United States v. Carolene Products* (1938), the Court began reviewing cases involving civil liberties differently.

Carolene Products dealt with a relatively boring object: filled milk. According to the Filled Milk Act of 1923, "filled milk" was defined as "any milk . . . to which has been added . . . any fat or oil other than milk fat, so that the resulting product is in imitation or semblance of milk." Congress banned this substance from being shipped in interstate commerce because it found it to be "an adulterated article of food, injurious to the public health." The Carolene Products Company was indicted for transporting "Milnut," a compound of condensed skimmed milk and coconut oil, across state lines. The company challenged the conviction under the Fifth Amendment's Due Process Clause, which reads "nor shall any person . . . be deprived of life, liberty, or property, without due process of law." In effect, Carolene Products claimed that their equal protection rights were violated, when compared to milk companies. The Supreme Court, however, found the law to be constitutional.[2]

The point of interest in this case, as it relates to civil liberties, was buried in the Court's annotations. In footnote number four, the Court stated the following: "There may be narrower scope for operation of the presumption of constitutionality when legislation appears on its face to be within a specific prohibition of the Constitution, such as those of the first ten amendments." The footnote went on to posit that it was unnecessary to consider at that time whether a "more exacting judicial scrutiny" or "more searching judicial inquiry" is required when the court is examining the constitutionality of legislation that touches on, among other things, First Amendment rights that are important to protect "political processes" or to protect the rights of "discrete and insular minorities." These rights included "the dissemination of information," "political organizations," "peaceable assembly," and the rights of "particular religions."[3]

Notice how the Court in footnote number four not only states Madison's vision of the courts being "guardians" of liberty but also does this partly for Madisonian reasons. The Court wanted to protect these rights because they had valuable secondary benefits to society. The secondary benefits in this case included making the political process work as well as ensuring that religious minorities would not have their rights trampled by a self-interested majority. From this time on, the view that legislation infringing on the Bill of Rights would have less presumption of constitutionality slowly became a reality on the Supreme Court.

Four years after *Carolene Products*, the Court heard *Skinner v. Oklahoma* (1942), a case involving the forced sterilization of a habitual felon. Chief Justice Harlan

Fiske Stone cited footnote number four in a concurring opinion, noting that "[t]here are limits to the extent to which the presumption of constitutionality can be pressed, especially where the liberty of the person is concerned."[4] In a 1948 case, Justice Wiley Rutledge wrote in a concurrence that "legislative judgment . . . is always entitled to respect." He then went on to cite footnote number four, claiming, "that judgment does not bear the same weight and is not entitled to the same presumption of validity, when the legislation on its face or in specific application restricts the rights of conscience, expression and assembly protected by the [First] Amendment."[5]

However, during this era, the significance of footnote number four was not yet fully accepted on the Court. In *Kovacs v. Cooper* (1949), Justice Felix Frankfurter wrote of *Carolene Products* that a "footnote hardly seems to be an appropriate way of announcing a new constitutional doctrine, and the *Carolene* footnote did not."[6] Justice Frankfurter composed this concurrence in response to Justice Stanley Reed's majority opinion, which spoke of the "preferred position of freedom of speech." Justice Rutledge in dissent reiterated that "the First Amendment guaranties of the freedoms of speech, press, assembly and religion occupy [a] preferred position."[7] Although Frankfurter was denying the utility of footnote number four, there is no question that civil liberties, particularly First Amendment rights at this point, were seen by the Court majority as having a special status. Justice Frankfurter would continue to mock footnote number four, as well as the preferred position analysis three years later in a concurrence in *Dennis v. United States* (1951): "It has been suggested, with the casualness of a footnote, that such legislation [touching on First Amendment freedoms] is not presumptively valid, and it has been weightily reiterated that freedom of speech has a 'preferred position' among constitutional safeguards."[8]

However, by the 1960s the notion that the Supreme Court would treat First Amendment rights issues the same as all other legal questions was dying, and the *Carolene Products* approach was gaining strength. In 1961, Justice William Brennan wrote, "The honored place of religious freedom in our constitutional hierarchy . . . foreshadowed by a prescient footnote in *United States v. Carolene Products Co.*, must now be taken to be settled."[9] By 2008, in the Second Amendment case *District of Columbia v. Heller,* it was clear the Court fully supported applying a higher level of judicial scrutiny. This more protective stance for liberties is required whenever "a legislature may regulate a specific, enumerated right, [including] the freedom of speech, the guarantee against double jeopardy, the right to counsel, or the right to keep and bear arms." In the course of making this point, the Court cited none other than footnote number four of *U.S. v. Carolene Products.*[10] *Heller* represented seven decades of footnote number four being cited by the Court in scores of cases. But why was this one little footnote so important to the Court when evaluating freedoms protected by the Bill of Rights?

Carolene Products was decided by the Court at a time when it was just beginning to differentiate how it reviewed government action. Traditionally, the Supreme Court had one standard of review when deciding if a law ran afoul of the Constitution: the rational basis test, also known as the rational relationship test. Going back to the nineteenth century, the Court held in Equal Protection Clause cases that laws that classify people differently "must always rest upon some difference which bears a reasonable and just relation to the act in respect to which the classification is proposed, and can never be made arbitrarily and without any such basis."[11] In other words, the Court required only that legislatures could not make arbitrary laws—legislatures just had to act reasonably. Put another way by the Court more recently, "The general rule is that legislation is presumed to be valid and will be sustained if the classification drawn by the statute is rationally related to a legitimate state interest."[12] The rational basis test is deferential to legislative bodies and their fact-finding ability. The test presumes that a legislative body acted in a constitutional manner when it passed a statute, and a great deal of evidence is needed by the party challenging the constitutionality of a statute to win a case under this test. The rational basis test is still the typical standard of review for legal questions.

Since *Carolene Products* dealt with something outside of the Bill of Rights or similarly valued freedoms (i.e., filled milk), the Court applied the rational basis test in that case: "[T]he existence of facts supporting the legislative judgment is to be presumed, for regulatory legislation affecting ordinary commercial transactions is not to be pronounced unconstitutional unless in the light of the facts made known or generally assumed it is of such a character as to preclude the assumption that it rests upon some *rational basis* within the knowledge and experience of the legislators."[13] However, footnote number four (which was the footnote at the end of the sentence quoted above) opened the door for a higher level of scrutiny. After *Carolene Products* was decided in 1938, the phrase "preferred position" was used by the Court many times to refer to First Amendment freedoms. In 1942, Chief Justice Stone, in dissent, stated that "[t]he First Amendment is not confined to safeguarding freedom of speech and freedom of religion against discriminatory attempts to wipe them out. On the contrary, the Constitution . . . has put those freedoms in a preferred position."[14] By the next year, 1943, this stance was taken by the Court majority: "Freedom of press, freedom of speech, freedom of religion are in a preferred position."[15] The preferred position analysis of First Amendment freedoms elevated those rights to be more important than any others. This First Amendment glory was short-lived, however. Although some individual Supreme Court justices (particularly Justices Hugo Black and William Douglas) continued to speak of First Amendment freedoms being in a "preferred position" well into the 1970s, the last time a majority opinion classified these rights as such was in the *Kovacs* case in 1949. Indeed, by 1953, the majority of the Court had already concluded that "[i]t is a *non sequitur* to say that First Amendment rights may not be regulated because they hold a preferred position in the hierarchy of the constitutional guarantees of the incidents of freedom. This Court has never so held and indeed has definitely indicated the contrary."[16]

This notwithstanding, the Court moved away from the preferred position test, in part, because it had come upon a new test—one that privileged, not just First Amendment freedoms, but many other liberties as well. This came to be called the strict scrutiny test, and it became the chief rival to the rational basis test in constitutional cases. The strict scrutiny test was the natural outgrowth of footnote number four in *Carolene Products*, which referred to a "narrower scope for operation of the presumption of constitutionality" of laws that affect the Bill of Rights. The test was first used by the Court in a civil liberties case in *Skinner v. Oklahoma*, the case where the Court struck down the forced sterilization of a felon. According to the majority in *Skinner*, "strict scrutiny of the classification which a State makes in a sterilization law is essential" by the Court because the rights involved were "fundamental."[17] This continued the emphasis in footnote number four to give less judicial deference to legislative action when the case dealt with important rights. In *Griswold v. Connecticut* (1965), a case where the Court struck down a law prohibiting the use of contraceptives by married couples, the majority opinion clarified the specifics of the strict scrutiny test: "The nature of the right invaded is pertinent, to be sure, for statutes regulating sensitive areas of liberty do, under the cases of this Court, require strict scrutiny, and must be viewed in the light of less drastic means for achieving the same basic purpose. Where there is a significant encroachment upon personal liberty, the State may prevail only upon showing a subordinating interest which is compelling."[18] Put another way, strict scrutiny "forbids the government to infringe certain 'fundamental' liberty interests . . . unless the infringement is narrowly tailored to serve a compelling state interest."[19] This test gives very little deference to legislatures. When dealing with fundamental liberties, the burden of proof is on the government to show that the law in question serves nothing short of a compelling goal, and that the means chosen are the ones that infringe on the liberty the least in order to achieve that governmental goal.

In addition to procreative rights such as freedom from forced sterilization and the right to use contraceptives, the Court has also found that strict scrutiny is the standard to be applied in abortion rights cases.[20] Beyond procreative freedoms, the Court has used strict scrutiny to judge the constitutionality of many of the liberties Madison predicted, including First Amendment rights (beyond the religion clauses) and the rights of the accused.[21] At one point, the Court also used strict scrutiny in Free Exercise Clause cases.[22] Ultimately, the strict scrutiny test brought footnote number four to fruition more than the preferred position stance, as the strict scrutiny test elevated many more provisions of the Bill of Rights to a "preferred position" than just First Amendment freedoms.

Finally, Madison's prediction that the judiciary would become the guardian of liberty has not gone unnoticed by Supreme Court justices. Several justices have cited this quote by Madison in Bill of Rights cases to demonstrate the need for the judiciary to intervene and protect freedoms that are threatened by the other two branches of government. Beginning in 1943, six justices in 15 different opinions have cited Madison's prediction that, under a Bill of Rights, "independent tribunals of justice will consider themselves in a peculiar manner the guardians of those rights." Of this group, Justice William Brennan cited this Madison quote five times, and Justice Hugo Black cited it the most of any justice, a total of seven times. Especially for Justice Black, this message from Madison was exactly how the Court should see its role; at one point he characterized this quote as "the injunction to Court and Congress made by Madison when he introduced the Bill of Rights."[23] Although no justice has cited the passage since 1993, it is clear that Madison's prediction has come true. And there is no doubt that, under the strict scrutiny test, the Supreme Court has become a Madisonian "guardian" of liberties. Indeed, one recent study of the Burger and Rehnquist Courts (1969–2005) found that the justices were significantly more likely to strike a law down as unconstitutional if the case involved civil liberties.[24]

The Court proved Madison correct with respect to his premonition that courts would jealously guard the liberties contained within the Bill of Rights, with some justices taking the quote to heart. Indeed, even without a Council of Revision, the freedom that Madison valued so dearly found a defender. Next, consider how the Court resurrected Madison's plan to protect rights against state infringement.

"NO STATE SHALL . . ."

Another way that Madison attempted to compensate for a major Constitutional Convention loss was his "most valuable amendment" limiting state powers. After failing to create a congressional "veto" power over state laws, Madison saw the need for a bill of rights, particularly with a provision to limit state powers. Therefore, Madison proposed his "most valuable amendment," which he later helped modify slightly in a congressional committee, to read as follows: "No State shall infringe the equal rights of conscience, nor the freedom of speech, or of the press, nor of the right of trial by jury in criminal cases." With basically the same wording, this amendment passed the House. However, as explained above, Madison's second attempt to limit state powers also failed, as the Senate stripped this proposal from the Bill of Rights. With this amendment gone, nothing in the Bill of Rights limited state powers. This fact was confirmed by Chief Justice John Marshall in *Barron v. Baltimore* (1833): "These amendments demanded security against the apprehended encroachments of the general [federal] government—not against those of the local [state] governments."[25] Thus, the freedoms listed in the Bill of Rights only limited the federal government, not the states. That point notwithstanding, with the help of nineteenth-century congressman John Bingham, the U.S. Supreme Court (eventually) restored Madison's original constitutional vision and limited state powers over certain individual liberties.[26]

This part of our story emerges from the ashes of the American Civil War. Within five years of the war's conclusion, three amendments, known collectively as the Civil War Amendments, were ratified. The first of these three amendments, the Thirteenth Amendment, was ratified in 1865 and prohibited slavery and involuntary servitude (except as punishment for a crime). The third of the Civil War Amendments, the Fifteenth Amendment, was ratified in 1870 and stated that the right to vote shall not be denied based on race. It is the middle amendment, the Fourteenth Amendment, which concerns us here. The Fourteenth Amendment, ratified in 1868, has five sections to it. Among other things, the Amendment defines citizenship, it bans former Confederates from serving in Congress or the presidency, and it prohibits states from denying anyone equal protection of the law.

Tucked away within section 1 of the Fourteenth Amendment is the following proclamation: "No state shall make or enforce any law which shall abridge the privileges or immunities of citizens of the United States; nor shall any state deprive any person of life, liberty, or property, without due process of law." These two clauses are known as the Privileges and Immunities Clause and the Due Process Clause, respectively. The primary architect of these clauses was Congressman John Bingham, a representative from Ohio. Bingham was an abolitionist Radical Republican who had previously served as a special judge advocate general, presiding over the trial of the conspirators responsible for the assassination of Abraham Lincoln.[27] During the 39th Congress in 1866, Bingham was a member of the Joint House-Senate Committee on Reconstruction, which held hearings and drafted legislation related to rebuilding the Union, especially the former Confederacy, after the Civil War.[28] On this committee, Bingham was charged with drafting the text cited above of the Fourteenth Amendment.[29] Bingham's initial language, which he proposed on February 26, 1866, stated that "Congress shall have power to make all laws which shall be necessary and proper to secure to the citizens of each State all privileges and immunities of citizens in the several States, and to all persons in the several States equal protection in the rights of life, liberty, and property."[30] Bingham had to redraft section 1 of the Amendment to mollify some of his colleagues who wanted states to maintain more power.[31] Bingham's task in 1866 was one with which Madison was painfully familiar in 1789. After some rewriting, Bingham's part of the Fourteenth Amendment for our purposes read as follows: "No state shall make or enforce any law which shall abridge the privileges or immunities of citizens of the United States; nor shall any state deprive any person of life, liberty or property without due process of law."[32] Although this language was moved to a different part of the amendment, it is the exact wording of the Fourteenth Amendment's section 1 today. Bingham's new language was approved by the Committee on Reconstruction on April 21 and introduced in the House on May 8.[33]

Bingham's importance in the formation of the Fourteenth Amendment cannot be underestimated. Much like Madison with the Bill of Rights, Bingham drafted the language, sat on the key committee, and made minor alterations that were ultimately passed by Congress and ratified by the states. For this reason, Justice Black once stated that "Congressman Bingham may, without extravagance, be called the Madison of the first section of the Fourteenth Amendment."[34] What, then, did Congressman Bingham have to say about his amendment? During House debate on May 10, Bingham referred to this part of section 1 and stated:

> [M]any instances of State injustice and oppression have already occurred in the State legislation of this Union, of flagrant violations of the guaranteed privileges of citizens of the United States, for which the national Government furnished and could furnish by law no remedy whatever. Contrary to the express letter of your Constitution, "cruel and unusual punishments" have been inflicted under State laws within this Union upon citizens . . . for which and against which the Government of the United States had provided no remedy and could provide none. . . . That great want of the citizen and stranger, protection by national law from unconstitutional State enactments, is supplied by the first section of this amendment.[35]

Bingham wanted to reverse the interpretation of *Barron v. Baltimore* and make the Bill of Rights applicable to the states. In effect, this would carry on Madison's vision with his "most valuable amendment," and it would even carry it farther, protecting many more rights against the states than even Madison had proposed in 1789. The Fourteenth Amendment passed both chambers of Congress later in 1866 and was ratified by the states in 1868.

John Bingham's interpretation of the amendment he drafted notwithstanding, early Supreme Court decisions of the Fourteenth Amendment did nothing to limit state power over any freedoms. This began with *The Slaughterhouse Cases* (1873), which began when a group of different butchers challenged a Louisiana law that created a monopoly for the slaughtering of cattle and pigs. The statute gave exclusive right to one company to slaughter livestock in the City of New Orleans, and the statute restricted how and where animal remains could be disposed. The slaughterhouses in existence at the time, which were effectively put out of business by this law, challenged the statute on several grounds, primarily because it violated the Privileges and Immunities Clause of the Fourteenth Amendment.[36] The Supreme Court, in a rather sweeping statement, denied the claims of the slaughterhouse owners. The Court noted that except for a few instances of specific limitations on state power in the original Constitution: "the entire domain of the privileges and immunities of citizens of the States . . . lay within the constitutional and legislative power of the States, and without that of the Federal government."[37] The Court went on to rhetorically ask and answer the following question:

> Was it the purpose of the fourteenth amendment, by the simple declaration that no State should make or enforce any law which shall abridge the privileges and immunities of citizens of the United States, to transfer the security and protection of all the civil rights which we have mentioned, from the States to the Federal government? . . . We are convinced that no such results were intended by the Congress which proposed these amendments, nor by the legislatures of the States which ratified them.[38]

The Court effectively read the Privileges and Immunities Clause as a dead letter, interpreting it as nothing more than a restatement of a similar clause in the original Constitution. After *The Slaughterhouse Cases*, it appeared as though Madison's vision of a constitutional scheme that limited state powers, which Bingham tried to resurrect, would not live.

More than a decade after *The Slaughterhouse Cases*, the Supreme Court was asked in *Hurtado v. California* (1884) to review a case in which the defendant had been indicted by information, instead of by grand jury. An indictment by information is a process in which a suspect is formally charged with a crime by a prosecutor. It involves the prosecutor signing a document that charges the suspect with the crime in question. This document is then reviewed by a judge to see if there is sufficient evidence to move a criminal case forward to trial, or if the matter should be dropped and the suspect released. Indictment by information is contrasted with the traditional method of indictment, which is indictment by a grand jury. A grand jury is a panel of citizens that hears cases from prosecutors and then decides whether to formally charge a suspect with a crime. Grand juries were instituted in medieval England as a check on governmental power—the theory was that a prosecutor needed first to convince a body of citizens (the grand jury) to issue charges, and then the prosecutor had to convince another body of citizens (the trial jury) that the defendant committed the crime. The grand jury was important enough to Madison that he proposed it in the Bill of Rights, and it was ultimately ratified as part of the Fifth

Amendment: "No person shall be held to answer for a capital, or otherwise infamous crime, unless on a presentment or indictment of a grand jury."

In *Hurtado*, California indicted the defendant by information, rather than by grand jury. If this had been a federal criminal case, it would have clearly violated the Fifth Amendment. However, since it was a *state* criminal case, the Court found that there was no grand jury requirement. Hurtado claimed that the Due Process Clause of the Fourteenth Amendment barred an indictment by information because having a grand jury was part of maintaining "due process of law." The Court, however, cited the Fifth Amendment, which includes both the Grand Jury Clause as well as a Due Process Clause that is almost identical in language to the Fourteenth Amendment's Due Process Clause (the Fifth Amendment states "nor shall any person . . . be deprived of life, liberty, or property, without due process of law," while the Fourteenth Amendment states "nor shall any state deprive any person of life, liberty, or property, without due process of law"). The majority claimed that no clause in the Constitution was meant to be superfluous, so if the Fifth Amendment included both a Grand Jury Clause and a Due Process Clause, that Due Process Clause could not, by itself, require grand jury indictments. Since the language was similar in the Fourteenth Amendment's Due Process Clause, it, analogously, could not require a grand jury indictment.[39] Again, the Supreme Court denied that the Fourteenth Amendment did anything to limit state power over civil liberties.

Something else interesting happened in *Hurtado* though. In a dissenting opinion, Justice John Marshall Harlan planted a germ with regard to protecting liberties against state governments. While stating that he thought states should also be bound by the same grand jury requirement as the federal government, Harlan claimed of the Fifth Amendment that "[t]his language is similar to that of the clause of the Fourteenth Amendment now under examination. That similarity was not accidental, but evinces a purpose to impose upon the States the same restrictions, in respect of proceedings involving life, liberty and property, which had been imposed upon the general government."[40] In his arguments, Harlan cited James Madison as an authority on the importance of protecting the rights of the accused, referring to Madison as a "sagacious statesman and jurist."[41] Although Harlan was on the losing side of this argument in 1884, the case for limiting state powers was now growing on the Court.

Nearly a quarter-century passed with the *Slaughterhouse* scheme intact. Then, in 1896, the Supreme Court decided a property rights case that began a slow progression that ultimately culminated in the states' being limited by much of the Bill of Rights. *Missouri Pacific Railway Co. v. Nebraska* involved a group of farmers who wanted to build a grain elevator at a railway station. The farmers obtained an order from the state board of transportation directing the railway company to grant the farmers the right to build the elevator at the station. The railway company claimed that this amounted to a taking of private property for *private* use in violation of the Fourteenth Amendment's Due Process Clause.[42] The Court found for the railway, stating the following: "The taking by a State of the private property of one person or corporation, without the owner's consent, for the private use of another, is not due process of law, and is a violation of the Fourteenth Article of Amendment of the Constitution of the United States."[43] This was the first time the Court found the Fourteenth Amendment's Due Process Clause to protect a liberty that was also in the Bill of Rights (the Fifth Amendment's Takings Clause) from state infringement. One year later, *Chicago, Burlington and Quincy Railroad Co. v. Chicago* involved the named city condemning land owned by a railroad company. The railroad sued, claiming that its Fourteenth Amendment Due Process rights had been violated. Specifically, the railroad wanted to be financially compensated for the city's seizure of its land. The Court again protected the property rights of the railroad.[44] Justice Harlan, now in the majority for a unanimous Court, stated that "private property . . . taken for the State or under its direction for public use, without compensation made or secured to the owner, is . . . wanting in the due process of law required by the Fourteenth Amendment."[45] Both of these railroad cases involved rights protected against infringement by the federal government via the Fifth Amendment's Takings Clause being applied by the Fourteenth Amendment's Due Process Clause to limit the states. However, the Court stopped there. Any elaboration on what else the Due Process Clause meant would have to wait until one quarter of the way through the twentieth century. In the meantime, the only right that had been given any limitation by the Court against state infringement was the right protecting private property from being taken for public use without just compensation.

In 1925, the Court was again asked to interpret the meaning of the Fourteenth Amendment's Due Process Clause, but now for the first time the Court was asked to interpret what this Clause meant for something other than property rights. *Gitlow v. New York* involved the criminal prosecution by New York State of Benjamin Gitlow for criminal anarchy. New York charged and convicted Gitlow for helping to publish a manifesto for the Socialist Party. Gitlow proceeded to challenge the law under the Fourteenth Amendment's Due Process Clause. Unfortunately for Mr. Gitlow, the Court rejected his claim and upheld his conviction.[46] Nevertheless, in the Opinion for the Court, Justice Edward Sanford wrote the following with little explanation: "For present purposes we may and do assume that freedom of speech and of the press—which are protected by the First Amendment from abridgment by Congress—are among the fundamental personal rights and 'liberties' protected by the due process clause of the Fourteenth Amendment from impairment by the States."[47] In one fell swoop, this statement fundamentally altered the balance of power between civil liberties and state powers. The Court began an open season on state powers and was well on its way to achieving the vision of Madison and Bingham.

The Court was now becoming more explicit in its interpretation of the Fourteenth Amendment's Due Process Clause as more than simply a restatement of the Fifth Amendment's Due Process Clause. Instead, it was something that protected a set of specified rights against infringement by the states. The application of provisions of the Bill of Rights to limit state powers is also known as incorporation because these rights are being "incorporated" to apply to the states by the Due Process Clause of the Fourteenth Amendment. Over the next several years, the Court specifically incorporated the First Amendment's freedom of the press (*Near v. Minnesota*, 1931) and freedom of association (*DeJonge v. Oregon*, 1937).[48] Even though the Supreme Court was stating in individual cases whether a right was incorporated, it still raised an important question. How would one know if a particular right was protected by the Fourteenth Amendment?

The Court answered this question in *Palko v. Connecticut* (1937). Frank Palka (note correct spelling) initially confessed to murdering two police officers, but he later recanted. At his trial; the judge barred evidence of the confession from being introduced. Palka was found guilty only of second-degree murder and was sentenced to life in prison. However, Connecticut appealed the case, and an appellate court reversed the verdict. At a new trial, the confession was allowed into evidence, Palka was convicted of first-degree murder, and he was sentenced to death. This time Mr. Palka appealed, claiming that his Fifth Amendment right against double jeopardy, as incorporated by the Fourteenth Amendment's Due Process Clause, had been violated.[49] Writing for the majority, Justice Benjamin Cardozo stated what was by then fact: "immunities that are valid as against the federal government by force of the specific pledges of particular amendments have been found to be implicit in the concept of ordered liberty, and thus, through the Fourteenth Amendment, become valid as against the states."[50] Both Madison and Bingham would be proud at this point in the opinion. But how do we know which rights are "implicit in the concept of ordered liberty"? According to Cardozo, these are the rights that are "of the very essence of a scheme of ordered liberty. To abolish them is . . . to violate a principle of justice so rooted in the traditions and conscience of our people as to be ranked as fundamental."[51] Cardozo went on to describe of these rights that "neither liberty nor justice would exist if they were sacrificed."[52] Cardozo subsequently gave an example of these incorporated rights: "This is true, for illustration, of freedom of thought, and speech. Of that freedom one may say that it is the matrix, the indispensable condition, of nearly every other form of freedom."[53] Madison and Bingham, had they been alive to read this statement, would have been elated.

However, the Court ultimately found in *Palko* that the right against double jeopardy did *not* apply to the states because trying Palka one more time afforded the state to "a trial free from the corrosion of substantial legal error."[54] In fact, during the course of his opinion Cardozo said that "[t]he right to trial by jury [is] not of the very essence of a scheme of ordered liberty."[55] Both points, but especially the latter statement, would have caused Madison consternation. Madison strongly believed that the right to a criminal jury trial was an important way of securing every other important liberty.

Nevertheless, the process of selective incorporation laid out by the Court in *Palko* was the catalyst to limit state power over fundamental liberties. Over time, the U.S. Supreme Court has incorporated almost every provision in the Bill of Rights, including the ones that most particularly concerned Madison. In addition to the freedoms of speech and press that had already been incorporated before *Palko,* the Court later incorporated the other core components of Madison's failed state amendment, including the freedom of religion and the right to a jury trial in criminal cases. In *Cantwell v. Connecticut* (1940), the Court proclaimed, "The First Amendment declares that Congress shall make no law respecting an establishment of religion or prohibiting the free exercise thereof. The Fourteenth Amendment has rendered the legislatures of the states as incompetent as Congress to enact such laws."[56] And in *Duncan v. Louisiana* (1968), the Court proudly declared that "the Fourteenth Amendment guarantees a right of jury trial in all criminal cases which—were they to be tried in a federal court—would come within the Sixth Amendment's guarantee."[57] By the 1970s, the Court had incorporated almost all provisions of the first eight amendments, even going farther than Madison proposed in his "most valuable amendment." The Supreme Court in the middle third of the twentieth century did something that Madison could not accomplish in 1789—it protected from state infringement the freedoms of religion, speech, and press as well as the right to a jury trial in criminal cases.

The Court as a whole has become the "guardian" of liberties, including guarding these freedoms against state infringement. Even though Madison lost his congressional veto and his "most valuable amendment," his vision of the Bill of Rights is with us in the twenty-first century because of decisions by the Supreme Court. That said, different justices on the Court have had varying degrees of success in citing Madison in context when they have used him in these types of cases. The next four chapters explore how individual justices have (or have not) truly understood Madison when citing him in Bill of Rights cases.

ten

DEVOTEES OF MADISON ON
THE SUPREME COURT

This chapter observes the opinions of four justices who fundamentally understood Madison. Justices Hugo Black, William Brennan, Anthony Kennedy, and David Souter have all made reference to Madison in multiple Bill of Rights cases. Some of them have cited Madison several times in these types of cases; some referred to Madison dozens of times. What all four of them share in common is the ability to comprehend Madison's political theory and view of human nature consistently throughout their careers.

As is the case with any manuscript, all of the possible evidence of the justices' use of Madison in Bill of Rights cases cannot be examined here. Given that Madison has been cited in 230 Supreme Court opinions in these types of cases, doing an in-depth analysis of all of these cases would make this book significantly longer. Thus, some illustrative examples are offered for justices of each of the four types, and even with each justice only a few samples are discussed here. Specifically regarding the devotees of Madison, there are other justices who fall into this category, including William Douglas, Lewis Powell, and Harry Blackmun. Of particular significance among devotees not discussed at length here is Justice William Douglas, who cited Madison in Bill of Rights cases 25 times—more than any other justice in Supreme Court history. However, since Douglas's treatment of Madison was very similar to those of both Justices Black and Brennan, a discussion of cases by Douglas would have been a bit redundant. That said, as is the case with any other justice, a list of all of the cases where Douglas cited Madison is available in appendix A.

JUSTICE HUGO BLACK

Hugo Black served on the Supreme Court from 1937 to 1971. Black was largely a strict construction textualist on the Court, looking to the language of the Constitution and deriving the meaning of a constitutional provision primarily or exclusively from interpreting the text itself. As an appointee of President Franklin Roosevelt, Black turned out to be a dependable liberal in his time on the Court. He was one of the earliest justices to extensively cite James Madison when interpreting provisions in the Bill of Rights. Justice Black referenced Madison in cases ranging from the Religion Clauses to other First Amendment freedoms to the right to a jury trial. In doing so, he appeared to recognize Madison's fears about the self-interested tendency of human nature, the importance of Madison's insistence on ensuring that the majority could not steal away rights from minority groups, and Madison's belief in natural rights.

Take, for instance, *Engel v. Vitale* (1962). The case revolved around a New York program of daily classroom prayers in public schools. Under the state law in question, the principal of each public school was directed to require each class to state the following prayer at the beginning of each school day: "Almighty God, we acknowledge our dependence upon Thee, and we beg Thy blessings upon us, our parents, our teachers and our Country." The parents of ten pupils sued, claiming that this practice violated the Establishment Clause. The Supreme Court ruled in favor of the suing parents.[1] Writing for the majority, Justice Black undertook an analysis of why the government-mandated prayer ran afoul of the First Amendment. In doing so, he cited Madison multiple times, including the following example from the Virginia assessment controversy: "[T]hose opposed to the established Church, led by James Madison and Thomas Jefferson, who, though themselves not members of any of these dissenting religious groups, opposed all religious establishments by law on grounds of principle, obtained the enactment of the famous 'Virginia Bill for Religious Liberty' by which all religious groups were placed on an equal footing so far as the State was concerned."[2]

Black understood Madison's fear of the government aligning with a majority religion to the detriment of minority religions. Black saw this as the driving force behind the Virginia assessment as well as the state-required prayer in *Engel*. Black continued his line of reasoning: "The history of governmentally established religion, both in England and in this country, showed that whenever government had allied itself with one particular form of religion, the inevitable result had been that it had incurred the hatred, disrespect and even contempt of those who held contrary beliefs."[3] At the end of this sentence, Black placed a footnote, in which he quoted Madison's "Memorial and Remonstrance" as it related to the dangers establishment poses to both religion and government.[4] Black then concluded, "The Establishment Clause thus stands as an expression of principle on the part of the Founders of our Constitution that religion is too personal, too sacred, too holy, to permit its 'unhallowed perversion' by a civil magistrate."[5]

As a final point in *Engel*, Black addressed the fact that this prayer involved was a short nondenominational prayer of only 22 words (which could probably be easily recited in less than 15 seconds). Even so, Black was not dissuaded: "To those who may subscribe to the view that because the Regents' official prayer is so brief and general there can be no danger to religious freedom in its governmental establishment, however, it may be appropriate to say in the words of James Madison, the author of the First Amendment: 'It is proper to take alarm at the first experiment on our liberties.'"[6] Again, Black's citation of Madison is well within context. Madison's fear of religious assessments in Virginia, even though they were for a paltry amount, was that they might grow into something much larger and more detrimental. Madison believed that separationism was the best way to protect against the slippery slope of minor infractions that could become great ones because Madison saw the corruptibility of human nature. Black expressed similar fears in his *Engel* opinion.

Galloway v. United States (1943) was another instance of how Black comprehended Madisonian theory. *Galloway* was a civil case in which a veteran sued the federal government, claiming that his military service during World War I eventually led to his experiencing a mental breakdown. After a federal trial court heard the evidence, the government requested from the judge, and received, a directed verdict. A directed verdict occurs when the judge rules for one party without the decision going to the jury, on the grounds that no jury could reasonably find for the other party. In this case, the trial judge reasoned that Galloway had not brought sufficient evidence for the jury to deliberate. Galloway claimed that his Seventh Amendment right to a jury trial in civil cases was violated, so he appealed the case. The Supreme Court, however, found in favor of the government.[7]

Justice Black did not agree with the majority in *Galloway*. Instead, Black reasoned that directed verdicts should rarely, if ever, be used in federal civil cases. In support of this proposition, Black noted:

> We should not fail to meet the expectation of James Madison, who, in advocating the adoption of the Bill of Rights, said: "Independent tribunals of justice will consider themselves in a peculiar manner the guardians of those rights" . . . a verdict should be directed, if at all, only when, without weighing the credibility of the witnesses, there is in the evidence no room whatever for honest difference of opinion over the factual issue in controversy. I shall continue to believe that in all other cases a judge should, in obedience to the command of the Seventh Amendment, not interfere with the jury's function.[8]

Justice Black's quotation here is within the spirit of Madison's constitutional vision. Black understood that Madison wanted secondary precautions taken to protect rights—this included not just putting the Bill of Rights down on parchment, but also entrusting both judges *and* juries with the ability to check governmental power. Black also underscored Madison's emphasis on having rights reinforce each other, as the right to a jury trial can be used to protect other rights. Finally, Black demonstrated an awareness of Madison's understanding of human nature, noting how difficult it will be for judges, who want to selfishly guard their own power, to yield it to juries, as per the command of the Seventh Amendment.

Justice Black also drew on Madison's thought in *Yates v. United States* (1957). Yates and 13 other Communist Party members were prosecuted by the federal government under the Smith Act, which prohibited advocating the overthrow of the U.S. government by force. Upon conviction, each defendant was sentenced to five years in prison and given a fine of $10,000. The Court, based on the evidence, found that the convictions of 5 of the Communist Party members should be reversed, and the other 9 were ordered to have new trials.[9]

Justice Black dissented in part in the *Yates* case. According to him, all 14 of the petitioners' convictions should have been reversed. To support his position on the absolute protection of the freedom of speech, Black cited Madison:

> Madison . . . believed that loyalty to the provisions of this Amendment was the best way to assure a long life for this new nation and its Government. Unless there is complete freedom for expression of all ideas, whether we like them or not, concerning the way government should be run and who shall run it, I doubt if any views in the long run can be secured against the censor. The First Amendment provides the only kind of security system that can preserve a free government—one that leaves the way wide open for people to favor, discuss, advocate, or incite causes and doctrines however obnoxious and antagonistic such views may be to the rest of us.[10]

Black once more captured the essence of Madison. Black recognized that Madison wanted to defend the expression of all ideas, regardless of how offensive they might be, because he saw the freedom of speech as a natural right that belonged to individuals. In addition, Madison regarded protecting a broad right to freedom of speech as important, given the partially self-interested nature of humanity; indeed, if one view can be censored today, then eventually the government might selfishly censor all views except those expressed by the ruling party. Justice Black was able to see this about Madison, and he properly cited Madison's name in *Yates*.

Before Justice Black arrived on the Court, no justice had cited Madison in more than two opinions in Bill of Rights cases. During his tenure on the Court, Black cited Madison in 16 opinions in these types of cases, helping to dawn a new era. Black was able to use Madison to defend his positions in ways consistent with Madison's political theory and views on human nature.

JUSTICE WILLIAM BRENNAN

William Brennan served on the Court from 1956 to 1990. Although Brennan shared a similar interpretation of Madison compared to Black and was just as liberal as Black, the method of constitutional interpretation used by these two justices could not be more different. While Justice Black wanted to look entirely or primarily at the text of the Constitution to interpret the meaning of the document, Justice Brennan used a more multifaceted approach called "living constitutionalism." For Brennan, this meant looking at the text, as well as the intervening history and modern-day understanding of the Constitution to interpret its meaning.

More than any other recent or former U.S. Supreme Court justice, Brennan was profoundly influenced by Madison's political theory when deciding cases involving provisions of the Bill of Rights. Throughout his time on the Court, Brennan cited Madison in cases involving many areas of the Bill of Rights, and in doing so he invoked Madison in ways consistent with Madison's political theory and view of human nature. Brennan saw Madison's complex and realistic view of human nature as well as Madison's commitment to protecting natural rights both for their own sake and as a way to promote virtue and the common good. Brennan also used Madison in his opinions to demonstrate that protecting certain rights in the Bill of Rights will help to protect the other rights listed therein.

For example, in *Marsh v. Chambers* (1983), the Court had to deal with a case where the Nebraska legislature employed a chaplain to open each legislative session with a prayer. A Nebraska taxpayer sued the state in federal court, claiming that this practice violated the Establishment Clause. The Court, however, found the practice constitutional on the grounds that it was steeped in history and tradition.[11]

In dissent, Justice Brennan claimed that what Nebraska was doing ran afoul of the Constitution, and he cited Madison's statements to support his position several times.[12] Brennan believed the legislative employment of a chaplain unconstitutional, in part, because

> It intrudes on the right to conscience by forcing some legislators either to participate in a 'prayer opportunity,' with which they are in basic disagreement, or to make their disagreement a matter of public comment by declining to participate. It forces all residents of the State to support a religious exercise that may be contrary to their own beliefs. It requires the State to commit itself on fundamental theological issues. It has the potential for degrading religion by allowing a religious call to worship to be intermeshed with a secular call to order. And it injects religion into the political sphere by creating the potential that each and every selection of a chaplain, or consideration of a particular prayer, or even reconsideration of the practice itself, will provoke a political battle along religious lines and ultimately alienate some religiously identified group of citizens.[13]

Brennan made this statement in the paragraph directly following one in which he quoted Madison's disapproval of the appointment of chaplains for Congress, which is discussed in chapter 7. Brennan advocated separationism here while expressing many of the themes in Madison's conception of human nature and political theory. Brennan was troubled by forcing nonadherent legislators to either stand in the chamber during prayer time or publicly get up to leave, either of which could be troubling to the free exercise rights of minority religions. Brennan was disturbed with the practice in part because it degraded religion by intermeshing it with government, which Madison saw as a roadblock to the private cultivation of individual virtue through religion. Brennan was also concerned that the process of appointing the chaplains could be politically charged and could create needless fighting on the legislative floor to the detriment of building consensus and compromise on other policy issues. In this way, Brennan argued that such acts are detrimental to the public good.

Finally, in *Marsh* Brennan needed to respond to a specific point made by Chief Justice Warren Burger in the Court's majority opinion. According to Burger, it was instructive that Madison was in the First Congress when it decided to open its session with prayer and pay the chaplains who performed the payers.[14] As noted above, Madison later repudiated this practice. In a similar vein, Justice Brennan made the following observation:

> Legislators, influenced by the passions and exigencies of the moment, the pressure of constituents and colleagues, and the press of business, do not always pass sober constitutional judgment on every piece of legislation they enact . . . the fact that James Madison, who voted for the bill authorizing the payment of the first congressional chaplains, later expressed the view that the practice was unconstitutional, is instructive on precisely this point. Madison's later views may not have represented so much a change of mind as a change of role, from a Member of Congress engaged in the hurly-burly of legislative activity to a detached observer engaged in unpressured reflection. Since the latter role is precisely the one with which this Court is charged, I am not at all sure that Madison's later writings should be any less influential in our deliberations than his earlier vote.[15]

Justice Brennan's points about Madison's statements as well as how the Court should heed them could not be expressed more accurately. In particular, Brennan recognized the proper "reflection" that the Court could and should give when serving as a guardian of civil liberties, a sentiment shared by Madison. Again in *Marsh*, Brennan was able to take the long view and understand the thoughts Madison had on liberties and political theory.

Another First Amendment case, *O'Lone v. Estate of Shabazz* (1987), involved a New Jersey state prison work detail outside the prison. All prisoners were expected to participate in the work program, which was held on days that conflicted with Muslim inmates' observance of the Jumu'ah weekly congregational service. Jumu'ah is commanded by the Koran and must be held every Friday after the sun reaches its zenith and before the Asr, or afternoon prayer. Believing that their religious liberties had been violated, some of the Muslim prisoners sued. The Court in *O'Lone* held that this practice did not violate the Free Exercise Clause because the prison policy met concerns of institutional order and stability.[16]

However, Justice Brennan in dissent supported a more accommodationist free exercise position, noting that he would "require prison officials to demonstrate that the restrictions they have imposed are necessary to further an important government interest, and that these restrictions are no greater than necessary to achieve prison objectives."[17] Brennan's jurisprudential theory behind this was that the "Constitution was not adopted as a means of enhancing the efficiency with which government officials conduct their affairs, nor as a blueprint for ensuring sufficient reliance on administrative expertise. Rather, it was meant to provide a bulwark against infringements that might otherwise be justified as necessary expedients of governing."[18] Brennan proceeded to cite Madison in support of this position: "The practice of Europe, wrote James Madison, was 'charters of liberty . . . granted by power'; of America, 'charters of power granted by liberty.' While we must give due consideration to the needs of those in power, this Court's role is to ensure that fundamental restraints on that power are enforced."[19] Thus, Brennan made use of Madison's statements to support his accommodationist free exercise position.

Brennan's dissent in *O'Lone* was consistent with Madison's theories. Brennan took this accommodationist stance by emphasizing the need for government officials to meet a heavy burden before infringing on the prisoners' religious rights. This was similar to Madison's prescription that religious freedom should be "unpunished and unrestrained by the magistrate, Unless the preservation of equal liberty and the existence of the State are manifestly endangered.[20] Additionally, the passage that Brennan drew from Madison's writings is on point, as it presumed that our system was built on a recognition that private liberty had granted power to government. This sounds reminiscent of a Lockean social contract theory, in which we are born with natural rights and choose to give up some of these rights to government in exchange for the government's protection of the remainder of our retained rights. In this sense, Brennan appropriately expressed Madison's theory.

Brennan also drew on Madison's thought in a case involving the freedom of speech, *Brown v. Hartlage* (1982), which was a dispute over a Kentucky law that prohibited candidates from offering material benefits to voters. A problem developed under the law when both candidates for a county commissioner position promised to take a reduced salary if elected. When the two candidates were informed that their respective promises violated the law, they both retracted their comments. However, after the election, the losing candidate petitioned for the results to be voided because the winner violated the law. The Court found that the law itself violated the First Amendment.[21] In the majority opinion in *Brown,* Justice Brennan explained that

> Candidate commitments enhance the accountability of government officials to the people whom they represent, and assist the voters in predicting the effect of their vote. The fact that some voters may find their self-interest reflected in a candidate's commitment does not place that commitment beyond the reach of the First Amendment. We have never insisted that the franchise be exercised without taint of individual benefit; indeed, our tradition of political pluralism is partly predicated on the expectation that voters will pursue their individual good through the political process, and that the summation of these individual pursuits will further the collective welfare.[22]

To support this theory of protecting individual rights in order to achieve the collective welfare, Brennan cited Madison: "The Madisonian democratic tradition extolled a system of political pluralism in which 'the private interest of every individual may be a sentinel over the public rights.'"[23] Brennan's position in *Brown* certainly fits Madison's liberalism and understanding of human nature. To Brennan, a candidate could, either for the selfish reason of winning an election or for the virtuous reason of being truthful to voters about saving taxpayer dollars, offer to reduce his salary if elected. In either case, Brennan found this scenario to provide a welcome benefit to voters. Either through the route of virtuous or selfish liberalism, Brennan's interpretation was consistent with Madison. Of course, it is also worth noting that Madison made campaign promises in real life that may have been done partially out of self-interest, as he promised his constituents that he would support a bill of rights if elected to the First Congress.

One final example of Brennan's understanding of Madison is found in *United States v. Verdugo-Urquidez* (1990). Recall from chapter 1 that in this case the Court held that the Fourth Amendment protection of "people" from unreasonable searches and seizures did not apply to the search and seizure by U.S. agents of property owned by a nonresident alien and located in a foreign country. In his *Verdugo-Urquidez* dissent, Justice Brennan concluded that the alien in this case was one of "the people" for Fourth Amendment purposes. According to Brennan, any alien is entitled to the protections of the Fourth Amendment when the U.S. government investigates him and attempts to hold him accountable under U.S. law, because the government has treated him as a member of our community for purposes of enforcing our laws.[24] Brennan claimed that this position of mutuality, where the government is to respect aliens' Fourth Amendment rights if aliens are expected to obey U.S. law, is one that Madison supported:

> James Madison, universally recognized as the primary architect of the Bill of Rights, emphasized the importance of mutuality when he spoke out against the Alien and Sedition Acts less than a decade after the adoption of the Fourth Amendment: "It does not follow, because aliens are not parties to the Constitution, as citizens are parties to it, that, whilst they actually conform to it, they have no right to its protection. Aliens are not more parties to the laws than they are parties to the Constitution; yet it will not be disputed that, as they owe, on one hand, a temporary obedience, they are entitled, in return, to their protection and advantage."[25]

For Brennan, Madison's statement here and his position as the "primary architect" of the Bill of Rights were sufficient evidence that Fourth Amendment rights ought to be interpreted expansively, including the application of those rights to individual aliens.

Brennan's position was consistent with Madison's view of rights. First, the items seized without a warrant in *Verdugo-Urquidez* were documents, or "papers"—something explicitly protected in Madison's proposal and something that is specifically tied to Madison's belief that strong protections for the rights of the accused were another way to protect First Amendment rights. Second, as Brennan's quote of Madison illuminated, Madison believed in the promotion of liberal rights for the purpose of advancing the public good. In this case, Brennan claimed that could be accomplished by adhering to the principle of mutuality, which would make aliens in the United States more likely to follow domestic laws if they are given the protections of the law. Third, this mutuality will, in turn, promote virtue among aliens by giving them more reason and opportunity to follow U.S. laws. Thus, not only did Brennan cite Madison as authority in this case, but he advanced a theory that was consistent with Madison's vision regarding the rights of the accused.

Overall, Justice Brennan invoked Madison's name in many cases, including 23 opinions in which provisions of the Bill of Rights were at issue. Brennan at times appeared to have been almost enamored with Madison, citing him approvingly on so many occasions. What is all the more remarkable is that Brennan consistently expressed Madison's theory correctly during more than a third of a century on the bench.

JUSTICE ANTHONY KENNEDY

Anthony Kennedy was appointed to the Supreme Court in 1988. Although a nominee of Republican President Ronald Reagan, Kennedy has wound up being a moderate, swing-vote justice. With the possible exception of Justice Brennan, no justice during the Supreme Court's recent history has as deep and acute a grasp of Madison's theory as Kennedy. As the five cases below demonstrate, Justice Kennedy has repeatedly given an accurate portrayal of Madison's political philosophy and view of human nature.

In his first full term on the Court, Kennedy dissented in part from the Court's opinion in *County of Allegheny v. American Civil Liberties Union* (1989). The case arose from two government-sponsored holiday displays in Pittsburgh, Pennsylvania. One of the displays was a crèche which included an angel bearing a banner that proclaimed, "Gloria in Excelsis Deo!" ("Glory to God in the Highest!"). The crèche was donated by the Holy Name Society and displayed on the grand staircase in the county courthouse in Allegheny, Pennsylvania. In addition, there was another holiday display outside an office building jointly owned by the city of Pittsburgh and Allegheny County, consisting of (1) a 45-foot Christmas tree, (2) an 18-foot menorah, and (3) a sign bearing a message that Pittsburgh "salutes liberty" during the holiday season. In response to a lawsuit from the American Civil Liberties Union (ACLU), the Court held that the crèche violated the Establishment Clause, but that the other display did not.[26]

Justice Kennedy believed that *both* displays were constitutional. According to Kennedy, the purpose of the Establishment Clause was to prevent government action that "further[s] the interests of religion through the coercive power of government."[27] Kennedy sustained this stance by quoting Madison:

> The freedom to worship as one pleases without government interference or oppression is the great object of both the Establishment and the Free Exercise Clauses. Barring all attempts to aid religion through government coercion goes far toward attainment of this object . . . James Madison, who proposed the First Amendment in Congress, "apprehended the meaning of the [Religion Clauses] to be, that Congress should not establish a religion, and enforce the legal observation of it by law, nor compel men to worship God in any manner contrary to their conscience."[28]

In his first citation of Madison in a Bill of Rights case, Kennedy demonstrated an acute awareness of Madison's political theory and view of human nature. Kennedy focused on the Establishment Clause as a bar to government's coercive power, which shows Kennedy's interest in protecting minority groups from the tyranny of a self-interested majority. Clearly, this points toward a realistic understanding of human nature on the part of Kennedy.

Additionally, Kennedy pointed out how Madison saw the Religion Clauses as reinforcing each other to protect the freedom of and from religion. Even though Kennedy ultimately took a nonpreferentialist stance in *Allegheny,* he appears to have understood Madison's general political theory.

Another Establishment Clause case confronted by Justice Kennedy is *Lee v. Weisman* (1992). This case revolved around a public middle school graduation ceremony in which the principal invited clergy to hold an invocation and benediction. In anticipation of the event, the principal gave the clergyperson a pamphlet entitled "Guidelines for Civic Occasions," which recommended that public prayers at civic ceremonies be composed with inclusiveness and sensitivity. Both prayers were nonsectarian and short in duration. However, the parent of one of the students objected, claiming an Establishment Clause violation. The Supreme Court found for the parent.[29]

Writing for the majority in *Lee,* Kennedy staked out the following separationist position:

> The First Amendment's Religion Clauses mean that religious beliefs and religious expression are too precious to be either proscribed or prescribed by the State. The design of the Constitution is that preservation and transmission of religious beliefs and worship is a responsibility and a choice committed to the private sphere, which itself is promised freedom to pursue that mission. It must not be forgotten then, that while concern must be given to define the protection granted to an objector or a dissenting nonbeliever, these same Clauses exist to protect religion from government interference.[30]

Kennedy proceeded to invoke Madison in support: "James Madison, the principal author of the Bill of Rights, did not rest his opposition to a religious establishment on the sole ground of its effect on the minority. A principal ground for his view was: 'Experience witnesseth that ecclesiastical establishments, instead of maintaining the purity and efficacy of Religion, have had a contrary operation.'"[31] For Kennedy, this interpretation of Madison justified striking down the government action in this case as detrimental to religion, because it can be corrupted when used as a tool of government. Kennedy's assessment of Madison was essentially correct. First, Kennedy emphasized Madison's aversion to establishments because of their effect on minorities. Kennedy recognized that Madison understood the dangers of giving too much power to a self-interested majority, given the realistic nature of humanity. His citation of Madison also accentuated Madison's commitment to disestablishment as a way to protect free exercise rights. Furthermore, Kennedy recognized that the rights to be protected here were private individual freedoms. In other words, Kennedy understood Madison to support a position where the government was instituted to protect freedom of religion. Finally, Kennedy also saw that disestablishment was a way for Madison to promote virtue, as it protected the "purity and efficacy" of religion. In *Lee,* Kennedy understood Madison's theory on multiple levels.

He also portrayed Madison accurately in *Austin v. Michigan State Chamber of Commerce* (1990). The case began when the State of Michigan passed a campaign-finance law. Contained within the law was a prohibition on corporations from using corporate treasury funds for independent expenditures in support of, or in opposition to, any candidate in elections for state office. The state chamber of commerce then filed a lawsuit, claiming that the law violated the First Amendment. In *Austin,* the Court sided with the state, finding the law to be constitutional.[32]

Justice Kennedy wrote a dissent in *Austin.* He criticized the majority for approving the constitutionality of a "value-laden, content-based speech suppression that permits some nonprofit corporate groups, but not others, to engage in political speech."[33] According to Kennedy, the majority interpreted associational rights incorrectly: "I reject any argument based on the idea that these groups and their views are not of importance and value to the self-fulfillment and self-expression of their members, and to the rich public dialogue that must be the mark of any free society."[34] Kennedy then cited Madison to buttress his arguments: "It is a distinctive part of the American character for individuals to join associations to enrich the public dialogue. . . . The theme of group identity is part of the history of American democracy. See, e.g., *The Federalist No. 10* (J. Madison)."[35] Kennedy did not elaborate much on Madison in *Austin,* but it is clear from the citation and its context that Kennedy properly understood Madison. Indeed, Kennedy packed several ideas into a few brief passages.

First, Kennedy stressed both the freedoms of speech and association. Thus, Kennedy understood more of Madison's complex thought, as he understood that Madison saw these rights as protecting one another. In this case, Kennedy seized upon the freedom of association as a way to promote and protect the right to freedom of expression. Second, in the paragraph before he mentioned Madison's name, Kennedy stated that the freedoms of association and speech in this case were important to the self-fulfillment of people who belong to groups. In this way, Kennedy understood the rights at issue to be freely exercised by the autonomous individual; in other words, Kennedy saw that these rights existed primarily as personal property to be exercised however individuals desire them, not that they existed primarily for the good of democracy. Finally, Kennedy understood Madison's correlation between protecting these liberal rights and the resulting common good when he stated that allowing such freedom would "enrich the public dialogue." *Austin* is another example of Kennedy getting Madison's theory right.

Kennedy dissented in another First Amendment case, *Alexander v. United States* (1993). Alexander owned 13 stores dealing in sexually explicit materials, and he was convicted of violating federal obscenity laws. Alexander was also convicted of violating the Racketeer Influenced and Corrupt Organizations Act (RICO), based on a finding that seven items sold at several stores were obscene and were thereby part of an ongoing criminal enterprise. In addition to imposing a prison term and fine, the trial judge ordered Alexander, as punishment for the RICO violations, to forfeit his businesses and almost $9 million acquired through racketeering activity. This forfeiture included destroying the magazines and videotapes located at Alexander's businesses, even if they had not been proven obscene. Alexander challenged this as a violation of his First Amendment rights. The Supreme Court held RICO, as applied in this case, constitutional.[36]

This decision disturbed Kennedy, however, and he chastised the majority for embracing a rule that "would find no affront to the First Amendment in the Government's destruction of a book and film business and its entire inventory of legitimate expression as punishment for a single past speech offense. . . . This ominous, onerous threat undermines free speech and press principles essential to our personal freedom."[37] According to Kennedy, this constituted a "prior restraint" on expression: "What is happening here is simple: Books and films are condemned and destroyed not for their own content but for the content of their owner's prior speech. Our law does not permit the government to burden future speech for this sort of taint."[38] When discussing how this runs counter to our history and tradition of freedom of expression, Kennedy reviewed how classical English law only defined freedom of the press as "laying no *previous* restraints upon publications."[39] Kennedy compared this to the more open view of freedom of expression rights in eighteenth-century America by quoting Madison:

> [T]olerance of subsequent punishments . . . would be in flagrant violation of the principles of free speech and press that we have come to know and understand as being fundamental to our First Amendment freedoms. Indeed, in the beginning of our Republic, James Madison argued against the adoption of [this] definition of free speech under the First Amendment. Said Madison: "This idea of the freedom of the press can never be admitted to be the American idea of it" because a law inflicting penalties would have the same effect as a law authorizing a prior restraint.[40]

Thus, Kennedy invoked Madison to assist him in defending a liberal position on freedom of expression.

Did Justice Kennedy use Madison appropriately? Yes, for multiple reasons. He referred to Madison as an authority in a case where Kennedy emphasized that the freedom of expression is a private freedom, which is true to Madison's position. Kennedy also demonstrated an awareness of Madison's belief that protecting the freedom of expression would be valuable for the common good, as he found protection of the freedoms of speech and press as "essential." Finally, Kennedy stated in *Alexander* that protecting the right to freedom of expression would protect "our personal freedom," which demonstrated Kennedy's agreement with Madison that protecting one set of rights could help to reinforce others. All of these positions were consistent with Madison.

Kennedy also made use of Madison in a case regarding the rights of the accused, *Roper v. Simmons* (2005). The facts of this case began when Christopher Simmons and two accomplices committed murder by breaking into a victim's home, tying up the victim, and throwing her off a bridge to her death. Simmons, who was 17 at the time of the crime, was tried and convicted as an adult. The prosecutor sought and received the death penalty. Simmons, however, claimed that executing someone who was a minor at the time of his crime violated the Eighth Amendment's Cruel and Unusual Punishment Clause. The Court held that the death penalty is unconstitutional for juveniles because they tend to have an underdeveloped character and sense of responsibility, and they are more susceptible to negative peer pressure than adults.[41]

According to Kennedy's majority opinion, "it would be misguided to equate the failings of a minor with those of an adult, for a greater possibility exists that a minor's character deficiencies will be reformed."[42] Based on this reasoning, Justice Kennedy found that "the death penalty is disproportionate punishment for offenders under 18."[43] In justifying a "living constitution" approach to constitutional interpretation, Kennedy used Madison:

> Over time, from one generation to the next, the Constitution has come to earn the high respect and even, as Madison dared to hope, the veneration of the American people. See *The Federalist No.* 49, p 314 (C. Rossiter ed. 1961). The document sets forth, and rests upon, innovative principles original to the American experience, such as federalism; a proven balance in political mechanisms through separation of powers; specific guarantees for the accused in criminal cases; and broad provisions to secure individual freedom and preserve human dignity.[44]

In Kennedy's view, Madison wanted the Constitution and its amendments to earn the veneration of the American people, and part of the reason we should have such veneration for the Constitution is its specific guarantees for the criminally accused and its emphasis on securing individual rights and preserving human dignity. Kennedy's position was again consistent with Madison. Madison was concerned about protecting individual human dignity, a concept that is related both to protecting natural rights and to the attainment of virtue.[45] For Madison, governments are bound to respect natural rights because to do so is to recognize the importance of individual human dignity. Indeed, Madison wanted to see the human person protected and to see people flourish. In this sense, Madison understood a residual natural right to life and liberty, a position that is certainly relevant when discussing the death penalty. Indeed, under Madison's theory of property rights, one's own life was the most valuable form of property. Furthermore, in addition to protecting the rights to life and human dignity as natural rights, one way of safeguarding those rights is through properly protecting the rights of the accused. Thus, Kennedy also appears to have seen the relationship Madison found between criminal procedures and individual rights. Kennedy also engaged in a Madisonian analysis by linking together the concepts of federalism, separation of powers, and freedoms in the Bill of Rights. Finally, Kennedy emphasized the importance of the age of the offenders and how minors have underdeveloped characters and senses of responsibility as reasons to bar executing them. In this way, Kennedy expressed a belief that protecting minors' right to life and the rights of the accused may result in these minors one day achieving virtue.

Overall, Justice Kennedy has comprehended and embraced Madison's understanding of human nature, his liberalism, and his focus on rights reinforcing each other as a way to promote virtue and to achieve the common good. Although Kennedy has cited Madison in only 5 Bill of Rights cases, far short of Brennan's 23 references, all of Kennedy's invocations have been accurate. Thus, it appears that Kennedy has been distinctly influenced by Madison and can be rightly classified as a devotee.

JUSTICE DAVID SOUTER

David Souter served on the Court from 1990 to 2009. When appointed by President George H. W. Bush, the media nicknamed him "The Stealth Candidate" because it was thought this quiet New Englander was going to be a covert conservative appointee. On the contrary, Souter became one of the Court's most liberal members. Outside of Tenth Amendment cases (which are beyond of the scope of this work), the only Bill of Rights cases in which Souter cited Madison involved the Establishment Clause. Nevertheless, when writing and ruling on Establishment Clause disputes, Justice Souter demonstrated his deep understanding of Madison's theory. Interestingly enough, when Souter joined the Court he took the seat of another Madison "devotee," William Brennan.

Recall the *Rosenberger* case from chapter 1, where the Court held that the Establishment Clause did not bar disbursement of funds from student activity fees at the University of Virginia to a religious organization, Wide Awake Publications (WAP).[46] Souter dissented from the majority's ruling, claiming that "[u]sing public funds for the direct subsidization of preaching the word is categorically forbidden under the Establishment Clause, and if the Clause was meant to accomplish nothing else, it was meant to bar this use of public money."[47] Souter then quoted Madison: "Who does not see that . . . the same authority which can force a citizen to contribute three pence only of his property for the support of any one establishment, may force him to conform to any other establishment in all cases whatsoever?"[48] According to Souter, "Madison's Remonstrance captured the colonists' 'conviction that individual religious liberty could be achieved best under a government which was stripped of all power to tax, to support, or otherwise to assist any or all religions, or to interfere with the beliefs of any religious individual or group,'" and his arguments led directly to the defeat of the Virginia Assessment Bill and the enactment of the Virginia Bill for Establishing Religious Freedom.[49] In a footnote, Souter elaborated on Madison's theoretical position:

> Madison strongly inveighed against the proposed aid for religion for a host of reasons . . . many of those reasons would have applied whether or not the state aid was being distributed equally among sects, and whether or not the aid was going to those sects in the context of an evenhanded government program. *See, e.g.,* Madison's Remonstrance. . . . "In matters of Religion, no man's right is abridged by the institution of Civil Society. . . . Religion is wholly exempt from its cognizance." . . . State support of religion "is a contradiction to the Christian Religion itself; for every page of it disavows a dependence on the powers of this world." . . . "Experience witnesseth that ecclesiastical establishments, instead of maintaining the purity and efficacy of Religion, have had a contrary operation."[50]

Souter concluded as follows: "The principle against direct funding with public money is patently violated by the contested use of today's student activity fee. Like today's taxes generally, the fee is Madison's threepence."[51]

Souter largely portrayed Madison accurately when he cited him in *Rosenberger.* The main thrust of Souter's Madison citations was that carefully patrolling the limits of the Establishment Clause helps protect the free exercise rights of minority religions. Not only does this show an awareness of Madison's idea that different rights protect each other, but also that we must be cautious of those in power advancing their interests to the detriment of minority groups in society. Second, Souter repeatedly implied that taking religion out of the public sphere will help avoid religious strife. Again, Souter hit the mark in citing Madison. For Madison it was more dangerous to allow religion into the public sphere, as he believed that this entailed the possible corruption of religion by government *and* of government by religion. Thus, Madison did not want these two institutions to be "fused" together over funding decisions. By keeping religion out of the public sphere, Madison believed that neither of these dangers was possible, and he even argued that religion would be stronger out of the public sphere because religious groups would be free to cultivate their virtue without government influence. Thus, Souter seized upon Madison's point that establishments destroy the purity and efficacy of religions. This demonstrated that Souter understood Madison's view that separationism would promote the independent development of religions, allowing individuals to cultivate virtue without the potentially corrupting influence of government.

One thing missing from Souter's analysis was the effect on WAP's free exercise rights if they were barred from funding. Madison conceived of a natural right to practice one's religion, including a natural right to religious speech. Souter's statement that Madison wanted a government that was "stripped of all power . . . to assist any or all religions" is a slight misrepresentation of Madison, given Madison's proclivity toward accommodationism on free exercise questions. This notwithstanding, Souter's assessment of Madison's theory regarding the Establishment Clause was largely accurate.

Souter also drew on Madison's theory in *Zelman v. Simmons-Harris* (2002). *Zelman* began with an Ohio pilot program designed to provide educational choices to families with children in the Cleveland City School District. The program offered aid to students to attend a participating public or private school of their parents' choosing—tuition aid for private schools and tutorial aid for public schools. Five years into the program's existence, some important information came to light about the program, including the fact that more than 96 percent of the students participating in the scholarship portion of the program were enrolled in religiously affiliated schools. Based on this data, some Ohio taxpayers sued. The Court found that the program did not violate the Establishment Clause, as it had a valid secular purpose and was a true private choice.[52]

In dissent, Justice Souter claimed the program to be unconstitutional because "the money will . . . pay for eligible students' instruction not only in secular subjects but in religion as well, in schools that can fairly be characterized as founded to teach religious doctrine and to imbue teaching in all subjects with a religious dimension."[53] Indeed, Souter found the Ohio program absolutely maddening, and Madison was included among the authorities he cited:

> It is virtually superfluous to point out that every objective underlying the prohibition of religious establishment is betrayed by this scheme, but something has to be said about the enormity of the violation. I anticipated these objectives . . . the first being respect for freedom of conscience. . . . Madison thought it violated by any "authority which can force a citizen to contribute three pence . . . of his property for the support of any . . . establishment." "Any tax to establish religion is antithetical to the command that the minds of men always be wholly free." Madison's objection to three pence has simply been lost in the majority's formalism.[54]

Souter elaborated on this point in a footnote: "As a historical matter, the protection of liberty of conscience may well have been the central objective served by the Establishment Clause."[55] This point ties together the two clauses, promoting the Madisonian idea that the two rights could reinforce one another, something Souter had neglected in his *Rosenberger* dissent. Likewise, Souter observed a need to have "respect" for freedom of conscience that would be threatened by establishment of religion.

Next, Souter described a second problem with the Ohio program under the Establishment Clause:

> As for the second objective, to save religion from its own corruption, Madison wrote of the "experience . . . that ecclesiastical establishments, instead of maintaining the purity and efficacy of Religion, have had a contrary operation." In Madison's time, the manifestations were "pride and indolence in the Clergy; ignorance and servility in the laity[,] in both, superstition, bigotry and persecution;" in the 21st century, the risk is one of "corrosive secularism" to religious schools, and the specific threat is to the primacy of the schools' mission to educate the children of the faithful according to the unaltered precepts of their faith.[56]

Souter here seized on the Establishment Clause as not only a protector of free exercise rights but also a way to promote the virtue of persons practicing religion free from "corrosive" government influence.

Finally, Souter discussed the majority's formalism, which he alluded to in the first passage above quoting Madison. In particular, Souter emphasized that even though the funds went to school children's parents, "96.6% of all voucher recipients go to religious schools, only 3.4% to nonreligious ones."[57] Souter then went on to posit that "One answer to these statistics . . . might be that 96.6% of families choosing to avail themselves of vouchers choose to educate their children in schools of their own religion. . . . Evidence shows, however, that almost two out of three families using vouchers to send their children to religious schools did not embrace the religion of those schools."[58] Based on this, Souter concluded, "There is, in any case, no way to interpret the 96.6% of current voucher money going to religious schools as reflecting a free and genuine choice by the families that apply for vouchers. The 96.6% reflects, instead, the fact that too few nonreligious school desks are available and few but religious schools can afford to accept more than a handful of voucher students."[59]

Souter recognized, much like Madison, that the majority had to be guarded from infringing on the rights of the minority. Likewise, Souter understood that government funding of religion, whether direct or indirect, could lead to the corruption of religion. In this case, Souter saw such corruption in a government program that promoted religious schools but which drew most of its funds from parents who did not practice the faith of that school. Based on his statements in *Zelman*, it is clear that Madison and Souter used the same type of reasoning when deciding establishment questions. Thus, Souter again demonstrated an awareness of Madison's political theory and Madison's view of the Bill of Rights.

As a final example, take Souter's majority opinion in *McCreary County v. ACLU* (2005). *McCreary* arose when two Kentucky counties each posted the King James Version of the Ten Commandments on the walls of their respective courthouses. The ACLU soon filed suit, challenging the constitutionality of the postings. The Supreme Court held that the Ten Commandments displays violated the Establishment Clause because neither one had a secular legislative purpose.[60]

At one point in his Opinion for the Court, Souter claimed that Justice Antonin Scalia's dissent (cited below) mischaracterized Madison. According to Souter, the "Framers and the citizens of their time intended not only to protect the integrity of individual conscience in religious matters, but to guard against the civic divisiveness that follows when the Government weighs in on one side of religious debate; nothing does a better job of roiling society."[61] Souter continued, accusing Scalia in dissent of cherry-picking facts: "The historical record, moreover, is complicated beyond the dissent's [Scalia's] account by the writings and practices of figures no less influential than Thomas Jefferson and James Madison."[62] In confirmation of his proposition that Madison was a separationist, Souter asserted that "Madison, whom the dissent claims as supporting its thesis . . . criticized Virginia's general assessment tax not just because it required people to donate 'three pence' to religion, but because 'it is itself a signal of persecution. It degrades from the equal rank of Citizens all those whose opinions in Religion do not bend to those of the Legislative authority.'"[63] In order to support his separationist position, Souter also cited Madison's statements that "'religion & Govt. will both exist in greater purity, the less they are mixed together,'" and that "with respect to religion and government the 'tendency to a usurpation on one side, or the other, or to a corrupting coalition or alliance between them, will be best guarded against by an entire abstinence of the Government from interference.'"[64]

Much like his *Rosenberger* and *Zelman* dissents, Souter properly used Madison in his *McCreary County* majority opinion. He highlighted Madison's fear that human nature would often compel those in power to act wickedly to the detriment of minority religions; hence, there is a need to police vigilantly the line of disestablishment. Souter again underscored how enforcing one constitutional provision (the Establishment Clause) would lead to more protection for another right (free exercise). And more explicitly than in *Rosenberger*, Souter emphasized how separationism would lead to the common good, by avoiding the "divisiveness" and "roiling" that establishment brings. Finally, Souter made reference to the protection of "the integrity of individual conscience in religious matters," as a paramount concern of the Religion Clauses, demonstrating his understanding of a liberal, individual right at stake here when invoking Madison in support. All of these propositions are properly in line with Madison's thoughts.

Overall, Justice Souter can properly be characterized as a devotee of Madison's political theory, at least in Establishment Clause cases. Souter ran almost to excess in the 10 relevant cases where he cited Madison. Indeed, in his first Establishment Clause case where he cited Madison, a concurrence in *Lee v. Weisman,* Souter invoked Madison's name no less than 35 times in the course of directly quoting Madison 17 times![65] However, Souter did not just blindly cite Madison in his opinions. Instead, Souter consistently captured the essence of Madison's political theory and understanding of human nature.

eleven

LEARNERS

Discussing the justices in the last chapter was relatively easy. They all demonstrated an acute awareness of Madison's theories when they cited the Father of the Constitution in their opinions. Beginning with this chapter, however, the justices discussed will have progressively less of an understanding of Madison, even though they may cite to him just as often as his "devotees" do.

There are two justices on the Court who appear to have undergone a transformation in their appreciation of Madison. Both Justice Potter Stewart and Justice Sandra Day O'Connor failed to fully grasp Madison's theories early in their careers on the Court. Yet, as time marched along, both of them came to have a better understanding of Madison and eventually embraced the spirit of Madison's thought. Although this transformation in thinking is more evident in O'Connor, it is also noticeable in the reasoning of Justice Stewart.

JUSTICE POTTER STEWART

Potter Stewart joined the Supreme Court in 1958 and remained there until 1981. While there, he usually was a swing vote on an often bitterly divided Court. With regard to his interpretation of Madison, Justice Stewart changed course in the middle of his term on the Court. Although he initially failed to grasp Madison's meaning, in later years Stewart got Madison right in a variety of cases.

The story of Justice Stewart's citations of Madison begins fairly early in his Supreme Court career in the case of *Engel v. Vitale* (1962). Recall that Justice Black accurately portrayed Madison's theory in this case dealing with a nondenominational prayer program in New York public schools. Dissenting from Black's majority opinion, Stewart did not see how such a prayer could violate the Establishment Clause. In support of his position, Stewart noted the public invocation of God by various presidents throughout U.S. history. As an example, Stewart placed the following in a footnote:

On March 4, 1809, President James Madison said: "But the source to which I look . . . is in . . . my fellow-citizens, and in the counsels of those representing them in the other departments associated in the care of the national interests. In these my confidence will under every difficulty be best placed, next to that which we have all been encouraged to feel in the guardianship and guidance of that Almighty Being whose power regulates the destiny of nations, whose blessings have been so conspicuously dispensed to this rising Republic, and to whom we are bound to address our devout gratitude for the past, as well as our fervent supplications and best hopes for the future."[1]

However, as noted above, Madison later explained that he did not want to make such references, and only did so after he was goaded into it. Upon careful reflection in his later years, Madison proclaimed that "[r]eligious proclamations by the Executive . . . imply a religious agency, making no part of the trust delegated to political rulers." Madison believed this because he saw the danger that government posed to religion if the two were not completely separated. Madison feared that religious strife could be instigated by having government involved in something as simple as a religious endorsement via a prayer. Thus, unlike his colleague Justice Black, Stewart's use of Madison in *Engel* is a bit shortsighted.

Justice Stewart also failed to comprehend Madison's theory in *Griswold v. Connecticut* (1965). In *Griswold,* the executive and medical directors of the Planned Parenthood League of Connecticut were convicted as accessories by giving information, instruction, and advice to married persons as to the means of preventing conception. At the time, Connecticut made the use of contraceptives, even by married couples, a criminal offense. The Court majority found that the statute was invalid as an unconstitutional invasion of the right of privacy of married persons.[2]

Writing in concurrence and dissent, Justice Arthur Goldberg and Justice Stewart, respectively, sparred over Madison's meaning when he introduced the Ninth Amendment. Justice Goldberg defended the Court's decision, and he volunteered an expansive reading of the Ninth Amendment:

> The Ninth Amendment reads, "The enumeration in the Constitution, of certain rights, shall not be construed to deny or disparage others retained by the people." The Amendment is almost entirely the work of James Madison. It was introduced in Congress by him and passed the House and Senate with little or no debate and virtually no change in language. It was proffered to quiet expressed fears that a bill of specifically enumerated rights could not be sufficiently broad to cover all essential rights and that the specific mention of certain rights would be interpreted as a denial that others were protected.[3]

Goldberg went on to cite a lengthy quote by Madison from his introduction of the Bill of Rights in Congress in 1789, before concluding as follows: "These statements of Madison . . . make clear that the Framers did not intend that the first eight amendments be construed to exhaust the basic and fundamental rights which the Constitution guaranteed to the people."[4]

However, Stewart disagreed with Goldberg on both the meaning of the Ninth Amendment and the use of Madison to defend such a position. According to Justice Stewart,

> The Court also quotes the Ninth Amendment, and my Brother GOLDBERG's concurring opinion relies heavily upon it. But to say that the Ninth Amendment has anything to do with this case is to turn somersaults with history. The Ninth Amendment, like its companion the Tenth, which this Court held "states but a truism that all is retained which has not been surrendered," was framed by James Madison and adopted by the States simply to make clear that the adoption of the Bill of Rights did not alter the plan that the Federal Government was to be a government of express and limited powers, and that all rights and powers not delegated to it were retained by the people and the individual States. Until today no member of this Court has ever suggested that the Ninth Amendment meant anything else.[5]

In the eyes of Stewart, the Ninth Amendment created no substantive rights to be enforced by the federal judiciary: "the idea that a federal court could ever use the Ninth Amendment to annul a law passed by the elected representatives of the people of the State of Connecticut would have caused James Madison no little wonder."[6]

Again, Justice Stewart was mistaken in his interpretation of Madison. One of Madison's greatest fears regarding a bill of rights was that something important might inadvertently be left off the list. If not on this list, a self-interested majority in Congress or a state legislature could try to violate that right. It was for this reason that Madison drafted the Ninth Amendment and charged judges as the "guardians" of such liberties. Madison was wary of the effects that a self-interested majority might have on the rights of a minority. If the limited virtue of the majority threatened to take away certain liberties, including ones not enumerated, the courts could step in and be the defenders of the minority. Thus, Goldberg was correct that Madison's idea behind penning the Ninth Amendment was to protect a group of rights that had not been enumerated in the first eight amendments to the Constitution, and Stewart missed this important point in Madison's political theory.

However, after his *Griswold* dissent, something changed in Stewart's thinking on Madison in Bill of Rights cases. Perhaps he began heeding the advice of his fellow justices on Madison, or perhaps he spent more time reading Madison's writings and speeches. Whatever the case, by the 1970s, Stewart began referring to Madison in ways that suggest he more fully understood Madison's philosophy.

One example is *Time, Inc. v. Pape* (1971). In this case, a police officer, Frank Pape, filed a libel lawsuit against *Time* for an article the magazine did on a report of the Civil Rights Commission. At one point, the article referred to civil rights complaints filed against certain Chicago policemen headed by Deputy Chief of Detectives Pape. *Time* magazine quoted from a summary of the complaint, without indicating that the charges were those of the complainant and not the independent findings of the Commission. The Supreme Court found no evidence of libel and upheld the First Amendment rights of *Time*.[7]

Writing for the majority, Stewart noted that the press must be given some leeway in reporting news stories; otherwise the government could effectively censor what is written. Part of this was premised on prior Supreme Court cases, which had narrowed the scope of libel law in the process of broadening the rights of the press. In doing this, Stewart noted that these prior cases were "premised on a recognition that, as Madison put it, 'Some degree of abuse is inseparable from the proper use of everything; and in no instance is this more true than in that of the press.'"[8] Stewart here recognized Madison's desire strongly to protect the press. Even though there is no question that some in the media will take advantage of an expanded press freedom, Madison thought it paramount to protect this freedom in the fullest latitude. By protecting a liberal right such as this, Madison saw generous secondary benefits to society, in that the people would be more aware of what their government was doing. Stewart caught on to Madison's line of thought in *Pape,* correctly spelling out Madison's stance on the freedom of the press.

Stewart's changed attitude on Madison can also be seen in *Abood v. Detroit Board of Education* (1977). *Abood* dealt with a Michigan "agency shop" law, in which every employee represented by a union, even though not a union member, was required to pay to the union a service fee equal in amount to union dues. An employee who did not meet this requirement could be fired. After a secret-ballot election, the Detroit Federation of Teachers (DFT) was certified as the exclusive representative of teachers employed by the Detroit Board of Education. Once DFT began implementing the agency shop law, several teachers filed a lawsuit, claiming that the law violated their freedom of association rights. The Court found that the agency shop clause was generally valid, but the Court also held that the teachers had the right to prevent the union from spending part of their required service fees to express ideological or political views unrelated to DFT's duties as an exclusive bargaining representative.[9]

Writing for the majority in *Abood,* Justice Stewart penned the following: "The fact that the appellants are compelled to make . . . contributions for political purposes [is] an infringement of their constitutional rights."[10] In a footnote, Stewart then explained, "This view has long been held. James Madison, the First Amendment's author, wrote in defense of religious liberty: 'Who does not see . . . [t]hat the same authority which can force a citizen to contribute three pence only of his property for the support of any one establishment, may force him to conform to any other establishment in all cases whatsoever?'"[11] Stewart once more captured the essence of Madisonian theory. While Madison's quote involved the tyranny of forcing one to contribute financially to a church in which they disbelieved, the sentiment applied equally for Madison to other First Amendment rights. Madison was distrustful of any governmental action that forced citizens to pay for ideas they did not believe in. Madison thought this was the slippery slope to taking more and more of citizens' money for a cause that the majority supported. His focus was religious establishments, but Madison held a similar position on government tilting the balance of power in political debates, which was evinced in his strong opposition to the Alien and Sedition Acts. Furthermore, Stewart was using Madison's statements about the freedom of religion to help protect other First Amendment rights, which was a practice that Madison routinely engaged in. Thus, Justice Stewart grasped some of the complexities of Madison's theory.

Justice Stewart did not cite Madison often in Bill of Rights cases. Though he only made use of Madison's writing six times in such cases, there was an evolution in his thought on Madison, where Stewart eventually figured out what Madison believed. For an even stronger progression on understanding Madison, one needs to turn to the justice who took Potter Stewart's seat on the Court upon his retirement: Justice O'Connor.

JUSTICE SANDRA DAY O'CONNOR

Sandra Day O'Connor sat on the Court from 1981 to 2006. O'Connor was the first woman to serve on the Supreme Court, and during her career she was a moderate justice and often a swing vote in narrowly divided cases. Similar to Potter Stewart, Justice O'Connor's understanding of Madison appears to have evolved over time. When she first took her seat on the Court, O'Connor improperly cited and quoted Madison to support theories on rights. However, during her service on the Court, owing either to the influence of other justices or to her own personal reflection, O'Connor eventually came to grasp Madison's political theory and understanding of human nature.

Take, for instance, a case from relatively early in O'Connor's career—
Tibbs v. Florida (1982). The facts of the case involve some complicated

legal technicalities that boil down to the following: the Court held that the Double Jeopardy Clause of the Fifth Amendment did not bar the retrial of an accused when an earlier conviction was reversed based on the weight, as opposed to the sufficiency, of the evidence.[12] In other words, an accused who successfully appealed a judgment against him based on the weight of the evidence could be tried again for the same offense. Writing for the majority, Justice O'Connor stated that past Supreme Court precedents "concluded that retrial after reversal of a conviction is not the type of governmental oppression targeted by the Double Jeopardy Clause."[13] O'Connor continued: "The rule also appears to coincide with the intent of the Fifth Amendment's drafters. James Madison's proposed version of the Double Jeopardy Clause provided that '[no] person shall be subject, except in cases of impeachment, to more than one punishment or one trial for the same offence.' . . . Madison's supporters explained that the language would not prevent a convicted defendant from seeking a new trial, and the House approved Madison's proposal."[14] O'Connor used as evidence Madison's proposal that became the Double Jeopardy Clause to prove that the Clause was intended to have a narrow interpretation for criminal defendants.

First, a note on O'Connor's resort to the proposed language of the Double Jeopardy Clause: Madison's relevant proposal regarding *Tibbs* was, "[n]o person shall be subject, except in cases of impeachment, to more than one punishment, or one trial for the same offence." Madison's draft was a broader protection of the rights of the accused than the clause as it was finally ratified: "nor shall any person be subject for the same offense to be twice put in jeopardy of life or limb." Indeed, Madison's proposal specifically stated that one could be "tried" only once by the government, with no exceptions. Madison's language would have prevented a second criminal trial for any reason, while the language as adopted could be interpreted to allow for a second prosecution if the defects with the first trial are deemed to not have actually put the accused "in jeopardy of life or limb," as was the case in *Tibbs*.

Madison's focus on the importance of a jury trial is telling here also, because Madison saw the trial by jury in criminal cases as a vital check on the power of the executive branch of government. Perhaps this was why Madison's proposed bill of rights included three separate provisions that specifically protected the right to a trial by jury in criminal cases. Allowing the government to subject one to more than one jury trial would be harassment, cheapening the right to a jury trial; hence, Madison proposed the Double Jeopardy Clause. Thus, there is nothing in Madison's proposals that necessarily supports O'Connor's invocation of Madison here.

More importantly for the present purposes, there is no evidence that O'Connor understood Madison's broader theory when she wrote her opinion in *Tibbs*. She failed to discuss the rights of the accused as a way to protect other rights, promote virtue, or enhance the public good. However, since *Tibbs* occurred relatively early in O'Connor's career on the Court, perhaps at this point she simply had not developed a comprehensive theory regarding Madison and the Bill of Rights. If this is correct, perhaps in this case O'Connor was simply using Madison's name as an appeal to authority.

An early Free Exercise Clause case in which O'Connor invoked Madison's name was *Lyng v. Northwest Indian Cemetery Protective Association* (1988). *Lyng* began when the U.S. Forest Service announced plans to complete a road between two California towns by building a six-mile connecting segment through an area within Six Rivers National Forest. The harvesting of timber, which had not previously been allowed, was also part of the proposal. Some Native Americans objected to the project because the area in question was used by members of three Native American tribes for many religious rituals. When the Forest Service decided to go ahead with the road construction anyway, the Native Americans sued the government, claiming a constitutional violation. The Court, however, held that the Free Exercise Clause did not prohibit the federal government from acting in this case.[15]

Writing for the majority, O'Connor avowed that "government simply could not operate if it were required to satisfy every citizen's religious needs and desires."[16] O'Connor continued to explain that the "Constitution does not, and courts cannot, offer to reconcile the various competing demands on government, many of them rooted in sincere religious belief, that inevitably arise in so diverse a society as ours. That task, to the extent that it is feasible, is for the legislatures and other institutions."[17] O'Connor cited *Federalist* 10 to support her position, as she claimed that this paper proposed that "the effects of religious factionalism are best restrained through competition among a multiplicity of religious sects."[18] O'Connor invoked Madison to support a neutrality-based decision on free exercise: instead of claiming that the Native Americans deserved an exemption from the normal operation of the law, O'Connor held that their free exercise rights were sufficiently protected by a law that applies to everyone and by their ability to lobby the legislature for a change in policy.

O'Connor's use of Madison was misplaced here, as she implied that Madison intended to leave religious freedom up to the market. While Madison was supportive of the market mechanism to sort out the best ideas, Madison was not enamored with leaving decisions about First Amendment *rights* up to the "market" of those comprising a majority in the legislature. Instead, Madison advocated protecting free exercise as a natural right, and because there would be valuable secondary benefits to such an approach. Madison believed this, in part, because he understood that there would be self-interested people in power who would attempt to take away the rights of minority religions. Thus, O'Connor's approach to Madison's theory—that Madison would have left a decision regarding the freedom of religion to the majority of a legislature—was misplaced.

O'Connor eventually rejected her neutrality-based approach to free exercise years later in *City of Boerne v. Flores* (1997). In *Boerne*, the Catholic archbishop of San Antonio applied for a building permit to enlarge a church in Boerne, Texas. Local zoning authorities denied the permit, relying on an ordinance governing historic preservation in a district which, they argued, included the church. The archbishop then filed a lawsuit challenging the permit denial. This case was heard after *Employment Division v. Smith* (discussed in chapters 1 and 7), a case in which the Court ended its decades-long accommodationist stance regarding free exercise. Thus, the Court majority dealt with the case under other constitutional provisions as well as a federal statute, the Religious Freedom Restoration Act of 1993.[19]

However, this did not stop Justices O'Connor and Scalia (see excerpts from Scalia's opinion below) from debating the relevant free exercise issues of the case. In a dissent, O'Connor used Madison's proposed amendment in the 1776 Virginia Provincial Convention as evidence that Madison supported an accommodationist vision of the Free Exercise Clause. O'Connor cited the fact that the original proposal for the Virginia Bill of Rights declared only "that all men should enjoy the fullest toleration in the exercise of religion, according to the dictates of conscience, unpunished and unrestrained by the magistrate, unless, under colour of religion, any man disturb the peace, the happiness, or safety of society."[20] However, O'Connor then stated that this weak proposal "did not go far enough for a 26-year-old James Madison,"[21] because he "objected first to [George] Mason's use of the term 'toleration,' contending that the word implied that the right to practice one's religion was a governmental favor, rather than an inalienable liberty."[22] Furthermore, O'Connor proclaimed that "Madison thought Mason's proposal countenanced too much state interference in religious matters, since the 'exercise of religion' would have yielded whenever it was deemed inimical to 'the peace, happiness, or safety of society.'"[23] O'Connor went on:

> Madison suggested the provision read instead: "That religion, or the duty we owe our Creator, and the manner of discharging it, being under the direction of reason and conviction only, not of violence or compulsion, all men are equally entitled to the full and free exercise of it, according to the dictates of conscience; and therefore that no man or class of men ought on account of religion to be invested with peculiar emoluments or privileges, nor subjected to any penalties or disabilities, unless under color of religion the preservation of equal liberty, and the existence of the State be manifestly endangered."[24]

Based on this, O'Connor stated that "under Madison's proposal, the State could interfere in a believer's religious exercise only if the State would otherwise 'be manifestly endangered,'" and that for Madison the idea of free exercise of religion "include[d] a right to be exempt from certain generally applicable laws."[25] O'Connor also emphasized Madison's "Memorial and Remonstrance": "By its very nature, Madison wrote, the right to free exercise is 'unalienable,' both because a person's opinion 'cannot follow the dictates of others,' and because it entails 'a duty toward the Creator.' Madison continued: 'This duty [owed the Creator] is precedent both in order of time and degree of obligation, to the claims of Civil Society.'"[26]

Finally, O'Connor summarized Madison's position on free exercise: "To Madison, then, duties to God were superior to duties to civil authorities. . . . The idea that civil obligations are subordinate to religious duty is consonant with the notion that government must accommodate, where possible, those religious practices that conflict with civil law."[27] In O'Connor's *Boerne* opinion, Madison wanted government to accommodate religious practices whenever feasible. In this case, O'Connor was consistent with Madison's theory. She saw Madison as supportive of a natural, unalienable right to practice one's faith, and of the idea that doing this would lead to the cultivation of virtue and the common good. Indeed, O'Connor had a fundamental change of heart regarding Madison and the Free Exercise Clause, moving from a neutrality-based position that misunderstood Madison to an accommodationist theory that embraced the ideas for which Madison stood.

Next, remember *McCreary,* where the Court held that Ten Commandments displays in two Kentucky courthouses violated the Establishment Clause. In this case, relatively late in O'Connor's career, she joined the Court's opinion but also wrote a concurrence. According to O'Connor, "the Religion Clauses were designed to safeguard the freedom of conscience and belief that those immigrants had sought. They embody an idea that was once considered radical: Free people are entitled to free and diverse thoughts, which government ought neither to constrain nor to direct."[28] In support of this proposition, O'Connor quoted Madison: "Our guiding principle has been James Madison's—that '[t]he Religion . . . of every man must be left to the conviction and conscience of every man.'"[29] In this case, O'Connor grasped much of Madison's theory. She understood Madison as supporting an individual right to religious freedom that was protected by a separationist form of disestablishment. In addition to seeing the interplay between the Religion Clauses, O'Connor explained another outgrowth of this type of disestablishment in the very next paragraph: "In the marketplace of ideas, the government has vast resources and special status. Government religious expression therefore risks crowding out private observance and distorting the natural interplay between competing beliefs."[30] Thus, O'Connor also understood Madison's love for the free market of ideas, including a free market of religious ideas, as a way to promote virtue (through private religious observance) and the common good (through the emergence of truth by the debate of ideas).

Finally, consider *Kelo v. City of New London* (2005). The dispute in this case was over the Fifth Amendment's Takings Clause ("nor shall private property be taken for public use, without just compensation"). In 1998, the pharmaceutical company Pfizer announced that it would build a $300 million research facility in New London, Connecticut. Shortly thereafter, the city council created an economic development plan that included purchasing residential land adjacent to the planned Pfizer facility, for the eventual building of a hotel, restaurants, and retail shopping stores. Property owners who did not sell to the city had their land condemned. Those property owners then filed suit, claiming a violation of the Takings Clause, specifically that their private property was being taken from them for private, not public, use. The Court majority in *Kelo* held that the city's economic redevelopment plan was constitutional because the plan served a "public purpose."[31]

Justice O'Connor vehemently dissented in *Kelo*. She claimed that the term "public use" in the Takings Clause should be narrowly defined, thereby putting a stronger limit on government power to seize property: "the Court today significantly expands the meaning of public use. It holds that the sovereign may take private property currently put to ordinary private use, and give it over for new, ordinary private use, so long as the new use is predicted to generate some secondary benefit for the public."[32] O'Connor then claimed that Madison would have opposed New London's practice:

> Any property may now be taken for the benefit of another private party, but the fallout from this decision will not be random. The beneficiaries are likely to be those citizens with disproportionate influence and power in the political process, including large corporations and development firms. As for the victims, the government now has license to transfer property from those with fewer resources to those with more. The Founders cannot have intended this perverse result. "That alone is a just government," wrote James Madison, "which impartially secures to every man, whatever is his own."[33]

O'Connor saw a broad definition of public use (or public purpose) as one that allows the government to give private property over to another private owner with no primary public benefit. Since O'Connor claimed this system would allow for abuse by the government in conjunction with corporations and development firms, she stated that Madison would have opposed this potentially biased system of property redistribution. Again, O'Connor accurately portrayed Madison's theory. She demonstrated an awareness that Madison wanted to protect liberal, individual property rights, and she appreciated Madison's wariness of allowing potentially self-interested persons in government too much authority to tinker with something as important as property rights.

When one examines all of Justice O'Connor's opinions on Madison and the Bill of Rights, one finds that she did not understand or was not influenced by Madison in early cases such as *Tibbs* and *Lyng*. However, before her tenure on the Court ended she had an accurate understanding of Madison. Indeed, by the 1990s O'Connor consistently invoked Madison in cases where she discussed rights as individual freedoms that protect one another as well as promoting virtue and the common good.

twelve

INCONSISTENTS

This chapter examines a sampling of the justices who sometimes make correct use of Madison yet at other times do not. They include Chief Justice Warren Burger, as well as Justices John Paul Stevens, Antonin Scalia, and Clarence Thomas. Their lack of consistency may be for any number of reasons. Perhaps they see Madison's theory only in some types of Bill of Rights cases but not others. Perhaps they are truly "name droppers" (see the next chapter) who just happen to randomly "drop" Madison's name—and in some cases they just happen to stumble upon the correct meaning of Madison's thought. Regardless of the reasons for their inconsistency, the justices in this chapter differ from those discussed in the two preceding chapters. These justices do not embrace Madison by articulating his theory every time they cite him; nor is there a progression of thought in these justices' thinking, where they move from lacking an understanding of Madison to eventually "getting" him. On the contrary, these justices are sometimes right and sometimes wrong on Madison's theory throughout their time on the Court. At the same time, the "inconsistents" are different from the name droppers of chapter 13 because they do sometimes appear to understand Madison.

CHIEF JUSTICE WARREN BURGER

Warren Burger sat on the Court from 1969 to 1986. He was largely a conservative vote on the Supreme Court, although less so than some of its other Nixon and Reagan appointees. Burger repeatedly cited and quoted Madison in various First Amendment cases throughout his career. However, he was not a devotee of Madison, as he misinterpreted Madison's theory on multiple occasions during his tenure. Likewise, he did not necessarily learn from Madison over time because some of his misconceptions occurred in cases later in his time as chief justice. Thus, he can best be characterized as inconsistent on Madison, as a few examples below demonstrate.

Wisconsin v. Yoder (1972) might be one of the most interesting cases to come before the Supreme Court. It involved Wisconsin's compulsory school-attendance law, which required children to attend public or private school until age 16. However, members of the Old Order Amish religion in the state declined to send their children, ages 14–15, to public school after they completed the eighth grade. The parents were charged with violating the law, and upon conviction they were each fined five dollars. The parents raised First Amendment objections to the law, claiming that their children's attendance at high school was contrary to the Amish religion, and that sending their children there would endanger their own salvation and that of their children. Upon review, the Court found for the parents, holding that the Free Exercise Clause required accommodation of the Amish religion and that state interests to the contrary did not outweigh the rights of the Amish.[1]

In *Yoder*, Chief Justice Burger wrote the majority opinion. In his reasoning, he made the following statement:

> Some States have developed working arrangements with the Amish regarding high school attendance. . . . However, the danger to the continued existence of an ancient religious faith cannot be ignored simply because of the assumption that its adherents will continue to be able, at considerable sacrifice, to relocate in some more tolerant State or country or work out accommodations under threat of criminal prosecution. Forced migration of religious minorities was an evil that lay at the heart of the Religion Clauses. See . . . Madison, Memorial and Remonstrance Against Religious Assessments.[2]

Burger's use of Madison here was consistent with Madison's political theory and beliefs on human nature. First, it emphasized one of Madison's major points about the freedom of religion—that it needed to be protected for minority groups against the possible exercise of power by an overbearing, self-interested majority. Second, its recognition of the threat to the very "existence" of a minority religion goes hand in hand with the Madisonian idea that one purpose of the freedom of religion was to protect the very survival of religion in its purest form from government intervention. Finally, it acknowledged that religious adherents should not need to work out accommodations of their faith with the government; instead, the Free Exercise Clause should automatically create that accommodation for them. There is no doubt that the chief justice made an appropriate citation to Madison in this case.

Burger's reference to Madison in *Yoder* becomes puzzling when you read his majority opinion a dozen years later in another case involving the Religion Clauses, *Lynch v. Donnelly* (1984). *Lynch* dealt with a holiday display by the City of Pawtucket, Rhode Island, which included a Santa Claus house, reindeer pulling Santa's sleigh, candy-striped poles, a Christmas tree, carolers, and a crèche. City residents and the ACLU sued on the grounds that the display violated the Establishment Clause. The Court, however, upheld the city's action.[3]

The chief justice, in defending the Court's decision, noted other official government action that involves religion, including religious proclamations. He cited President Washington's 1789 Thanksgiving proclamation, and then stated that "Presidents Adams and Madison also issued Thanksgiving Proclamations, as have almost all our Presidents."[4] Although it is true that Madison issued such proclamations as president, he later repudiated this practice, a point noted above. Failure to concede Madison's change of position was a bit of intellectual malpractice on the part of Burger. It missed Madison's concern about those in government exercising official power on religious matters to the detriment of certain religious groups.

Chief Justice Burger had inconsistencies in other areas of the First Amendment as well. For a case where he offered an accurate interpretation of Madison, one needs to look no further than *First National Bank v. Bellotti* (1978). *Bellotti* involved a Massachusetts statute that prohibited banks and business corporations from spending money to influence the vote on referenda. There was an exception in the law that allowed these businesses to spend money if a referendum was one "materially affecting" the business; otherwise, businesses were barred from spending funds on any state referendum. Businesses that wanted to oppose a referendum proposing a state graduated income tax filed a lawsuit, claiming that the statute violated their First Amendment rights. The Court ruled that the law was unconstitutional, finding that there was no compelling state interest that justified the prohibition of speech by corporations.[5]

The chief justice wrote a concurrence in *Bellotti*, in which he emphasized that the First Amendment protected everyone's rights, not just those of certain groups. Burger went on to stress that the "freedom of speech" protected more forms of expression than just speech: "The simplest explanation of the Speech and Press Clauses might be that the former protects oral communications; the latter, written. But the historical evidence does not strongly support this explanation."[6] According to Burger, James Madison's draft of the First Amendment and the slight modifications made to it in the First Congress were proof of this point:

> The first draft of what became the free expression provisions of the First Amendment, one proposed by Madison . . . read: "The people shall not be deprived or abridged of their right to speak, to write, or to publish their sentiments; and the freedom of the press, as one of the great bulwarks of liberty, shall be inviolable." . . . It seems likely that the Committee [of Eleven] shortened Madison's language preceding the semicolon in his draft to "freedom of speech" without intending to diminish the scope of protection contemplated by Madison's phrase; in short, it was a stylistic change.[7]

Burger's citation here of Madison works quite well. Madison conceived of the freedom of speech as a natural right; indeed, for Madison, this was a natural "property" that individuals possessed. Thus, the method that individuals wanted to use to express themselves was something Madison believed should be protected. Furthermore, Burger here has a full understanding of the historical record (something lacking in his opinion in *Lynch*). Consequently, Burger's use of Madison in this context reflects a comprehension of the man's theory.

Now compare Burger's statements about Madison and the freedom in speech in *Schad v. Mt. Ephraim* (1981), where the Court heard an appeal over a case involving a municipal ordinance that prohibited nude entertainment. An adult bookstore in the city installed a coin-operated mechanism permitting customers to watch a live dancer, usually nude, performing behind a glass panel. The bookstore was found guilty of violating the ordinance and fined. During the trial, the owners of the bookstore claimed that the ordinance violated the First Amendment, in that other, non-nude forms of live entertainment were permitted. When the case reached the Court, the majority ruled that there were no needs advanced by the city that justified the restriction on the bookstore.[8]

Writing in dissent in *Schad*, Burger opined the following:

> In Federalist Paper No. 51, Madison observed: "In framing a government which is to be administered by men over men, the great difficulty lies in this: you must first enable the government to control the governed; and in the next place oblige it to control itself." This expresses the balancing indispensable in all governing, and the Bill of Rights is one of the checks to control overreaching by government. But it is a check to be exercised sparingly by federal authority over local expressions of choice going to essentially local concerns. . . . To say that there is a First Amendment right to impose every form of expression on every community, including the kind of "expression" involved here, is sheer nonsense.[9]

There are some problems with Burger's understanding of Madison here. First, although Burger uses Madison's name in conjunction with the Bill of Rights and discusses the Bill of Rights as an important check on government "overreaching," Burger subsequently emphasizes his own point: that federal authority (the Supreme Court in this case) should be exercised sparingly over local governments. This completely ignores Madison's "most valuable amendment" and his concerns about freedom being breached by state power, as well as Madison's notion that judges should be "guardians of liberty." Second, Burger implies that communities, if they want, may place significant limits on the forms of expression that one utilizes. While Burger may have a valid point here, citing Madison to make that point is out of place. For Madison, the freedom of speech was a natural right that belonged to the individual. If it limited one's choices of expression, the government infringed upon this personal liberty. Thus, Burger's treatment of Madison in *Schad* is completely different from *Bellotti*.

Burger cited Madison in a total of 10 Bill of Rights cases, almost exclusively in cases related to First Amendment freedoms. Overall, Chief Justice Burger's record on citing Madison was varied. He was able to articulate Madison's theories in some cases, but not in others.

JUSTICE JOHN PAUL STEVENS

John Paul Stevens has served on the Supreme Court since 1975. Although named to the Court by Republican President Gerald Ford, Stevens has become one of the most ardent liberals on the country's highest judicial body. Like Chief Justice Burger, Justice Stevens is more of a mixed bag regarding Madison and the Bill of Rights. Either Stevens has been influenced by Madison's theory in only some areas of the Bill of Rights, or he has made use of Madison as an authority in cases where it was wholly inappropriate.

Stevens showed an understanding of Madison in *Van Orden v. Perry* (2005), the companion case to *McCreary*. *Van Orden* litigated a dispute on the 22 acres surrounding the Texas State Capitol. This area contains 17 monuments and 21 historical markers, including a monument six feet high and three and a half feet wide containing the text of the Ten Commandments. Thomas Van Orden, a Texas resident, sued the state, claiming that this monument violated the Establishment Clause. Upon review, the Court found that the Decalogue monument was constitutional, given the monument's history, context, and passive nature.[10]

Stevens dissented in *Van Orden,* and he opened his opinion by quoting from the Ten Commandments monument at issue, which begins by stating, "I AM the LORD thy God. Thou shalt have no other gods before me."[11] In response to other opinions in *Van Orden* that referenced Congress's appointment of chaplains as evidence of an early nonpreferentialist approach, Stevens proceeded to cite several writings by Madison, including a letter in which Madison stated that "Congress' appointment of Chaplains to be paid from the National Treasury was 'not with my approbation' and was a 'deviation' from the principle of 'immunity of Religion from civil jurisdiction.'"[12] Stevens trailed this Madison quote with the following one:

> Madison more than once repudiated the views attributed to him by many, stating unequivocally that with respect to government's involvement with religion, the "tendency to a usurpation on one side, or the other, or to a corrupting coalition or alliance between them, will be best guarded against by an entire abstinence of the Government from interference, in any way

whatever, beyond the necessity of preserving public order, & protecting each sect against trespasses on its legal rights by others."[13]

By emphasizing Madison's position as one where religion should be immune from civil jurisdiction and chaplains should not be appointed or paid by public funds, Stevens correctly characterized Madison as a separationist. Additionally, Stevens utilized quotes that emphasized Madison's realistic understanding of human nature: we need to be wary of allowing two large power conglomerates such as religion and government to combine, as this consolidation of influence could allow those with self-interested motives to be oppressive and interfere with the public good. Stevens also understood Madison's conception of various liberties in the Bill of Rights as reinforcing one another, as disestablishment would lead to the protection of the "legal rights" of every religious sect from one another's possibly corrupting influence.

A free speech and association case where Stevens found support from Madison was *McIntyre v. Ohio Elections Commission* (1990). This case arose owing to an Ohio statute that prohibited the distribution of anonymous campaign literature. Margaret McIntyre distributed leaflets opposing a proposed school tax levy. Some of the leaflets purported to express only the views of "CONCERNED PARENTS AND TAX PAYERS." Based on this, the Ohio Elections Commission imposed a $100 fine on Mrs. McIntyre. When this case reached the Supreme Court, the justices found the law to violate the freedom of speech.[14]

In the majority opinion, Justice Stevens stated, "On occasion, quite apart from any threat of persecution, an advocate may believe her ideas will be more persuasive if her readers are unaware of her identity. Anonymity thereby provides a way for a writer who may be personally unpopular to ensure that readers will not prejudge her message simply because they do not like its proponent."[15] Thus, Stevens defended the right of the individual to speak anonymously, even given the interest advanced by the state that "the statute under review is a reasonable regulation of the electoral process."[16] In support of his position that anonymity is protected by the First Amendment, Stevens cited Madison: "That tradition is most famously embodied in the *Federalist Papers,* authored by James Madison, Alexander Hamilton, and John Jay, but signed 'Publius.'"[17] Given that Stevens understood Madison's commitment to protecting the individual's right to exercise freedom of speech as he or she sees fit in *McIntyre,* Stevens portrayed Madison in a manner consistent with Madison's political theory. In addition, Stevens grasped the Madisonian idea that protecting this individual right would benefit the public good, by allowing readers of an anonymous tract to evaluate the quality of the ideas contained therein without giving the opportunity for pundits to attack the writer personally.

However, Stevens's understanding of Madison and First Amendment rights was less accurate in *California Democratic Party v. Jones* (2000). This case involved the California "blanket primary," whereby (1) anyone who was entitled to vote, including persons who were not registered members of any party, could vote for any candidate of any party for a given office, and (2) the candidate of each party who won the greatest number of votes became that party's nominee. Four political parties in California, each of which had party rules prohibiting persons who were not registered members of the parties from voting in their primaries, sued. The Supreme Court then ruled that the associational rights of political parties to select their nominees were violated by the blanket primary.[18]

In dissent, Justice Stevens defended the constitutionality of the blanket primary because he saw it as a state's way of furthering democracy, and he did not find a political party's right to association to be a compelling interest:

> Prominent members of the founding generation would have disagreed with the Court's suggestion that representative democracy is "unimaginable" without political parties. . . . At best, some members of that generation viewed parties as an unavoidable product of a free state that were an evil to be endured, though most viewed them as an evil to be abolished or suppressed. Indeed, parties ranked high on the list of evils that the Constitution was designed to check . . . see *The Federalist No. 10* (J. Madison).[19]

Stevens placed *Federalist* 10 at the center of a dominant political theory at the Founding, one which he claimed denounced parties as an "evil" that needed to be checked. Because he interpreted Madison's essay in this way, it helped Stevens justify a democracy-centered reading of the freedom of association for political parties. However, Madison believed that parties have rights to form as they wish without undue hindrance from the government. Under Madison's theory, government must be respectful of the natural rights of political party members. Inability to decide their own membership threatens parties' ability to assemble and collectively to choose the candidates that they think could best achieve their vision of the common good. Even though some of these parties may comprise persons solely seeking their own interests, Madison believed that protecting liberal association rights would enhance our elections by enabling more voices to advance new ideas. In this way, Stevens cited Madison out of context in his dissent.

Next, there is a notable free press case in which Stevens invoked Madison: *Houchins v. KQED* (1978). In *Houchins,* the Alameda County, California, sheriff (who runs the Alameda County Jail) refused a request from KQED to inspect and take pictures within the jail. Specifically, KQED wanted to report on a recent prisoner's suicide as well as stories about alleged rapes, beatings, and generally poor physical conditions. After being refused entry,

KQED sued the sheriff, claiming a constitutional right to report. The Court, however, held that the press had no First Amendment right of access to a jail greater than that of the public generally.[20]

Stevens dissented in *Houchins,* advancing his view that "the First Amendment serves an essential societal function. Our system of self-government assumes the existence of an informed citizenry."[21] Stevens continued:

> As Madison wrote: "A popular Government, without popular information, or the means of acquiring it, is but a Prologue to a Farce or a Tragedy; or, perhaps both. Knowledge will forever govern ignorance: And a people who mean to be their own Governors, must arm themselves with the power which knowledge gives." It is not sufficient, therefore, that the channels of communication be free of governmental restraints. Without some protection for the acquisition of information about the operation of public institutions such as prisons by the public at large, the process of self-governance contemplated by the Framers would be stripped of its substance.[22]

Thus, although Justice Stevens wanted to protect a broader press right under the First Amendment than the Court did in *Houchins,* Stevens emphasized the need to guard press rights *only* when it is in the best interest of democracy. However, under Madison's theory of the Bill of Rights members of the media have individual rights, and the amount of access they have should be based on this, not the ultimate societal good that may result. Stevens's reasoning differed from that of Madison in that Stevens focused on the protection of the press only when the press is acting to keep the democratic public informed. However, Madison reversed the equation, and he advocated protecting a liberal right to the press because it is a natural right. Madison believed that by protecting a liberal press right, a natural outgrowth would be a promotion of the public good in the long run via the press reporting information to the public, but Madison did *not* think that the press should be protected *only* when the result would be a more informed citizenry. For Madison, even if granting such a liberal freedom to the press would result in a few "noxious branches" taking advantage of their freedom and publishing trash (i.e., tabloids), on the whole society would be better served by an unrestrained press. In *Houchins,* Stevens's analysis was the opposite of Madison's.

However, in another case litigating the freedom of speech and the press, *Ft. Wayne Books v. Indiana,* Stevens evoked Madison in a way consistent with Madison's theory. In *Ft. Wayne Books,* the Court held that booksellers are liable to Indiana RICO prosecutions (similar to the RICO prosecution described in *Alexander*). The *Ft. Wayne Books* Court, however, also ruled that the seizure of allegedly obscene books and films before they were judicially determined to be obscene violated the First Amendment.[23]

In an opinion partially concurring with and partially dissenting from the majority, Stevens found that the Indiana law unconstitutionally "authorized wide-ranging civil sanctions against both protected and unprotected speech."[24] In support of this position, Stevens made the following statement, including a quote by Madison:

> Many sexually explicit materials are little more than noxious appendages to a sprawling media industry. . . . Indiana's RICO/CRRA statutes arm prosecutors not with scalpels to excise obscene portions of an adult bookstore's inventory but with sickles to mow down the entire undesired use. This the First Amendment will not tolerate. "[I]t is better to leave a few . . . noxious branches to their luxuriant growth, than, by pruning them away, to injure the vigour of those yielding the proper fruits."[25]

Stevens cited Madison to support a theoretical position compatible with Madison's political philosophy. Stevens recognized that it is better to protect the liberal right to possess expressive materials, which may include protecting sexually explicit materials, than it is to allow government the power to seize and punish a broad amount of media. Stevens recognized Madison's concern with limiting those in power as a way to protect against self-interested tyrants, and he acknowledged Madison's emphasis on protecting a liberal right in order to achieve the common good. Given the intersection of property rights and First Amendment rights in this case, Stevens's ability to grasp Madison's theory was especially important.

Finally, Stevens cited Madison in one Takings Clause case—*Lucas v. South Carolina Coastal Council* (1992). In 1986, David Lucas bought two residential lots on a South Carolina barrier island, intending to build single-family homes there. In 1988, however, the South Carolina legislature prohibited the building of any permanent habitable structures on an area that included Lucas's parcels. Lucas then filed suit against the state, contending that the ban on construction deprived him of all economically viable use of his property, making it a "taking" under the Fifth Amendment that required just compensation. The Supreme Court agreed with Lucas, finding that the Takings Clause had been violated by South Carolina.[26]

Stevens dissented in the case, claiming that "one of the central concerns of our takings jurisprudence is preventing the public from loading upon one individual more than his just share of the burdens of government. We have, therefore, in our takings law frequently looked to the generality of a regulation of property."[27] Stevens then explained, "This principle of generality is well rooted in our broader understandings of the Constitution as designed in part to control the 'mischiefs of faction.' See *The Federalist No. 10* . . . (J. Madison)."[28] For Stevens, Madison intended the Takings Clause to apply only if some members of the community were being forced by a faction to give up more than their fair share of property. However, a general regulation that applies to everyone would not be an unconstitutional taking under this understanding of the clause. Did Stevens appropriately apply Madisonian theory in *Lucas?*

Stevens's position on Madison and the Takings Clause is complicated, but largely consistent, with Madisonian theory. Property was a right that had special importance for Madison. He also wanted to protect property owners from an unpropertied majority that might try to redistribute their wealth. Madison feared that a self-interested majority might try to seize the land of the minority. For this reason, Stevens's focus on preventing government from "loading upon one individual more than his just share" when determining the constitutionality of a general regulation of property was consistent with a Madisonian analysis. In Madison's view, if government must regulate, what saved us from those in power tyrannically taking our property was that they must regulate all of us equally. In this sense, Stevens correctly identified Madison's fears of self-interested factions, based on Madison's understanding of human nature. Where Stevens is slightly incorrect in his use of Madison, however, is that what was at issue in *Lucas* was ultimately a regulation, not a physical taking of property. Madison's intent with the Takings Clause was only to prevent government from physically seizing property without just compensation. Indeed, Madison's original draft of the Takings Clause only required compensation if land were completely taken: "No person shall . . . be obliged to relinquish his property, where it may be necessary for public use, without a just compensation." Thus, although Stevens correctly understood Madison's general theory in *Lucas*, he applied his analysis to the wrong clause. The principle of generality would be more appropriate when interpreting the Due Process Clause, which under Madison's theory allows regulation and even deprivation of property as long as it conforms to due process.

The amount of influence that Madison has on Justice Stevens is questionable. In some areas, such as the Establishment Clause and property rights, Stevens has appropriately cited Madison and has largely understood Madison's political theory and conception of human nature. However, in areas of the First Amendment outside of the Religion Clauses, such as the freedoms of speech and press, Stevens has failed to consistently draw the connections he saw in other areas. This pattern holds throughout the 19 Bill of Rights cases where Stevens has cited Madison.

JUSTICE ANTONIN SCALIA

Antonin Scalia was appointed to the Court in 1986 by President Reagan. He is one of the Court's most outspoken conservatives. His method of constitutional interpretation is a mixture of textualism (similar to that of Justice

Hugo Black) and original meaning, which tries to decipher what reasonable persons alive when a provision of the Constitution was ratified thought it meant. He has frequently invoked Madison in Bill of Rights cases, but not always in ways consistent with Madison's theory. As demonstrated in the pages that follow, this leaves Justice Scalia in the same category of Chief Justice Burger and Justice Stevens.

In *Lee v. Weisman*, recall that the Court held unconstitutional a public school graduation ceremony in which the principal invited a member of the clergy to give prayers. In his *Lee* dissent, Scalia disagreed with the characterization of Madison as a separationist by Justice Kennedy in the Opinion of the Court. According to Scalia, "'A test for implementing the protections of the Establishment Clause that, if applied with consistency, would invalidate longstanding traditions cannot be a proper reading of the Clause.'"[29] Scalia proceeded to accuse the majority of "lay[ing to] waste a tradition that is as old as public school graduation ceremonies themselves, and that is a component of an even more longstanding American tradition of nonsectarian prayer to God at public celebrations generally."[30] Instead of citing Madison's "Memorial and Remonstrance" as Kennedy did, Scalia followed Justice Stewart in *Engel* and Chief Justice Burger in *Lynch*—he emphasized Madison's First Inaugural Address as evidence that Madison would have approved of the prayer at issue in *Lee*: "James Madison, in his first inaugural address, placed his confidence 'in the guardianship and guidance of that Almighty Being whose power regulates the destiny of nations, whose blessings have been so conspicuously dispensed to this rising Republic, and to whom we are bound to address our devout gratitude for the past, as well as our fervent supplications and best hopes for the future.'"[31] Thus, Scalia claimed that Madison's speech supported his accommodationist reading of the Establishment Clause in *Lee*.

However, much like Stewart and Burger, Scalia's reliance here on Madison was sorely misplaced. As noted above, Madison later renounced his presidential invocations of God. Madison claimed that such practices exacerbated the potential strife that could follow from religious differences. Madison believed that it could eventually lead to government unfairly bending public policy to support certain sects. Madison also thought that such proclamations were likely the result of religion having undue influence in government. Understanding humans to be primarily self-interested power-seekers, Madison disfavored those in government combining their power with religious institutions. Thus, Scalia's use of Madison in *Lee* was inconsistent with Madison's political theory and views on human nature, especially given how Madison subsequently rejected his own proclamation.

Turning to Free Exercise Clause concerns, Justice Scalia wrote a concurring opinion in *Boerne*, and he cited Madison as supporting his position. Scalia debated the merits and demerits of the Court's recent approach to the clause with Justice O'Connor (whose opinion in this case is cited above). In Scalia's defense of a neutrality-based reading of the Clause, he cited Madison as supporting his position. Scalia claimed that Madison's "Memorial and Remonstrance" did "not argue that the assessment would violate the 'free exercise' provision in the Virginia Declaration of Rights."[32] Instead, according to Scalia, in his "Memorial and Remonstrance" Madison "argues that the assessment wrongly placed civil society ahead of personal religious belief and, thus, should not be approved by the legislators."[33] For Scalia, "There is no reason to think [the statements of Madison and others] were meant to describe what was constitutionally required (and judicially enforceable), as opposed to what was thought to be legislatively or even morally desirable."[34] Even though Madison made accommodationist arguments in his "Memorial and Remonstrance," Scalia understood this as Madison supporting only what he thought was good policy. For Scalia, Madison's statements did not contradict a neutrality-based understanding of free exercise rights under the Constitution.

However, Madison maintained a strong accommodationist position throughout his political career. Since Madison believed that the freedom of religion was a natural right, it was also something he wanted protected against all governments at all times, not left up to legislators. By characterizing Madison's position on free exercise as solely a policy argument for legislators, Scalia misconstrued Madison's commitment to natural rights. In addition, Scalia failed to grasp Madison's fear of tyrannical majorities. Given Madison's realistic understanding of human nature, Madison believed that religious freedom needed constitutional protection so that self-interested majorities would not take away the rights of minorities. All of this was lost on Scalia in *Boerne*.

Now take *Locke v. Davey* (2004), a case involving the Washington State "Promise Scholarship" program, which was created to help students from low- and middle-income families pay for college. However, since the Washington constitution prohibited state funds from being used for religious instruction, the scholarship program did not offer financial assistance to students pursuing a degree in theology. Theology major Joshua Davey, who otherwise qualified for the scholarship, was denied funding. Davey sued, claiming that his free exercise rights had been violated. In *Locke*, the Court held that denying scholarships to students pursuing degrees in theology was constitutional.[35]

In his *Locke* dissent Justice Scalia maintained a neutrality approach to free exercise rights, which he claimed was reason enough to find the program unconstitutional: "When the State makes a public benefit generally available, that benefit becomes part of the baseline against which burdens on religion are measured; and when the State withholds that benefit from some individuals solely on the basis of religion, it violates the Free Exercise

Clause no less than if it had imposed a special tax."[36] In defense of this proposition, Scalia cited Madison as a supporter of the neutrality approach, for, in Scalia's opinion, Madison and others did not oppose

> the inclusion of religious ministers in public benefits programs like the one at issue here, but laws that singled them out for financial aid. For example, the Virginia bill at which Madison's Remonstrance was directed provided: "[F]or the support of Christian teachers . . . [a] sum payable for tax on the property within this Commonwealth, is hereby assessed." . . . One can concede the Framers' hostility to funding the clergy specifically, but that says nothing about whether the clergy had to be excluded from benefits the State made available to all.[37]

In other words, Scalia understood Madison's "Memorial and Remonstrance" to place the clergy on a plane equal to that of all others, which is consistent with Scalia's neutrality approach to free exercise questions.

Given Madison's understanding of human nature, government funding to religion presents special problems. Scalia was right to make the connection in Madison's theory that was opposed to government selectively giving funds to one religious group and not others. However, Scalia glossed over Madison's fear that *any* government funding to religion could be damaging to religion, government, and the common good. The latter concern was more at issue in *Locke* than the former one: Washington State's approach was to refrain from funding any religious group, while Scalia's approach would have provided direct government funding for the training of ministers. Scalia did not seem aware of Madison's desire to have strong disestablishment as a way to reinforce free exercise rights. Thus, while Scalia found a thread of Madison's theory in *Locke,* he neglected to mention another important part of Madison's political philosophy.

Another First Amendment case example involving Justice Scalia is the *Austin* case cited earlier. Remember that in this case the Court held constitutional a state law prohibiting corporations from using their treasury funds for independent expenditures in support of, or in opposition to, any candidate in elections for state office. Like Justice Kennedy, Scalia dissented, rejecting the majority's approach to free speech: "the Court today endorses the principle that too much speech is an evil that the democratic majority can proscribe."[38] Scalia continued: "I dissent because that principle is contrary to our case law and incompatible with the absolutely central truth of the First Amendment: that government cannot be trusted to assure, through censorship, the 'fairness' of political debate."[39] Scalia then cited Madison in support:

> I doubt that those who framed and adopted the First Amendment would agree that avoiding the New Corruption, that is, calibrating political speech to the

degree of public opinion that supports it, is even a desirable objective, much less one that is important enough to qualify as a compelling state interest. Those Founders designed, of course, a system in which popular ideas would ultimately prevail; but also, through the First Amendment, a system in which true ideas could readily become popular. For the latter purpose, the calibration that the Court today endorses is precisely backwards: To the extent a valid proposition has scant public support, it should have wider rather than narrower public circulation. I am confident, in other words, that Jefferson and Madison would not have sat at these controls; but if they did, they would have turned them in the opposite direction.[40]

Here, Scalia accurately portrayed Madison's ideas, rejecting a democracy-centered approach to the First Amendment in the process. Madison wanted a broad, liberal protection for free speech rights in part because it would allow people to hear a multitude of voices and to learn from and succumb to great ideas. Madison believed that government existed to protect an individual right such as the freedom of speech, not that the right existed at the whim of the government. Madison's theory is all the more relevant in this case where the "speech" was expressed through dispensing money, as it involved the mutual reinforcement of First Amendment rights and property rights. Although Scalia did not discuss this last point, he at least discovered Madison's liberalism regarding the freedom of speech.

In *Lucas*, a case involving the Takings Clause, Justice Scalia wrote for the majority and cited Madison. Scalia specifically targeted the dissent of Justice Blackmun, who argued that "James Madison, author of the Takings Clause, apparently intended it to apply only to direct, physical takings of property by the Federal Government."[41] Scalia stated that Blackmun's discussion of the early history of the Clause "is largely true, but entirely irrelevant."[42] Indeed, Scalia agreed that Madison wanted only to prohibit physical seizure of land, not regulatory takings:

> JUSTICE BLACKMUN is correct that early constitutional theorists did not believe the Takings Clause embraced regulations of property at all, but even he does not suggest (explicitly, at least) that we renounce the Court's contrary conclusion. . . . Since the text of the Clause can be read to encompass regulatory as well as physical deprivations[,] in contrast to the text originally proposed by Madison, ("No person shall be . . . obliged to relinquish his property, where it may be necessary for public use, without a just compensation"), we decline to do so as well.[43]

For Scalia, it was perfectly obvious that when Madison proposed the initial language of the Takings Clause he did not intend for it to apply to regulatory takings. However, this original intent of Madison was irrelevant to Scalia, as the final text of the Fifth Amendment can be read as requiring compensation for regulatory takings.

Did Scalia properly characterize Madison? Yes. First, Scalia correctly cited Madison's original proposal. In Madison's early thoughts on the topic in 1785, he wrote about prohibiting the government "from seizing private property," which implies that the government would have to seize the land physically in order to rise to the level of a taking.[44] Likewise, Madison's draft of the Takings Clause in Congress used the word "relinquish," implying that Madison did not personally think a regulation should require compensation. This interpretation of Madisonian theory is consistent with a liberal understanding of rights, as the government is instituted to protect our property and must compensate us for taking it. However, there is no evidence that Madison opposed all regulation of property, and nothing in Madison's statements or political theory implied that Madison wanted government to provide compensation for a regulation. Thus, Scalia noticed Madison's liberal commitment to property rights as well as the limits that Madison had for property rights.

Finally, Justice Scalia took a narrow approach to the rights of the accused in *Harmelin v. Michigan* (1991), and he used Madison to support his position. Ronald Harmelin was convicted of possessing 672 grams of cocaine. Under Michigan law, possessing anymore than 650 grams of cocaine mandates a prison sentence of life without possibility of parole, which is what Harmelin received. Harmelin appealed, claiming that this mandatory sentence violated his Eighth Amendment right against cruel and unusual punishment because the punishment received was not proportional to the crime committed. The Court upheld his sentence.[45]

In his opinion, Scalia expressed the view that the Eighth Amendment contains no proportionality guarantee because while "[s]evere mandatory penalties might be cruel . . . they are not unusual in the constitutional sense, having been employed in various forms throughout our Nation's history."[46] For Scalia, "to use the phrase 'cruel and unusual punishment' to describe a requirement of proportionality would have been an exceedingly vague and oblique way of saying what Americans were well accustomed to saying more directly."[47] Scalia then went on to cite some early state constitutions that had a requirement of proportionality in addition to their respective prohibitions on cruel and unusual punishment (New Hampshire's 1784 Bill of Rights and the 1802 Ohio Constitution).[48] In support of his nonproportionality position on the Eighth Amendment, Justice Scalia implied that Madison knew of these provisions but refrained from using the term "proportionality" when drafting the Eighth Amendment: "Printed collections of State Constitutions were available to the Founders, see . . . [*The Federalist*]

No. 47, pp. 304–307 [(C. Rossiter ed. 1961)] (J. Madison) (comparing constitutions of all 13 States)."[49] Thus, Scalia used Madison's knowledge of state constitutions as evidence that Madison could have made the Cruel and Unusual Punishment Clause more protective of the rights of the accused by including a separate proportionality clause in his draft bill of rights. That Madison could have done this but did not was evidence for Scalia that Madison and the other Framers did not intend the Eighth Amendment to have a proportionality component.

First, Justice Scalia's use of evidence in *Harmelin* merits special consideration. Madison wrote *Federalist* 47 in 1788. Therefore, it was unreasonable for Scalia to claim Madison knew of a provision in the Ohio Constitution that did not exist until 1802. Scalia's insinuation that Madison had given a close reading to the New Hampshire Constitution before he wrote *Federalist* 47 is equally disingenuous. In that essay, Madison cited the respective constitutions of each state to make a specific argument regarding the separation of powers among the legislative, executive, and judicial departments. It had nothing to do with punishments.[50] Thus, there is no direct evidence that Madison specifically studied either the New Hampshire or Ohio constitutions' relevant clauses, either before or after he contributed to *The Federalist*.

Second, and more relevant for the present purposes, Scalia invoked Madison to represent a position that was inconsistent with Madison's avowed political theory. Madison believed in a natural, unalienable right to life, liberty, and property. Thus, government must have a great justification before taking away one's liberty or life. In addition, using either of Madison's justifications of liberalism, the punishment given to Harmelin would raise serious issues. Indeed, if an individual is capable of doing virtuous things, then having him in prison for the rest of his natural life either will hinder his ability to achieve virtue, or it will keep him from using his virtue for good. And if an individual is incapable of virtue, then if free he or she could contribute more to society by doing things such as working and spending the money he or she earns, which is much more than one could contribute by sitting in a prison cell. This is why Madison opposed excessive punishments that took away one's ability to contribute to the community, but such analysis is absent from Scalia's opinion when he made reference to Madison.

Overall, Scalia's record is inconsistent with Madison in the 12 Bill of Rights cases where he cites the Father of the Constitution. Scalia appears to understand Madisonian theory in freedom of speech and takings cases, but Madison's theory has been largely lost on Scalia in cases dealing with religion or the rights of the accused. In these latter cases, discussions about virtue, the common good, rights reinforcing each other, and a realistic understanding of human nature are wholly lacking when Scalia refers to Madison.

JUSTICE CLARENCE THOMAS

Clarence Thomas arrived on the Supreme Court in 1991. Like Justice Scalia, Justice Thomas has become a regular conservative vote, perhaps the most conservative justice in recent history. Also like his colleague Scalia, Thomas has largely adopted originalism as his method of constitutional interpretation. And much like Scalia, Thomas uses Madison inconsistently in Bill of Rights cases. Sometimes he uses Madison correctly and sometimes not. At times, he appears to be projecting two different theoretical visions of Madison in the same opinion.

Take *Rosenberger*, where Thomas joined the Court's opinion in full but wrote separately to express his disagreement with the historical analysis in Souter's dissent. According to Thomas, the Virginia assessment controversy was not necessarily "indicative of the principles embodied in the Establishment Clause," and even if it were, the controversy over the bill was that the "assessment was to be imposed for the support of clergy in the performance of their function of teaching religion."[51] In other words, Thomas believed that the Virginia assessment was not opposed for separationist reasons, but for nonpreferentialist ones, as most objectors did not want to see certain religious proselytizing funded by the government at the exclusion of other religious groups. Thomas's proof of this was Madison's opposition to the Virginia assessment. Thomas claimed that Madison did not oppose the tax in principle in his "Memorial and Remonstrance," but only because it did not treat all religions equally:

> Contrary to the dissent's suggestion, Madison's objection to the assessment bill did not rest on the premise that religious entities may never participate on equal terms in neutral government programs. Nor did Madison embrace the argument that forms the linchpin of the dissent: that monetary subsidies are constitutionally different from other neutral benefits programs. Instead, Madison's comments are more consistent with the neutrality principle that the dissent inexplicably discards. According to Madison, the Virginia assessment was flawed because it "violated that equality which ought to be the basis of every law."[52]

Thomas then repeated the following line from the "Memorial and Remonstrance": "Who does not see that the same authority which can establish Christianity, in exclusion of all other Religions, may establish with the same ease any particular sect of Christians, in exclusion of all other Sects."[53] For Thomas, the focus of Madison's "Memorial and Remonstrance" was that the chief flaw of the religious "tax" was its unequal application among different sects. To the extent that one can find separationist sentiment in Madison's work, Thomas stated the following: "Even if more extreme notions of the separation of church and state can be attributed to Madison, many of them clearly stem from 'arguments reflecting the concepts of natural law, natural rights, and the social contract between government and a civil society,' rather than the principle of nonestablishment in the Constitution."[54] According to Thomas, since the "Memorial and Remonstrance" was written before the First Amendment was ratified, any argument that Madison made that the religious assessment was a violation of natural law was no longer relevant after ratification. Thomas then concluded: "Even if Madison believed that the principle of nonestablishment of religion precluded government financial support for religion per se (in the sense of government benefits specifically targeting religion), there is no indication that at the time of the framing [of the Bill of Rights] he took the dissent's extreme view that the government must discriminate against religious adherents by excluding them from more generally available financial subsidies."[55] For Thomas, Madison was a nonpreferentialist, and to the extent that there were separationist strands of thought in his earlier work, it is irrelevant. Indeed, Thomas even stated of Madison that "the views of one man do not establish the original understanding of the First Amendment."[56]

Thomas's understanding of Madison in *Rosenberger* is a bit of a mixed bag. On one hand, Thomas correctly recognized that Madison advocated an approach to religious freedom questions that emphasized natural rights and the social contract. However, Thomas failed to grasp the relevance of Madison's views on the realism of human nature as it related to the government giving funds to a majority religious group. The strife that would be inimical to the common good and the loss of virtue due to potential government corruption of religion were also themes in Madison's thought that escaped Thomas in *Rosenberger*. Thomas also failed to draw the important link in Madison's thought between protecting free exercise and free speech rights. Finally, Thomas mistakenly implied that Madison had changed his views on disestablishment between the Virginia assessment controversy and the framing of the Establishment Clause. As shown above, Madison maintained a consistency in his beliefs about religious freedom during that entire period, and long after.

Thomas's inability to grasp Madisonian theory regarding the Establishment Clause was confirmed in *Elk Grove Unified School District v. Newdow* (2004). The *Newdow* case gained national attention because it involved an atheist father of a child who attended a public school in California. The father objected to his daughter sitting through class each day where the Pledge of Allegiance was recited—the father's main objection was the phrase "under God" contained within the Pledge. The Ninth Circuit Court of Appeals found for the father, holding that the Establishment Clause was violated by the school district requirement that students recite the Pledge in school every day. However, the Supreme Court found that *Newdow* lacked standing to bring the suit forward on behalf of his minor daughter.

Newdow was not married to the mother of the child in question, nor was he the custodial parent. Furthermore, the child's mother held no objections to her daughter's presence in class where the Pledge is recited. Thus, the Court did not deal with the ultimate issue presented in the *Newdow* case—whether the school district's requirement of beginning each day with the Pledge violates the First Amendment.[57]

Even though the Court did not answer the constitutional question in *Newdow,* Thomas wrote a concurring opinion on this issue. Thomas quoted his *Rosenberger* concurrence (including some of his Madison quotations) while making a bold assertion that threatened to upend more than a half century of settled law: "I would acknowledge that the Establishment Clause is a federalism provision, which, for this reason, resists incorporation."[58] For Thomas, the Establishment Clause was "intended to prevent Congress from interfering with state establishments."[59] Instead of seeing the Establishment Clause as protecting an individual right against the federal government establishing religion to the detriment of the citizen, Thomas sees it as restricting the federal government from interfering with state religious establishments. Since no individual right is protected by the clause in Thomas's eyes, the right cannot be incorporated by the Fourteenth Amendment.

Using Madison to justify such an argument is untenable. Madison had strong objections to any type of religious establishment, whether it was by the national or a state government. Madison saw the freedom of religion and disestablishment as two sides of the same coin, as rights that mutually reinforced each other. Defending state religious establishments is far afield of Madison's true position.

Moving on to other areas of the First Amendment, Justice Thomas concurred in *McIntyre,* a case where the Court found an Ohio statute prohibiting the distribution of anonymous campaign literature to violate the freedom of speech. Continuing Stevens's theme that unsigned publications are protected by the First Amendment, Thomas stated that "[t]he use of anonymous writing extended to issues as well as candidates . . . James Madison and Alexander Hamilton, for example, resorted to pseudonyms in the famous 'Helvidius' and 'Pacificus' debates over President Washington's declaration of neutrality in the war between the British and French."[60] Certainly, Madison's contributions to public debate as "Helvidius" are consistent with his approach to protecting liberal rights because they are natural and inalienable, and because doing so would benefit the common good. Thomas may have grasped that this is an expressive right that Madison did not think should ever be taken away by government, but it is unclear based on the reasoning he used. Thomas referred to Madison's writings, but Thomas did not attempt to reveal any theory that Madison had behind them, nor did he argue any political theory in his concurrence beyond the proposition that "[w]e should seek the original understanding when we interpret the Speech and Press Clauses."[61]

Thomas also explored Madison's political theory in his *Nixon v. Shrink Missouri Government PAC* (2000). The *Nixon* case began with a Missouri law that limited campaign contributions to $1,075 for state political candidates. Shrink Missouri Government PAC gave a candidate for state auditor, Zev David Fredman, the maximum amount allowed by law. The PAC then filed a lawsuit, claiming it would have given Fredman more money if that had been legal. The Court, however, held the law constitutional under the rationale that this prevented corruption and the appearance of corruption.[62]

Justice Thomas disagreed in *Nixon,* and he quoted Madison in the process:

> The Founders sought to protect the rights of individuals to engage in political speech because a self-governing people depends upon the free exchange of political information. And that free exchange should receive the most protection when it matters the most—during campaigns for elective office. "The value and efficacy of [the right to elect the members of government] depends on the knowledge of the comparative merits and demerits of the candidates for public trust, and on the equal freedom, consequently, of examining and discussing these merits and demerits of the candidates respectively."[63]

Thomas took a democracy-centered stance on free speech rights by stating that we protect the freedom of speech to the extent that it is good for democracy. At the same time, however, Thomas characterized this as an individual right. Thomas then offered an interpretation of *Federalist* 10 that strongly supported liberal associational rights. Thomas stated that

> Presumably, the majority does not mean that politicians should be free of attachments to constituent groups. . . . The Framers of course thought such attachments inevitable in a free society and that faction would infest the political process. As to controlling faction, James Madison explained, "There are again two methods of removing the causes of faction: the one, by destroying the liberty which is essential to its existence; the other, by giving to every citizen the same opinions, the same passions, and the same interests." Contribution caps are an example of the first method, which Madison contemptuously dismissed: "It could never be more truly said than of the first remedy that it was worse than the disease. Liberty is to faction what air is to fire, an aliment without which it instantly expires. But it could not be a less folly to abolish liberty, which is essential to political life, because it nourishes faction than it would be to wish the annihilation of air, which is essential to animal life, because it imparts to fire its destructive agency."[64]

For Thomas, Madison would have disavowed contribution caps because it violates our liberal freedom to "speak" and "associate" through campaign donations. Thomas concluded by citing Madison again: "The Framers preferred a political system that harnessed such faction for good, preserving liberty while also ensuring good government. Rather than adopting the repressive 'cure' for faction that the majority today endorses, the Framers armed individual citizens with a remedy. 'If a faction consists of less than a majority, relief is supplied by the republican principle, which enables the majority to defeat its sinister views by regular vote.'"[65]

Thomas asserted that Madison believed government should not try to "destroy liberty" by limiting the ability of individuals to form groups to interact with politicians and engage in elective politics. Instead, freedom to form groups and associate with others should be preserved. If there truly are minority groups that are inimical to the public good, then the majority of voters will achieve victory in the next election and remove from office any corrupt politicians who are tied to these groups. Overall, Thomas made use of Madison in these last two passages to support an individual, liberal position regarding First Amendment rights.

There is at least some support for the idea that Thomas understood Madison here, though he applied Madison's theory a bit haphazardly. Certainly, Thomas made a claim that the rights at stake in *Nixon* were individual ones to speak and to associate. He also identified that Madison had multiple objectives when protecting rights: (1) "preserving liberty" for its own sake; (2) "ensuring good government," which could be interpreted to mean protecting rights to lead to the cultivation of virtue in politicians; and (3) "harness[ing] such faction for good," even when some of these factions may be acting out of self-interest. This seems to be a comprehensive understanding of Madison's political theory. However, in the first quote above Thomas reversed Madison's equation by claiming these rights are to be protected only to the extent that they are "political speech" that fosters democratic governance. Madison, though, believed that we first protect a natural right to freedoms of speech and association because this is why government was instituted, and Madison further believed that a natural outgrowth of this would be an increase in valuable information during elections. While there is some evidence that Thomas understood Madison in *Nixon,* Thomas was not completely consistent in his treatment of Madison.

In *Kelo,* Justice Thomas cited Madison in dissent to support his claim that Madison intended the term "public use" in the Takings Clause to be narrowly defined, therefore putting a stronger limit on government power to seize property. According to Thomas, the *Kelo* "decision is simply the latest in a string of our cases construing the Public Use Clause to be a virtual nullity, without the slightest nod to its original meaning. In my view, the Public Use Clause, originally understood, is a meaningful limit on the government's eminent domain power."[66] Thomas then explained why he held this position:

Though one component of the protection provided by the Takings Clause is that the government can take private property only if it provides "just compensation" for the taking, the Takings Clause also prohibits the government from taking property except "for public use." Were it otherwise, the Takings Clause would either be meaningless or empty. If the Public Use Clause served no function other than to state that the government may take property through its eminent domain power—for public or private uses—then it would be surplusage. Alternatively, the Clause could distinguish those takings that require compensation from those that do not. That interpretation, however, would permit private property to be taken or appropriated for private use without any compensation whatever. In other words, the Clause would require the government to compensate for takings done "for public use," leaving it free to take property for purely private uses without the payment of compensation. This would contradict a bedrock principle well established by the time of the founding: that all takings required the payment of compensation.[67]

According to Thomas, Madison would have opposed this type of "nullification" of the public use requirement, because in one of his "Property" essays Madison "argu[ed] that no property 'shall be taken *directly* even for public use without indemnification to the owner.'"[68] Thomas here interpreted Madison's statement as support for a strict requirement of public use, thus disallowing both (1) takings for private use, and (2) takings for public use that failed to offer just compensation. Thomas understood Madison when he penned his *Kelo* opinion. Madison wanted property rights, as a type of natural rights, to be vigorously protected against government infringement. Madison also wrote the Takings Clause because he feared the government seizure of property (as opposed to the regulation of property), which Thomas recognized.

Finally, Thomas wrote a concurrence in *United States v. Hubbell* (2000), a case dealing with the act of production doctrine. In the course of the Independent Counsel's investigation of President Bill Clinton's involvement with the Whitewater Development Corporation, information was uncovered that led to the former Associate Attorney General Webster Hubbell being charged with mail fraud and tax evasion. In *Hubbell,* the Court held that Hubbell's act of producing documents to the Independent Counsel had a testimonial aspect, the details of which are not important for the present purposes. However, according to the majority, Hubbell could not be compelled to produce the requested documents without first receiving a grant of immunity under federal law. Put another way, someone compelled to turn over incriminating papers or other physical evidence pursuant to a subpoena may invoke his or her Fifth Amendment privilege against self-incrimination if the act of producing that evidence would contain testimonial features. Based on this ruling, the Court dismissed the indictment against Hubbell.[69]

In his concurrence, Thomas stated that he joined the Court's opinion on the act of production doctrine but wrote separately because "this doctrine may be inconsistent with the original meaning of the Fifth Amendment's Self-Incrimination Clause. A substantial body of evidence suggests that the Fifth Amendment privilege protects against the compelled production not just of incriminating testimony, but of any incriminating evidence."[70] According to Thomas,

> [D]uring ratification of the Federal Constitution, the four States that proposed bills of rights put forward draft proposals employing similar wording for a federal constitutional provision guaranteeing the right against compelled self-incrimination. Each of the proposals broadly sought to protect a citizen from "being compelled to give evidence against himself." Similarly worded proposals to protect against compelling a person "to furnish evidence" against himself came from prominent voices outside the conventions.[71]

Thomas then used Madison as part of the foundation of his argument:

> In response to such calls, James Madison penned the Fifth Amendment. In so doing, Madison substituted the phrase "to be a witness" for the proposed language "to give evidence" and "to furnish evidence." But it seems likely that Madison's phrasing was synonymous with that of the proposals. The definitions of the word "witness" and the background history of the privilege against self-incrimination, both discussed above, support this view. And this may explain why Madison's unique phrasing—phrasing that none of the proposals had suggested—apparently attracted no attention, much less opposition, in Congress, the state legislatures that ratified the Bill of Rights, or anywhere else.[72]

Essentially, Thomas claimed that Madison's proposal for the Fifth Amendment did not differ in substance from what others in the 1780s wanted to protect—a privilege not just against compelled production of incriminating testimony but against production of *any* incriminating evidence. Again, Thomas correctly assessed Madison's theory, as it is a strong protection of the rights of the accused to protect other rights. In particular, Thomas emphasized the need to have criminal procedural rights to reinforce First Amendment rights to freedom of speech and press as well as property rights to documents.

Overall, Justice Thomas has used Madison in seven Bill of Rights cases. With regard to property rights and the rights of the accused, Thomas is able to cite Madison within context quite well. In cases involving First Amendment freedoms, however, Thomas has had less success. With the Establishment Clause in particular, Thomas has missed the mark completely in his interpretation of Madison. Overall, though, Thomas has employed Madison accurately multiple times, earning him a place in the "inconsistent" category. He is not merely a "name dropper," a category explored in the next chapter.

thirteen

NAME DROPPERS

The justices in this chapter cited Madison in Bill of Rights cases on repeated occasions, but they also made reference to Madison in ways incompatible with Madison's political theory or his view of human nature, or both. They include Justice Felix Frankfurter, Justice Robert Jackson, and Chief Justice William Rehnquist. Although there may be a case here and there where each of these justices managed to comprehend Madison's theory, on the whole each one failed in this endeavor. It is impossible to tell whether these justices fundamentally misunderstood Madison, or if they knew they were misquoting him and just wanted to appeal to Madison as an authority figure on the Bill of Rights. What is clear, however, is that the justices below cited and quoted Madison inappropriately and out of context.

JUSTICE FELIX FRANKFURTER

Felix Frankfurter served on the U.S. Supreme Court from 1939 to 1962. Although personally a liberal and appointed by Democratic President Franklin Roosevelt, on the Court Frankfurter became an advocate of judicial restraint, viewing the Court's role as limited, especially with regard to the other two branches of the federal government. Throughout his Court career, Justice Frankfurter was a consistent moderate. Frankfurter's references to Madison occurred throughout his time on the Court, but it was regularly marked with a misunderstanding of Madison's vision.

For an early example of Frankfurter's inability to grasp Madison's theory, take his majority opinion in *Minersville School District v. Gobitis* (1940). The case dealt with two students, ages 10 and 12, expelled from the public schools of Minersville, Pennsylvania. They were kicked out of school for failing to salute the American flag and recite the Pledge of Allegiance, which was required daily by state law for all students and teachers in public schools. The students and their parents, who were Jehovah's Witnesses, believed that saluting the flag was tantamount to worshipping a graven image, which was prohibited by their faith. The Court found the law to be constitutional and upheld the decision to expel the students.[1]

According to Frankfurter's Opinion for the Court, there was no violation of the children's free exercise rights. Frankfurter claimed, "Conscientious scruples have not, in the course of the long struggle for religious toleration, relieved the individual from obedience to a general law not aimed at the promotion or restriction of religious beliefs."[2] At the end of this sentence, Frankfurter wrote a footnote in which he cited several sources to this effect, including James Madison.[3] However, the use of Madison in this context is misleading. Madison was a strong proponent of accommodating religions, especially minority religions, so that a self-interested majority could not impose its view of "proper" religious beliefs on everyone. By referring to Madison, Frankfurter was failing to recognize that a legislative majority could pass a law to force the Jehovah's Witnesses to assimilate to the religious beliefs of the majority.

This failure to understand Madison on religious freedom was confirmed three years later in Frankfurter's dissenting opinion in *West Virginia v. Barnette*. The facts in *Barnette* were strikingly similar to those in *Gobitis*. The West Virginia State Board of Education required all public school teachers and pupils to salute the American flag and recite the Pledge of Allegiance daily. A group of Jehovah's Witnesses filed a lawsuit, claiming that forcing them to engage in the salute and pledge violated their First Amendment rights. This time, the Court found for the Jehovah's Witnesses and struck down the law.[4]

The Court's decision in *Barnette* left Frankfurter in dissent. He proceeded to write the following: "[T]he history out of which grew constitutional provisions for religious equality and the writings of the great exponents of religious freedom[, including] Madison . . . are totally wanting in justification for a claim by dissidents of exceptional immunity from civic measures of general applicability, measures not in fact disguised assaults upon such dissident views."[5] Frankfurter's use of Madison here was quite similar to his citation in *Gobitis*. Frankfurter made Madison out to be a supporter of a very formal definition of religious equality, and he assumed Madison to support laws that have general applicability. Again, Frankfurter failed to notice Madison's fear of a self-interested religious majority. This is a misconception of Madison's political theory as well as his understanding of human nature.

Moving away from religious freedom, Frankfurter's track record on Madison does not improve for other rights in the First Amendment. As noted earlier, Justice Frankfurter was critical of the Court's use of *Carolene Products* footnote number four to place First Amendment rights in a more protected category. One of the cases where he voiced his opposition to this approach was in *Dennis v. United States* (1951). *Dennis* involved Communist Party members being prosecuted for advocating the violent overthrow of the United States in violation of the Smith Act. After a nine-month trial, all defendants were found guilty. Although Dennis and his fellow defendants appealed the decision on the grounds that the Smith Act violated the Free Speech Clause, the Supreme Court affirmed their convictions.[6]

Frankfurter wrote a concurring opinion that defended the constitutionality of the Smith Act, and he misread Madison more than once in his text. First, as documented above, Frankfurter essentially mocked the idea that First Amendment rights should be considered as "preferred freedoms" that are more closely guarded by the courts than other constitutional rights; Madison was clearly of a different opinion. That general point notwithstanding, Frankfurter first cited Madison in the following passage: "The right of a government to maintain its existence—self-preservation—is the most pervasive aspect of sovereignty. 'Security against foreign danger,' wrote Madison, 'is one of the primitive objects of civil society.'"[7] The citation is from *Federalist* 41, a paper that generally dealt with the powers being given to the national government in the Constitution. Although Frankfurter correctly quoted each word Madison wrote, the justice took those words out of context. The powers Madison cited in *Federalist* 41 that help provide "[s]ecurity against foreign danger" include only the "power of declaring war" and the "power of raising troops, as well as providing fleets; and of maintaining both in peace, as well as in war."[8] Nowhere does Madison imply in this essay that restricting the freedom of speech of U.S. citizens is necessary to provide national security.

Furthermore, Madison warned that the "security" provided by having a strong military can be a grave threat to freedom:

> Not less true is it, that the liberties of Rome proved the final victim to her military triumphs; and that the liberties of Europe, as far as they ever existed, have, with few exceptions, been the price of her military establishments. A standing force, therefore, is a dangerous, at the same time that it may be a necessary, provision . . . A wise nation will combine all these considerations; and, whilst it does not rashly preclude itself from any resource which may become essential to its safety, will exert all its prudence in diminishing both the necessity and the danger of resorting to one which may be inauspicious to its liberties.[9]

Thus, even in the same passage where Madison promoted the idea of taking precautions for national security, he quickly retreated back to his emphasis of protecting civil liberties. In fact, Madison used the word "liberty" or "liberties" 10 times in *Federalist* 41. Madison's driving argument in this essay was that freedom would be better protected under the Constitution than under the Articles of Confederation, in part, because there would be only one standing army in America, as opposed to 13. Madison wanted the federal and state governments collectively to put fewer resources into national security than he feared would eventually be the case if the Confederation were allowed to continue: "[N]othing short of a Constitution fully adequate to the national defense and the preservation of the Union, can save America from as many standing armies as it may be split into States or Confederacies, and from such a progressive augmentation, of these establishments in each, as will render them as burdensome to the properties and ominous to the liberties of the people."[10] Here again, Madison cannot conclude without emphasizing the importance to maintaining liberty—one of the things that Madison thought was so paramount to securing against any danger, whether foreign or domestic. One of the liberties very important to Madison was the freedom of speech, which was at issue in *Dennis*. Frankfurter's quote of Madison here might be the textbook example of how to quote someone out of context.

Justice Frankfurter was not done referring to Madison in *Dennis,* however. Frankfurter went on to cite how various states early in the history of the Republic made laws outlawing certain types of speech. When chronicling a law from Virginia, he wrote that "Madison's own State put on its books in 1792 a statute confining the abusive exercise of the right of utterance."[11] Frankfurter's implication was that, since Madison lived in Virginia at a time when a serious limitation was put on the freedom of speech, Madison must have supported it. This position by Frankfurter cannot even be defended as a misinterpretation of Madison—it is nothing more than a bald name drop. Madison was in Congress in 1792, not in the Virginia legislature, and there is no evidence that he supported the passage of this law. Again, Madison was cited out of context. Furthermore, Frankfurter's citations of Madison in *Dennis* demonstrate no awareness of Madison's political theory or his view of human nature.

Frankfurter's misunderstanding of Madison regarding the freedom of speech was confirmed one year later in *Joseph Burstyn, Inc. v. Wilson* (1952). This case revolved around a New York statute that authorized the New York State Board of Regents to ban any film it deemed to be "sacrilegious." The law required companies exhibiting motion pictures for an admission fee to obtain first a license from the state department of education, which is how films could then be screened by the board. Joseph Burstyn, Inc., displayed a movie called "The Miracle," which was about a female goat herder who was apparently impregnated by St. Joseph. After receiving hundreds of letters and calls about the motion picture, the board of regents reviewed the film, found it to be sacrilegious, and rescinded the company's license to show the film in the state. The company challenged this regulation as violating the First Amendment. The Court agreed, holding that the state had no legitimate interest in putting in place prior restraints on the freedom of speech and press to protect religions from views they found distasteful.[12]

Justice Frankfurter concurred in the result of the case, as he found the standard by which New York State was judging films—whether or not they were sacrilegious—to be far too vague. However, Frankfurter wanted to condemn any absolutist approach to the First Amendment, regardless of whether it protected or denigrated the freedom of speech. In the course of doing this, Frankfurter cited Madison as an authority: "It would startle Madison and Jefferson and George Mason, could they adjust themselves to our day, to be told that the freedom of speech which they espoused in the Bill of Rights authorizes a showing of "The Miracle" from windows facing St. Patrick's Cathedral in the forenoon of Easter Sunday, just as it would startle them to be told that any picture, whatever its theme and its expression, could be barred from being commercially exhibited."[13]

Frankfurter gave no explanation why Madison and his contemporaries would have been startled by this. That said, Frankfurter is half correct in his assessment. Madison believed that both property rights and the freedom of speech were natural rights belonging to autonomous individuals. Madison thought that the expression one wanted to engage in, especially on one's own property, was a freedom that government could not take away. Thus, Madison would have been startled at the power of the government to limit one's free expression rights—the second example given by Frankfurter—but he would not necessarily have been startled at the first example of people freely expressing themselves.

Overall, Justice Frankfurter missed the mark on Madison. His misconceptions ranged from quoting Madison out of context to dropping Madison's name without any textual support that Madison espoused the vision that Frankfurter was ascribing to him. Although Frankfurter cited Madison in 17 cases involving the Bill of Rights, time and time again he failed to understand Madison's thinking on human nature or his political theory.

JUSTICE ROBERT JACKSON

Robert Jackson first took his seat on the Supreme Court in 1941, resigning his position as the U.S. attorney general to work on the Court. He took a leave of absence during 1945–1946 to serve as U.S. chief of counsel for the prosecution of Nazi war criminals at Nuremberg. After the Nuremberg trials he returned to the Court, where he remained until his untimely death in 1954. As a justice, Jackson had a largely moderate record. When it came to citing Madison in Bill of Rights cases, Jackson had some mistaken impressions when ruling on both the rights of the accused and the First Amendment.

One example of this occurred in *Johnson v. Eisentrager* (1950), which involved 21 German nationals who were in the service of the German armed forces in China during World War II. After Germany surrendered, these nationals continued gathering intelligence for the Japanese armed forces. They were taken into custody by the U.S. Army after the Japanese surrendered and were tried and convicted by a U.S. military commission in China. The German nationals were then sent to Landsberg Prison in Germany, which was run by the army. The prisoners then petitioned a U.S. federal court for a writ of habeas corpus, claiming that they were being held illegally, in part because it was in violation of the Fifth Amendment's Due Process Clause. The Supreme Court denied the request, stating that nonresident enemy aliens have no access to our courts in wartime.[14]

Justice Jackson wrote for the majority in *Eisentrager*. To help defend the Court's ruling, Jackson looked for guidance to the Alien and Sedition Acts of 1798. Jackson found the acts relevant because "this enactment was never repealed" and "was enacted or suffered to continue by men who helped found the Republic and formulate the Bill of Rights."[15] According to Jackson, "although it obviously denies enemy aliens the constitutional immunities of citizens, it seems not then to have been supposed that a nation's obligations to its foes could ever be put on a parity with those to its defenders."[16] At this point in his opinion, Jackson turned to Madison for support:

> [T]he 5th Congress passed [the Alien and Sedition Acts] in rapid succession. . . . Madison was the author of the Virginia Resolutions, and in his report to the Virginia House of Delegates the ensuing year after the deluge of controversy, he carefully and with some tartness asserted a distinction between alien members of a hostile nation and alien members of a friendly nation, disavowed any relation of the Resolutions to alien enemies, and declared, "With respect to alien enemies, no doubt has been intimated as to the federal authority over them; the Constitution having expressly delegated to Congress the power to declare war against any nation, and of course to treat it and all its members as enemies."[17]

Madison wrote those words, but citing Madison in this context fails to reflect Madison's true position on the rights of the accused. Simply because Madison agreed that Congress may treat alien enemies as enemies does not mean that Madison condoned denying them constitutional rights. Madison believed that criminal procedures were essential to protecting natural rights—if allowed to violate habeas corpus and due process, government may strip all of one's natural rights away. This is all the more relevant when aliens are involved, as they certainly would constitute a disadvantaged minority that could be taken advantage of by a majority faction. For this reason, citing Madison in *Eisentrager* was not within the spirit of Madison's political philosophy.

Jackson's failure to understand Madison was also on display in *Kunz v. New York* (1951). *Kunz* involved a New York City ordinance which made it unlawful to hold public worship meetings on the streets without first obtaining an annual permit. Carl Jacob Kunz, an ordained Baptist minister, had his permit revoked after the police commissioner found that Kunz had ridiculed and denounced other religious beliefs in his meetings. Kunz reapplied for the permit in 1947 and 1948, but he was denied both years. In September 1948 Kunz was arrested for speaking without a permit, and upon conviction he was fined $10. On appeal, the Supreme Court found the law to be an unconstitutional prior restraint on First Amendment rights.[18]

Jackson dissented in *Kunz*, finding New York's permit system constitutional. Jackson chided the majority for its cavalier attitude toward public safety: "The Court holds . . . that Kunz must not be required to get permission, the City must sit by until some incident, perhaps a sanguinary one, occurs and then there are unspecified 'appropriate public remedies.'"[19] In a footnote, Jackson quoted a line from a prior Supreme Court opinion that referred to Madison: "[T]he First Amendment while prohibiting legislation against free speech as such cannot have been, and obviously was not, intended to give immunity for every possible use of language . . . neither Hamilton nor Madison, nor any other competent person then or later, ever supposed that to make criminal the counselling of a murder within the jurisdiction of Congress would be an unconstitutional interference with free speech."[20] To be sure, the statement made by Jackson is a correct one—Madison would have no problem with outlawing conspiracy to commit murder under the First Amendment. However, the applicability of this statement to the question in *Kunz* is questionable at best. *Kunz* had nothing to do with committing murder. Instead, the case involved a street preacher's ability to proselytize without being required first to earn a government permit. This entails three of Madison's core rights: the freedom of religion, the freedom of speech, and the rights of criminal defendants. Casually referring to Madison and counseling a homicide is far afield from the many statements Madison made about protecting these rights and how they reinforced each other. Thus, Jackson's appeal to Madison was misplaced.

It was also ironic that Jackson used Madison to defend the fining of a Baptist minister for preaching without a permit. In a well-known letter to his good friend William Bradford in 1774, Madison closed his correspondence with the following irate words: "This vexes me the most of anything whatsoever. There are at this in the adjacent County not less than 5 or 6 well meaning men in close Goal for publishing their religious Sentiments. . . . I have squabbled and scolded and abused and ridiculed so long about it, to so little purpose that I am without common patience. So I leave you to pity me and pray for Liberty of Conscience to revive among us."[21] What could possibly have been done to these six men that vexed Madison and left him without patience? They were Baptist ministers who had been jailed for preaching without a license.[22]

Finally, Justice Jackson wrote a concurrence in *Dennis*, the facts of which are recounted in the section on Justice Frankfurter above. Although agreeing with the Court's decision to uphold the convictions of Communist Party members, Jackson wrote separately to note that advocacy of the violent overthrow of the government may be constitutionally prohibited, even in cases where there is no clear and present danger of a violent overthrow of government. To make his point, Jackson used the same passage that he cited above in *Kunz*.[23] The use of this quote again raises similar problems as in *Kunz*. Jackson's summary appeal once more neglects any real connection to the facts of the case, as well as any comprehensive description of Madison's position on free speech issues. Although *Dennis* dealt at least with violence similar to a murder conspiracy, Jackson does not explain why Madison's thoughts were applicable to the case. Instead, Jackson drops Madison's name without further explanation.

Robert Jackson only referred to Madison in three cases involving the Bill of Rights during his career on the Court. It is lucky that he *only* made these three references because more citations to Madison might have resulted in Jackson misapplying Madison more times. For a final example of a justice who misunderstood Madison, we need look no further than one of Jackson's former law clerks at the Supreme Court, William Hubbs Rehnquist.

CHIEF JUSTICE WILLIAM REHNQUIST

William Rehnquist was appointed as an associate justice in 1972 and was elevated to chief justice in 1986; he served on the Court until his unfortunate death in 2005. Throughout that time, Rehnquist was a dependable conservative vote on the Court. When initially appointed he was nicknamed "The Lone Ranger" because he was often the sole dissenter on the Court, but by the time he was chief justice he was frequently forging conservative majorities. During his tenure on the Court, Rehnquist did not correctly express Madison's theory very often in cases litigating the Bill of Rights. Either Rehnquist did not understand Madison or he simply used Madison's words as a convenient appeal to authority. Indeed, with the exception of one citation in one case, Rehnquist never correctly assessed Madison's political theory or Madison's conception of human nature.

Rehnquist's longest elaboration on Madison in a Bill of Rights case took place when he was an associate justice in *Wallace v. Jaffree* (1985). The *Wallace* case began with a 1981 Alabama statute that authorized a one-minute period of silence in all public schools "for meditation or voluntary prayer."

Ishmael Jaffree, who had three children in Alabama public schools, filed a lawsuit, arguing that the law violated the Establishment Clause. The Supreme Court agreed, holding that the statute was intended to convey a message of state approval of prayer in the public schools.[24]

In dissent, then-Justice Rehnquist stated his belief that the majority's wall of separation theory of the Establishment Clause was incorrect, and that "[n]othing in the Establishment Clause of the First Amendment, properly understood, prohibits any such generalized 'endorsement' of prayer."[25] Instead, according to Rehnquist, the clause only "forbade establishment of a national religion, and forbade preference among religious sects or denominations."[26] To support this nonpreferentialist position on establishment, Rehnquist detailed the history of the Establishment Clause, including Madison's involvement therein.

Rehnquist began by broadly stating that "Madison . . . did play as large a part as anyone in the drafting of the Bill of Rights," but cautioned that when "we turn to the record of the proceedings in the First Congress leading up to the adoption of the Establishment Clause of the Constitution, including Madison's significant contributions thereto, we see a far different picture of its purpose than the highly simplified 'wall of separation between church and State.'"[27]

Rehnquist began his analysis by describing the language introduced by Madison: "The civil rights of none shall be abridged on account of religious belief or worship, nor shall any national religion be established, nor shall the full and equal rights of conscience be in any manner, or on any pretext, infringed."[28] Rehnquist then avowed, "The Committee [of Eleven] revised Madison's proposal regarding the establishment of religion to read: '[No] religion shall be established by law, nor shall the equal rights of conscience be infringed.'"[29] Rehnquist subsequently described the debate in the House on the clause, particularly emphasizing how Representative Benjamin Huntington "expressed the view that the Committee's language might 'be taken in such latitude as to be extremely hurtful to the cause of religion.'"[30] According to Rehnquist, Huntington represented Connecticut, so he was concerned that in "New England States, where state-established religions were the rule rather than the exception, the federal courts might not be able to entertain claims based upon an obligation under the bylaws of a religious organization to contribute to the support of a minister or the building of a place of worship."[31] Rehnquist then described how "Madison responded that the insertion of the word 'national' before the word 'religion' in the Committee version should satisfy the minds of those who had criticized the language."[32] However, Rehnquist claimed that Madison withdrew this proposal owing to "opposition to the use of the word 'national' because of strong feelings expressed during the ratification debates that a federal government, not a national government, was created by the Constitution."[33] Rehnquist then detailed how the language progressed from the House to the Senate to the House-Senate conference committee, which constituted the final wording of the Religion Clauses ("Congress shall make no law respecting an establishment of religion, or prohibiting the free exercise thereof").[34]

Rehnquist then seized upon the following:

> James Madison was undoubtedly the most important architect among the Members of the House of the Amendments which became the Bill of Rights, but it was James Madison speaking as an advocate of sensible legislative compromise, not as an advocate of incorporating the Virginia Statute of Religious Liberty into the United States Constitution. During the ratification debate in the Virginia Convention, Madison had actually opposed the idea of any Bill of Rights. His sponsorship of the Amendments in the House was obviously not that of a zealous believer in the necessity of the Religion Clauses, but of one who felt it might do some good, could do no harm, and would satisfy those who had ratified the Constitution on the condition that Congress propose a Bill of Rights. His original language "nor shall any national religion be established" obviously does not conform to the "wall of separation" between church and State idea which latter-day commentators have ascribed to him. His explanation on the floor of the meaning of his language—"that Congress should not establish a religion, and enforce the legal observation of it by law" is of the same ilk. When he replied to Huntington in the debate over the proposal which came from the Select Committee of the House, he urged that the language "no religion shall be established by law" should be amended by inserting the word "national" in front of the word "religion."[35]

Based on this, Rehnquist deduced, "It seems indisputable from these glimpses of Madison's thinking, as reflected by actions on the floor of the House in 1789, that he saw the Amendment as designed to prohibit the establishment of a national religion, and perhaps to prevent discrimination among sects. He did not see it as requiring neutrality on the part of government between religion and irreligion."[36] Rehnquist then concluded with the following: "Thus the Court's opinion in *Everson*—while correct in bracketing Madison and Jefferson together in their exertions in their home State leading to the enactment of the Virginia Statute of Religious Liberty—is totally incorrect in suggesting that Madison carried these views onto the floor of the United States House of Representatives when he proposed the language which would ultimately become the Bill of Rights."[37]

To sum up, Rehnquist's argument in *Wallace* was as follows: Madison was an important member of the First Congress, which drafted the Establishment Clause, but he was only one member, who had lukewarm support for the Bill of Rights generally. And to the extent that Madison was influential, he intended a nonpreferentialist protection when he was in Congress, not the more separationist stance he vigorously advocated in Virginia three years earlier. Rehnquist closed his analysis of Madison's involvement with the history and tradition of the clause by confirming that, while president, Madison issued thanksgiving proclamations.[38]

First, Rehnquist neglected some important historical facts in his analysis. Madison's involvement with the Bill of Rights went beyond simply introducing the Establishment Clause, speaking on it, and offering an amendment to insert the word "national" in front of the word "religion." Madison had to prod the House to consider the amendments, he was one of the most vocal members on the amendments, and he served on the Committee of Eleven—all facts that Rehnquist either neglected or downplayed. And, as Rehnquist pointed out, Madison moved to place the word "national" in front of the word "religion" in the Committee of Eleven proposal; however, when Madison proposed that amendment, he also stated that he "believed that the people feared one sect might obtain a pre-eminence, or two combine together, and establish a religion which they would *compel* on others to conform."[39] There is nothing in this statement that would have been inconsistent with a separationist position, as it points to Madison's condemnation of one religion dominating the political landscape, or multiple religions combining into one religion to exercise power over others. Furthermore, only three years previously Madison championed the Virginia Act for Establishing Religious Freedom, which stated, "to *compel* a man to furnish contributions of money for the propagation of opinions which he disbelieves, is sinful and tyrannical."[40] In both the debate on the Establishment Clause and in the Virginia bill, Madison spoke of the dangers of government and religions combining to "compel" others to conform or contribute to a cause in which they did not believe. Furthermore, Rehnquist failed to mention that Madison withdrew his "national" amendment after only short comments by two other representatives, so he could not have been very committed to the use of the word "national" in that amendment.[41] Rehnquist also overlooked the fact that Madison was the chair of the conference committee that finalized the Establishment Clause's language ("Congress shall make no law respecting an establishment of religion"), which was decidedly more separationist than the Senate's version ("Congress shall make no law establishing articles of faith or a mode of worship"). Indeed, the final language was not only more separationist but also closer to what Madison had intended in his original proposal ("nor shall any national religion be established"). Finally, Rehnquist neglected to mention that, although Madison gave religious proclamations, he later repudiated his actions. For these reasons, it is no wonder that several scholars have derided Rehnquist's account of the Establishment Clause in *Wallace* as nothing short of a cherry-picking of facts.[42]

However, historical inaccuracies or misconceptions aside, the greater error made by Rehnquist for present purposes was that he misconstrued Madison's theoretical stance on the Establishment Clause. Rehnquist failed to draw the important connection that Madison found between protecting disestablishment as a way to protect natural rights, such as free exercise rights. In fact, his amendment after Huntington's comment appears to have been aimed at this very point. Rehnquist did not discuss Madison's emphasis on virtue and the common good, or Madison's understanding of human nature. Instead, Rehnquist appeared to have selected a set of facts that allowed him to characterize Madison in 1789 as a nonpreferentialist, even when Rehnquist essentially admitted that Madison had taken a separationist position only a few years earlier. Rehnquist offered no explanations for this purported switch by Madison, with the exception that in 1789 Madison was acting out of "legislative compromise."

Rehnquist made similar mistakes in other First Amendment cases, most notably in *Anderson v. Celebrezze* (1983). The case began on April 24, 1980, when John Anderson announced that he was going to be an independent candidate for president of the United States in the 1980 general election. His supporters gathered the required number of signatures to get his name on the ballot in Ohio and turned the petition in to the Ohio secretary of state on May 16. However, state law required that the deadline to get one's name on the ballot for the November presidential election was March 20. Anderson's supporters sued, claiming that their associational rights were violated by such an early filing deadline. The Supreme Court agreed, finding the burden to be unconstitutional.[43]

In dissent, Rehnquist rejected the majority's broad understanding of associational rights, claiming that Ohio "apparently believes with the Founding Fathers that splintered parties and unrestrained factionalism may do significant damage to the fabric of government. See *The Federalist, No. 10* (Madison)."[44] Rehnquist used Madison to justify an interpretation of the freedom of association where individual rights to join groups may be significantly tailored by a state's interests in promoting orderly democracy.

This is in direct contradiction to Madison's political theory. Although Madison thought that government could justifiably control the effects of factions, he did not think it acceptable for government to attack the liberty that is the cause of faction. In *Anderson*, Rehnquist implicated that the freedom of association was a right dependent on the needs of state elections. Madison, however, reversed the equation, believing that how elections are run is dependent upon the natural right to association. Madison also feared government power to control parties directly, as he thought at least some parties were capable of good for society. Thus, Madison suggested in *Federalist 10* that the Constitution control factions in two ways only, by the principle of representation and by extending the size of the republic. At no point in *Federalist* 10 did Madison suggest an invasive or direct regulation of parties, as that would have been contrary to his political theory. Finally, Madison assisted Jefferson in building America's first opposition party, which at its inception was clearly a minority party and was attacked by the majority Federalist Party via the passage of the Alien and Sedition Acts. Madison adamantly opposed this Federalist Party action, in part, because it attacked his minority party's ability to form and run campaigns. For all of the foregoing reasons, Rehnquist misconstrued Madison's intent when he penned his dissent in *Anderson.*

Rehnquist also cited Madison in his opinion in *Verdugo-Urquidez*, the case involving the Fourth Amendment rights of a nonresident alien. Writing for the majority, Chief Justice Rehnquist stated that the Fourth Amendment's purpose "was to restrict searches and seizures which might be conducted by the United States in domestic matters."[45] Accordingly, "The Framers originally decided not to include a provision like the Fourth Amendment, because they believed the National Government lacked power to conduct searches and seizures. *See* . . . 1 Annals of Cong. 437 (1789) (statement of J. Madison)."[46] Rehnquist then explained that Madison feared that Congress might abuse its powers under the Necessary and Proper Clause to harm the rights of U.S. citizens: "Madison . . . argued that 'there is a clause granting to Congress the power to make all laws which shall be necessary and proper for carrying into execution all of the powers vested in the Government of the United States,' and that general warrants might be considered 'necessary' for the purpose of collecting revenue."[47] Based on this, Rehnquist concluded that

> The driving force behind the adoption of the Amendment, as suggested by Madison's advocacy, was widespread hostility among the former colonists to the issuance of writs of assistance empowering revenue officers to search suspected places for smuggled goods, and general search warrants permitting the search of private houses, often to uncover papers that might be used to convict persons of libel. The available historical data show, therefore, that the purpose of the Fourth Amendment was to protect the people of the United States against arbitrary action by their own Government; it was never suggested that the provision was intended to restrain the actions of the Federal Government against aliens outside of the United States territory.[48]

Rehnquist invoked Madison's statements in his defense of a narrow, "citizen-only" interpretation of the Fourth Amendment. This interpretation is not a classically liberal one, as it does not focus on people as rights-bearing individuals; rather, it focuses on the protection of members of the political community against actions by their own government or by the government in the country where they happen to be physically located. Madison was concerned with the protection of individual autonomy for all persons, as he believed that all of us are endowed with natural rights. However, this analysis was not present in Rehnquist's citation of Madison. In addition, Rehnquist failed to see that Madison valued criminal procedural rights for *all* persons because they protect other important rights, and because they may promote virtue (as Brennan pointed out with his mutuality theory). Thus, Rehnquist's interpretation of Madison is contrary to both Madison's theory and Brennan's use of Madison in the same case.

The only case in which Rehnquist cited Madison and appeared to understand Madison's theory regarding the Bill of Rights was *Locke v. Davey*. Recall that in *Locke* the Court held that denying scholarships to students pursuing degrees in theology did not violate the Free Exercise Clause. In writing the majority opinion, Rehnquist noted that, "[s]ince the founding of our country, there have been popular uprisings against procuring taxpayer funds to support church leaders, which was one of the hallmarks of an 'established' religion."[49] To support this point Rehnquist utilized the "Memorial and Remonstrance," a document in which Rehnquist claimed that Madison was "noting the dangers to civil liberties from supporting clergy with public funds."[50] In this case, Rehnquist properly appreciated that Madison wanted disestablishment as a way to protect other liberties, most notably the free exercise of religion. Although Rehnquist ultimately used Madison to support a nonpreferentialist position, he was able to grasp some of Madison's other thoughts on human freedom.

It interesting, however, that Rehnquist in *Locke* was willing to cite Madison's "Memorial and Remonstrance" to support his interpretation of the Religion Clauses. Years earlier in *Wallace*, Rehnquist claimed that Madison's statements in his "Memorial and Remonstrance" were not dispositive of Madison's views on the First Amendment. Perhaps this case, which was decided barely one year before Rehnquist's death, could have been the beginning of a Madison "learning" period for Rehnquist. If he had lived longer, Rehnquist might have moved into the same category as Justices Stewart and O'Connor regarding Madison and the Bill of Rights. Unfortunately, we will never know whether Chief Justice Rehnquist was beginning to understand Madison, as *Locke* was one of his last opinions about the Father of the Constitution.

Overall, it appears that Rehnquist either misunderstood Madison or he purposely invoked Madison's name inappropriately. Indeed, outside of *Locke,* each of the other seven times that Rehnquist cited Madison in Bill of Rights cases he did not perceive Madison's theory properly or understand the nuances of Madison's thought.

Fourteen

CONCLUSIONS

The Supreme Court's treatment of James Madison in cases involving the Bill of Rights is as diverse as the different rights protected by the Constitution. Indeed, whether measuring justices by political philosophy or favored method of constitutional interpretation, there is significant variation in their ability to figure out the Father of the Constitution.

For instance, liberal justices have varying degrees of success in applying Madison's theory correctly. It was true that the liberals Hugo Black, William Brennan, and David Souter managed to figure out Madison on the Bill of Rights. However, other liberals, most notably Justice John Paul Stevens, have struggled with Madison in some types of cases. Likewise, the moderates in the Court's history have had varying degrees of success. Anthony Kennedy has pegged Madison time and time again, but Felix Frankfurter and Robert Jackson were largely off the mark in this regard. The other moderates examined here, Potter Stewart and Sandra Day O'Connor, took time to figure Madison out. Finally, there is no consensus about Madison among conservatives on the Court. William Rehnquist failed to appreciate Madison's political theory, but Antonin Scalia, Clarence Thomas, and Warren Burger have often been able to discern Madison's views and to apply his theories in context.

The same discrepancies occur if one analyzes the justices from their methods of constitutional interpretation. For example, look to the textualism of Black and Scalia. Black used this method of interpretation and easily assessed Madison. But for Scalia, this method of interpretation has proven to be a less reliable way to interpret Madison's ideas about freedom. The other justices examined here, who had more diverse and multiple methods of interpreting the Constitution, stand all over the map among devotees, learners, inconsistents, and name droppers with regard to Madison and the Bill of Rights.

Individual justices may vary in their understanding of Madison. Although the devotees and (eventually) the learners have comprehended Madison's theory and applied it to each right, not every justice falls into those two categories. For instance, some justices understand Madison and can apply his theory in cases involving the Religion Clauses or the First Amendment generally, but they appear clueless when applying his writings to their decisions on other rights. Other justices appear to have Madison figured out for all freedoms *except* for religious liberty. And a few justices are consistently wrong on Madison, regardless of the right in question.

That said, the continued citation in recent decades of Madison by the justices is warranted. Madison is important because he was the major player in securing the Bill of Rights for us. Madison at first believed that a bill of rights would not be an effective way of protecting liberal rights, given his understanding of human nature, because he feared that mere words on paper could not stop a self-interested majority faction. However, over time he was persuaded that a bill of rights could serve as an additional shield to protect liberty, and that it could be employed for strategic purposes as well. For these reasons, what he thought about the Bill of Rights is relevant when we try to figure out what that document means.

It is rare to find justices who can fully articulate Madison's multifaceted theories and his diverse influences, especially his teacher John Witherspoon, his friend Thomas Jefferson, and the authors David Hume, John Locke, and Adam Smith. Many of the justices fail to completely see that Madison understood that human nature is not fixed for us all but, rather, that some of us will be capable of virtue and others of us not. However, some of the justices have figured out that Madison believed that we are prone to act selfishly *and* that we are capable of virtue in an age of enlightenment. While it is rare, some justices have consistently seen that this understanding of human nature influenced Madison's political philosophy, in which he defended a classically liberal understanding of natural rights. Madison thought that government was instituted to protect natural rights, a belief that some of the justices have pieced together. Madison also believed that society would be best if it protected liberal rights, because it would allow us the freedom to cultivate our capacities for virtue. Furthermore, if we failed to become virtuous and acted solely in our self-interest, society overall would still benefit from the increased productivity that Madison believed would come from the exercise of our freedoms. Some of the justices grasp these points about Madison. When Madison proposed his amendments, he sought to create an organic whole of rights that mutually reinforced each other, another point not lost on every justice. For Madison, protecting a core set of liberal rights—freedom of religion; freedoms of speech, press, and association; property rights; and rights of the criminally accused—would be the best method for achieving both individual virtue and the common good. Many justices have recognized this, citing Madison repeatedly in these types of cases.

What ties together all of the devotees, as well as the learners in their later years, is their understanding of most or all of the points above. This includes the ability to recognize the importance of liberal rights to Madison and how that conception fits with Madison's natural-rights theory, his secondary benefits theory, and his theory regarding the diversity of human nature. If justices are to continue using Madison, they need to study his works and make these connections in Madison's thought. It is only by undertaking this endeavor that the justices on the Court can have a full understanding of Madison and what he thought about individual rights such as the freedom of religion or the right to a jury trial in criminal cases.

Although not every justice examined here has truly understood Madison, they all deserve kudos for realizing that Madison is important in these types of cases. Furthermore, the Supreme Court has largely fulfilled Madison's dream of being the "guardian" of rights, and the Court has long carried out the mission of Madison's failed Council of Revision. What is more, through the assistance of John Bingham, the Court has effectively resurrected Madison's "most valuable amendment" regarding a federal veto power over state laws, and this has been an effective substitute for Madison's failed congressional veto. These victories for freedom made Madison's vision of the Bill of Rights *our* Bill of Rights, even if they were rather belated triumphs.

Interestingly enough, Madison has become used more frequently by the Court over the last century. As noted above (and as listed in appendix A), Madison was used in 230 opinions in Bill of Rights cases between 1869 and 2009. The first point to be made here is that no justice cited Madison when interpreting the Bill of Rights before 1869. The justices on the Court during its first 80 or so years apparently did not feel it necessary to write about Madison in these types of cases. This would slowly begin to change, however. Before the end of the nineteenth century, Madison would be cited in eight Supreme Court opinions. Still, this means that only 3 percent of Madison citations in Bill of Rights cases were made before the twentieth century. Even up to 1937, Madison was only cited in 14 Bill of Rights opinions, or 6 percent of all such citations made through 2009.

Then, a sea change began on the Court beginning in 1937. In that year, the Court decided *Palko,* which formally stated the process of selective incorporation, eventually paving the way for almost all of the Bill of Rights to limit the states. In 1938, the Court began giving more protection to civil liberties in *Carolene Products* footnote number four. Also during this era, Franklin Roosevelt began naming justices to the Court. Justice Black in 1937 was the first of nine Roosevelt appointees. Eight of these Roosevelt appointees cited Madison in 68 opinions, accounting for 30 percent of all Madison citations over the Court's history, which was probably, at least in part, due to the fact that many of Roosevelt's Court nominees worked in the executive branch and the Senate before their appointments. Perhaps this left these men with a broader understanding of how to interpret the Constitution, going far beyond previously decided Supreme Court cases.

Once these Roosevelt appointees began citing Madison, the genie could not be put back in the bottle. Their citations of Madison were then in Court opinions, and these opinions, with their citations of Madison, were bound to be read and cited by later justices when interpreting these same provisions of the Bill of Rights.

Even this process of citing Madison by Roosevelt appointees was a relatively slow one. The overwhelming majority of citations by the Roosevelt appointees were made by three justices—Black, Frankfurter, and William Douglas. But these three made most of their citations later in their Court careers. Partially for this reason, as well as the 1956 appointment of Madison devotee William Brennan, 186 of these opinions, or 81 percent, have been written in the last half century (1959–2009). Indeed, not really until the 1960s, when incorporation was in full swing and the strict scrutiny test had become standard, did the frequency of citations to Madison take off.

The march of time has certainly not slowed Madison citations. As mentioned in chapter 1, Madison has been cited in 65 opinions in Bill of Rights cases during the Rehnquist and Roberts Courts (1986–2009). As of this writing, that is a period of less than a quarter century. In that time, 28 percent of all opinions that make any reference to Madison were written. No doubt, Madison has continued to be relevant in these types of cases. This is partly because of renewed interest in originalism brought about by justices such as Scalia and Thomas. Of course, other justices who do not limit themselves to originalism have also cited Madison in this current period, too, so originalism cannot be the sole explanation for Madison's continued use.

With each passing year, as the Bill of Rights becomes more a part of a distant past, the justices have more frequently turned to Madison to help explain what these eighteenth-century words mean. Perhaps the justices have done this *because* the Bill of Rights is now so far in our past, and thus the justices need some sort of intellectual grounding when making their decisions, a problem that simply would not have existed in the nineteenth century. For example, Chief Justice Marshall's opinion in *Barron v. Baltimore*, in which he declared that the Bill of Rights did not limit state government powers, was decided in 1833. Marshall did not cite Madison, but why would he? Madison was still alive. Both Madison and Marshall were members of the founding generation, and many other people were still alive who lived through that era. Appealing to Madison at that time to help people understand what the Bill of Rights meant would have seemed out of place.

Yet, at the dawn of the twentieth, and later the twenty-first, centuries, the Founders were all dead and buried. No one with any personal experience of the Founding remained alive. Looking to the text alone cannot fully determine the meaning of vague phrases such as "Congress shall make no law . . . abridging the freedom of speech," or "nor shall any person . . . be deprived of life, liberty, or property, without due process of law." Even Justice Black, who often purported to derive the meaning of the Constitution only from reading the text, cited and quoted Madison many times in Bill of Rights cases. Madison's writing and speeches are now ways to give context to the language of the document that he drafted and was so instrumental in passing.

In the end, it is quite likely as we forge into the future that Madison will continue to exercise influence from the grave over what we think the Bill of Rights means. There is every reason to believe that this will continue on the Supreme Court as well as in the American public generally. It is inspiring to think that the rights Madison helped enshrine in the Constitution in 1789 are still with us, and they are still respected by government. Madison's freedom has endured. If James Madison—the Father of the Constitution, the Father of the Bill of Rights—were alive today, he would be quite proud to find the Supreme Court justices serving as guardians of freedom, helping to secure the liberty of the people.

APPENDIX A

SUPREME COURT CITATIONS OF JAMES MADISON
IN BILL OF RIGHTS CASES

Below is a list of all opinions in which a justice wrote in his or her opinion a reference to "Madison" or "Federalist No. 10" when interpreting the First Amendment, property rights under the Constitution, constitutional rights of the criminally accused, or the Bill of Rights generally. This list does not include citations to "the Framers" or any other similar generic term. Categorization is based on a justice's treatment of Madison and is not necessarily based on the clause upon which the Court decided the case.

Next to each justice is listed the case name, the case citation, the pages on which the citation appear, the year the case was decided, the type of opinion (majority, plurality, concurrence, dissent), and the provision in the Bill of Rights being interpreted. Each amendment is abbreviated by its number and a capital letter "A," so that the First Amendment is abbreviated as "1A." More specific abbreviations are to the following clauses:

1A	EST = Establishment
	FE = Free Exercise
	FS = Freedom of Speech
	FP = Freedom of the Press
	FA = Freedom of Assembly/Association
5A	GJ = Grand Jury
	DJ = Double Jeopardy
	CSI = Compelled Self–Incrimination
	DP = Due Process
	TC = Takings Clause
6A	SPT = Speedy and Public Trial
	JT = Jury Trial
	AOC = Assistance of Counsel
8A	CUP = Cruel and Unusual Punishment
BOR	Bill of Rights (generally)

Justices are listed below in the order that they arrived on the Court. The years of service for each justice are listed in parentheses, with chief justices denoted by the abbreviation "C.J."

Samuel Nelson (1845–1872)
Justices v. Murray, 76 U.S. 274, 282 (1869), Majority, 7A

Stephen J. Field (1863–1897)
Fong Yue Ting v. United States, 149 U.S. 698, 747–49, 759 (1893),
Dissent, 5A (DP)

Morrison R. Waite (1874–1888 C.J.)
Reynolds v. United States, 98 U.S. 145, 163–64 (1879), Majority, 1A (FE)

John M. Harlan (1877–1911)
Hurtado v. California, 110 U.S. 516, 549 (1884), Dissent, 6A (JT)
Callan v. Wilson, 127 U.S. 540, 550 (1888), Majority, 6A (JT)

Horace Gray (1882–1902)
Ex parte Wilson, 114 U.S. 417, 424 (1885), Majority, 5A (GJ)
Capital Traction Co. v. Hof, 174 U.S. 1, 7–8 (1899), Majority, 7A

David J. Brewer (1889–1910)
Fong Yue Ting v. United States, 149 U.S. 698, 740–41 (1893),
Dissent, 5A (DP)
United States v. Ju Toy, 198 U.S. 253, 270 (1905), Dissent, 5A (DP)

Edward D. White (1894–1910; 1910–1921 C.J.)
Weems v. United States, 217 U.S. 349, 397 (1910), Dissent, 8A (CUP)

Oliver W. Holmes (1902–1932)
Frohwerk v. United States, 249 U.S. 204, 206 (1919), Majority, 1A (FS)

Charles E. Hughes (1910–1916; 1930–1941 C.J.)
Near v. Minnesota, 283 U.S. 697, 714, 717, 722 (1931), Majority, 1A (FP)

George Sutherland (1922–1938)
Lambert v. Yellowley, 272 U.S. 581, 604 (1926), Dissent, 10A

Pierce Butler (1923–1939)
Near v. Minnesota, 283 U.S. 697, 734 (1931), Dissent, 1A (FP)

Harlan F. Stone (1925–1941; 1941–1946 C.J.)
Ex parte Quirin, 317 U.S. 1, 42 (1942), Majority, 6A (JT)

Hugo L. Black (1937–1971)
Bridges v. California, 314 U.S. 252, 264–65 (1941), Majority, 1A (FS, FP)

Galloway v. United States, 319 U.S. 372, 407 (1943), Dissent, 7A

Everson v. Board of Education, 330 U.S. 1, 11–13 (1947), Majority, 1A (EST)

Reid v. Covert, 354 U.S. 1, 8, 24 (1957), Plurality, 6A (JT)

Yates v. United States, 354 U.S. 298, 344 (1957), Concurrence/Dissent, 1A (FS, FP, FA)

Barenblatt v. United States, 360 U.S. 109, 143 (1959), Dissent, 1A (FS, FP, FA, PET)

Smith v. California, 361 U.S. 147, 157–58 (1959), Concurrence, 1A (FS, FP)

Konigsberg v. State Bar of California, 366 U.S. 36, 61 (1961), Dissent, 1A (FS)

Communist Party of United States v. Subversive Activities Control Bd., 367 U.S. 1, 168 (1961), Dissent, 1A (FS, FP, FA, PET)

International Ass'n of Machinists v. Street, 367 U.S. 740, 790 (1961), Dissent, 1A

Mapp v. Ohio, 367 U.S. 643, 663 (1961), Concurrence, 4A, 5A (CSI)

Torcaso v. Watkins, 367 U.S. 488, 491 (1961), Majority, 1A (EST)

Engel v. Vitale, 370 U.S. 421, 428, 431–32, 436 (1962), Majority, 1A (EST)

Chapman v. California, 386 U.S. 18, 21 (1967), Majority, 5A (CSI)

California v. Byers, 402 U.S. 424, 459 (1971), Dissent, 5A (CSI)

New York Times Co. v. United States, 403 U.S. 713, 716–17, 719 (1971), Concurrence, 1A (FP)

Stanley F. Reed (1938–1957)

Murdock v. Pennsylvania, 319 U.S. 105, 124–25 (1943), Dissent, 1A (FE, FS, FP)

Illinois ex rel. McCollum v. Bd. of Edu., 333 U.S. 203, 244–48 (1948), Dissent, 1A (EST)

Felix Frankfurter (1939–1962)

Minersville School Dist. v. Gobitis, 310 U.S. 586, 594 (1940), Majority, 1A (FE)

West Virginia v. Barnette, 319 U.S. 624, 652–53 (1943), Dissent, 1A (FE)

Malinski v. New York, 324 U.S. 401, 414–15 (1945), Concurrence, 5A (DP)

Davis v. United States, 328 U.S. 582, 604–5 (1946), Dissent, 4A

Harris v. United States, 331 U.S. 145, 158 (1947), Dissent, 4A

Adamson v. California, 332 U.S. 46, 66 (1947), Concurrence, 5A (DP)

Illinois ex rel. McCollum v. Bd. of Edu., 333 U.S. 203, 214, 216 (1948), Concurrence, 1A (EST)

Ludecke v. Watkins, 335 U.S. 160, 171–72 (1948), Majority, 5A (DP)

Kovacs v. Cooper, 336 U.S. 77, 96 (1949), Concurrence, 1A (FS)

Dennis v. United States, 341 U.S. 494, 519, 521–23 (1951), Concurrence, 1A (FS)

Joseph Burstyn, Inc. v. Wilson, 343 U.S. 495, 518 (1952), Concurrence, 1A (FS)

Green v. United States, 355 U.S. 184, 201–2 (1957), Dissent, 5A (DJ)
Green v. United States, 356 U.S. 165, 190 (1958), Concurrence, 6A (JT)
Knapp v. Schweitzer, 357 U.S. 371, 376–77 (1958), Majority, 5A (CSI)
Smith v. California, 361 U.S. 147, 163 (1959), Concurrence, 1A (FS)
McGowan v. Maryland, 366 U.S. 420, 463–65, 486, 492–95 (1961),
  Separate, 1A (EST)
International Ass'n of Machinists v. Street, 367 U.S. 740, 816 (1961),
  Dissent, 1A

William O. Douglas (1939–1975)
Dennis v. United States, 341 U.S. 494, 591 (1951), Dissent, 1A (FS)
McGowan v. Maryland, 366 U.S. 420, 577–78 (1961), Dissent, 1A (EST)
United States v. Oregon, 366 U.S. 643, 653 (1961), Dissent, 10A
Scales v. United States, 367 U.S. 203, 271–72 (1961), Dissent, 1A (FS)
International Ass'n of Machinists v. Street, 367 U.S. 740, 778 (1961),
  Concurrence, 1A
Engel v. Vitale, 370 U.S. 421, 444 (1962), Concurrence, 1A (EST)
Gibson v. Florida Legislative Investigation Committee, 372 U.S. 539, 574
  (1963), Concurrence, 1A (FA)
Garrison v. Louisiana, 379 U.S. 64, 83–88 (1964), Concurrence, 1A (FS)
*A Book Named "John Cleland's Memoirs of a Woman of Pleasure" v.
  Attorney General of Massachusetts*, 383 U.S. 413, 429–30 (1966),
  Concurrence, 1A (FS, FP)
Board of Education v. Allen, 392 U.S. 236, 266 (1968), Dissent, 1A (EST)
Flast v. Cohen, 392 U.S. 83, 107–8 (1968), Concurrence, 1A (EST)
North Carolina v. Pearce, 395 U.S. 711, 728–29 (1969), Concurrence, 5A
  (DJ)
Walz v. Tax Com. of New York, 397 U.S. 664, 704–6, 710–13, 715, 719–27
  (1970), Dissent, 1A (EST, FE)
Tilton v. Richardson, 403 U.S. 672, 696–97 (1971), Dissent, 1A (EST)
Lemon v. Kurtzman, 403 U.S. 602, 630, 633–34, 637 (1971), Concur-
  rence, 1A (EST)
Dun & Bradstreet, Inc. v. Grove, 404 U.S. 898, 900–1 (1971), Dissent from
  Denial of Cert., 1A (FS, FP)
Healy v. James, 408 U.S. 169, 197 (1972), Concurrence, 1A (FS, FA)
Laird v. Tatum, 408 U.S. 1, 21–22, 28–29 (1972), Dissent, 1A (FS, FA)
Branzburg v. Hayes, 408 U.S. 665, 723 (1972), Dissent, 1A (FP)
Lemon v. Kurtzman, 411 U.S. 192, 209–12 (1973), Dissent, 1A (EST)
CBS, Inc. v. Democratic Nat'l Committee, 412 U.S. 94, 148 (1973), Concur-
  rence, 1A (FP)
United States v. 12 200-Ft. Reels of Super 8mm Film, 413 U.S. 123, 131–33,
  135 (1973), Dissent, 1A (FS, FP)
United States v. Matlock, 415 U.S. 164, 183 (1974), Dissent, 4A

Wheeler v. Barrera, 417 U.S. 402, 430 (1974), Dissent, 1A (EST)
Hamling v. United States, 418 U.S. 87, 141 (1974), Dissent, 1A (FS, FP)

Frank Murphy (1940–1949)
Thornhill v. Alabama, 310 U.S. 88, 98 (1940), Majority, 1A (FS, FP)
Jones v. Opelika, 316 U.S. 584, 622 (1942), Dissent, 1A (FE)
Schneiderman v. United States, 320 U.S. 118, 133 (1943), Majority, 1A (FS)

Robert H. Jackson (1941–1954)
Johnson v. Eisentrager, 339 U.S. 763, 774 (1950), Majority, 5A (DP)
Kunz v. New York, 340 U.S. 290, 310 (1951), Dissent, 1A (FS)
Dennis v. United States, 341 U.S. 494, 571 (1951), Concurrence, 1A (FS)

Wiley B. Rutledge (1943–1949)
Everson v. Board of Education, 330 U.S. 1, 31–46, 49, 51–54, 57, 60, 63–72
(1947), Dissent, 1A (EST)

Tom C. Clark (1949–1967)
Mapp v. Ohio, 367 U.S. 643, 647 (1961), Majority, 4A
Abington v. Schempp, 374 U.S. 203, 213–14, 225 (1963), Majority, 1A (EST)
United States v. Barnett, 376 U.S. 681, 693 (1964), Majority, 6A (JT)
Schneider v. Rusk, 377 U.S. 163, 170–71 (1964), Dissent, 5A (DP)

Earl Warren (1953–1969 C.J.)
McGowan v. Maryland, 366 U.S. 420, 430, 437–41 (1961), Majority, 1A (EST)
Sperry v. Florida, 373 U.S. 379, 403 (1963), Majority, 10A
Bond v. Floyd, 385 U.S. 116, 135–36 (1966), Majority, 1A (FS)
Flast v. Cohen, 392 U.S. 83, 103–4 (1968), Majority, 1A (EST)

John M. Harlan (1955–1971)
Time, Inc. v. Hill, 385 U.S. 374, 410 (1967), Concurrence/Dissent, 1A (FS, FP)
Duncan v. Louisiana, 391 U.S. 145, 173 (1968), Dissent, 6A (JT)
Flast v. Cohen, 392 U.S. 83, 126, 128, 130 (1968), Dissent, 1A (EST)
Williams v. Florida, 399 U.S. 78, 124 (1970), Concurrence/Dissent, 6A (JT)
Bivens v. Six Unknown Named Agents of Federal Bureau of Narcotics, 403
U.S. 388, 401 (1971), Concurrence, 4A

William J. Brennan (1956–1990)
Roth v. United States, 354 U.S. 476, 488 (1957), Majority, 1A (FS, FP)
Reina v. United States, 364 U.S. 507, 512 (1960), Majority, 10A
Abington v. Schempp, 374 U.S. 203, 233–35, 238–41, 259, 286, 296
(1963), Concurrence, 1A (EST)
New York Times Co. v. Sullivan, 376 U.S. 254, 271, 274–75, 282 (1964),
Majority, 1A (FS & FP)

Time, Inc. v. Hill, 385 U.S. 374, 388–89 (1967), Majority, 1A (FS, FP)

Walz v. Tax Com. of New York, 397 U.S. 664, 684–85 (1970), Concurrence, 1A (EST)

Rosenbloom v. Metromedia, 403 U.S. 29, 51 (1971), Plurality, 1A (FS, FP)

United States v. Calandra, 414 U.S. 338, 356–57, 366 (1974), Dissent, 4A

Meek v. Pittenger, 421 U.S. 349, 382 (1975), Dissent, 1A (EST)

National League of Cities v. Usery, 426 U.S. 833, 876 (1976), Dissent, 10A

McDaniel v. Paty, 435 U.S. 618, 632 (1978), Concurrence, 1A (FE)

Davis v. Passman, 442 U.S. 228, 241–42 (1979), Majority, 5A (DP)

*Valley Forge Christian College v. Americans United for Separation of Church
   and State, Inc.*, 454 U.S. 464, 494, 502–4, 512 (1982), Dissent, 1A (EST)

Brown v. Hartlage, 456 U.S. 45, 56 (1982), Majority, 1A (FS)

Larson v. Valente, 456 U.S. 228, 245 (1982), Majority, 1A (FE)

Board of Education v. Pico, 457 U.S. 853, 867 (1982), Plurality, 1A (FS, FP)

Marsh v. Chambers, 463 U.S. 783, 804, 807–8, 815, 817 (1983), Dissent,
   1A (EST)

United States v. Leon, 468 U.S. 897, 930 (1984), Dissent, 4A

Wainwright v. Witt, 469 U.S. 412, 463 (1985), Dissent, BOR

McDonald v. Smith, 472 U.S. 479, 489 (1985), Concurrence, 1A

O'Lone v. Estate of Shabazz, 482 U.S. 342, 356 (1987), Dissent, 1A (FE)

Church of Jesus Christ of Latter–Day Saints v. Amos, 483 U.S. 327, 341
   (1987), Concurrence, 1A (FE)

United States v. Verdugo-Urquidez, 494 U.S. 259, 284 (1990), Dissent, 4A

Potter Stewart (1958–1981)

Engel v. Vitale, 370 U.S. 421, 447 (1962), Dissent, 1A (EST)

Griswold v. Connecticut, 381 U.S. 479, 529–30 (1965), Dissent, 9A

Time, Inc. v. Pape, 401 U.S. 279, 290 (1971), Majority, 1A (FS, FP)

Branzburg v. Hayes, 408 U.S. 665, 728 (1972), Dissent, 1A (FP)

Faretta v. California, 422 U.S. 806, 831 (1975), Majority, 6A (AOC)

Abood v. Detroit Bd. of Education, 431 U.S. 209, 234 (1977), Majority,
   1A (FS, FA)

Byron R. White (1962–1993)

United States v. Robel, 389 U.S. 258, 289 (1967), Dissent, 1A (FA)

Williams v. Florida, 399 U.S. 78, 94–96 (1970), Majority, 6A (JT)

United States v. Marion, 404 U.S. 307, 314 (1971), Majority, 6A (SPT)

Apodaca v. Oregon, 406 U.S. 404, 409 (1972), Plurality, 6A (JT)

Storer v. Brown, 415 U.S. 724, 736 (1974), Majority, 1A (FA)

Gertz v. Robert Welch, Inc., 418 U.S. 323, 384 (1974), Dissent, 1A
   (FS, FP)

Payton v. New York, 445 U.S. 573, 610–11 (1980), Dissent, 4A

Brecht v. Abrahamson, 507 U.S. 619, 645 (1993), Dissent, BOR

Arthur J. Goldberg (1962–1965)
Griswold v. Connecticut, 381 U.S. 479, 488–90 (1965), Concurrence, 9A

Thurgood Marshall (1967–1991)
Colgrove v. Battin, 413 U.S. 149, 172–73 (1973), Dissent, 7A
United States v. Wilson, 420 U.S. 332, 340–41 (1975), Majority, 5A (DJ)

Warren E. Burger (1969–1986 C.J.)
Walz v. Tax Com. of New York, 397 U.S. 664, 675 (1970), Majority, 1A (EST, FE)
Wisconsin v. Yoder, 406 U.S. 205, 218 (1972), Majority, 1A (FE)
McDaniel v. Paty, 435 U.S. 618, 623–24, 626, 628 (1978), Plurality, 1A (FE)
First Nat'l Bank v. Bellotti, 435 U.S. 765, 799–800 (1978), Concurrence,
    1A (FS, FP)
Richmond Newspapers v. Virginia, 448 U.S. 555, 579–80 (1980), Majority,
    1A (FS, FP), 9A
Schad v. Mt. Ephraim, 452 U.S. 61, 87–88 (1981), Dissent, 1A (FS)
Board of Education v. Pico, 457 U.S. 853, 888 (1982), Dissent, 1A (FS, FP)
Marsh v. Chambers, 463 U.S. 783, 788, 791 (1983), Majority, 1A (EST)
Lynch v. Donnelly, 465 U.S. 668, 675 (1984), Majority, 1A (EST)
McDonald v. Smith, 472 U.S. 479, 482 (1985), Majority, 1A (PET)

Harry A. Blackmun (1970–1994)
G.M. Leasing Corp. v. United States, 429 U.S. 338, 355 (1977), Majority, 4A
Garcia v. SAMTA, 469 U.S. 528, 549–52 (1985), Majority, 10A
United States v. Halper, 490 U.S. 435, 440 (1989), Majority, 5A (DJ)
Lee v. Weisman, 505 U.S. 577, 603, 607–8 (1992), Concurrence, 1A (EST)
Lucas v. South Carolina Coastal Council, 505 U.S. 1003, 1057 (1992),
    Dissent, 5A (TC)

Lewis F. Powell (1972–1987)
Committee for Public Education & Religious Liberty v. Nyquist, 413 U.S.
    756, 760, 770–71, 783, 798 (1973), Majority, 1A (EST)
Gertz v. Robert Welch, Inc., 418 U.S. 323, 340 (1974), Majority, 1A (FS, FP)
Elrod v. Burns, 427 U.S. 347, 378 (1976), Dissent, 1A (FS, FA)
EEOC v. Wyoming, 460 U.S. 226, 267–68, 270–72 (1983), Dissent, 10A
Oliver v. United States, 466 U.S. 170, 176–77 (1984), Majority, 4A
Garcia v. SAMTA, 469 U.S. 528, 569–73 (1985), Dissent, 10A
Edwards v. Aguillard, 482 U.S. 578, 605–6 (1987), Concurrence, 1A (EST)

William H. Rehnquist (1972–1986; 1986–2005 C.J.)
Smith v. Goguen, 415 U.S. 566, 600 (1974), Dissent, 1A (FS)
Carey v. Population Services International, 431 U.S. 678, 717 (1977),
    Dissent, 1A (FS)

Anderson v. Celebrezze, 460 U.S. 780, 813 (1983), Dissent, 1A (FA)

Wallace v. Jaffree, 472 U.S. 38, 92–100, 103 (1985), Dissent, 1A (EST)

United States v. Verdugo-Urquidez, 494 U.S. 259, 266 (1990), Majority, 4A

Timmons v. Twin Cities Area New Party, 520 U.S. 351, 368 (1997), Majority, 1A (FA)

Locke v. Davey, 540 U.S. 712, 722–23 (2004), Majority, 1A (EST)

Van Orden v. Perry, 125 S. Ct. 2854, 2859 (2005), Plurality, 1A (EST)

John Paul Stevens (1975–)

Houchins v. KQED, Inc., 438 U.S. 1, 31–32 (1978), Dissent, 1A (FP)

EEOC v. Wyoming, 460 U.S. 226, 249 (1983), Concurrence, 10A

Press-Enterprise Co. v. Superior Court of California, 464 U.S. 501, 518 (1984), Concurrence, 1A (FS, FP)

Massachusetts v. Upton, 466 U.S. 727, 737 (1984), Concurrence, 9A

Wallace v. Jaffree, 472 U.S. 38, 53–54 (1985), Majority, 1A (EST)

Chicago Teachers Union, Local No. 1 v. Hudson, 475 U.S. 292, 305 (1986), Majority, 1A (FS, FA)

Press-Enterprise Co. v. Superior Court, 478 U.S. 1, 18 (1986), Dissent, 1A (FP)

Ft. Wayne Books v. Indiana, 489 U.S. 46, 85 (1989), Concurrence/Dissent, 1A (FS, FP)

Harte-Hanks Communications v. Connaughton, 491 U.S. 657, 687 (1989), Majority, 1A (FS, FP)

Allegheny County v. ACLU 492 U.S. 573, 647 (1989), Concurrence/Dissent, 1A (EST)

Rutan v. Republican Party, 497 U.S. 62, 82 (1990), Concurrence, 1A (FS, FA)

Lucas v. South Carolina Coastal Council, 505 U.S. 1003, 1072 (1992), Dissent, 5A (TC)

McIntyre v. Ohio Elections Commission, 514 U.S. 334, 343 (1995), Majority, 1A (FS)

Adarand Constructors v. Pena, 515 U.S. 200, 251 (1995), Dissent, 5A (DP)

Printz v. United States, 521 U.S. 898, 942 (1997), Dissent, 10A

California Democratic Party v. Jones, 530 U.S. 567, 591 (2000), Dissent, 1A (FA)

Cook v. Gralike, 531 U.S. 510, 521 (2001), Majority, 1A (PET)

Van Orden v. Perry, 125 S. Ct. 2854, 2884 (2005), Dissent, 1A (EST)

District of Columbia v. Heller, 128 S. Ct. 2783, 2833–35 (2008), Dissent, 2A

Sandra Day O'Connor (1981–2005)

Federal Energy Regulatory Commission v. Mississippi, 456 U.S. 742, 793–96 (1982), Concurrence, Dissent, 10A

Tibbs v. Florida, 457 U.S. 31, 40 (1982), Majority, 5A (DJ)

Minneapolis Star & Tribune Co. v. Minn. Comm'r of Revenue, 460 U.S. 575, 583 (1983), Majority, 1A (FP)

Minnesota State Bd. for Community Colleges v. Knight, 465 U.S. 271, 285 (1984), Majority, 1A (FS,FA, PET)

Garcia v. SAMTA, 469 U.S. 528, 582 (1985), Dissent, 10A

Lyng v. Northwest Indian Cemetery Protective Association, 485 U.S. 439, 452 (1988), Majority, 1A (FE)

Gregory v. Ashcroft, 501 U.S. 452, 457–59 (1991), Majority, 10A

New York v. United States, 505 U.S. 144, 164, 180 (1992), Majority, 10A

City of Boerne v. Flores, 521 U.S. 507, 549, 555–57, 560–61, 563–64 (1997), Dissent, 1A (FE)

Kelo v. City of New London, 125 S. Ct. 2655, 2677 (2005), Dissent, 5A (TC)

McCreary County v. ACLU, 125 S. Ct. 2722, 2746 (2005), Concurrence, 1A (EST)

Antonin Scalia (1986–)

Austin v. Michigan State Chamber of Commerce, 494 U.S. 652, 693 (1990), Dissent, 1A (FS)

Harmelin v. Michigan, 501 U.S. 957, 977 (1991), Plurality, 8A (CUP)

Norman v. Reed, 502 U.S. 279, 299–300 (1992), Dissent, 1A (FA)

Lee v. Weisman, 505 U.S. 577, 634 (1992), Dissent, 1A (EST)

Lucas v. South Carolina Coastal Council, 505 U.S. 1003, 1028 (1992), Majority, 5A (TC)

Board of Education v. Grumet, 512 U.S. 687, 736 (1994), Dissent, 1A (EST, FE)

City of Boerne v. Flores, 521 U.S. 507, 540–42 (1997), Concurrence, 1A (FE)

Printz v. United States, 521 U.S. 898, 918–22 (1997), Majority, 10A

Locke v. Davey, 540 U.S. 712, 727 (2004), Dissent, 1A (FE)

McCreary County v. ACLU, 125 S. Ct. 2722, 2749–50, 2754 (2005), 1A (EST)

Hein v. Freedom from Religion Foundation, 127 S. Ct. 2553, 2576–77, 2583 (2007), Concurrence, 1A (EST)

District of Columbia v. Heller, 128 S. Ct. 2783, 2796, 2799 (2008), Majority, 2A

Anthony M. Kennedy (1988–)

Allegheny County v. ACLU 492 U.S. 573, 660 (1989), Concurrence/Dissent, 1A (EST)

Austin v. Michigan State Chamber of Commerce, 494 U.S. 652, 710 (1990), Dissent, 1A (FA)

Lee v. Weisman, 505 U.S. 577, 590 (1992), Majority, 1A (EST)

Alexander v. United States, 509 U.S. 544, 568 (1993), Dissent, 1A (FS, FP)

Roper v. Simmons, 543 U.S. 551, 578 (2005), Majority, 8A (CUP)

David H. Souter (1990–2009)

Lee v. Weisman, 505 U.S. 577, 612–13, 615–18, 620–27, 630–31 (1992), Concurrence, 1A (EST, FE)

Rosenberger v. Rector & Visitors of the University of Virginia, 515 U.S. 819, 868–73, 890–91 (1995), Dissent, 1A (EST)

Seminole Tribe v. Florida, 517 U.S. 44, 183 (1996), Dissent, 10A

Agostini v. Felton, 521 U.S. 203, 243 (1997), Dissent, 1A (EST)

United States v. Morrison, 529 U.S. 598, 647–48 (2000), Dissent, 10A

Mitchell v. Helms, 530 U.S. 793, 870–71, 899, 909 (2000), Dissent, 1A (EST)

Zelman v. Simmons-Harris, 536 U.S. 639, 711–12 (2002), Dissent, 1A (EST)

McCreary County v. ACLU, 125 S. Ct. 2722, 2743–44 (2005), Majority, 1A (EST)

Van Orden v. Perry, 125 S. Ct. 2854, 2892 (2005), Dissent, 1A (EST)

Hein v. Freedom from Religion Foundation, 127 S. Ct. 2553, 2585, 2587–88 (2007), Dissent, 1A (EST)

Clarence Thomas (1991–)

McIntyre v. Ohio Elections Commission, 514 U.S. 334, 369 (1995), Concurrence, 1A (FS, FP)

Rosenberger v. Rector & Visitors of the University of Virginia, 515 U.S. 819, 853–58 (1995), Concurrence, 1A (EST)

Nixon v. Shrink Missouri Government PAC, 528 U.S. 377, 411, 424 (2000), Dissent, 1A (FS)

United States v. Hubbell, 530 U.S. 27, 53 (2000), Concurrence, 5A (CSI)

Elk Grove Unified School District v. Newdow, 542 U.S. 1, 53–54 (2004), Concurrence, 1A (EST)

Cutter v. Wilkinson, 544 U.S. 709, 729 (2005), Concurrence, 1A (EST)

Kelo v. City of New London, 125 S. Ct. 2655, 2679 (2005), Dissent, 5A (TC)

Stephen G. Breyer (1994–)

Eldred v. Ashcroft, 537 U.S. 186, 246–47, 260–61 (2003), Dissent, 1A

Appendix B

The Bill of Rights Proposed by James Madison

The amendments which have occurred to me, proper to be recommended by Congress to the State Legislatures, are these:

First, That there be prefixed to the constitution a declaration, that all power is originally vested in, and consequently derived from the people.

That Government is instituted, and ought to be exercised for the benefit of the people; which consists in the enjoyment of life and liberty, with the right of acquiring and using property, and generally of pursuing and obtaining happiness and safety.

That the people have an indubitable, unalienable, and indefeasible right to reform or change their Government, whenever it be found adverse or inadequate to the purposes of its institution.

Secondly. That in article 1st, section 2, clause 3, these words be struck out, to wit, "The number of representatives shall not exceed one for every thirty thousand, but each state shall have at least one representative, and until such enumeration shall be made;" and that in place thereof be inserted these words, to wit, "After the first actual enumeration, there shall be one representative for every thirty thousand, until the number amount to —, after which the proportion shall be so regulated by Congress, that the number shall never be less than —, nor more —, than but each State shall after the first enumeration, have at least two Representatives; and prior thereto."

Thirdly. That in article 1st, section 6, clause 1, there be added to the end of the first sentence, these words, to wit, "But no law varying the compensation last ascertained shall operate before the next ensuing election of Representatives."

Fourthly. That in article 1st, section 9, between clauses 3 and 4, be inserted these clauses, to wit: The civil rights of none shall be abridged on account of religious belief or worship, nor shall any national religion be established, nor shall the full and equal rights of conscience be in any manner, or on any pretext infringed.

The people shall not be deprived or abridged of their right to speak, to write, or to publish their sentiments; and the freedom of the press, as one of the great bulwarks of liberty, shall be inviolable.

The people shall not be restrained from peaceably assembling and consulting for their common good; nor from applying to the Legislature by petitions, or remonstrances for redress of their grievances.

The right of the people to keep and bear arms shall not be infringed; a well armed, and well regulated militia being the best security of a free country: but no person religiously scrupulous of bearing arms, shall be compelled to render military service in person.

No soldier shall in time of peace be quartered in any house without the consent of the owner; nor at any time, but in a manner warranted by law.

No person shall be subject, except in cases of impeachment, to more than one punishment, or one trial for the same offence; nor shall be compelled to be a witness against himself; nor be deprived of life, liberty, or property without due process of law; nor be obliged to relinquish his property, where it may be necessary for public use, without a just compensation.

Excessive bail shall not be required, nor excessive fines imposed, nor cruel and unusual punishments inflicted.

The rights of the people to be secured in their persons; their houses, their papers, and their other property from all unreasonable searches and seizures, shall not be violated by warrants issued without probable cause, supported by oath or affirmation, or not particularly describing the places to be searched, or the persons or things to be seized.

In all criminal prosecutions, the accused shall enjoy the right to a speedy and public trial, to be informed of the cause and nature of the accusation, to be confronted with his accusers, and the witnesses against him; to have a compulsory process for obtaining witnesses in his favor; and to have the assistance of counsel for his defence.

The exceptions here or elsewhere in the constitution, made in favor of particular rights, shall not be so construed as to diminish the just importance of other rights retained by the people, or as to enlarge the powers delegated by the constitution; but either as actual limitations of such powers, or as inserted merely for greater caution.

Fifthly. That in article 1st, section 10, between clauses 1 and 2, be inserted this clause, to wit:

No state shall violate the equal rights of conscience, or the freedom of the press, or the trial by jury in criminal cases.

Sixthly. That, in article 3d, section 2, be annexed to the end of clause 2d, these words to wit:

But no appeal to such court shall be allowed where the value in controversy shall not amount to—dollars: nor shall any fact triable by jury, according to the course of common law, be otherwise re-examinable than may consist with the principles of common law.

Seventhly. That in article 3d, section 2, the third clause be struck out, and in its place be inserted the clauses following, to wit:

The trial of all crimes (except in cases of impeachments, and cases arising in the land or naval forces, or the militia when on actual service in time of war or public danger) shall be by an impartial jury of freeholders of the vicinage, with the requisite of unanimity for conviction, of the right of challenge, and other accustomed requisites; and in all crimes punishable with loss of life or member, presentment or indictment by a grand jury, shall be an essential preliminary, provided that in cases of crimes committed within any county which may be in possession of an enemy, or in which a general insurrection may prevail, the trial may by law be authorized in some other county of the same state, as near as may be to the seat of the offence.

In cases of crimes committed not within any county, the trial may by law be in such county as the laws shall have prescribed. In suits at common law, between man and man, the trial by jury, as one of the best securities to the rights of the people, ought to remain inviolate.

Eighthly. That immediately after article 6th, be inserted, as article 7th, the clauses following, to wit:

The powers delegated by this constitution, are appropriated to the departments to which they are respectively distributed: so that the legislative department shall never exercise the powers vested in the executive or judicial, nor the executive exercise the powers vested in the legislative or judicial, nor the judicial exercise the powers vested in the legislative or executive departments.

The powers not delegated by this constitution, nor prohibited by it to the States, are reserved to the States respectively.

Ninthly. That article 7th, be numbered as article 8th.

Appendix C

The Bill of Rights

Amendment I—Congress shall make no law respecting an establishment of religion, or prohibiting the free exercise thereof; or abridging the freedom of speech, or of the press; or the right of the people peaceably to assemble, and to petition the government for a redress of grievances.

Amendment II—A well regulated militia, being necessary to the security of a free state, the right of the people to keep and bear arms, shall not be infringed.

Amendment III—No soldier shall, in time of peace be quartered in any house, without the consent of the owner, nor in time of war, but in a manner to be prescribed by law.

Amendment IV—The right of the people to be secure in their persons, houses, papers, and effects, against unreasonable searches and seizures, shall not be violated, and no warrants shall issue, but upon probable cause, supported by oath or affirmation, and particularly describing the place to be searched, and the persons or things to be seized.

Amendment V—No person shall be held to answer for a capital, or otherwise infamous crime, unless on a presentment or indictment of a grand jury, except in cases arising in the land or naval forces, or in the militia, when in actual service in time of war or public danger; nor shall any person be subject for the same offense to be twice put in jeopardy of life or limb; nor shall be compelled in any criminal case to be a witness against himself, nor be deprived of life, liberty, or property, without due process of law; nor shall private property be taken for public use, without just compensation.

Amendment VI—In all criminal prosecutions, the accused shall enjoy the right to a speedy and public trial, by an impartial jury of the state and district wherein the crime shall have been committed, which district shall have been previously ascertained by law, and to be informed of the nature and cause of the accusation; to be confronted with the witnesses against him; to have compulsory process for obtaining witnesses in his favor, and to have the assistance of counsel for his defense.

Amendment VII—In suits at common law, where the value in controversy shall exceed twenty dollars, the right of trial by jury shall be preserved, and no fact tried by a jury, shall be otherwise reexamined in any court of the United States, than according to the rules of the common law.

Amendment VIII—Excessive bail shall not be required, nor excessive fines imposed, nor cruel and unusual punishments inflicted.

Amendment IX—The enumeration in the Constitution, of certain rights, shall not be construed to deny or disparage others retained by the people.

Amendment X—The powers not delegated to the United States by the Constitution, nor prohibited by it to the states, are reserved to the states respectively, or to the people.

NOTES

1—THE SUPREME COURT, THE BILL OF RIGHTS, AND JAMES MADISON

1. *See* RICHARD LABUNSKI, JAMES MADISON AND THE STRUGGLE FOR THE BILL OF RIGHTS 2 (New York: Oxford University Press, 2006).

2. *See* Commission as Colonel (Oct. 2, 1775), *in* 1 THE PAPERS OF JAMES MADISON, at 163, 164 n.1 (William T. Hutchinson & William M.E. Rachal, eds., Chicago: University of Chicago Press, 1962); Letter from Edmund Pendleton to James Madison (Sept. 25, 1780), *in* 2 THE PAPERS OF JAMES MADISON 99, 99 & n.1 (William T. Hutchinson & William M.E. Rachal, eds., Chicago: University of Chicago Press, 1962); Letter from James Madison to Alexander Hamilton (June 9, 1788), *in* 11 THE PAPERS OF JAMES MADISON 101 (Robert A. Rutland & Charles F. Hobson, eds., Charlottesville: University Press of Virginia, 1977); Letter from James Madison to George Washington (Jan. 4, 1790), *in* 12 THE PAPERS OF JAMES MADISON 466, 466 (Charles F. Hobson & Robert A. Rutland, eds., Charlottesville: University Press of Virginia, 1979); Letter from James Madison to James Madison, Sr. (May 2, 1790), *in* 13 THE PAPERS OF JAMES MADISON 183, 183 (Charles F. Hobson & Robert A. Rutland, eds., Charlottesville: University Press of Virginia, 1981); Letter from James Madison to Thomas Jefferson (July 1, 1791), *in* 14 THE PAPERS OF JAMES MADISON 39, 39 (Robert A. Rutland & Thomas A Mason, eds., Charlottesville: University Press of Virginia, 1983); Letters from James Madison to Thomas Jefferson (Aug. 5, 1797) and James Madison to Thomas Jefferson (Jan. 10, 1801), *in* 17 THE PAPERS OF JAMES MADISON 38, 39–40, 453, 455 (David B. Mattern et al., eds., Charlottesville: University Press of Virginia, 1991).

3. *See* LABUNSKI, *supra* note 1, at 2, 84; James Madison, Speech in the Virginia Ratifying Convention in Defense of the Constitution (June 6, 1788), *in* JAMES MADISON: WRITINGS 354, 354 (Jack N. Rakove, ed., New York: Library of America, 1999); James Madison, Power of Congress to Regulate the Militia (June 14, 1788) and Judicial Powers of the National Government (June 20, 1788) *in* 11 THE PAPERS OF JAMES MADISON, *supra* note 2, at 142, 144, 158, 164.

4. Rosenberger v. Rector, 515 U.S. 819 (1995).

5. *Id.* at 854 (Thomas, J., concurring, quoting Madison, *Memorial and Remonstrance against Religious Assessments*).

6. *Id.* at 855.

7. JAMES MADISON, *Memorial and Remonstrance against Religious Assessments*, *in* JAMES MADISON: WRITINGS, *supra* note 3, at 29, 30.

8. *Id.* at 32.

9. Rosenberger, 515 U.S. at 856 (Thomas, J., concurring) (internal citation and quotation omitted).

10. *Id.* at 856–57 (Thomas, J., concurring).

11. *Id.* at 868 (Souter, J., dissenting, quoting Madison, *Memorial and Remonstrance*).

12. *Id.* at 869–70 (Souter, J., dissenting, quoting Everson v. Bd. of Educ., 330 U.S. 1, 11 (1947)).

13. *Id.* at 869–70 n.1 (Souter, J., dissenting).

14. U.S. v. Verdugo-Urquidez, 494 U.S. 259 (1990).

15. *Id.* at 266.

16. *Id.*

17. *Id.* (quoting 1 ANNALS OF CONG. 438 (1789)).

18. *Id.* (internal citations omitted).

19. *Id.* at 284 (Brennan, J., dissenting).

20. *Id.* (quoting MADISON, *Report on the Virginia Resolutions* (Jan. 1800), reprinted in 4 ELLIOT'S DEBATES 556 (2d ed. 1836)).

21. For those seeing Madison as a separationist, *see* Irving Brant, *Madison: On the Separation of Church and State*, 8 WM. & MARY Q. 3, 3 (1951); IRVING BRANT, JAMES MADISON: FATHER OF THE CONSTITUTION, 1787–1800 272 (Indianapolis: Bobbs-Merrill, 1950); Thomas Lindsay, *James Madison on Religion and Politics: Rhetoric and Reality*, 85 AM. POL. SCI. REV. 1321, 1321 (1991); JACK N. RAKOVE, JAMES MADISON AND THE CREATION OF THE AMERICAN REPUBLIC 15 (New York: Longman, 2002); Robert S. Alley, *How Much God in the Schools? Public Education and the Public Good*, 4 WM. & MARY BILL RTS. J. 277, 335 (1995); RALPH KETCHAM, JAMES MADISON: A BIOGRAPHY 163 (Charlottesville: University Press of Virginia, 1990); LEONARD W. LEVY, ORIGINS OF THE BILL OF RIGHTS 86 (New Haven: Yale Nota Bene, 1999); Charles J. Reid Jr., *The Fundamental Freedom: Judge John T. Noonan Jr.'s Historiography of Religious Liberty*, 83 MARQ. L. REV. 367, 412 (1999); Daniel R. Gordon, *Due North: James Madison, the American Modern Wall of Separation, and the Canadian Indian Residential Schools*, 32 CUMB. L. REV. 281, 288 (2001/2002); David Reiss, *Jefferson and Madison as Icons in Judicial History: A Study of Religion Clause Jurisprudence*, 61 MD. L. REV. 94, 103 (2002); David P. Currie, *God & Caesar & President Madison*, 3 GREEN BAG 2d 11, 11 (1999); Kurt T. Lash, *Power and the Subject of Religion*, 59 OHIO ST. L.J. 1069 (1998); Steven G. Gey, *When Is Religious Speech Not "Free Speech"?* 2000 U. ILL. L. REV. 379 (2000). For those understanding Madison to be a nonpreferentialist, *see* Thomas M. Franck, *Is Personal Freedom a Western Value?* 91 AM. J. INT'L L. 593, 596 (1997); Steven D. Smith, *Blooming Confusion: Madison's Mixed Legacy*, 75 IND. L.J. 61, 62 (2000); John S. Baker Jr., *The Establishment Clause as Intended: No Preference among Sects and Pluralism in a Large Commercial Republic*, in THE BILL OF RIGHTS: ORIGINAL MEANING AND CURRENT UNDERSTANDING 41, 50–51 (Eugene W. Hickok Jr., ed., Charlottesville: University Press of Virginia, 1991).

22. Employment Div. v. Smith, 494 U.S. 872, 894 (1990) (O'Connor, J., concurring).

23. Smith at 879 (internal quotations omitted).

24. For those understanding Madison to be an accommodationist, *see* Rodney K. Smith, *James Madison, John Witherspoon, and Oliver Cowdery: The First Amendment and the 134th Section of the Doctrine and Covenants*, 2003 BYU L. REV. 891, 903 (2003); RICHARD K. MATTHEWS, IF MEN WERE ANGELS: JAMES MADISON AND THE HEARTLESS EMPIRE OF REASON 121, 124 (Lawrence: University Press of Kansas, 1995); JACK N. RAKOVE, ORIGINAL MEANINGS: POLITICS AND IDEAS IN THE MAKING OF THE CONSTITUTION 312 (New York: Knopf, 1996); KETCHAM, JAMES MADISON: A BIOGRAPHY, *supra* note 21, at 319; Michael McConnell, *The Origins and Historical Understandings of Free Exercise of Religion*, 103 HARV. L. REV. 1409, 1454 (1990); Walter Berns, *James Madison on Religion and Politics*, in JAMES MADISON AND THE FUTURE OF LIMITED GOVERNMENT 135, 139 (John Samples, ed., Washington,

D.C.: Cato Institute, 2002); Rodney A. Grunes, *James Madison and Religious Freedom, in* JAMES MADISON: PHILOSOPHER, FOUNDER, AND STATESMAN 105, 115 (John R. Vile et al., eds., Athens: Ohio University Press, 2008). For those who think Madison took a neutrality position for free exercise, *see* Steven D. Smith, *Blooming Confusion, supra* note 21, at 65; Vincent Blasi, *School Vouchers and Religious Liberty: Seven Questions from Madison's Memorial and Remonstrance,* 87 CORNELL L. REV. 783, 808 (2002); Vincent Phillip Muñoz, *James Madison's Principle of Religious Liberty,* 97 AM. POL. SCI. REV. 17, 31 (2003); Mark W. Cordes, *Politics, Religion, and the First Amendment,* 50 DEPAUL L. REV. 111 (2000).

25. For those seeing Madison as a classical liberal for First Amendment purposes, *see* J.M. Balkin, *Populism and Progressivism as Constitutional Categories,* 104 YALE L.J. 1935, 1955 (1995) (reviewing SUNSTEIN, DEMOCRACY AND THE PROBLEM OF FREE SPEECH, *infra*); John O. McGinnis, *The Once and Future Property-Based Vision of the First Amendment,* 63 U. CHI. L. REV. 49, 56–57 (1996); Steven J. Heyman, *Righting the Balance: An Inquiry into the Foundations and Limits of Freedom of Expression,* 78 B.U.L. REV. 1275, 1290–91 (1998); Reid, *The Fundamental Freedom, supra* note 21, at 416; Solveig Singleton, *Reviving a First Amendment Absolutism for the Internet,* 3 TEX. REV. L. & POL. 279, 312 (1999); Samuel R. Olken, *The Business of Expression: Economic Liberty, Political Factions, and the Forgotten First Amendment Legacy of Justice George Sutherland,* 10 WM. & MARY BILL RTS. J. 249, 281 (2002); LANCE BANNING, THE SACRED FIRE OF LIBERTY: JAMES MADISON AND THE FOUNDING OF THE FEDERAL REPUBLIC 391 (Ithaca, N.Y.: Cornell University Press, 1995); LEVY, ORIGINS, *supra* note 21, at 108; Daniel E. Troy, *Advertising: Not "Low Value" Speech,* 16 YALE J. ON REG. 85 (1999); John R. Vile, *James Madison's* Report of 1800 *in* JAMES MADISON: PHILOSOPHER, FOUNDER, AND STATESMAN, *supra* note 24, at 133. For those who thought Madison employed a democracy-centered approach to these rights, *see* CASS R. SUNSTEIN, DEMOCRACY AND THE PROBLEM OF FREE SPEECH xvi–xviii, 119 (New York: Free Press, 1995); Adrienne Koch & Harry Ammon, *The Virginia and Kentucky Resolutions: An Episode in Jefferson's and Madison's Defense of Civil Liberties,* 5 WM. & MARY Q. 145, 172 (1948); Neal Riemer, *Two Conceptions of the Genius of American Politics,* 20 J. POL. 695, 712 (1958); Robert A. Rutland, *The Trivialization of the Bill of Rights: One Historian's View of How the Purposes of the First Ten Amendments Have Been Defiled,* 31 WM. & MARY L. REV. 287, 287–88 (1990); MICHAEL KENT CURTIS, FREE SPEECH, "THE PEOPLE'S DARLING PRIVILEGE": STRUGGLES FOR FREEDOM OF EXPRESSION IN AMERICAN HISTORY 195 (Durham, N.C.: Duke University Press, 2000); Ron Smith, *Compelled Cost Disclosure of Grass Roots Lobbying Expenses: Necessary Government Voyeurism or Chilled Political Speech?,* 6 KAN J.L. & PUB. POL'Y 115 (1996).

26. For those understanding Madison to be a classical liberal on property rights, *see* SAMUEL H. BEER, TO MAKE A NATION: THE REDISCOVERY OF AMERICAN FEDERALISM 273 (Cambridge, Mass.: Belknap Press, 1993); James A. Dorn, *The Rule of Law and Freedom in Emerging Democracies: A Madisonian Perspective, in* JAMES MADISON AND THE FUTURE OF LIMITED GOVERNMENT, *supra* note 24, at 191, 196; MATTHEWS, *supra* note 24, at xvi, 153; JAMES W. ELY, JR., THE GUARDIAN OF EVERY OTHER RIGHT: A CONSTITUTIONAL HISTORY OF PROPERTY RIGHTS 53, 55 (New York: Oxford University Press, 1998); NEDELSKY, PRIVATE PROPERTY AND THE LIMITS OF AMERICAN CONSTITUTIONALISM: THE MADISONIAN

FRAMEWORK AND ITS LEGACY 153 (Chicago: University of Chicago Press, 1990), 35, 152. For those scholars interpreting Madison to have a more classical republican stance on property, *see* Jack N. Rakove, *The Madisonian Theory of Rights*, 31 WM. & MARY L. REV. 245, 261 (1990); RAKOVE, ORIGINAL MEANINGS, *supra* note 24, at 315; Matthew Harrington, *"Public Use" and the Original Understanding of the So-Called "Takings" Clause*, 53 HASTINGS L.J. 1245, 1248 (2002); Walter J. Kendall III, *Madison and the Market Economy*, 23 QUINNIPIAC L. REV. 1097, 1101 (2005); GUY PADULA, MADISON V. MARSHALL: POPULAR SOVEREIGNTY, NATURAL LAW, AND THE UNITED STATES CONSTITUTION 148 (Lanham, Md.: Lexington, 2001); NEAL RIEMER, JAMES MADISON: CREATING THE AMERICAN CONSTITUTION 127 (Washington, D.C.: Congressional Quarterly, 1986); KETCHAM, JAMES MADISON: A BIOGRAPHY, *supra* note 21, at 221.

27. For more description of classical republican political theory, *see generally* Isaac Kramnick, *The "Great National Discussion": This Discourse of Politics in 1787, in* WHAT DID THE CONSTITUTION MEAN TO EARLY AMERICANS? 36–37 (Edward Countryman, ed., Boston: Bedford, 1999); GARRETT WARD SHELDON, THE POLITICAL PHILOSOPHY OF JAMES MADISON 80 (Baltimore: The Johns Hopkins University Press, 2001); GORDON S. WOOD, THE CREATION OF THE AMERICAN REPUBLIC, 1776–1787 24, 49–53, 68 (Chapel Hill: University of North Carolina Press, 1969); FORREST MCDONALD, NOVUS ORDO SECLORUM: THE INTELLECTUAL ORIGINS OF THE CONSTITUTION 70–75, 87 (Lawrence: University Press of Kansas, 1985); James T. Kloppenberg, *The Virtues of Liberalism: Christianity, Republicanism, and Ethics in Early American Political Discourse*, 74 J. AM. HIST. 9, 14 (1987); J.G.A. POCOCK, THE MACHIAVELLIAN MOMENT: FLORENTINE POLITICAL THOUGHT AND THE ATLANTIC REPUBLICAN TRADITION 520–23 (Princeton, N.J.: Princeton University Press, 1975); DANIEL A. FARBER & SUZANNA SHERRY, A HISTORY OF THE AMERICAN CONSTITUTION 11–14 (St. Paul, Minn.: West, 1990).

28. For more description of classical liberal political theory, *see generally* Kramnick, *supra* note 27, at 36–37; FARBER & SHERRY, *supra* note 27, at 12–13; R. Randall Kelso, *The Natural Law Tradition on the Modern Supreme Court: Not Burke, but the Enlightenment Tradition Represented by Locke, Madison, and Marshall*, 26 ST. MARY'S L.J. 1051, 1065 (1995); JOHN P. DIGGINS, THE LOST SOUL OF AMERICAN POLITICS: VIRTUE, SELF-INTEREST, AND THE FOUNDATIONS OF LIBERALISM 16 (Chicago: University of Chicago Press, 1984).

29. JOHN LOCKE, SECOND TREATISE OF GOVERNMENT 32 (C.B. Macpherson, ed., Indianapolis: Hackett, 1980). For more on Locke's theory of liberty, *see* SHELDON S. WOLIN, POLITICS AND VISION: CONTINUITY AND INNOVATION IN WESTERN POLITICAL THOUGHT 278 (Princeton, N.J.: Princeton University Press, 2004).

30. For more on the tie between liberalism and virtue, *see* JAMES T. KLOPPENBERG, THE VIRTUES OF LIBERALISM 6 (New York: Oxford University Press, 1998); Kloppenberg, *The Virtues of Liberalism*, *supra* note 27, at 16–18; GARY ROSEN, AMERICAN COMPACT: JAMES MADISON AND THE PROBLEM OF FOUNDING 5 (Lawrence: University Press of Kansas, 1999); Steven J. Heyman, *Ideologial Conflict and the First Amendment*, 78 CHI.-KENT L. REV. 531, 571–72 (2003).

31. *See* LEVY, ORIGINS, *supra* note 21, at 180, 181; Ralph Rossum, *"Self-Incrimination": The Original Intent, in* THE BILL OF RIGHTS: ORIGINAL MEANING, *supra*

note 21, at 273, 280; Michael Edmund O'Neill, *The Fifth Amendment in Congress: Revisiting the Privilege against Compelled Self-Incrimination*, 90 GEO. L.J. 2445, 2481 (2002); RAKOVE, JAMES MADISON, *supra* note 21, at 95. Almost all of these inquiries are based solely on the language Madison proposed in Congress on June 8, 1789: "No person . . . shall be compelled to be a witness against himself."

32. BERNARD SCHWARTZ, THE GREAT RIGHTS OF MANKIND: A HISTORY OF THE AMERICAN BILL OF RIGHTS 151–52 (Madison, Wisc.: Madison House, 1992); Thomas Y. Davies, *The Fictional Character of Law-and-Order Originalism: A Case Study of the Distortions and Evasions of Framing-Era Arrest Doctrine in* Atwater v. Lago Vista, 37 WAKE FOREST L. REV. 239, 251 (2002); SHELDON, *supra* note 27, at 90; IRVING BRANT, THE BILL OF RIGHTS: ITS ORIGIN AND MEANING 392 (Indianapolis: Bobbs-Merrill, 1965); James W. Ely, Jr., *The Oxymoron Reconsidered: Myth and Reality in the Origins of Substantive Due Process*, 16 CONST. COMMENT. 315, 325 (1999); Robert E. Riggs, *Substantive Due Process in 1791*, 1990 WIS. L. REV. 941, 994 (1990). There is very little that scholars use as evidence of Madison's intent beyond his June 8, 1789, speech in Congress.

33. For a liberal view of Madison on the Fourth Amendment, *see* AKHIL REED AMAR, THE BILL OF RIGHTS: CREATION AND RECONSTRUCTION 65 (New Haven, Conn.: Yale University Press, 1998). For the contrary position, *see* Clark D. Cunningham, *A Linguistic Analysis of the Meanings of "Search" in the Fourth Amendment: A Search for Common Sense*, 73 IOWA L. REV. 541, 551–52 (1988); Tracey Maclin, *The Central Meaning of the Fourth Amendment*, 35 WM. & MARY L. REV. 197, 249 n.35 (1993); Thomas K. Clancy, *The Role of Individualized Suspicion in Assessing the Reasonableness of Searches and Seizures*, 25 U. MEM. L. REV. 483, 635 (1994).

34. *See, e.g.*, Rosenberger v. Rector, 515 U.S. 819, 856 (1995) (Thomas, J., concurring) (quoting ROBERT L. CORD, SEPARATION OF CHURCH AND STATE: HISTORICAL FACT AND CURRENT FICTION 22 (Cambridge, Mass.: Lambeth Press, 1982)); Lucas v. S.C. Coastal Council, 505 U.S. 1003, 1057 n.23 (1992) (Blackmun, J., dissenting) (quoting Joseph L. Sax, *Takings and the Police Power*, 74 YALE L.J. 36, 58 (1964)); Wallace v. Jaffree, 472 U.S. 38, 97, 100 (1985) (Rehnquist, J., dissenting) (quoting C. ANTIEAU, A. DOWNEY, & E. ROBERTS, FREEDOM FROM FEDERAL ESTABLISHMENT 130, 163 (1964)).

35. For authors who have attempted a more comprehensive study of the Bill of Rights as a whole and have said more about Madison in this regard, *see* LEVY, ORIGINS, *supra* note 21; AMAR, *supra* note 33; 2 BERNARD SCHWARTZ, THE BILL OF RIGHTS: A DOCUMENTARY HISTORY 1006 (New York: Chelsea House, 1971).

36. THE FEDERALIST NO. 10, at 161 (James Madison) *in* JAMES MADISON: WRITINGS, *supra* note 3.

37. MADISON, *Memorial and Remonstrance, supra, in* JAMES MADISON: WRITINGS, *supra* note 3, at 30.

38. James Madison, Speech in Congress on "Self-Created Societies" (Nov. 27, 1794), *in* JAMES MADISON: WRITINGS, *supra* note 3, 551, 552.

39. 1 ANNALS OF CONG. 451 (1789).

40. *Id.*

41. *Id.* at 452.

42. *Id.* at 453.

43. For those understanding Madison to be a classical republican, *see* WOOD,

supra note 27, at 429; Lawrence Claus, *Protecting Rights from Rights: Enumeration, Disparagement, and the Ninth Amendment*, 79 NOTRE DAME L. REV. 585, 630 (2004); GARRY WILLS, EXPLAINING AMERICA: THE FEDERALIST 268, 269 (Garden City, N.Y.: Doubleday, 1981); Douglass Adair, *The Tenth Federalist Revisited*, 8 WM. & MARY Q. 48 (1951) and Douglass Adair, *"That Politics May be Reduced to a Science": David Hume, James Madison, and the Tenth* Federalist, 20 HUNTINGTON LIBR. Q. 343 (1957); Norman B. Smith, *"Shall Make No Law Abridging": An Analysis of the Neglected, but Nearly Absolute, Right of Petition*, 54 U. CIN. L. REV. 1153, 1182–83 (1986); A.E. Dick Howard, *James Madison and the Founding of the Republic, in* JAMES MADISON ON RELIGIOUS LIBERTY 21, 24 (Robert S. Alley, ed., Buffalo, N.Y.: Prometheus Books, 1985); Colleen A. Sheehan, *The Politics of Public Opinion: James Madison's "Notes on Government,"* 49 WM. & MARY Q. 609, 611 (1992); COLLEEN A. SHEEHAN, JAMES MADISON AND THE SPIRIT OF REPUBLICAN SELF-GOVERNMENT (New York: Cambridge University Press, 2009). For those understanding Madison to be a classical liberal, *see* Laura S. Underkuffler, *On Property: An Essay*, 100 YALE L.J. 127, 137–38 (1990); Larry D. Kramer, *Madison's Audience*, 112 HARV. L. REV. 611, 672 (1999); Heyman, *Ideological Conflict and the First Amendment, supra* note 30, at 541–42; ROSEN, *supra* note 30, at 3; MATTHEWS, *supra* note 24, at 18–19; Joseph P. Viteritti & Gerald J. Russello, *Community and American Federalism: Images Romantic and Real*, 4 VA. J. SOC. POL'Y & L. 683, 694 (1997); Robert H. Horwitz, *John Locke and the Preservation of Liberty: A Perennial Problem of Civic Education, in* THE MORAL FOUNDATIONS OF THE AMERICAN REPUBLIC 129, 132–33 (Robert H. Horwitz, ed., Charlottesville: University Press of Virginia, 1977); Balkin, *supra* note 25, at 1955; Charles F. Hobson, *James Madison, the Bill of Rights, and the Problem of the States*, 31 WM. & MARY L. REV. 267, 268 (1990); Muñoz, *supra* note 24, at 22; Olken, *supra* note 25, at 281; Roger Pilon, *Madison's Constitutional Vision: The Legacy of Enumerated Powers, in* JAMES MADISON AND THE FUTURE, *supra* note 24, 25, 27–28; LEONARD R. SORENSON, MADISON ON THE "GENERAL WELFARE" OF AMERICA: HIS CONSISTENT CONSTITUTIONAL VISION 109 (Lanham, Md.: Rowman & Littlefield, 1995). For those understanding Madison to be something more complex or something in between classical liberalism and classical republicanism, *see* Ralph L. Ketcham, *James Madison and the Nature of Man*, 19 J. HIST. IDEAS 62, 62, 68 (1958); KETCHAM, JAMES MADISON: A BIOGRAPHY, *supra* note 21, at ix; BANNING, THE SACRED FIRE, *supra* note 25, at 9–10; SHELDON, *supra* note 27, at xii; NEDELSKY, *supra* note 26, at 181–82; Kloppenberg, *The Virtues of Liberalism, supra* note 27, at 30; James H. Read, *"Our Complicated System": James Madison on Power and Liberty*, 23 POL. THEORY 452, 455 (1995).

2—MADISON'S CONCEPTION OF HUMAN NATURE

1. *See* THE FEDERALIST NO. 55, at 316 (James Madison) (Jack N. Rakove, ed., 1999); JAMES MADISON, *Government* (Jan. 2, 1792), *in* JAMES MADISON: WRITINGS, *supra* chap. 1, note 3, at 501, 502; JAMES MADISON, *Universal Peace* (Feb. 2, 1792), *in* JAMES MADISON: WRITINGS, *supra* chap. 1, note 3, at 505–7; Letter from James Madison to James Monroe (July 6, 1807), *in* JAMES MADISON: WRITINGS, *supra* chap. 1, note 3, at 673, 676; James Madison, Speech in Congress Opposing the National Bank (Feb. 2, 1791), *in* JAMES MADISON: WRITINGS, *supra* chap. 1, note 3, at 480, 481.

2. KETCHAM, JAMES MADISON: A BIOGRAPHY, *supra* chap. 1, note 21, at 20.

3. Commonplace Book, Editorial Note, *in* 1 THE PAPERS OF JAMES MADISON, *supra* chap. 1, note 2, at 4, 5.

4. *Id.* at 28–29, 33.

5. PADULA, MADISON V. MARSHALL, *supra* chap. 1, note 26, at 23.

6. James Madison, Report on Books for Congress (Jan. 23, 1783), *in* 6 THE PAPERS OF JAMES MADISON, at 62–90 (William T. Hutchinson & William M.E. Rachal, eds., Chicago: University of Chicago Press, 1969).

7. *See* Rodney K. Smith, *supra* chap. 1, note 24, at 895–96; KETCHAM, JAMES MADISON: A BIOGRAPHY, *supra* chap. 1, note 21, at 25; WILLS, *supra* chap. 1, note 43, at 17; RAKOVE, JAMES MADISON, *supra* chap. 1, note 21, at 3; Thomas Miller, Introduction, *in* JOHN WITHERSPOON, THE SELECTED WRITINGS OF JOHN WITHERSPOON 1, 36–37 (Thomas Miller, ed., Carbondale: Southern Illinois University Press, 1990); Roy Branson, *James Madison and the Scottish Enlightenment*, 40 J. HIST. IDEAS 235, 236 (1979); PADULA, MADISON V. MARSHALL, *supra* chap. 1, note 26, at 23.

8. John Witherspoon, Lectures in Moral Philosophy, *in* WITHERSPOON, *supra* note 7, at 152, 171.

9. *Id.* at 161.

10. Dennis F. Thompson, *The Education of a Founding Father: The Reading List for John Witherspoon's Course in Political Theory, as Taken by James Madison*, 4 POL. THEORY 523, 523 (1976).

11. *Id.* at 528.

12. Madison, Report on Books for Congress, *supra*, *in* 6 THE PAPERS OF JAMES MADISON, *supra* note 6, at 65–115. Witherspoon helped Madison choose the books for this list. *Id.* at 63.

13. 1 JOHN CALVIN, INSTITUTES OF THE CHRISTIAN RELIGION 251 (John T. McNeill, ed., Ford Lewis Battles, trans., Philadelphia: Westminster, 1960).

14. *Id.* at 252.

15. *Id.* at 250.

16. John Witherspoon, Christian Magnanimity, *in* WITHERSPOON, *supra* note 7, at 116, 120.

17. John Witherspoon, Dominion of Providence, *in* WITHERSPOON, *supra* note 7, at 126, 128.

18. *Id.* at 129.

19. Witherspoon, Lectures on Moral Philosophy, *supra*, *in* WITHERSPOON, *supra* note 7, at 154.

20. Witherspoon, Dominion of Providence, *supra*, *in* WITHERSPOON, *supra* note 7, at 130.

21. *Id.* at 136.

22. Witherspoon, Lectures on Moral Philosophy, *supra*, *in* WITHERSPOON, *supra* note 7, at 203.

23. *See* Adair, *"That Politics May be Reduced to a Science," supra* chap. 1, note 43, at 348–56; Marc M. Arkin, *"The Intractable Principle": David Hume, James Madison, Religion, and the Tenth Federalist*, 39 AM. J. LEGAL HIST. 148, 157 (1995); BANNING, THE SACRED FIRE, *supra* chap. 1, note 25, at 204; BEER, *supra* chap. 1, note 26, at 269; Branson, *supra* note 7, at 244, 247; Franklin A. Kalinowski, *David Hume on*

the Philosophic Underpinnings of Interest Group Politics, 25 POLITY 355, 356 (1993); Ralph L. Ketcham, *Notes on James Madison's Sources for the Tenth Federalist Paper*, 1 MIDWEST J. OF POL. SCI. 20, 23 (1958); MATTHEWS, *supra* chap. 1, note 24, at 77; John M. Werner, *David Hume and America*, 33 J. HIST. IDEAS 439, 452 (1972).

24. DAVID HUME, A TREATISE OF HUMAN NATURE 193 (David Fate Norton & Mary J. Norton, eds., Oxford: Oxford University Press, 2000).

25. *Id.* at 268.

26. *Id.* at 266.

27. *Id.* at 320.

28. *Id.* at 320–21.

29. Madison, Report on Books for Congress, *supra*, *in* 6 THE PAPERS OF JAMES MADISON, *supra* note 6, at 80, 87.

30. *See* THE FEDERALIST NO. 10, at 270 n.1 (James Madison) *in* 10 THE PAPERS OF JAMES MADISON (Robert A. Rutland et al., eds., Chicago: University of Chicago Press, 1977).

31. For others holding this view of Madison, *see* Ketcham, *James Madison and the Nature of Man*, *supra* chap. 1, note 43, at 67; Joseph F. Kobylka & Bradley Kent Carter, *Madison, The Federalist, & the Constitutional Order: Human Nature & Institutional Structure*, 20 POLITY 190, 190–95 (1987); James Q. Wilson, *Interests and Deliberation in the American Republic; or, Why James Madison Would Never Have Won the James Madison Award*, 23 PS: POL. SCI. & POL. 558, 562 (1990); RIEMER, JAMES MADISON, *supra* chap. 1, note 26, at xvi; KETCHAM, JAMES MADISON: A BIOGRAPHY, *supra* chap. 1, note 21, at 50; WILLS, *supra* chap. 1, note 43, at 187–88. However, there are also scholars who understand Madison as having a pessimistic view of human nature. For those, *see generally* FARBER & SHERRY, *supra* chap. 1, note 27, at 211; SHELDON, *supra* chap. 1, note 27, at ix, xv; MATTHEWS, *supra* chap. 1, note 24, at 51; WOLIN, *supra* chap. 1, note 29, at 349; NEDELSKY, *supra* chap. 1, note 26, at 208.

32. James Madison, Vices of the Political System of the United States (Apr. 1787), *in* JAMES MADISON: WRITINGS, *supra* chap. 1, note 3, at 69, 75–76.

33. *Id.* at 75.

34. *Id.* at 77.

35. *Id.*

36. Letter from James Madison to Thomas Jefferson (Oct. 24, 1787), *in* JAMES MADISON: WRITINGS, *supra* chap. 1, note 3, at 142, 150.

37. *Id.*

38. *Id.*

39. *Id.*

40. *Id.* at 151.

41. *Id.*

42. *Id.*

43. THE FEDERALIST NO. 10, at 161 (James Madison) (Jack N. Rakove, ed., 1999).

44. *Id.*

45. *Id.* at 163.

46. THE FEDERALIST NO. 37, at 200 (James Madison) (Jack N. Rakove, ed., 1999).

47. *Id.* at 201.

48. THE FEDERALIST NO. 51, at 295 (James Madison) (Jack N. Rakove, ed., 1999).

49. *Id.*

50. *Id.*

51. THE FEDERALIST NO. 55, at 319–20 (James Madison) (Jack N. Rakove, ed., 1999).

52. THE FEDERALIST NO. 57, at 327 (James Madison) (Jack N. Rakove, ed., 1999).

53. James Madison, Speech at the Constitutional Convention (July 11, 1787), *in* JAMES MADISON, NOTES OF DEBATES IN THE FEDERAL CONVENTION OF 1787 272 (James Madison, ed., New York: Norton, 1966) (emphasis added).

54. Letter from James Madison to Thomas Jefferson (Oct. 17, 1788), *in* JAMES MADISON: WRITINGS, *supra* chap. 1, note 3, at 421 (emphasis added).

55. JAMES MADISON, *Helvidius No. 5* (Sept. 18, 1793), *in* 15 THE PAPERS OF JAMES MADISON, at 113, 118 (Thomas A. Mason et al., eds., Charlottesville: University Press of Virginia, 1985) (emphasis added).

56. James Madison, Speech in the Virginia Constitutional Convention (Dec. 2, 1829), *in* JAMES MADISON: WRITINGS, *supra* chap. 1, note 3, at 824.

57. James Madison, Speech in the Virginia Ratifying Convention on the Judicial Power (June 20, 1788), *in* JAMES MADISON: WRITINGS, *supra* chap. 1, note 3, at 393, 398.

58. *Id.*

3—MADISON'S MULTIFACETED LIBERALISM

1. Witherspoon, Lectures on Moral Philosophy, *supra*, *in* WITHERSPOON, *supra* chap. 2, note 7, at 181.

2. *Id.* at 191.

3. *Id.*

4. James Madison, Amendments to the Virginia Declaration of Rights (June 12, 1776), *in* JAMES MADISON: WRITINGS, *supra* chap. 1, note 3, at 10.

5. MADISON, *Memorial and Remonstrance, supra, in* JAMES MADISON: WRITINGS, *supra* chap. 1, note 3, at 30.

6. *Id.*

7. *Id.*

8. *Id.* at 31.

9. *Id.* at 35.

10. THE FEDERALIST NO. 43, at 250–51 (James Madison) (Jack N. Rakove, ed., 1999).

11. THE FEDERALIST NO. 44, at 253 (James Madison) (Jack N. Rakove, ed., 1999).

12. LOCKE, *supra* chap. 1, note 29, at 89.

13. *Id.* at 68.

14. Witherspoon, Lectures on Moral Philosophy, *supra, in* WITHERSPOON, *supra* chap. 2, note 7, at 191.

15. 1 ANNALS OF CONG. 451 (1789).

16. LOCKE, *supra* chap. 1, note 29, at 46.

17. *Id.* at 47–48.

18. *Id.* at 69.

19. *Id.* at 124.

20. Thompson, *supra* chap. 2, note 10, at 527.

21. *Id.*

22. 1 ANNALS OF CONG. 452 (1789).

23. *Id.* at 454 (emphasis added).

24. Letter from James Madison to Thomas Jefferson (Feb. 4, 1790), *in* JAMES MADISON: WRITINGS, *supra* chap. 1, note 3, at 473, 476.

25. LOCKE, *supra* chap. 1, note 29, at 52.

26. *Id.* at 64.

27. THE FEDERALIST NO. 43, at 250 (James Madison) (Jack N. Rakove, ed., 1999).

28. LOCKE, *supra* chap. 1, note 29, at 7, 8, 9, 10, 12, 14, 17, 20, 24, 33, 36, 41, 46, 47, 56, 66, 67, 70, 71, 84, 88, 89, 95, 97, 105, 118.

29. JAMES MADISON, *Spirit of Governments* (Feb. 20, 1792), *in* JAMES MADISON: WRITINGS, *supra* chap. 1, note 3, at 509, 510.

30. JAMES MADISON, *Helvidius No. 1* (Aug. 24, 1793), *in* 15 THE PAPERS OF JAMES MADISON, *supra* chap. 2, note 55, at 66, 68.

31. JAMES MADISON, *Property* (Mar. 29, 1792), *in* JAMES MADISON: WRITINGS, *supra* chap. 1, note 3, at 515 (internal quotation unknown).

32. *Id.*

33. LOCKE, *supra* chap. 1, note 29, at 21.

34. MADISON, *Property*, *supra*, *in* JAMES MADISON: WRITINGS, *supra* chap. 1, note 3, at 515.

35. LOCKE, *supra* chap. 1, note 29, at 19.

36. *Id.* at 46.

37. *Id.* at 90.

38. MADISON, *Property*, *supra*, *in* JAMES MADISON: WRITINGS, *supra* chap. 1, note 3, at 515.

39. *Id.* at 517.

40. LOCKE, *supra* chap. 1, note 29, at 66.

41. ADAM SMITH, AN INQUIRY INTO THE NATURE AND CAUSES OF THE WEALTH OF NATIONS 15 (Edwin Cannan, ed., New York: Modern Library, 1994).

42. *Id.* at 484–85 (emphasis added).

43. *Id.* at 444.

44. ADAM SMITH, THE THEORY OF MORAL SENTIMENTS 3 (Amherst, N.Y.: Prometheus Books, 2000).

45. For scholarship on Smith's promotion of virtue and Madison's support for this position, *see* Kloppenberg, *The Virtues of Liberalism*, *supra* chap. 1, note 27, at 18; KLOPPENBERG, THE VIRTUES OF LIBERALISM, *supra* chap. 1, note 30, at 26; GERTRUDE HIMMELFARB, THE IDEA OF POVERTY: ENGLAND IN THE EARLY INDUSTRIAL AGE 63 (New York: Knopf, 1984); MATTHEWS, *supra* chap. 1, note 24, at 86.

46. For others adhering to this position, *see* MCDONALD, *supra* chap. 1, note 27, at 74–75; FARBER & SHERRY, *supra* chap. 1, note 27, at 13–14.

47. THOMAS JEFFERSON, *Notes on the State of Virginia*, *in* THE LIFE AND

SELECTED WORKS OF THOMAS JEFFERSON 173, 259 (Adrienne Koch & William Peden, eds., New York: Modern Library, 1993).

48. *Id.*

49. Letter from Thomas Jefferson to John Jay (Aug. 23, 1785), *in* THE LIFE AND SELECTED WORKS OF THOMAS JEFFERSON, *supra* note 47, at 351.

50. *Id.*

51. For scholars who believe Madison found self-interest to lead to virtue, *see* McGinnis, *supra* chap. 1, note 25, at 70; Sheehan, *supra* chap. 1, note 43, at 611; Frank H. Easterbrook, *The State of Madison's Vision of the State: A Public Choice Perspective*, 107 HARV. L. REV. 1328, 1333 (1994).

52. Letter from James Madison to William Bradford (Jan. 24, 1774), *in* JAMES MADISON: WRITINGS, *supra* chap. 1, note 3, at 5, 7.

53. Letter from James Madison to William Bradford (Apr. 1, 1774), *in* JAMES MADISON: WRITINGS, *supra* chap. 1, note 3, at 7, 9.

54. MADISON, *Memorial and Remonstrance, supra, in* JAMES MADISON: WRITINGS, *supra* chap. 1, note 3, at 32.

55. *Id.* at 33.

56. Letter from James Madison to James Monroe (Aug. 7, 1785), *in* 8 THE PAPERS OF JAMES MADISON, at 333 (Robert A. Rutland et al., eds., Chicago: University of Chicago Press, 1973).

57. James Madison, Import and Tonnage Duties, *in* 12 THE PAPERS OF JAMES MADISON, *supra* chap. 1, note 2, at 69, 71.

58. *See id.* at 70–73; Letter from James Madison to James Monroe (June 21, 1786) and Letter from James Madison to Edmund Pendleton (Jan. 9, 1787), *in* 9 THE PAPERS OF JAMES MADISON, at 82, 84 n.9, 244 (Robert A. Rutland & William M.E. Rachal, eds., Chicago: University of Chicago Press, 1975), *in id.* at 244; *see also* DREW R. MCCOY, THE ELUSIVE REPUBLIC: POLITICAL ECONOMY IN JEFFERSONIAN AMERICA 143 (Chapel Hill: University of North Carolina Press, 1980).

59. James Madison, Notes for Speech in Congress (ca. Apr. 9, 1789), *in* 12 THE PAPERS OF JAMES MADISON, *supra* chap. 1, note 2, at 68.

60. ANNALS OF CONG. 454 (1789).

61. *Id.* at 455.

62. JAMES MADISON, *Republican Distribution of Citizens* (Mar. 5, 1792), *in* JAMES MADISON: WRITINGS, *supra* chap. 1, note 3, at 511, 512–13.

63. JAMES MADISON, *Fashion* (Mar. 22, 1792), *in* JAMES MADISON: WRITINGS, *supra* chap. 1, note 3, at 513, 514.

64. Letter from James Madison to Thomas Jefferson (Sept. 2, 1793), *in* 15 THE PAPERS OF JAMES MADISON, *supra* chap. 2, note 55, at 92, 93. *See also* letter from James Madison to James Monroe (June 21, 1785), *in* 8 THE PAPERS OF JAMES MADISON, *supra* note 56, at 306, 307.

65. James Madison, Address of the House of Representatives to the President (May 5, 1789), *in* 12 THE PAPERS OF JAMES MADISON, *supra* chap. 1, note 2, at 132, 133. Interestingly enough, Madison *also* wrote Washington's First Inaugural Address. George Washington, Address of the President to Congress (Apr. 30, 1789), *in* 12 THE PAPERS OF JAMES MADISON, *supra* chap. 1, note 2, at 120.

66. Madison, Report on Books for Congress, *supra, in* 6 THE PAPERS OF JAMES MADISON, *supra* chap. 2, note 6, at 86.

67. James Madison, The Bank Bill (Feb. 2, 1791), *in* 13 THE PAPERS OF JAMES MADISON, *supra* chap. 1, note 2, at 372, 373.

68. Letter from Fisher Ames to George Richards Minot (May 29, 1789), *in* 1 WORKS OF FISHER AMES AS PUBLISHED BY SETH AMES 635, 638 (W.B. Allen, ed., Indianapolis: Liberty Fund, 1983).

69. MADISON, *Memorial and Remonstrance, supra, in* JAMES MADISON: WRITINGS, *supra* chap. 1, note 3, at 31.

70. THE FEDERALIST NO. 10, at 160 (James Madison) (Jack N. Rakove, ed., 1999).

71. *Id.* at 161.

72. *Id.*

73. *Id.* at 162.

74. *Id.* at 163, 165.

75. *Id.* at 165.

76. THE FEDERALIST NO. 51, at 295 (James Madison) (Jack N. Rakove, ed., 1999).

77. *Id.*

78. *Id.*

79. *Id.*

80. THE FEDERALIST NO. 43, at 243 (James Madison) (Jack N. Rakove, ed., 1999).

81. JAMES MADISON, REPORT ON THE ALIEN AND SEDITION ACTS (Jan. 7, 1800), *in* JAMES MADISON: WRITINGS, *supra* chap. 1, note 3, at 608, 647.

82. Madison, Import and Tonnage Duties, *supra, in* 12 THE PAPERS OF JAMES MADISON, *supra* chap. 1, note 2, at 71.

83. James Madison, Property and Suffrage: Second Thoughts on the Constitutional Convention (1821), *in* THE MIND OF THE FOUNDER: SOURCES OF THE POLITICAL THOUGHT OF JAMES MADISON 501, 503 (Marvin Myers, ed., Indianapolis: Bobbs-Merrill, 1973).

4—MADISON OPPOSES A BILL OF RIGHTS, THEN SEES ITS STRATEGIC VALUE

1. THE FEDERALIST NO. 38, at 208 (James Madison) (Jack N. Rakove, ed., 1999).

2. James Madison, Speech in the Virginia Ratifying Convention on Ratification and Amendments (June 24, 1788), *in* JAMES MADISON: WRITINGS, *supra* chap. 1, note 3, at 401, 404–5.

3. THE FEDERALIST NO. 45, at 265 (James Madison) (Jack N. Rakove, ed., 1999). Hamilton made a similar argument in *Federalist* 84: "the Constitution is itself, in every rational sense, and to every useful purpose, A BILL OF RIGHTS." THE FEDERALIST NO. 84, at 515 (Alexander Hamilton) (Clinton Rossiter, ed., New York: Mentor, 1961).

4. In fact, before the 1787 Constitutional Convention, Madison often expressed his concern about the powerlessness of the national government under the Articles of Confederation. *See* James Madison, Motion to Inform States of Financial Crisis (May 20, 1782), *in* 4 THE PAPERS OF JAMES MADISON 254, 254–55 (William

T. Hutchinson & William M.E. Rachal, eds., Chicago: University of Chicago Press, 1965); Letters from James Madison to Edmund Randolph (July 28, 1783), and to Thomas Jefferson (Sept. 20, 1783), *in* 7 THE PAPERS OF JAMES MADISON 256, 257, 352–53 (William T. Hutchinson & William M.E. Rachal, eds., Chicago: University of Chicago Press, 1971); Letter from James Madison to Thomas Jefferson (Apr. 25, 1784), *in* 8 THE PAPERS OF JAMES MADISON, *supra* chap. 3, note 56, at 19, 21 (Madison refers to "the impotency of the federal Govt.").

5. THE FEDERALIST NO. 41, at 233 (James Madison) (Jack N. Rakove, ed., 1999).

6. Madison, Speech in the Virginia Ratifying Convention in Defense of the Constitution (June 6, 1788), *supra, in* JAMES MADISON: WRITINGS, *supra* chap. 1, note 3, at 361.

7. James Madison, Speech in the Virginia Ratifying Convention on Taxation, a Bill of Rights, and the Mississippi (June 12, 1788), *in* JAMES MADISON: WRITINGS, *supra* chap. 1, note 3, at 380, 382.

8. Letter from James Madison to Thomas Jefferson (Oct. 17, 1788), *in* JAMES MADISON: WRITINGS, *supra* chap. 1, note 3, at 418, 420.

9. THE FEDERALIST NO. 10, at 163 (James Madison) (Jack N. Rakove, ed., 1999).

10. THE FEDERALIST NO. 52, at 300 (James Madison) (Jack N. Rakove, ed., 1999).

11. THE FEDERALIST NO. 10, at 166 (James Madison) (Jack N. Rakove, ed., 1999).

12. THE FEDERALIST NO. 51, at 296–97 (James Madison) (Jack N. Rakove, ed., 1999).

13. THE FEDERALIST NO. 46, at 269 (James Madison) (Jack N. Rakove, ed., 1999).

14. James Madison, Speech at the Constitutional Convention (July 17, 1787), *in* MADISON, NOTES OF DEBATES, *supra* chap. 2, note 53, at 311.

15. THE FEDERALIST NO. 47, at 273 (James Madison) (Jack N. Rakove, ed., 1999). Madison may have been influenced in this belief by Witherspoon, who claimed the following: "Monarchy everyone knows is but another name for tyranny, where the arbitrary will of one capricious man disposes of the lives and properties of all ranks." Witherspoon, Lectures on Moral Philosophy, *supra, in* WITHERSPOON, *supra* chap. 2, note 7, at 202.

16. *Id.*

17. Letter from Madison to Jefferson (Oct. 17, 1788), *supra, in* JAMES MADISON: WRITINGS, *supra* chap. 1, note 3, at 420.

18. *Id.* at 422.

19. *Id.*

20. James Madison, Observations on the "Draught of a Constitution for Virginia" (c. Oct. 15, 1788), *in* JAMES MADISON: WRITINGS, *supra* chap. 1, note 3, at 409, 417.

21. THE FEDERALIST NO. 37, at 196 (James Madison) (Jack N. Rakove, ed., 1999).

22. THE FEDERALIST NO. 45, at 260 (James Madison) (Jack N. Rakove, ed., 1999).

23. THE FEDERALIST NO. 18, at 179 (James Madison) (Jack N. Rakove, ed., 1999).

24. *See* LABUNSKI, *supra* chap. 1, note 1, at 114.

25. *Id.*

26. Letter from James Madison to Alexander Hamilton (June 27, 1788), *in* 11 THE PAPERS OF JAMES MADISON, *supra* chap. 1, note 2, at 181, 181.

27. Letter from Madison to Jefferson (Oct. 17, 1788), *supra*, *in* JAMES MADISON: WRITINGS, *supra* chap. 1, note 3, at 420.

28. *Id.* at 422–23.

29. *Id.* at 420.

30. Madison, Speech in the Virginia Ratifying Convention on Taxation, a Bill of Rights, and the Mississippi, *supra*, *in* JAMES MADISON: WRITINGS, *supra* chap. 1, note 3, at 381.

31. Letter from Madison to Jefferson (Oct. 17, 1788), *supra*, *in* JAMES MADISON: WRITINGS, *supra* chap. 1, note 3, at 421.

32. *Id.*

33. Kenneth R. Bowling, *"A Tub to the Whale": The Founding Fathers and Adoption of the Federal Bill of Rights*, 8 J. EARLY REPUBLIC 223, 224 (1988).

34. For those believing Madison supported the Bill of Rights purely for tactical reasons, *see id.*; FARBER & SHERRY, *supra* chap. 1, note 27, at 225, 227; BERNARD A. WEISBERGER, AMERICA AFIRE: JEFFERSON, ADAMS, AND THE FIRST CONTESTED ELECTION 53–54 (New York: Perennial, 2000); Christopher Wolfe, *The Original Meaning of the Due Process Clause*, *in* THE BILL OF RIGHTS: ORIGINAL MEANING, *supra* chap. 1, note 21, at 213, 220; RAKOVE, JAMES MADISON, *supra* chap. 1, note 21, at 91; ROBERT A. GOLDWIN, FROM PARCHMENT TO POWER: HOW JAMES MADISON USED THE BILL OF RIGHTS TO SAVE THE CONSTITUTION 93 (Washington, D.C.: American Enterprise, 1997); ROBERT ALLEN RUTLAND, JAMES MADISON: THE FOUNDING FATHER 61–62 (Columbia: University of Missouri Press, 1987); Paul Finkelman, *James Madison and the Bill of Rights: A Reluctant Paternity*, 1990 SUP. CT. REV. 301 (1990). For those thinking Madison supported the Bill for substantive reasons, *see* LABUNSKI, *supra* chap. 1, note 1, at 63; Stuart Leibiger, *James Madison and Amendments to the Constitution, 1787–1789: "Parchment Barriers,"* 59 J. S. HIST. 441, 442–43 (1993); Heyman, *Ideological Conflict and the First Amendment*, *supra* chap. 1, note 30, at 540–41; BANNING, THE SACRED FIRE, *supra* chap. 1, note 25, at 281; KETCHAM, JAMES MADISON: A BIOGRAPHY, *supra* chap. 1, note 21, at 303.

35. Letter from James Madison to Edmond Randolph (Jan. 10, 1788), *in* JAMES MADISON: WRITINGS, *supra* chap. 1, note 3, at 190, 190–91.

36. *Id.* at 191.

37. *Id.*

38. *See* LABUNSKI, *supra* chap. 1, note 1, at 17–18.

39. Letter from James Madison to George Eve (Jan. 2, 1789), *in* JAMES MADISON: WRITINGS, *supra* chap. 1, note 3, at 427, 428.

40. *Id.*

41. Letter from James Madison to George Nicholas (Apr. 8, 1788), *in* 11 THE PAPERS OF JAMES MADISON, *supra* chap. 1, note 2, at 11, 12–13.

42. Letter from James Madison to Edmund Randolph (Apr. 10, 1788), *in* 11 THE PAPERS OF JAMES MADISON, *supra* chap. 1, note 2, at 18, 19.

43. Letter from James Madison to Thomas Jefferson (Apr. 22, 1788), *in* 11 THE PAPERS OF JAMES MADISON, *supra* chap. 1, note 2, at 27, 28.

44. Letter from James Madison to Thomas Jefferson (Aug. 10, 1788), *in* 11 THE PAPERS OF JAMES MADISON, *supra* chap. 1, note 2, at 225, 226.

45. Letter from James Madison to Thomas Jefferson (Aug. 23, 1788), *in* 11 THE PAPERS OF JAMES MADISON, *supra* chap. 1, note 2, at 238.

46. Letter from James Madison to Thomas Jefferson (Dec. 12, 1788), *in* 11 THE PAPERS OF JAMES MADISON, *supra* chap. 1, note 2, at 390.

47. Letter from James Madison to George Washington (Aug. 11, 1788), *in* 11 THE PAPERS OF JAMES MADISON, *supra* chap. 1, note 2, at 229, 230.

48. Letter from James Madison to George Lee Turberville (Nov. 2, 1788), *in* 11 THE PAPERS OF JAMES MADISON, *supra* chap. 1, note 2, at 330, 331.

49. Letter from James Madison to Phillip Mazzei (Dec. 10, 1788), *in* 11 THE PAPERS OF JAMES MADISON, *supra* chap. 1, note 2, at 388, 389.

50. THE FEDERALIST NO. 37, at 200 (James Madison) (Jack N. Rakove, ed., 1999).

51. *Id.* at 200–201.

52. THE FEDERALIST NO. 38, at 207 (James Madison) (Jack N. Rakove, ed., 1999).

53. 1 ANNALS OF CONG. 450 (1789).

54. *See* BANNING, THE SACRED FIRE, *supra* chap. 1, note 25, at 240. *See also* Letter from Thomas Jefferson to James Madison (Dec. 20, 1787), *in* THE LIFE AND SELECTED WORKS OF THOMAS JEFFERSON, *supra* chap. 3, note 47, at 403, 404–5; Letter from Thomas Jefferson to James Madison (July 31, 1788), *in* THE LIFE AND SELECTED WORKS OF THOMAS JEFFERSON, *supra* chap. 3, note 47, at 416, 416–17; Letter from Thomas Jefferson to James Madison (Mar. 15, 1789), *in* THE LIFE AND SELECTED WORKS OF THOMAS JEFFERSON, *supra* chap. 3, note 47, at 426, 426–28; Letters of Centinel, No. 2 (Oct. 24, 1787), *in* 2 THE COMPLETE ANTI-FEDERALIST 144 &152 (Herbert J. Storing, ed., Chicago: University of Chicago Press, 1981); An Old Whig, No. 8 (Fall, 1787), *in* 3 THE COMPLETE ANTI-FEDERALIST 46, 49 (Herbert J. Storing, ed., Chicago: University of Chicago Press, 1981); Letter by An Officer of the Late Continental Army (Nov. 6, 1787), *in* 3 THE COMPLETE ANTI-FEDERALIST, *supra*, at 91, 93; Philadelphiensis No. 6 (1787–88), *in* 3 THE COMPLETE ANTI-FEDERALIST, *supra*, at 119, 122; The Address and Reasons of Dissent of the Minority of the Convention of Pennsylvania to Their Constituents (Dec. 18, 1787), *in* 3 THE COMPLETE ANTI-FEDERALIST, *supra*, at 150–53; Letters of Agrippa, No. 12 (Jan. 14, 1788), *in* 4 THE COMPLETE ANTI-FEDERALIST 94, 96 (Herbert J. Storing, ed., Chicago: University of Chicago Press, 1981).

55. 1 ANNALS OF CONG. 444 (1789).

56. *Id.*

57. *Id.*

58. *Id.* at 448.

59. *Id.* at 449.

60. *Id.*

61. Letter from James Madison to Richard Peters (Aug. 19, 1789), *in* JAMES MADISON: WRITINGS, *supra* chap. 1, note 3, at 471, 472.

62. 1 ANNALS OF CONG. 457 (1789).

63. Letter from Madison to Peters (Aug. 19, 1789), *supra, in* JAMES MADISON: WRITINGS, *supra* chap. 1, note 3, at 471–72 (emphasis added).

64. 1 ANNALS OF CONG. 444 (1789).

65. *Id.* at 448.

66. *Id.* at 449.

67. *Id.* at 450.

68. *Id.* at 444.

69. Leibiger, *supra* note 34, at 458–59.

70. Letter from Madison to Eve (Jan. 2, 1789), *supra, in* JAMES MADISON: WRITINGS, *supra* chap. 1, note 3, at 427–28.

71. *Id.* at 459.

72. 1 ANNALS OF CONG. 444 (1789).

73. *Id.* at 448.

74. *Id.* at 459.

5—MADISON SEES THAT A BILL OF RIGHTS CAN PROTECT LIBERAL FREEDOMS

1. Letter from Madison to Jefferson (Oct. 17, 1788), *supra, in* JAMES MADISON: WRITINGS, *supra* chap. 1, note 3, at 420.

2. Letter from Madison to Eve (Jan. 2, 1789), *supra, in* JAMES MADISON: WRITINGS, *supra* chap. 1, note 3, at 428.

3. 1 ANNALS OF CONG. 453 (1789).

4. *Id.* at 459.

5. Letter from James Madison to Edmund Pendleton (Apr. 8, 1789), *in* 12 THE PAPERS OF JAMES MADISON, *supra* chap. 1, note 2, at 51.

6. Washington, Address of the President to Congress (Apr. 30, 1789), *supra, in* 12 THE PAPERS OF JAMES MADISON, *supra* chap. 1, note 2, at 123.

7. James Madison, Address of the House of Representatives to the President (May 5, 1789), *supra, in* 12 THE PAPERS OF JAMES MADISON, *supra* chap. 1, note 2, at 133.

8. Letter from James Madison to Thomas Jefferson (May 27, 1789), *in* 12 THE PAPERS OF JAMES MADISON, *supra* chap. 1, note 2, at 185, 186; Letter from James Madison to Thomas Jefferson (June 30, 1789), *in* 12 THE PAPERS OF JAMES MADISON, *supra* chap. 1, note 2, at 267, 272; Letter from James Madison to Edmund Randolph (June 15, 1789), *in* 12 THE PAPERS OF JAMES MADISON, *supra* chap. 1, note 2, at 219; Letter from James Madison to Samuel Johnston (June 21, 1789), *in* 12 THE PAPERS OF JAMES MADISON, *supra* chap. 1, note 2, at 249, 250; Letter from James Madison to Samuel Johnston (July 31, 1789), *in* 12 THE PAPERS OF JAMES MADISON, *supra* chap. 1, note 2, at 317; Letter from James Madison to Edmund Pendleton (June 21, 1789), *in* 12 THE PAPERS OF JAMES MADISON, *supra* chap. 1, note 2 , at 251, 253; Letter from James Madison to Tench Coxe (June 24, 1789), *in* 12 THE PAPERS OF JAMES MADISON, *supra* chap. 1, note 2, at 257; Letter from James Madison to James Madison, Sr. (July 5, 1789), *in* 12 THE PAPERS OF JAMES MADISON, *supra* chap. 1, note 2, at 278, 279; Letter from James Madison to George Nicholas (July 5, 1789), *in* 12 THE PAPERS OF JAMES MADISON, *supra* chap. 1, note 2, at 279, 282; Letter from James Madison to Wilson Cary Nicholas (July 18, 1789),

in 12 THE PAPERS OF JAMES MADISON, *supra* chap. 1, note 2, at 294, 295; Letter from James Madison to Wilson Cary Nicholas (Aug. 2, 1789), *in* 12 THE PAPERS OF JAMES MADISON, *supra* chap. 1, note 2, at 320, 321; Letter from Madison to Peters (Aug. 19, 1789), *supra, in* 12 THE PAPERS OF JAMES MADISON, *supra* chap. 1, note 2, at 346–48; Letter from James Madison to George Washington (Nov. 20, 1789), *in* 12 THE PAPERS OF JAMES MADISON, *supra* chap. 1, note 2, at 451, 453; Letter from James Madison to George Washington (Dec. 5, 1789), *in* 12 THE PAPERS OF JAMES MADISON, *supra* chap. 1, note 2, at 458, 459; Letter from James Madison to George Washington (Jan. 4, 1790), *supra, in* 12 THE PAPERS OF JAMES MADISON, *supra* chap. 1, note 2, at 466, 467.

9. Letter from James Madison to Thomas Jefferson (Dec. 8, 1788), *in* 11 THE PAPERS OF JAMES MADISON, *supra* chap. 1, note 2, at 381, 382.

10. 1 ANNALS OF CONG. 444, 449, 453, 458 (1789).

11. *Id.* at 448.

12. *Id.* at 450, 457, 459.

13. *Id.* at 775.

14. *Id.* at 784.

15. Letter from Madison to Peters (Aug. 19, 1789), *supra, in* 12 THE PAPERS OF JAMES MADISON, *supra* chap. 1, note 2, at 471.

16. Letter from James Madison to Alexander Hamilton (July 20, 1788), *in* JAMES MADISON: WRITINGS, *supra* chap. 1, note 3, at 408.

17. Letter from James Madison to George Washington (Dec. 20, 1787), *in* 10 THE PAPERS OF JAMES MADISON, *supra* chap. 2, note 30, at 333, 333–34.

18. *See also* Letter from Madison to Nicholas (Apr. 8, 1788), *supra, in* 11 THE PAPERS OF JAMES MADISON, *supra* chap. 1, note 2, at 12; Letter from Madison to Randolph (Apr. 10, 1788), *supra, in* 11 THE PAPERS OF JAMES MADISON, *supra* chap. 1, note 2, at 19; Letter from Madison to Jefferson (Apr. 22, 1788), *supra, in* 11 THE PAPERS OF JAMES MADISON, *supra* chap. 1, note 2, at 28.

19. Letter from Madison to Jefferson (Oct. 17, 1788), *supra, in* JAMES MADISON: WRITINGS, *supra* chap. 1, note 3, at 420.

20. Letter from James Madison to Henry Lee (Nov. 30, 1788), *in* 11 THE PAPERS OF JAMES MADISON, *supra* chap. 1, note 2, at 371, 372.

21. Letter from James Madison to Edmund Pendleton (Oct. 20, 1788), *in* 11 THE PAPERS OF JAMES MADISON, *supra* chap. 1, note 2, at 306, 307.

22. Letter from James Madison to George Washington (Nov. 5, 1788), *in* 11 THE PAPERS OF JAMES MADISON, *supra* chap. 1, note 2, at 334.

23. Letter from James Madison to George Eve (Jan. 2, 1789), *supra, in* JAMES MADISON: WRITINGS, *supra* chap. 1, note 3, at 427.

24. Letter from James Madison to Thomas Mann Randolph (Jan. 13, 1789), *in* 11 THE PAPERS OF JAMES MADISON, *supra* chap. 1, note 2, at 415, 416.

25. JAMES MADISON, *To a Resident of Spotsylvania County* (Jan. 27, 1789), *in* 11 THE PAPERS OF JAMES MADISON, *supra* chap. 1, note 2, at 428, 429.

26. *See* SCHWARTZ, THE GREAT RIGHTS OF MANKIND, *supra* chap. 1, note 32, at 104.

27. THE FEDERALIST NO. 44, at 253–54 (James Madison) (Jack N. Rakove, ed., 1999).

28. THE FEDERALIST NO. 48, at 285 (James Madison) (Jack N. Rakove, ed., 1999).

29. 1 ANNALS OF CONG. 449–50 (1789).

30. *Id.* at 458.

31. *Id.* at 458–59.

32. *Id.* at 455.

33. *Id.* at 455–56.

34. *Id.* at 758.

35. *Id.* at 457.

36. 1 ANNALS OF CONG. 458 (1789).

37. JAMES MADISON, *Virginia Resolutions Against the Alien and Sedition Acts, in* JAMES MADISON: WRITINGS, *supra* chap. 1, note 3, at 589.

38. *Id.*

39. Resolutions Proposed by Mr. Randolph in Convention (May 29, 1787), *in* MADISON, NOTES OF DEBATES, *supra* chap. 2, note 53, at 32.

40. Letter from James Madison to Edmund Randolph (Apr. 8, 1787), *in* 9 THE PAPERS OF JAMES MADISON, *supra* chap. 3, note 58, at 368, 370.

41. Letter from James Madison to George Washington (Apr. 16, 1787), *in* 9 THE PAPERS OF JAMES MADISON, *supra* chap. 3, note 58, at 382, 385.

42. The Virginia Plan (May 27, 1787), *in* 10 THE PAPERS OF JAMES MADISON, *supra* chap. 2, note 30, at 12, 12–13, 16.

43. MADISON, NOTES OF DEBATES, *supra* chap. 2, note 53, at 79, 337, 461.

44. James Madison, Speech at the Constitutional Convention (July 21, 1787), *in* MADISON, NOTES OF DEBATES, *supra* chap. 2, note 53, at 337, 338. *See also* Revisionary Power of the Executive and the Judiciary (June 4, 1787), *in* 10 THE PAPERS OF JAMES MADISON, *supra* chap. 2, note 30, at 25. For the importance of a Council of Revision to Madison, *see also* Steven P. Brown, *Mirroring Madison, in* JAMES MADISON: PHILOSOPHER, FOUNDER, AND STATESMAN, *supra* chap. 1, note 24, at 157, 159.

45. *See generally* Madison, Vices of the Political System of the United States (Apr. 1787), *supra, in* JAMES MADISON: WRITINGS, *supra* chap. 1, note 3, at 69–80; Letter from James Madison to George Washington (Apr. 16, 1787), *supra, in* 9 THE PAPERS OF JAMES MADISON, *supra* chap. 3, note 58, at 384.

46. For others finding this link in Madison's thought, *see* Madison at the First Session of the First Federal Congress 8 April–29 September 1789, Editorial Note, *in* 12 THE PAPERS OF JAMES MADISON, *supra* chap. 1, note 2, at 52, 58–59; Charles F. Hobson, *The Negative on State Laws: James Madison, the Constitution, and the Crisis of Republican Government*, 36 WM. & MARY Q. 215, 216 (1979); Rakove, *The Madisonian Theory of Rights, supra* chap. 1, note 26, at 253; MATTHEWS, *supra* chap. 1, note 24, at 189; Brown, *supra* note 44, at 158.

47. Letter from James Madison to Thomas Jefferson (Mar. 19, 1787), *in* 9 THE PAPERS OF JAMES MADISON, *supra* chap. 3, note 58, at 317, 318.

48. Letter from Madison to Randolph (Apr. 8, 1787), *supra, in* 9 THE PAPERS OF JAMES MADISON, *supra* chap. 3, note 58, at 370.

49. Letter from Madison to Washington (Apr. 16, 1787), *supra, in* 9 THE PAPERS OF JAMES MADISON, *supra* chap. 3, note 58, at 383.

50. MADISON, NOTES OF DEBATES, *supra* chap. 2, note 53, at 88.

51. James Madison, Speech at the Constitutional Convention (June 8, 1787), *in* MADISON, NOTES OF DEBATES, *supra* chap. 2, note 53, at 88.

52. James Madison, Speech at the Constitutional Convention (July 17, 1787), *in* MADISON, NOTES OF DEBATES, *supra* chap. 2, note 53, at 304.

53. Letter from Madison to Jefferson (Oct. 24, 1787), *supra*, *in* JAMES MADISON: WRITINGS, *supra* chap. 1, note 3, at 149.

54. 1 ANNALS OF CONG. 452 (1789).

55. *Id.* at 784.

56. *Id.* at 456.

57. *Id.* at 455.

58. Letter from Madison to Jefferson (Oct. 17, 1788), *supra*, *in* JAMES MADISON: WRITINGS, *supra* chap. 1, note 3, at 421–22.

59. THE FEDERALIST NO. 51, at 295 (James Madison) (Jack N. Rakove, ed., 1999).

60. Letter from Madison to Jefferson (Oct. 17, 1788), *supra*, *in* JAMES MADISON: WRITINGS, *supra* chap. 1, note 3, at 422.

61. *See* THE FEDERALIST NO. 84, at 513–15 (Alexander Hamilton) (Clinton Rossiter, ed., 1961).

62. 1 ANNALS OF CONG. 452 (1789).

63. *Id.* at 456.

64. *Id.*

65. *Id.*

66. Letter from Thomas Jefferson to James Madison (Dec. 20, 1787), *supra*, *in* THE LIFE AND SELECTED WORKS OF THOMAS JEFFERSON, *supra* chap. 3, note 47, at 404.

67. 1 ANNALS OF CONG. 451–53 (1789).

68. Letter from Jefferson to Madison (Dec. 20, 1787), *supra*, *in* THE LIFE AND SELECTED WORKS OF THOMAS JEFFERSON, *supra* chap. 3, note 47, at 404.

69. *See* 1 ANNALS OF CONG. 455–56 (1789).

70. Letter from Jefferson to Madison (Dec. 20, 1787), *supra*, *in* THE LIFE AND SELECTED WORKS OF THOMAS JEFFERSON, *supra* chap. 3, note 47, at 405.

71. Letter from Jefferson to Madison (July 31, 1788), *supra*, *in* THE LIFE AND SELECTED WORKS OF THOMAS JEFFERSON, *supra* chap. 3, note 47, at 416.

72. *Id.*

73. *Id.* at 417.

74. Letter from Thomas Jefferson to James Madison (Nov. 18, 1788), *in* THE LIFE AND SELECTED WORKS OF THOMAS JEFFERSON, *supra* chap. 3, note 47, at 417, 418.

75. Letter from Thomas Jefferson to James Madison (Mar. 15, 1789), *supra*, *in* THE LIFE AND SELECTED WORKS OF THOMAS JEFFERSON, *supra* chap. 3, note 47, at 426.

76. *Id.* at 426.

77. *Id.* at 426–27.

78. Letter from Madison to Jefferson (Oct. 17, 1788), *supra*, *in* JAMES MADISON: WRITINGS, *supra* chap. 1, note 3, at 420.

79. Letter from Jefferson to Madison (Mar. 15, 1789), *supra*, *in* THE LIFE AND SELECTED WORKS OF THOMAS JEFFERSON, *supra* chap. 3, note 47, at 427.

80. Letter from Madison to Jefferson (Oct. 17, 1788), *supra*, *in* JAMES MADISON: WRITINGS, *supra* chap. 1, note 3, at 420.

81. Letter from Jefferson to Madison (Mar. 15, 1789), *supra, in* THE LIFE AND SELECTED WORKS OF THOMAS JEFFERSON, *supra* chap. 3, note 47, at 427.

82. Letter from Madison to Jefferson (Oct. 17, 1788), *supra, in* JAMES MADISON: WRITINGS, *supra* chap. 1, note 3, at 420.

83. Letter from Jefferson to Madison (Mar. 15, 1789), *supra, in* THE LIFE AND SELECTED WORKS OF THOMAS JEFFERSON, *supra* chap. 3, note 47, at 427.

84. Letter from Madison to Jefferson (Oct. 17, 1788), *supra, in* JAMES MADISON: WRITINGS, *supra* chap. 1, note 3, at 420.

85. Letter from Jefferson to Madison (Mar. 15, 1789), *supra, in* THE LIFE AND SELECTED WORKS OF THOMAS JEFFERSON, *supra* chap. 3, note 47, at 427–28.

86. 1 ANNALS OF CONG. 449–50 (1789).

6—MADISON'S SYSTEM OF RIGHTS

1. 1 ANNALS OF CONG. 454 (1789).

2. *Id.*

3. For others who have a holistic approach to Madison or the Bill of Rights, *see* BANNING, THE SACRED FIRE, *supra* chap. 1, note 25, at 126; AMAR, *supra* chap. 1, note 33, at xii; RAKOVE, ORIGINAL MEANINGS, *supra* chap. 1, note 24, at 289; Burt Neuborne, *The House Was Quiet and the World Was Calm: The Reader Became the Book,* 57 VAND. L. REV. 2007, 2015–16 (2004).

4. MADISON, REPORT ON THE ALIEN AND SEDITION ACTS, *supra, in* JAMES MADISON: WRITINGS, *supra* chap. 1, note 3, at 657.

5. *Id.* at 657–58.

6. *Id.* at 658.

7. Letter from James Madison to Thomas Jefferson (Jan. 22, 1786), *in* 8 THE PAPERS OF JAMES MADISON, *supra* chap. 3, note 56, at 472, 474.

8. *See* also Burt Neuborne, *Toward a Democracy-Centered Reading of the First Amendment,* 93 NW. U.L. REV. 1055, 1069–70 (1999).

9. For others finding a link among First Amendment rights like this, *see* AMAR, *supra* chap. 1, note 33, at 239; MATTHEWS, *supra* chap. 1, note 24, at 125; Neuborne, *Toward a Democracy-Centered Reading, supra* note 8, at 1069–70.

10. JAMES MADISON, *Public Opinion* (Dec. 19, 1791), *in* JAMES MADISON: WRITINGS, *supra* chap. 1, note 3, at 500.

11. MADISON, *Virginia Resolutions, supra, in* JAMES MADISON: WRITINGS, *supra* chap. 1, note 3, at 590.

12. Letter from Madison to Bradford (Jan. 24, 1774), *supra, in* JAMES MADISON: WRITINGS, *supra* chap. 1, note 3, at 5.

13. Letter from Madison to Bradford (Apr. 1, 1774), *supra, in* JAMES MADISON: WRITINGS, *supra* chap. 1, note 3, at 8.

14. MADISON, *Memorial and Remonstrance, supra, in* JAMES MADISON: WRITINGS, *supra* chap. 1, note 3, at 33.

15. *Id.* at 35.

16. *Id.* at 35–36.

17. *See* BRANT, THE BILL OF RIGHTS, *supra* chap. 1, note 32, at 67; BANNING, THE SACRED FIRE, *supra* chap. 1, note 25, at 102; Neuborne, *The House Was Quiet, supra* note 3, at 2058; RIEMER, JAMES MADISON, *supra* chap. 1, note 26, at 150.

18. Letter from Madison to Bradford (Apr. 1, 1774), *supra, in* JAMES MADISON: WRITINGS, *supra* chap. 1, note 3, at 9.

19. THE FEDERALIST NO. 53, at 307 (James Madison) (Jack N. Rakove, ed., 1999).

20. MADISON, *Public Opinion* (Dec. 19, 1791), *supra, in* JAMES MADISON: WRITINGS, *supra* chap. 1, note 3, at 501.

21. *See* James Madison, Motion on Protection of Commerce (May 2, 1782), *in* 4 THE PAPERS OF JAMES MADISON, *supra* chap. 4, note 4, at 204–5; James Madison, Motion to Request France to Protect American Commerce (May 14, 1782), *in* 4 THE PAPERS OF JAMES MADISON, *supra* chap. 4, note 4, at 235; James Madison, Notes on Debates (Dec. 31, 1782), *in* 5 THE PAPERS OF JAMES MADISON, at 476 (William T. Hutchinson & William M.E. Rachal, eds., Chicago: University of Chicago Press, 1967); Letter from James Madison to Edmund Randolph (May 20, 1783), *in* 7 THE PAPERS OF JAMES MADISON, *supra* chap. 4, note 4, at 58, 60–61; Letter from James Madison to James Monroe (Apr. 9, 1786), *in* 9 THE PAPERS OF JAMES MADISON, *supra* chap. 3, note 58, at 25; Letter from James Madison to James Monroe (June 21, 1786), *supra, in* 9 THE PAPERS OF JAMES MADISON, *supra* chap. 3, note 58, at 82; THE FEDERALIST NO. 42, at 238–39 (James Madison) (Jack N. Rakove, ed., 1999); James Madison, Notes for Speech in Congress (ca. Apr. 9, 1789), *supra, in* 12 THE PAPERS OF JAMES MADISON, *supra* chap. 1, note 2, at 68; Madison, Import and Tonnage Duties, *supra, in* 12 THE PAPERS OF JAMES MADISON, *supra* chap. 1, note 2, at 70–71. For other scholars finding a link between these two sets of rights, *see* Baker, *The Establishment Clause as Intended, supra* chap. 1, note 21, at 51; McGinnis, *supra* chap. 1, note 25, at 79.

22. MADISON, *Memorial and Remonstrance, supra, in* JAMES MADISON: WRITINGS, *supra* chap. 1, note 3, at 32.

23. *Id.* at 33.

24. Letter from James Madison to Edmund Randolph (July 26, 1785), *in* 8 THE PAPERS OF JAMES MADISON, *supra* chap. 3, note 56, at 327.

25. MADISON, REPORT ON THE ALIEN AND SEDITION ACTS, *supra, in* JAMES MADISON: WRITINGS, *supra* chap. 1, note 3, at 654.

26. *Id.* at 654–55.

27. Letter from James Madison to James Monroe (Dec. 4, 1794), *in* 15 THE PAPERS OF JAMES MADISON, *supra* chap. 2, note 55, at 405, 407.

28. THE FEDERALIST NO. 10, at 162 (James Madison) (Jack N. Rakove, ed., 1999).

29. *See* SHELDON, *supra* chap. 1, note 27, at 27; LABUNSKI, *supra* chap. 1, note 1, at 162.

30. *See* LEVY, ORIGINS, *supra* chap. 1, note 21, at 232–36.

31. BRANT, THE BILL OF RIGHTS, *supra* chap. 1, note 32, at 107. *See also* Madison, Report on Books for Congress, *supra, in* 6 THE PAPERS OF JAMES MADISON, *supra* chap. 2, note 6, at 80–81.

32. MADISON, *Republican Distribution of Citizens* (Mar. 5, 1792), *supra, in* JAMES MADISON: WRITINGS, *supra* chap. 1, note 3, at 512–13.

33. MADISON, *Property* (Mar. 29, 1792), *supra, in* JAMES MADISON: WRITINGS, *supra* chap. 1, note 3, at 516.

34. James Madison, Speech at the Constitutional Convention (Aug. 7, 1787),

supra, in MADISON, NOTES OF DEBATES, *supra* chap. 2, note 53, at 403–4. *See also* ROBERT J. MORGAN, JAMES MADISON ON THE CONSTITUTION AND THE BILL OF RIGHTS 118 (New York: Greenwood Press, 1988).

35. MADISON, *Fashion, supra, in* JAMES MADISON: WRITINGS, *supra* chap. 1, note 3, at 514.

36. 1 ANNALS OF CONG. 452 (1789).

37. *Id.* at 451–52.

38. MADISON, *Property* (Mar. 29, 1792), *supra, in* JAMES MADISON: WRITINGS, *supra* chap. 1, note 3, at 516–17.

39. THE FEDERALIST NO. 10, at 161 (James Madison) (Jack N. Rakove, ed., 1999).

40. *Id.*

41. *Id.*

42. MADISON, *Property* (Mar. 29, 1792), *supra, in* JAMES MADISON: WRITINGS, *supra* chap. 1, note 3, at 515.

43. For other writers advocating this position on Madison, *see* Harrington, *"Public Use," supra* chap. 1, note 26, at 1299; Harrington, *Regulatory Takings and the Original Understanding of the Takings Clause,* 45 WM. & MARY L. REV. 2053, 2073; ELY, THE GUARDIAN OF EVERY OTHER RIGHT, *supra* chap. 1, note 26, at 54 ; OLKEN, *supra* chap. 1, note 25, at 281; ROSEN, *supra* chap. 1, note 30, at 87; BANNING, THE SACRED FIRE, *supra* chap. 1, note 25, at 63; Dorn, *supra* chap. 1, note 26, at 196; MATTHEWS, *supra* chap. 1, note 24, at 84; NEDELSKY, *supra* chap. 1, note 26, at 205.

44. 1 ANNALS OF CONG. 454 (1789).

45. *Id.* at 458.

46. *Id.* at 457.

47. MADISON, REPORT ON THE ALIEN AND SEDITION ACTS, *supra, in* JAMES MADISON: WRITINGS, *supra* chap. 1, note 3, at 624.

48. MADISON, *Memorial and Remonstrance, supra, in* JAMES MADISON: WRITINGS, *supra* chap. 1, note 3, at 30.

49. Madison, Speech in the Virginia Ratifying Convention on Taxation, a Bill of Rights, and the Mississippi, *supra, in* JAMES MADISON: WRITINGS, *supra* chap. 1, note 3, at 382 (emphasis added).

50. 1 ANNALS OF CONG. 451 (1789).

51. James Madison, Speech in Congress on Religious Exemptions from Militia Duty (Dec. 22, 1796), *in* JAMES MADISON: WRITINGS, *supra* chap. 1, note 3, at 478, 479.

52. MADISON, *Property* (Mar. 29, 1792), *supra, in* JAMES MADISON: WRITINGS, *supra* chap. 1, note 3, at 516.

53. James Madison, First Inaugural Address (Mar. 4, 1809), *in* JAMES MADISON: WRITINGS, *supra* chap. 1, note 3, at 680, 681.

54. Letter from James Madison to Edward Livingston (July 10, 1822), *in* JAMES MADISON: WRITINGS, *supra* chap. 1, note 3, at 786, 787–88.

55. For others finding this, *see* BANNING, THE SACRED FIRE, *supra* chap. 1, note 25, at 84; BRANT, JAMES MADISON, *supra* chap. 1, note 21, at 268; KETCHAM, JAMES MADISON: A BIOGRAPHY, *supra* chap. 1, note 21, at 57–58; SHELDON, *supra* chap. 1, note 27, at 27; PADULA, MADISON V. MARSHALL, *supra* chap. 1, note 26, at 33; RIEMER, JAMES MADISON, *supra* chap. 1, note 26, at 32.

56. THE FEDERALIST NO. 10, at 161 (James Madison) (Jack N. Rakove, ed., 1999).

57. THE FEDERALIST NO. 49, at 287 (James Madison) (Jack N. Rakove, ed., 1999).

58. MADISON, *Public Opinion* (Dec. 19, 1791), *supra, in* JAMES MADISON: WRITINGS, *supra* chap. 1, note 3, at 500.

59. JAMES MADISON, *Charters* (Jan. 19, 1792), *in* JAMES MADISON: WRITINGS, *supra* chap. 1, note 3, at 502, 503.

60. MADISON, *Virginia Resolutions, supra, in* JAMES MADISON: WRITINGS, *supra* chap. 1, note 3, at 590.

61. JAMES MADISON, *Foreign Influence* (Jan. 23, 1799), *in* JAMES MADISON: WRITINGS, *supra* chap. 1, note 3, at 592, 599.

62. MADISON, REPORT ON THE ALIEN AND SEDITION ACTS, *supra, in* JAMES MADISON: WRITINGS, *supra* chap. 1, note 3, at 645.

63. Madison, First Inaugural Address, *supra, in* JAMES MADISON: WRITINGS, *supra* chap. 1, note 3, at 681.

64. For others stating this position, *see* RIEMER, JAMES MADISON, *supra* chap. 1, note 26, at 142; SHELDON, *supra* chap. 1, note 27, at 84; KETCHAM, JAMES MADISON: A BIOGRAPHY, *supra* chap. 1, note 21, at 295–96.

65. Madison, Speech in the Virginia Ratifying Convention on the Judicial Power (June 20, 1788), *supra, in* JAMES MADISON: WRITINGS, *supra* chap. 1, note 3, at 399.

66. 1 ANNALS OF CONG. 452 (1789).

67. *Id.* at 454.

68. MADISON, REPORT ON THE ALIEN AND SEDITION ACTS, *supra, in* JAMES MADISON: WRITINGS, *supra* chap. 1, note 3, at 624.

69. THE FEDERALIST NO. 10, at 161 (James Madison) (Jack N. Rakove, ed., 1999).

70. MADISON, *Property* (Mar. 29, 1792), *supra, in* JAMES MADISON: WRITINGS, *supra* chap. 1, note 3, at 515.

71. *Id.*

72. *Id.*

73. 1 ANNALS OF CONG. 451 (1789).

74. Letter from James Madison to Caleb Wallace (Aug. 23, 1785), *in* JAMES MADISON: WRITINGS, *supra* chap. 1, note 3, at 39, 41 (emphasis added).

75. THE FEDERALIST NO. 41, at 233 (James Madison) (Jack N. Rakove, ed., 1999) (emphasis added).

76. THE FEDERALIST NO. 54, at 313 (James Madison) (Jack N. Rakove, ed., 1999).

77. Letter from Madison to Eve (Jan. 2, 1789), *supra, in* JAMES MADISON: WRITINGS, *supra* chap. 1, note 3, at 428 (emphasis added).

78. Letter from James Madison to Thomas Mann Randolph (Jan. 13, 1789), *supra, in* 11 THE PAPERS OF JAMES MADISON, *supra* chap. 1, note 2, at 416 (emphasis added).

79. 1 ANNALS OF CONG. 451–53 (1789).

80. *Id.* at 452 (emphasis added).

81. *Id.*

82. *Id.* at 458.

83. HELEN E. VEIT ET AL., CREATING THE BILL OF RIGHTS: THE DOCUMEN-TARY RECORD FROM THE FIRST FEDERAL CONGRESS 31 (Baltimore: The Johns Hopkins University Press, 1991).

84. 1 ANNALS OF CONG. 453 (1789).

85. *Id.*

86. *Id.* at 775 (emphasis added).

87. Madison, Speech in Congress Opposing the National Bank (Feb. 2, 1791), *supra, in* JAMES MADISON: WRITINGS, *supra* chap. 1, note 3, at 488.

88. *Id.* at 488–89 (emphasis added).

89. MADISON, *Property* (Mar. 29, 1792), *supra, in* JAMES MADISON: WRIT-INGS, *supra* chap. 1, note 3, at 517 (emphasis added).

90. MADISON, REPORT ON THE ALIEN AND SEDITION ACTS, *supra, in* JAMES MADISON: WRITINGS, *supra* chap. 1, note 3, at 627 (emphasis added).

91. *Id.* at 648.

92. *Id.* at 657.

93. *Id.* (emphasis added).

94. *Id.* (emphasis added).

95. For scholars discovering that Madison wanted special protection of this core set of rights *see* KETCHAM, JAMES MADISON: A BIOGRAPHY, *supra* chap. 1, note 21, at 290; MATTHEWS, *supra* chap. 1, note 24, at 19; RAKOVE, JAMES MADI-SON, *supra* chap. 1, note 21, at 96; RIEMER, JAMES MADISON, *supra* chap. 1, note 26, at 161; ROSEN, *supra* chap. 1, note 30, at 21.

96. THE FEDERALIST NO. 47, at 273 (James Madison) (Jack N. Rakove, ed., 1999).

97. James Madison, Speech at the Constitutional Convention (July 17, 1787), *in* MADISON, NOTES OF DEBATES, *supra* chap. 2, note 53, at 311.

98. 1 ANNALS OF CONG. 453 (1789).

99. *Id.* at 454.

100. *Id.* at 457.

101. MADISON, *Virginia Resolutions, supra, in* JAMES MADISON: WRITINGS, *supra* chap. 1, note 3, at 590.

102. MADISON, REPORT ON THE ALIEN AND SEDITION ACTS, *supra, in* JAMES MADISON: WRITINGS, *supra* chap. 1, note 3, at 629.

103. *Id.* at 631.

104. *See also* Rossum, *"Self-Incrimination": The Original Intent, supra* chap. 1, note 31, at 282.

105. 1 ANNALS OF CONG. 453 (1789).

106. *Id.* at 458.

107. *Id.* at 457.

108. MADISON, *Virginia Resolutions, supra, in* JAMES MADISON: WRITINGS, *supra* chap. 1, note 3, at 589.

109. *Id.*

110. MADISON, REPORT ON THE ALIEN AND SEDITION ACTS, *supra, in* JAMES MADISON: WRITINGS, *supra* chap. 1, note 3, at 611.

111. 1 ANNALS OF CONG. 454 (1789).

112. *Id.* at 455.

113. MADISON, REPORT ON THE ALIEN AND SEDITION ACTS, *supra, in* JAMES MADISON: WRITINGS, *supra* chap. 1, note 3, at 609.

114. *Id.* at 642.

115. 1 ANNALS OF CONG. 452 (1789).

116. *Id.* at 456.

117. THE FEDERALIST NO. 52, at 300 (James Madison) (Jack N. Rakove, ed., 1999).

118. 1 ANNALS OF CONG. 766 (1789).

119. Madison, Speech in Congress on "Self-Created Societies," *supra, in* JAMES MADISON: WRITINGS, *supra* chap. 1, note 3, at 552.

120. James Madison, Speech in Congress on the Jay Treaty (Apr. 6, 1796), *in* JAMES MADISON: WRITINGS, *supra* chap. 1, note 3, at 569.

121. MADISON, REPORT ON THE ALIEN AND SEDITION ACTS, *supra, in* JAMES MADISON: WRITINGS, *supra* chap. 1, note 3, at 655.

122. *See id.* at 652–55.

123. For other scholars advocating this position on Madison *see* AMAR, *supra* chap. 1, note 33, at 29; MATTHEWS, *supra* chap. 1, note 24, at 217; SHELDON, *supra* chap. 1, note 27, at 96; Berns, *Religion and the Founding Principle, in* Horwitz, *supra* chap. 1, note 43, at 157, 179–80; RUTLAND, JAMES MADISON, *supra* chap. 4, note 34, at 157.

7—MADISON'S VISION OF SPECIFIC FREEDOMS IN THE BILL OF RIGHTS

1. Madison, Speech in the Virginia Ratifying Convention in Defense of the Constitution (June 6, 1788), *supra, in* JAMES MADISON: WRITINGS, *supra* chap. 1, note 3, at 361.

2. James Madison, Detached Memoranda (1819?), *in* JAMES MADISON: WRITINGS, *supra* chap. 1, note 3, at 745, 760.

3. MADISON, *Memorial and Remonstrance, supra, in* JAMES MADISON: WRITINGS, *supra* chap. 1, note 3, at 31.

4. *Id.*

5. Letter from James Madison to Edmund Pendleton (Oct. 28, 1787), *in* 10 THE PAPERS OF JAMES MADISON, *supra* chap. 2, note 30, at 223.

6. THOMAS JEFFERSON, *An Act for Establishing Religious Freedom* (1779), *in* THE LIFE AND SELECTED WORKS OF THOMAS JEFFERSON, *supra* chap. 3, note 47, at 289.

7. Letter from Madison to Jefferson (Oct. 24, 1787), *supra, in* JAMES MADISON: WRITINGS, *supra* chap. 1, note 3, at 148.

8. MADISON, *Memorial and Remonstrance, supra, in* JAMES MADISON: WRITINGS, *supra* chap. 1, note 3, at 32.

9. *Id.* at 33.

10. *Id.* at 32–33.

11. James Madison, Naturalization (Jan. 1, 1795), *in* 15 THE PAPERS OF JAMES MADISON, *supra* chap. 2, note 55, at 432.

12. Letter from Madison to Jefferson (Jan. 22, 1786), *supra, in* 8 THE PAPERS OF JAMES MADISON, *supra* chap. 3, note 56, at 474.

13. Letter from James Madison to Robert Walsh (Mar. 2, 1819), *in* JAMES

MADISON: WRITINGS, *supra* chap. 1, note 3, at 723, 727 (emphasis added).

14. MADISON, *Memorial and Remonstrance, supra, in* JAMES MADISON: WRITINGS, *supra* chap. 1, note 3, at 32.

15. James Madison, Speech at the Constitutional Convention (Sept. 14, 1787), *in* MADISON, NOTES OF DEBATES, *supra* chap. 2, note 53, at 639. Madison also tried to establish a national university in Congress and during his presidency. *See* Madison in the Fourth Congress 7 December 1795–3 March 1797, Editorial Note, *in* 16 THE PAPERS OF JAMES MADISON, at 141, 151–52 (J.C.A. Stagg et al., eds., Charlottesville: University Press of Virginia, 1989); James Madison, National University (Dec. 12, 26, 1796), *in* 16 THE PAPERS OF JAMES MADISON, *supra*, at 225–26, 436–38.

16. Letter from James Madison to Edward Everett (Mar. 19, 1823), *in* JAMES MADISON: WRITINGS, *supra* chap. 1, note 3, at 794, 795.

17. THE FEDERALIST NO. 10, at 162 (James Madison) (Jack N. Rakove, ed., 1999).

18. MADISON, *Memorial and Remonstrance, supra, in* JAMES MADISON: WRITINGS, *supra* chap. 1, note 3, at 34.

19. James Madison, Speech in the Federal Convention on Factions (June 6, 1787), *in* JAMES MADISON: WRITINGS, *supra* chap. 1, note 3, at 92, 93.

20. MADISON, *Memorial and Remonstrance, supra, in* JAMES MADISON: WRITINGS, *supra* chap. 1, note 3, at 31.

21. Letter from Madison to Jefferson (Oct. 17, 1788), *supra, in* JAMES MADISON: WRITINGS, *supra* chap. 1, note 3, at 420.

22. MADISON, *Memorial and Remonstrance, supra, in* JAMES MADISON: WRITINGS, *supra* chap. 1, note 3, at 33–34.

23. *Id.* at 31.

24. *Id.* at 35.

25. *Id.* at 29.

26. Letter from Madison to Jefferson (Oct. 24, 1787), *supra, in* JAMES MADISON: WRITINGS, *supra* chap. 1, note 3, at 151.

27. Madison, Detached Memoranda, *supra, in* JAMES MADISON: WRITINGS, *supra* chap. 1, note 3, at 762.

28. *Id.* at 763.

29. *Id.*

30. *Id.*

31. *Id.* at 766.

32. *Id.* at 764.

33. Madison, Detached Memoranda, *supra, in* JAMES MADISON: WRITINGS, *supra* chap. 1, note 3, at 764.

34. *Id.* at 765.

35. *Id.*

36. Letter from Madison to Everett (Mar. 19, 1823), *supra, in* JAMES MADISON: WRITINGS, *supra* chap. 1, note 3, at 796.

37. MADISON, *Memorial and Remonstrance, supra, in* JAMES MADISON: WRITINGS, *supra* chap. 1, note 3, at 30; *see also* MORGAN, *supra*, at 147.

38. Madison, First Inaugural Address, *supra, in* JAMES MADISON: WRITINGS, *supra* chap. 1, note 3, at 681.

39. MADISON, *Property* (Mar. 29, 1792), *supra, in* JAMES MADISON: WRIT-

INGS, *supra* chap. 1, note 3, at 515.

40. MADISON, *Memorial and Remonstrance, supra, in* JAMES MADISON: WRITINGS, *supra* chap. 1, note 3, at 31.

41. *Id.*

42. Madison, Amendments to the Virginia Declaration of Rights, *supra, in* JAMES MADISON: WRITINGS, *supra* chap. 1, note 3, at 10.

43. 1 ANNALS OF CONG. 451 (1789).

44. Employment Div., 494 U.S. at 894 (O'Connor, J., concurring).

45. Employment Div., 494 U.S. 872.

46. THE FEDERALIST NO. 10, at 160 (James Madison) (Jack N. Rakove, ed., 1999).

47. Madison, Speech in the Virginia Ratifying Convention on Taxation, a Bill of Rights, and the Mississippi, *supra, in* JAMES MADISON: WRITINGS, *supra* chap. 1, note 3, at 382.

48. 1 ANNALS OF CONG. 451 (1789).

49. *Id.* at 452

50. MADISON, *Memorial and Remonstrance, supra, in* JAMES MADISON: WRITINGS, *supra* chap. 1, note 3, at 34.

51. *Id.* at 31.

52. Madison, Observations on the "Draught of a Constitution for Virginia," *supra, in* JAMES MADISON: WRITINGS, *supra* chap. 1, note 3, at 412.

53. Veto Message from President James Madison (Feb. 28, 1811), *in* 3 THE PAPERS OF JAMES MADISON: PRESIDENTIAL SERIES, 193 (J.C.A. Stagg et al., eds., Charlottesville: University Press of Virginia, 1996).

54. 1 ANNALS OF CONG. 451 (1789).

55. *Id.* at 452.

56. VEIT ET AL., *supra* chap. 6, note 83, at 31.

57. 1 ANNALS OF CONG. 451 (1789). Of course, Madison did not use the term "association," instead referring to the concept of "assembly." I cannot find a reason why Madison's concept of "assembly" would be substantially different from the U.S. Supreme Court's resort to using "association." However, there may be a distinction here that is beyond the scope of this work.

58. MADISON, *Property* (Mar. 29, 1792), *supra, in* JAMES MADISON: WRITINGS, *supra* chap. 1, note 3, at 515.

59. Madison, Speech in Congress on "Self-Created Societies," *supra, in* JAMES MADISON: WRITINGS, *supra* chap. 1, note 3, at 551.

60. Letter from James Madison to Archibald Stuart (Oct. 30, 1787), *in* 10 THE PAPERS OF JAMES MADISON, *supra* chap. 2, note 30, at 232.

61. MADISON, REPORT ON THE ALIEN AND SEDITION ACTS, *supra, in* JAMES MADISON: WRITINGS, *supra* chap. 1, note 3, at 647.

62. James Madison, Address of the House of Representatives to the President (Nov. 9, 1792), *in* 14 THE PAPERS OF JAMES MADISON, *supra* chap. 1, note 2, at 403, 404.

63. Letter from James Madison to Thomas Jefferson (May 5, 1798), *in* 17 THE PAPERS OF JAMES MADISON, *supra* chap. 1, note 2, at 126.

64. Letter from James Madison to Thomas Jefferson (June 12, 1792), *in* 14 THE PAPERS OF JAMES MADISON, *supra* chap. 1, note 2, at 316, 317. While in Congress,

Madison also advocated lower mailing costs for newspapers. *See* The Origins of Freneau's *National Gazette* 25 July 1791, Editorial Note, *in* 14 THE PAPERS OF JAMES MADISON, *supra* chap. 1, note 2, at 56, 56–57; James Madison, Low Postage for Newspapers (Jan. 9, 1792), *in* 14 THE PAPERS OF JAMES MADISON, *supra* chap. 1, note 2, at 186.

65. JAMES MADISON, *Who Are the Best Keepers of the People's Liberties?* (Dec. 22, 1792), *in* JAMES MADISON: WRITINGS, *supra* chap. 1, note 3, at 532, 533.

66. MADISON, *Foreign Influence* (Jan. 23, 1799), *supra*, *in* JAMES MADISON: WRITINGS, *supra* chap. 1, note 3, at 599.

67. THE FEDERALIST NO. 10, at 161 (James Madison) (Jack N. Rakove, ed., 1999).

68. Letter from James Madison to Thomas Jefferson (Nov. 30, 1794), *in* 15 THE PAPERS OF JAMES MADISON, *supra* chap. 2, note 55, at 396.

69. MADISON, *Property* (Mar. 29, 1792), *supra*, *in* JAMES MADISON: WRITINGS, *supra* chap. 1, note 3, at 516.

70. Madison, Speech in Congress on "Self-Created Societies," *supra*, *in* JAMES MADISON: WRITINGS, *supra* chap. 1, note 3, at 552.

71. *Id.*

72. MADISON, REPORT ON THE ALIEN AND SEDITION ACTS, *supra*, *in* JAMES MADISON: WRITINGS, *supra* chap. 1, note 3, at 655.

73. Madison, Speech in Congress on "Self-Created Societies," *supra*, *in* JAMES MADISON: WRITINGS, *supra* chap. 1, note 3, at 552.

74. MADISON, *Virginia Resolutions, supra, in* JAMES MADISON: WRITINGS, *supra* chap. 1, note 3, at 590.

75. Letter from Madison to Jefferson (Oct. 17, 1788), *supra*, *in* JAMES MADISON: WRITINGS, *supra* chap. 1, note 3, at 421.

76. MADISON, *Memorial and Remonstrance, supra, in* JAMES MADISON: WRITINGS, *supra* chap. 1, note 3, at 33; *see also* MORGAN, *supra*, at 149.

77. MADISON, *Property* (Mar. 29, 1792), *supra*, *in* JAMES MADISON: WRITINGS, *supra* chap. 1, note 3, at 515.

78. Madison, Speech in the Virginia Constitutional Convention (Dec. 2, 1829), *supra*, *in* JAMES MADISON: WRITINGS, *supra* chap. 1, note 3, at 824.

79. 1 ANNALS OF CONG. 451 (1789) (emphasis added).

80. For a similar view, *see* NEDELSKY, *supra* chap. 1, note 26, at 38.

81. Bill Prohibiting Further Confiscation of British Property (Dec. 3, 1784), *in* 8 THE PAPERS OF JAMES MADISON, *supra* chap. 3, note 56, at 173–74.

82. Letter from Madison to Wallace (Aug. 23, 1785), *supra*, *in* JAMES MADISON: WRITINGS, *supra* chap. 1, note 3, at 41.

83. 1 ANNALS OF CONG. 451–52 (1789).

84. *Id.* (emphasis added).

85. MADISON, *Property* (Mar. 29, 1792), *supra*, *in* JAMES MADISON: WRITINGS, *supra* chap. 1, note 3, at 516.

86. THE FEDERALIST NO. 10, at 162 (James Madison) (Jack N. Rakove, ed., 1999).

87. *Id.* at 167.

88. 1 ANNALS OF CONG. 454 (1789).

89. Apodaca v. Or., 406 U.S. 404, 409 (1972).

90. MADISON, REPORT ON THE ALIEN AND SEDITION ACTS, *supra, in* JAMES MADISON: WRITINGS, *supra* chap. 1, note 3, at 654–55.

91. 1 ANNALS OF CONG. 452 (1789).

92. MADISON, *Property* (Mar. 29, 1792), *supra, in* JAMES MADISON: WRITINGS, *supra* chap. 1, note 3, at 516.

93. 1 ANNALS OF CONG. 457 (1789).

94. *Id.* at 452; U.S. CONST. amend V.

95. James Madison, Amendments to a Bill for Proportioning Crimes and Punishments (Dec. 10, 1785), *in* 17 THE PAPERS OF JAMES MADISON, *supra* chap. 1, note 2, at 510, 511 n.1.

96. *Id.* at 510.

97. 1 ANNALS OF CONG. 451–52 (1789).

98. *See also* SCHWARTZ, THE GREAT RIGHTS OF MANKIND, *supra* chap. 1, note 32, at 151–52; Thomas Y. Davies, *The Fictional Character of Law-and-Order Originalism, supra* chap. 1, note 32, at 251.

99. *See also* Leibiger, *supra* chap. 4, note 34, at 461; RAKOVE, ORIGINAL MEANINGS, *supra* chap. 1, note 24, at 308; 2 SCHWARTZ, THE BILL OF RIGHTS, *supra* chap. 1, note 35, at 1008; SCHWARTZ, THE GREAT RIGHTS OF MANKIND, *supra* chap. 1, note 32, at 170.

100. MADISON, REPORT ON THE ALIEN AND SEDITION ACTS, *supra, in* JAMES MADISON: WRITINGS, *supra* chap. 1, note 3, at 622.

8—THE RELATION OF MADISON'S BILL OF RIGHTS TO OUR BILL OF RIGHTS

1. *See* LANCE BANNING, JEFFERSON AND MADISON: THREE CONVERSATIONS FROM THE FOUNDING 3 (Madison, Wisc.: Madison House, 1995); Alley, *Public Education and the Public Good, supra* chap. 1, note 21, at 304; SCHWARTZ, THE GREAT RIGHTS OF MANKIND, *supra* chap. 1, note 32, at 162; RAKOVE, ORIGINAL MEANINGS, *supra* chap. 1, note 24, at 330; BANNING, THE SACRED FIRE, *supra* chap. 1, note 25, at 308; LABUNSKI, *supra* chap. 1, note 1, at 2; FARBER & SHERRY, *supra* chap. 1, note 27, at 226–27; Reid, *The Fundamental Freedom, supra* chap. 1, note 21, at 416.

2. 1 ANNALS OF CONG. 257 (1789).

3. 2 SCHWARTZ, THE BILL OF RIGHTS, *supra* chap. 1, note 35, at 1006.

4. 1 ANNALS OF CONG. 440–41 (1789).

5. *Id.* at 448.

6. 2 SCHWARTZ, THE BILL OF RIGHTS, *supra* chap. 1, note 35, at 1006.

7. 1 ANNALS OF CONG. 442 (1789).

8. *Id.* at 443.

9. *Id.* at 445.

10. *Id.* at 443.

11. *Id.* at 445.

12. *Id.* at 459 (emphasis added). Of course, Madison had made similar arguments about a bill of rights in 1787–1788.

13. *Id.* at 460.

14. *Id.* at 461 (emphasis added).

15. *Id.* at 462.
16. *Id.* at 467.
17. *Id.* at 468.
18. *Id.* at 685–86.
19. *Id.* at 686.
20. *Id.* at 686–91. North Carolina and Rhode Island had not yet ratified the Constitution, so only 11 states were represented in Congress in July 1789.
21. *Id.* at 699.
22. *Id.*
23. *Id.* at 700; 2 SCHWARTZ, THE BILL OF RIGHTS, *supra* chap. 1, note 35, at 1050.
24. 1 ANNALS OF CONG. 725–30 (1789).
25. *Id.* at 731.
26. *Id.* at 731–32.
27. *Id.* at 734.
28. FARBER & SHERRY, *supra* chap. 1, note 27, at 226–27; LEVY, ORIGINS, *supra* chap. 1, note 21, at 34.
29. LEONARD W. LEVY, LEGACY OF SUPPRESSION: FREEDOM OF SPEECH AND PRESS IN EARLY AMERICAN HISTORY 227–28 (New York: Harper Torchbooks, 1963).
30. 1 ANNALS OF CONG. 790–92 (1789).
31. *Id.* at 790, 797.
32. *Id.* at 803.
33. *Id.* at 790.
34. *See id.* at 798, 800, 802.
35. *Id.* at 758–59.
36. *Id.* at 766–69.
37. *Id.* at 784.
38. 1 SENATE JOURNAL 72 (1789).
39. Letter from Madison to Peters (Aug. 19, 1789), *supra, in* JAMES MADISON: WRITINGS, *supra* chap. 1, note 3, at 471.
40. *See generally* Leonard W. Levy, *The Legacy Reexamined*, 37 STAN. L. REV. 767, 782 (1985); Leonard W. Levy, *Bill of Rights, in* ESSAYS ON THE MAKING OF THE CONSTITUTION 258 (Leonard W. Levy, ed., New York: Oxford University Press, 1987); Michael M. Maddigan, *The Establishment Clause, Civil Religion, and the Public Church*, 81 CAL. L. REV. 293, 305 (1993); Jonathan Duncan, *Looks Like a Waiting Period for the Brady Bill: Tenth Amendment Challenges to a Controversial Unfunded Mandate*, 43 KAN. L. REV. 835, 848 (1995); David L. Abney, *Constitutional Interpretation: Moving toward a Jurisprudence of Commonsense*, 67 TEMP. L. REV. 931, 939 (1994); Bradley C. Bobertz, *The Brandeis Gambit: The Making of America's "First Freedom," 1909–1931*, 40 WM. & MARY L. REV. 557, 647 (1999).
41. Letter from Richard Peters to James Madison (July 20, 1789), *in* 12 THE PAPERS OF JAMES MADISON, *supra* chap. 1, note 2, at 301–3.
42. Letter from James Madison to Edmund Pendleton (Aug. 21, 1789), *in* 12 THE PAPERS OF JAMES MADISON, *supra* chap. 1, note 2, at 348
43. Letter from James Madison to Edmund Randolph (Aug. 21, 1789), *in* 12 THE PAPERS OF JAMES MADISON, *supra* chap. 1, note 2, at 348.

44. Letter from James Madison to Edmund Pendleton (Sept. 14, 1789), *in* 12 THE PAPERS OF JAMES MADISON, *supra* chap. 1, note 2, at 402; Letter from James Madison to Edmund Pendleton (Sept. 23, 1789), *in* 12 THE PAPERS OF JAMES MADISON, *supra* chap. 1, note 2, at 418, 418–19.

45. *See* SHELDON, *supra* chap. 1, note 27, at 1; PADULA, MADISON V. MARSHALL, *supra* chap. 1, note 26, at 73; LEVY, ORIGINS, *supra* chap. 1, note 21, at 263–68; VEIT ET AL., *supra* chap. 6, note 83, at xi.

46. 1 ANNALS OF CONG. 690–91 (1789).

47. *See* FARBER & SHERRY, *supra* chap. 1, note 27, at 231; Leibiger, *supra* chap. 4, note 34, at 466; Neuborne, *The House Was Quiet, supra* chap. 6, note 3, at 2058.

48. *See* 1 ANNALS OF CONG. 730–808 (1789).

49. *Id.* at 15.

50. *See* FARBER & SHERRY, *supra* chap. 1, note 27, at 241–42.

51. 1 ANNALS OF CONG. 939 (1789).

52. BRANT, JAMES MADISON, *supra* chap. 1, note 21, at 271.

53. 1 ANNALS OF CONG. 451 (1789).

54. *Id.* at 757.

55. 1 SENATE JOURNAL 63 (1789).

56. *Id.* at 77

57. 1 ANNALS OF CONG. 451 (1789).

58. *Id.* at 451–52.

59. *Id.* at 452.

60. *Id.*

61. *Id.*

62. *Id.*

63. *Id.*

64. *Id.*

65. *Id.* at 467.

66. *Id.* at 730, 734.

67. *Id.* at 734–44.

68. *Id.* at 745–46.

69. Compare *id.* 451 with *id.* 759.

70. 1 SENATE JOURNAL 72 (1789).

71. 1 ANNALS OF CONG. 757–59 (1789).

72. *Id.* at 783.

73. *Id.* at 797.

74. 1 SENATE JOURNAL 70, 77 (1789).

75. *Id.* at 77.

76. Letter from James Madison to William Cogswell (Mar. 10, 1834), *in* 9 THE WRITINGS OF JAMES MADISON 533 (Galliard Hunt, ed.; New York: Putnam, 1910).

77. Letter from James Madison to Thomas Ritchie (Sept. 15, 1821), *in* 3 LETTERS AND OTHER WRITINGS OF JAMES MADISON 228 (Philadelphia: Lippincott, 1865).

78. Madison, Speech in Congress on the Jay Treaty (Apr. 6, 1796), *supra, in* JAMES MADISON: WRITINGS, *supra* chap. 1, note 3, at 574.

79. Madison, Speech in Congress Opposing the National Bank (Feb. 2, 1791), *supra, in* JAMES MADISON: WRITINGS, *supra* chap. 1, note 3, at 482.

80. THE FEDERALIST NO. 14, at 172 (James Madison) (Jack N. Rakove, ed., 1999).

81. James Madison, Speech at the Constitutional Convention (June 25, 1787), *in* MADISON, NOTES OF DEBATES, *supra* chap. 2, note 53, at 194.

82. THE FEDERALIST NO. 40, at 225 (James Madison) (Jack N. Rakove, ed., 1999).

9—MADISON AND THE BILL OF RIGHTS IN THE U.S. SUPREME COURT

1. 1 ANNALS OF CONG. 457 (1789).

2. United States v. Carolene Products, Co., 304 U.S. 144 (1938).

3. *Id.* at 153 n.4.

4. Skinner v. Oklahoma, 316 U.S. 535, 544 (1942) (Stone, C.J., concurring).

5. United States v. Congress of Industrial Organizations, 335 U.S. 106, 140 (1948) (Rutledge, J., concurring).

6. Kovacs v. Cooper, 336 U.S. 77, 90–91 (1949) (Frankfurter, J., concurring).

7. *Id.* at 88; *id.* at 106 (Rutledge, J., dissenting).

8. Dennis v. United States, 341 U.S. 494, 526–27 (1951) (Frankfurter, J., concurring).

9. Braunfeld v. Brown, 366 U.S. 599, 613 (1961) (Brennan, J., concurring and dissenting).

10. District of Columbia v. Heller, 128 S. Ct. 2783, 2817 n.27 (2008).

11. Gulf, Colorado and Santa Fe Railway Co. v. Ellis, 165 U.S. 150, 155 (1897).

12. City of Cleburne v. Cleburne Living Center, 473 U.S. 432, 440 (1985).

13. Carolene Products, 304 U.S. 153 (emphasis added).

14. Jones v. Opelika, 316 U.S. 584, 608 (1942).

15. Murdock v. Pennsylvania, 319 U.S. 105, 115 (1943).

16. Poulos v. New Hampshire, 345 U.S. 395, 405 (1953).

17. Skinner, 316 U.S. 541.

18. Griswold, 381 U.S. 503–4 (internal citations and quotations omitted).

19. Reno v. Flores, 507 U.S. 292, 302 (1993).

20. Planned Parenthood v. Casey, 505 U.S. 833, 871 (1992).

21. *See* Republican Party of Minnesota v. White, 536 U.S. 765 (2002): Brigham City v. Stuart, 547 U.S. 398 (2006); New York v. Quarles, 467 U.S. 649 (1984); United States v. Salerno, 481 U.S. 739, 755, 107 S. Ct. 2095, 95 L. Ed. 2d 697 (1987).

22. Hobbie v. Unemployment Appeals Commission of Florida, 480 U.S. 136 (1987).

23. Barenblatt v. United States, 360 U.S. 109, 143 (1959) (Black, H., dissenting).

24. Stefanie A. Lindquist and Rorie Spill Solberg, *Judicial Review by the Burger and Rehnquist Courts: Explaining Justices' Responses to Constitutional Challenges*, 60 POL. RESEARCH QUARTERLY 71 (2007).

25. Barron v. Baltimore, 32 U.S. 243, 250 (1833).

26. *See also* Brown, *supra* chap. 5, note 44, at 164.

27. *See* Richard L. Aynes, *The Antislavery and Abolitionist Background of John A. Bingham*, 37 CATH. U.L. REV. 881 (1988); Carol Chomsky, *The United States–Dakota War Trials: A Study in Military Injustice*, 43 STAN. L. REV. 13 (1990).

28. Bryan H. Wildenthal, *Nationalizing the Bill of Rights: Revisiting the Original*

Understanding of the Fourteenth Amendment in 1866–67, 68 OHIO ST. L.J. 1509, 1532 (2007).

29. *Id.*

30. CONG. GLOBE, 39th Cong., 1st Sess. 1034 (1866).

31. Wildenthal, *supra* note 28, at 1539.

32. Benjamin B. Kendrick, THE JOURNAL OF THE JOINT COMMITTEE OF FIFTEEN ON RECONSTRUCTION, 39TH CONGRESS, 1865–1867, 87 (New York: Longman's and Green, 1914).

33. Adamson v. California, 332 U.S. 46, 103–4 (1947) (Black, H., dissenting).

34. *Id.* at 73–74.

35. CONG. GLOBE, 39th Cong., 1st Sess. 2542–43 (1866).

36. The Slaughterhouse Cases, 83 U.S. 36 (1873).

37. *Id.* at 77.

38. *Id.* at 77–78.

39. Hurtado v. California, 110 U.S. 516 (1884).

40. *Id.* at 541 (Harlan, J., dissenting).

41. *Id.* at 549.

42. Missouri Pacific Railway Co. v. Nebraska, 164 U.S. 403 (1896).

43. *Id.* at 417.

44. Chicago, Burlington and Quincy Railroad Co. v. Chicago, 166 U.S. 226 (1897).

45. *Id.* at 241.

46. Gitlow v. New York, 268 U.S. 652 (1925).

47. *Id.* at 666.

48. Near v. Minnesota, 283 U.S. 697 (1931); DeJonge v. Oregon, 299 U.S. 353 (1937).

49. Palko v. Connecticut, 302 U.S. 319 (1937).

50. *Id.* at 324–25.

51. *Id.* at 325 (internal citations omitted).

52. *Id.* at 326.

53. *Id.* at 326–27.

54. *Id.* at 328.

55. *Id.* at 325.

56. Cantwell v. Connecticut, 310 U.S. 296, 303 (1940).

57. Duncan v. Louisiana, 391 U.S. 145, 149 (1968).

10—DEVOTEES OF MADISON ON THE SUPREME COURT

1. Engel v. Vitale, 370 U.S. 421 (1962).

2. *Id.* at 428.

3. *Id.* at 431.

4. *Id.* (internal citations omitted).

5. *Id.* at 431–32 (internal citations omitted).

6. *Id.* at 436 (internal citations omitted).

7. Galloway v. United States, 319 U.S. 372 (1943).

8. *Id.* at 407 (Black, H., dissenting).

9. Yates v. United States, 354 U.S. 298 (1957).

10. *Id.* at 344 (Black, H., dissenting in part).

11. Marsh v. Chambers, 463 U.S. 783 (1983).

12. *Id.* at 804, 807–8, 815, 817 (Brennan, J., dissenting).

13. *Id.* at 808 (Brennan, J., dissenting) (internal citations omitted).

14. *Id.* at 788, 788 n.8.

15. *Id.* at 814–15 (Brennan, J., dissenting)(internal citations omitted).

16. O'Lone v. Estate of Shabazz, 482 U.S. 342 (1987).

17. *Id.* at 354 (Brennan, J., dissenting).

18. *Id.* at 356 (Brennan, J., dissenting).

19. *Id.* (Brennan, J., dissenting) (quoting 6 WRITINGS OF JAMES MADISON 83 (G. Hunt, ed., 1906) (citations omitted).

20. Madison, Amendments to the Virginia Declaration of Rights, *supra, in* JAMES MADISON: WRITINGS, *supra* chap. 1, note 3, at 10.

21. Brown v. Hartlage, 456 U.S. 45 (1982).

22. *Id.* at 55–56.

23. *Id.* at 56 n.7 (quoting THE FEDERALIST NO. 51, at 324 (James Madison) (H. Lodge, ed., 1888)).

24. *Id.* at 284 (Brennan, J., dissenting).

25. *Id.* (Brennan, J., dissenting) (quoting MADISON, *Report on the Virginia Resolutions* (Jan. 1800), reprinted in 4 ELLIOT'S DEBATES 556 (2d ed., 1836)).

26. County of Allegheny v. ACLU, 492 U.S. 573 (1989).

27. *Id.* at 660 (Kennedy, J., concurring in judgment in part and dissenting in part).

28. *Id.* (Kennedy, J., concurring in judgment in part and dissenting in part) (quoting McGowan v. Md., 366 U.S. 420, 441 (1961) (quoting 1 ANNALS OF CONG. 730 (1789))) (internal citations omitted).

29. Lee v. Weisman, 505 U.S. 577 (1992).

30. *Id.* at 589.

31. *Id.* at 590 (quoting MADISON, *Memorial and Remonstrance against Religious Assessments* (1785), *in* 8 THE PAPERS OF JAMES MADISON, *supra* chap. 3, note 56, at 301).

32. Austin v. Michigan State Chamber of Commerce, 494 U.S. 652 (1990).

33. *Id.* at 695–96 (Kennedy, J., dissenting).

34. *Id.* at 710 (Kennedy, J., dissenting).

35. *Id.* (Kennedy, J., dissenting).

36. Alexander v. U.S., 509 U.S. 544 (1993).

37. *Id.* at 560 (Kennedy, J., dissenting).

38. *Id.* at 574 (Kennedy, J., dissenting).

39. *Id.* at 567 (Kennedy, J., dissenting) (quoting 4 WILLIAM BLACKSTONE, COMMENTARIES ON THE LAWS OF ENGLAND 151 (Chicago: University of Chicago Press, 1979) (1769)).

40. *Id.* at 568 (Kennedy, J., dissenting) (quoting 6 WRITINGS OF JAMES MADISON 386 (G. Hunt, ed., 1906)).

41. Roper v. Simmons, 543 U.S. 551 (2005).

42. *Id.* at 570.

43. *Id.* at 575.

44. *Id.* at 578.

45. For others who have understood Madison and his desire to protect human dignity in the Bill of Rights, *see* ROBERT ALLEN RUTLAND, THE BIRTH OF THE BILL OF RIGHTS, 1776–1791 222 (New York: Collier Books, 1962); Nash E. Long, *The "Constitutional Remand": Judicial Review of Constitutionally Dubious Statutes*, 14 J. L. & POLITICS 667, 700 (1998); Marc Chase McAllister, *Human Dignity and Individual Liberty in Germany and the United States as Examined Through Each Country's Leading Abortion Cases*, 11 TULSA J. COMP. & INT'L L. 491, 501 (2004).

46. Rosenberger, 515 U.S. 819.

47. *Id.* at 868 (Souter, J., dissenting).

48. *Id.* (Souter. J., dissenting, quoting Madison's *Memorial and Remonstrance*).

49. *Id.* at 869–70 (Souter. J., dissenting) (internal citations omitted).

50. *Id.* at 869–70 n.1 (Souter, J., dissenting).

51. *Id.* at 873 (Souter, J., dissenting).

52. Zelman v. Simmons-Harris, 536 U.S. 639 (2002).

53. *Id.* at 687 (Souter, J., dissenting).

54. *Id.* at 711 (Souter, J., dissenting) (quoting Madison's *Memorial and Remonstrance* P3, reprinted *in* Everson, 330 U.S. at 65–66; and quoting Mitchell v. Helms, 530 U.S. 793, 871 (2000) (Souter, J., dissenting)) (internal citations and quotation marks omitted).

55. *Id.* at 711 n.22 (Souter, J., dissenting).

56. *Id.* at 711–12 (Souter, J., dissenting) (quoting Madison's *Memorial and Remonstrance* P7, reprinted *in* Everson 330 U.S. at 67) (internal citations and quotation marks omitted).

57. *Id.* at 703 (Souter, J., dissenting).

58. *Id.* at 703–4 (Souter, J., dissenting).

59. *Id.* at 707 (Souter, J., dissenting).

60. McCreary County v. ACLU, 125 S. Ct. 2722 (2005).

61. McCreary County, 125 S. Ct. at 2742 (internal citations omitted).

62. *Id.* at 2744.

63. *Id.* (quoting Lee v. Weisman, 505 U.S. 577, 622 (Souter, J., concurring, quoting Madison, *Memorial and Remonstrance against Religious Assessments* (1785), *in* 5 THE FOUNDERS' CONSTITUTION 83 (P. Kurland & R. Lerner, eds., 1987))).

64. *Id.* (quoting Letter from James Madison to Edward Livingston (July 10, 1822), *in* 5 THE FOUNDERS' CONSTITUTION, *supra* note 63, at 106, and Letter from James Madison to J. Adams (Sept. 1833) *in* RELIGION AND POLITICS IN THE EARLY REPUBLIC 120 (D. Dreisbach, ed., 1996)).

65. Lee, 505 U.S. at 612–13, 615–18, 620–27, 630–31 (Souter, J., concurring).

11—LEARNERS

1. Engel, 370 U.S. at 447 n.3 (Stewart, J., dissenting).

2. Planned Parenthood v. Connecticut, 381 U.S. 479 (1965).

3. *Id.* at 488–89 (Goldberg, J., concurring).

4. *Id.* at 490.

5. *Id.* at 529–30 (Stewart, J., dissenting) (quoting U.S. v. Darby, 312 U.S. 100, 124 (1941)).

6. *Id.* at 530.

7. Time, Inc. v. Pape, 401 U.S. 279 (1971).

8. *Id.* at 290.

9. Abood v. Detroit Bd. of Education, 431 U.S. 209 (1977).

10. *Id.* at 234.

11. *Id.* at 234 n.31.

12. Tibbs v. Florida, 457 U.S. 31 (1982).

13. *Id.* at 40.

14. *Id.* at 40 n.14 (quoting 1 ANNALS OF CONG. 434 (1789)).

15. Lyng v. Northwest Indian Cemetery Protective Ass'n, 485 U.S. 439 (1988).

16. *Id.* at 452.

17. *Id.*

18. *Id.* (quoting THE FEDERALIST NO. 10 (James Madison)).

19. City of Boerne v. Flores, 521 U.S. 507 (1997).

20. *Id.* at 555 (O'Connor, J., dissenting) (quoting Committee Draft of the Virginia Declaration of Rights, 1 PAPERS OF GEORGE MASON 284–85 (R. Rutland ed. 1970)).

21. *Id.* (O'Connor, J., dissenting).

22. *Id.* (O'Connor, J., dissenting) (quoting Galliard Hunt, *James Madison and Religious Liberty*, 1 ANNUAL REPORT OF THE AMERICAN HISTORICAL ASSOCIATION 163, 166–167 (1901)).

23. *Id.* (O'Connor, J., dissenting).

24. *Id.* at 555–56 (O'Connor, J., dissenting) (quoting Hunt, *James Madison and Religious Liberty*, *supra* note 22, at 166–67).

25. *Id.* at 556–57 (O'Connor, J., dissenting).

26. *Id.* at 561 (O'Connor, J., dissenting) (quoting MADISON, *Memorial and Remonstrance*, *in* 2 WRITINGS OF JAMES MADISON 184–85 (G. Hunt, ed., 1901)) (alteration in original) (citations omitted).

27. *Id.* at 561 (O'Connor, J., dissenting).

28. *Id.* at 2746 (O'Connor, J., concurring).

29. *Id.* (O'Connor, J., concurring) (quoting MADISON, *Memorial and Remonstrance*, *in* 2 WRITINGS OF JAMES MADISON 183, 184 (G. Hunt, ed., 1901)).

30. *Id.* at 2747 (O'Connor, J., concurring).

31. Kelo v. City of New London, 125 S. Ct. 2655 (2005).

32. *Id.* at 2675 (O'Connor, J., dissenting).

33. *Id.* at 2677 (O'Connor, J., dissenting) (quoting JAMES MADISON, *Property* (Mar. 29, 1792), *in* 14 THE PAPERS OF JAMES MADISON, *supra* chap. 1, note 2, at 266).

12—Inconsistents

1. Wisconsin v. Yoder, 406 U.S. 205 (1972).

2. *Id.* at 218 n.9.

3. Lynch v. Donnelly, 465 U.S. 668 (1984).

4. *Id.* at 675 n.2.

5. First Nat'l Bank v. Bellotti, 435 U.S. 765 (1978).

6. *Id.* at 799 n.4 (Burger, C.J., concurring).

7. *Id.* (internal citations omitted).

8. Schad v. Mt. Ephraim, 452 U.S. 61 (1981).

9. *Id.* at 87–88 (Burger, C.J., dissenting) (internal citations omitted).

10. Van Orden v. Perry, 125 S. Ct. 2854 (2005).

11. *Id.* at 2873 (Stevens, J., dissenting).

12. *Id.* (quoting Letter from James Madison to Edward Livingston (July 10, 1822), *in* 5 THE FOUNDERS' CONSTITUTION, *supra* chap. 10, note 63, at 105–6).

13. *Id.* at 2884 (Stevens, J., dissenting).

14. McIntyre v. Ohio Elections Comm'n, 514 U.S. 334 (1990).

15. *Id.* at 342.

16. *Id.* at 341.

17. *Id.* at 343 n.6.

18. California Dem. Party v. Jones, 530 U.S. 567 (2000).

19. *Id.* at 591 n.2 (Stevens, J., dissenting).

20. Houchins v. KQED, Inc., 438 U.S. 1 (1978).

21. *Id.* at 31 (Stevens, J., dissenting).

22. *Id.* at 31–32 (quoting Madison 9 WRITINGS OF JAMES MADISON 103 (G. Hunt, ed., 1910)).

23. Ft. Wayne Books v. Ind., 489 U.S. 46 (1989).

24. *Id.* at 72 (Stevens, J., concurring in part and dissenting in part).

25. *Id.* at 85 (Stevens, J., concurring in part and dissenting in part) (quoting Near v. Minn. ex rel. Olson, 283 U.S. 697, 718 (quoting 4 WRITINGS OF JAMES MADISON 544 (1865))) (internal citations omitted).

26. Lucas v. South Carolina Coastal Council, 505 U.S. 1003 (1992).

27. *Id.* at 1071–72 (Stevens, J., dissenting) (internal citations omitted).

28. *Id.* at 1072 n.7 (Stevens, J., dissenting).

29. Lee, 505 U.S. at 631 (Scalia, J., dissenting) (quoting County of Allegheny v. ACLU, 492 U.S. 573, 670 (1989) (Kennedy, J., concurring in judgment in part and dissenting in part)).

30. *Id.* at 632 (Scalia, J., dissenting).

31. *Id.* at 634 (Scalia, J., dissenting) (quoting INAUGURAL ADDRESSES OF THE PRESIDENTS OF THE UNITED STATES, S. Doc. 101–10 at 28 (1989)).

32. City of Boerne v. Flores, 521 U.S. 507, 542 (1997) (Scalia, J., concurring).

33. City of Boerne, 521 U.S. at 542 (Scalia, J., concurring).

34. *Id.* at 541.

35. Locke v. Davey, 540 U.S. 712 (2004).

36. Locke, 540 U.S. at 726–27 (Scalia, J., dissenting).

37. *Id.* at 727 (Scalia, J., dissenting) (quoting A Bill Establishing a Provision for Teachers of the Christian Religion (1784), reprinted *in* Everson, 330 U.S. at 72) (alterations in original).

38. *Id.* at 679 (Scalia, J., dissenting).

39. *Id.* at 679–80 (Scalia, J., dissenting).

40. *Id.* at 693 (Scalia, J., dissenting).

41. Lucas, 505 U.S. at 1057 n.23 (Blackmun, J., dissenting).

42. *Id.* at 1028 n.15.

43. *Id.* at 1028 n.15 (internal citations omitted) (quoting James Madison, Speech Proposing Bill of Rights (June 8, 1789), *in* 12 THE PAPERS OF JAMES MADISON, *supra* chap. 1, note 2, at 201).

44. Letter from Madison to Wallace (Aug. 23, 1785), *supra, in* JAMES MADISON: WRITINGS, *supra* chap. 1, note 3, at 41.

45. Harmelin v. Michigan, 501 U.S. 957 (1991).

46. *Id.* at 995–96 (Scalia, J., plurality opinion).

47. *Id.* at 977.

48. *Id.* at 977–78.

49. *Id.* at 977 n.7 (internal citations omitted).

50. THE FEDERALIST NO. 47, at 276–79 (James Madison) (Jack N. Rakove, ed., 1999).

51. *Id.* at 853 (Thomas, J., concurring).

52. *Id.* at 854 (Thomas, J., concurring) (quoting Madison, Memorial and Remonstrance against Religious Assessments, reprinted *in* Everson, 330 U.S. at 66 (appendix to dissent of Rutledge, J.)).

53. *Id.* at 855 (Thomas, J., concurring) (quoting Madison, Memorial and Remonstrance against Religious Assessments).

54. *Id.* at 856 (Thomas, J., concurring) (quoting SEPARATION OF CHURCH AND STATE, *supra* chap. 1, note 34, at 22) (internal citation omitted).

55. *Id.* at 856–57 (Thomas, J., concurring).

56. *Id.* at 856 (Thomas, J., concurring).

57. Elk Grove Unified School District v. Newdow, 542 U.S. 1 (2004).

58. *Id.* at 45 (Thomas, J., concurring).

59. *Id.* at 49.

60. McIntyre, 514 U.S. at 369 (Thomas, J., concurring).

61. *Id.* at 359 (Thomas, J., concurring).

62. Nixon v. Shrink Missouri Gov't PAC, 528 U.S. 377 (2000).

63. *Id.* at 410–11 (Thomas, J., dissenting) (quoting MADISON, *Report on the Resolutions* (1799), *in* 6 WRITINGS OF JAMES MADISON 397 (G. Hunt, ed., 1906)) (internal citations omitted).

64. *Id.* at 424 & n.9 (Thomas, J., dissenting) (quoting THE FEDERALIST NO. 10, at 78 (James Madison) (Clinton Rossiter, ed., New York: Mentor, 1961)) (internal citation omitted).

65. *Id.* (Thomas, J., dissenting) (quoting THE FEDERALIST NO. 10, at 80 (James Madison) (Clinton Rossiter, ed., New York: Mentor, 1961)).

66. Kelo, 125 S. Ct. at 2678 (Thomas, J., dissenting).

67. *Id.* at 2678–79 (Thomas, J., dissenting) (internal citations and quotations omitted).

68. *Id.* at 2679 (Thomas, J., dissenting) (quoting JAMES MADISON, *Property* (Mar. 29, 1792), *in* 14 THE PAPERS OF JAMES MADISON, *supra* chap. 1, note 2, at 267).

69. U.S. v. Hubbell, 530 U.S. 27 (2000).

70. *Id.* at 49 (Thomas, J., concurring).

71. *Id.* at 52–53 (Thomas, J., concurring) (internal citations omitted).

72. *Id.* at 53 (Thomas, J., concurring).

13—NAME DROPPERS

1. Minersville School Dist. v. Gobitis, 310 U.S. 586 (1940).

2. *Id.* at 594.

3. *Id.*
4. West Virginia v. Barnette, 319 U.S. 624 (1943).
5. *Id.* at 652–53 (Frankfurter, J., dissenting).
6. Dennis v. United States, 341 U.S. 494 (1951).
7. *Id.* at 519 (Frankfurter, J., concurring) (quoting THE FEDERALIST NO. 41).
8. THE FEDERALIST NO. 41, at 227 (James Madison) (Jack N. Rakove, ed., 1999).
9. *Id.* at 228.
10. *Id.* at 231.
11. Dennis, 341 U.S. at 521 (Frankfurter, J., concurring).
12. Joseph Burstyn, Inc. v. Wilson, 343 U.S. 495 (1952).
13. *Id.* at 518 (Frankfurter, J., concurring).
14. Johnson v. Eisentrager, 339 U.S. 763 (1950).
15. *Id.* at 774–75.
16. *Id.* at 775.
17. *Id.* at 774 n.6.
18. Kunz v. New York, 340 U.S. 290 (1951).
19. *Id.* at 310 (Jackson, J., dissenting).
20. *Id.* at 310 n.9 (quoting Frohwerk v. United States, 249 U.S. 204 (1919)) (internal citations omitted).
21. Letter from Madison to Bradford (Jan. 24, 1774), *supra*, *in* JAMES MADISON: WRITINGS, *supra* chap. 1, note 3, at 7.
22. Jack N. Rakove, *Notes*, *in* JAMES MADISON: WRITINGS, *supra* chap. 1, note 3, at 924, 924.
23. Dennis, 341 U.S. at 571.
24. Wallace v. Jaffree, 472 U.S. 38 (1985).
25. *Id.* at 113–14 (Rehnquist, J., dissenting).
26. *Id.* at 106 (Rehnquist, J., dissenting).
27. *Id.* at 92 (Rehnquist, J., dissenting).
28. *Id.* at 94 (Rehnquist, J., dissenting) (quoting 1 ANNALS OF CONG. 434 (1789)).
29. *Id.* at 95 (Rehnquist, J., dissenting).
30. *Id.* at 96 (Rehnquist, J., dissenting) (quoting 1 ANNALS OF CONG. 730–31 (1789)). Rehnquist cited this passage in the Annals of Congress at 730–31; however, the quote occurs on 758.
31. *Id.* (Rehnquist, J., dissenting).
32. *Id.* (Rehnquist, J., dissenting).
33. *Id.* at 96–97 (Rehnquist, J., dissenting).
34. *Id.*
35. *Id.* at 97–98 (Rehnquist, J., dissenting).
36. *Id.* at 98 (Rehnquist, J., dissenting).
37. *Id.* at 98–99 (Rehnquist, J., dissenting).
38. *Id.* at 103 (Rehnquist, J., dissenting).
39. 1 ANNALS OF CONG. 758 (1789) (emphasis added).
40. JEFFERSON, *An Act for Establishing Religious Freedom* (1779), *supra*, *in* THE LIFE AND SELECTED WORKS OF THOMAS JEFFERSON, *supra* chap. 3, note 47, at 289 (emphasis added).

41. 1 ANNALS OF CONG. 759 (1789).

42. *See* SCHWARTZ, THE GREAT RIGHTS OF MANKIND, *supra* chap. 1, note 32, at 242–43; Alley, *Public Education and the Public Good, supra* chap. 1, note 21, at 306; Douglas Laycock, *"Nonpreferential" Aid to Religion: A False Claim about Original Intent,* 27 WM. & MARY L. REV. 875, 876, 882–83 (1986); TINSLEY E. YARBROUGH, THE REHNQUIST COURT AND THE CONSTITUTION 163 (New York: Oxford University Press, 2000).

43. Anderson v. Celebrezze, 460 U.S. 780 (1983).

44. *Id.* at 813 (Rehnquist, J., dissenting) (quoting Storer v. Brown, 415 U.S. 724, 736 (1974)) (internal citations omitted).

45. Verdugo-Urquidez, 494 U.S. at 266.

46. *Id.*

47. *Id.* (quoting 1 ANNALS OF CONG. 438 (1789)).

48. *Id.* (internal citations omitted).

49. *Id.* at 722.

50. *Id.* at 722–23.

TABLE OF CASES

References

Abney, David L. 1994. Constitutional Interpretation: Moving toward a Jurisprudence of Commonsense. *Temple Law Review* 67:931.

Adair, Douglass. 1951. The Tenth Federalist Revisited. *William and Mary Quarterly* 8:48.

———. 1957. "That Politics May be Reduced to a Science": David Hume, James Madison, and the Tenth *Federalist*. *Huntington Library Quarterly* 20:343.

Alley, Robert S. 1995. How Much God in the Schools? Public Education and the Public Good. *William and Mary Bill of Rights Journal*. J. 4:277.

Amar, Akhil Reed. 1998. *The Bill of Rights: Creation and Reconstruction*. New Haven: Yale University Press.

Ames, Fisher. 1983. *Works of Fisher Ames as Published by Seth Ames*, edited by W. B. Allen. 2 volumes. Indianapolis: Liberty Fund.

Arkin, Marc M. 1995. "The Intractable Principle": David Hume, James Madison, Religion, and the Tenth Federalist. *American Journal of Legal History* 39:148.

Aynes, Richard L. 1988. The Antislavery and Abolitionist Background of John A. Bingham. *Catholic University Law Review* 37:881.

Baker, John S., Jr. 1991. The Establishment Clause as Intended: No Preference among Sects and Pluralism in a Large Commercial Republic. In *The Bill of Rights: Original Meaning and Current Understanding*, edited by Eugene W. Hickok, Jr. Charlottesville: University Press of Virginia.

Balkin, J. M. 1995. Populism and Progressivism as Constitutional Categories. *Yale Law Journal* 104:1935.

Banning, Lance. 1995a. *Jefferson & Madison: Three Conversations from the Founding*. Madison, Wisc.: Madison House.

———. 1995b. *The Sacred Fire of Liberty: James Madison and the Founding of the Federal Republic*. Ithaca: Cornell University Press.

Beer, Samuel H. 1993. *To Make a Nation: The Rediscovery of American Federalism*. Cambridge, Mass.: Belknap.

Berns, Walter. 1977. Religion and the Founding Principle. In *The Moral Foundations of the American Republic*, edited by Robert H. Horwitz. Charlottesville: University Press of Virginia.

———. 2002. James Madison on Religion and Politics. In *James Madison and the Future of Limited Government*, edited by John Samples. Washington, D.C.: Cato Institute.

Blasi, Vincent. 2002. School Vouchers and Religious Liberty: Seven Questions from Madison's Memorial and Remonstrance. *Cornell Law Review* 87:783.

Bobertz, Bradley C. 1999. The Brandeis Gambit: The Making of America's "First Freedom," 1909–1931. *William and Mary Law Review* 40:557.

Bowling, Kenneth R. 1988. "A Tub to the Whale": The Founding Fathers and Adoption of the Federal Bill of Rights. *Journal of the Early Republic* 8:223.

Branson, Roy. 1979. James Madison and the Scottish Enlightenment. *Journal of the History of Ideas* 40:235.

Brant, Irving. 1950. *James Madison: Father of the Constitution, 1787–1800*. Indianapolis: Bobbs-Merrill.

———. 1951. Madison: On the Separation of Church and State. *William and Mary Quarterly* 8:3.

———. 1965. *The Bill of Rights: Its Origin and Meaning*. Indianapolis: Bobbs-Merrill.

Brown, Steven P. 2008. Mirroring Madison. In *James Madison: Philosopher, Founder, and Statesman*, edited by John R. Vile et al. Athens: Ohio University Press.

Calvin, John. 1960. *Institutes of the Christian Religion*, edited by John T. McNeill, translated by Ford Lewis Battles. 2 volumes. Philadelphia: Westminster.

Chomsky, Carol. 1990. The United States–Dakota War Trials: A Study in Military Injustice. *Stanford Law Review* 43:13.

Clancy, Thomas K. 1994. The Role of Individualized Suspicion in Assessing the Reasonableness of Searches and Seizures. *University of Memphis Law Review* 25:483.

Claus, Lawrence. 2004. Protecting Rights from Rights: Enumeration, Disparagement, and the Ninth Amendment. *Notre Dame Law Review* 79:585.

Cordes, Mark W. 2000. Politics, Religion, and the First Amendment. *DePaul Law Review* 50:111.

Cunningham, Clark D. 1988. A Linguistic Analysis of the Meanings of "Search" in the Fourth Amendment: A Search for Common Sense. *Iowa Law Review* 73:541.

Currie, David P. 1999. God & Caesar & President Madison. *The Green Bag* 3(2):11.

Curtis, Michael Kent. 2000. *Free Speech, "The People's Darling Privilege": Struggles for Freedom of Expression in American History*. Durham, N.C.: Duke University Press.

Davies, Thomas Y. 1999. Recovering the Original Fourth Amendment. *Michigan Law Review* 98:547.

———. 2002. The Fictional Character of Law-and-Order Originalism: A Case Study of the Distortions and Evasions of Framing-Era Arrest Doctrine in *Atwater v. Lago Vista*. *Wake Forest Law Review* 37:239.

Diggins, John P. 1984. *The Lost Soul of American Politics: Virtue, Self-Interest, and the Foundations of Liberalism*. Chicago: University of Chicago Press.

Dorn, James A. 2002. The Rule of Law and Freedom in Emerging Democracies: A Madisonian Perspective. In *James Madison and the Future of Limited Government*, edited by John Samples. Washington, D.C.: Cato Institute.

Duncan, Jonathan. 1995. Looks Like a Waiting Period for the Brady Bill: Tenth Amendment Challenges to a Controversial Unfunded Mandate. *Kansas Law Review* 43:835.

Easterbrook, Frank H. 1994. The State of Madison's Vision of the State: A Public Choice Perspective. *Harvard Law Review* 107:1328.

Ely, James W., Jr. 1998. *The Guardian of Every Other Right: A Constitutional History of Property Rights*. New York: Oxford University Press.

———. 1999. The Oxymoron Reconsidered: Myth and Reality in the Origins of Substantive Due Process. *Constitutional Commentary* 16:315.

Farber, Daniel A., and Suzanna Sherry. 1990. *A History of the American Constitution*. St. Paul: West Publishing.

Finkelman, Paul. 1990. James Madison and the Bill of Rights: A Reluctant Paternity. Supreme Court Review 1990:301.

Franck, Thomas M. 1997. Is Personal Freedom a Western Value? *American Journal of International Law* 91:593.

Gey, Steven G. 2000. When Is Religious Speech Not "Free Speech"? *University of Illinois Law Review* 2000:379.

Goldwin,.Robert A. 1997. *From Parchment to Power: How James Madison Used the Bill of Rights to Save the Constitution.* Washington, D.C.: American Enterprise Institute Press.

Gordon, Daniel R. 2001/2002. Due North: James Madison, the American Modern Wall of Separation, and the Canadian Indian Residential Schools. *Cumberland Law Review* 32:281.

Grunes, Rodney A. 2008. James Madison and Religious Freedom. In *James Madison: Philosopher, Founder, and Statesman,* edited by John R. Vile, et al., Athens: Ohio University Press.

Hamilton, Alexander, James Madison, and John Jay. 1961. *The Federalist Papers,* edited by Clinton Rossiter. New York: Mentor.

Harrington, Matthew. 2002. "Public Use" and the Original Understanding of the So-Called "Takings" Clause. *Hastings Law Journal* 53:1245.

———. 2004. Regulatory Takings and the Original Understanding of the Takings Clause. *William and Mary Law Review* 45:2053.

Heyman, Steven J. 1998. Righting the Balance: An Inquiry into the Foundations and Limits of Freedom of Expression. *Boston University Law Review* 78:1275.

———. 2003. Ideological Conflict and the First Amendment. *Chicago-Kent Law Review* 78:531.

Himmelfarb, Gertrude. 1984. *The Idea of Poverty: England in the Early Industrial Age.* New York: Knopf.

Hobson, Charles F. 1979. The Negative on State Laws: James Madison, the Constitution, and the Crisis of Republican Government. *William and Mary Quarterly* 36:215.

———. 1990. James Madison, the Bill of Rights, and the Problem of the States. *William and Mary Law Review* 31:267.

Horwitz, Robert H. 1977. John Locke and the Preservation of Liberty: A Perennial Problem of Civic Education. In *The Moral Foundations of the American Republic,* edited by Robert H. Horwitz. Charlottesville: University Press of Virginia.

Howard, A. E. Dick. 1985. James Madison and the Founding of the Republic. In *James Madison on Religious Liberty,* edited by Robert S. Alley. Buffalo: Prometheus Books.

Hume, David. 2000. *A Treatise of Human Nature,* edited by David Fate Norton & Mary J. Norton. Oxford: Oxford University Press.

Jefferson, Thomas. 1993. *The Life and Selected Writings of Thomas Jefferson,* edited by Adrienne Koch and William Peden. New York: Modern Library.

Kalinowski, Franklin A. 1993. David Hume on the Philosophic Underpinnings of Interest Group Politics. *Polity* 25:355.

Kelso, R. Randall. 1995. The Natural Law Tradition on the Modern Supreme Court: Not Burke, but the Enlightenment Tradition Represented by Locke, Madison, and Marshall. *St. Mary's Law Journal* 26:1051.

Kendall, Walter J., III. 2005. Madison and the Market Economy. *Quinnipac Law Review* 23:1097.

Kendrick, Benjamin B. 1914. *The Journal of the Joint Committee of Fifteen on Reconstruction, 39th Congress, 1865–1867.* New York: Longman's and Green.

Ketcham, Ralph L. 1958a. James Madison and the Nature of Man. *Journal of the History of Ideas* 19:62.

———. 1958b. Notes on James Madison's Sources for the Tenth Federalist Paper. *Midwest Journal of Political Science* 1:20.

———. 1990. *James Madison: A Biography*. Charlottesville: University Press of Virginia.

Kloppenberg, James T. 1987. The Virtues of Liberalism: Christianity, Republicanism, and Ethics in Early American Political Discourse. *Journal of American History* 74:9.

———. 1998. *The Virtues of Liberalism*. New York: Oxford University Press.

Kobylka, Joseph F., and Bradley Kent Carter. 1987. Madison, *The Federalist*, & the Constitutional Order: Human Nature & Institutional Structure. *Polity* 20:190.

Koch, Adrienne, and Harry Ammon. 1948. The Virginia and Kentucky Resolutions: An Episode in Jefferson's and Madison's Defense of Civil Liberties. *William and Mary Quarterly* 5:145.

Kramer, Larry D. 1999. Madison's Audience. *Harvard Law Review* 112:611.

Kramnick, Isaac. 1999. The "Great National Discussion": This Discourse of Politics in 1787. In *What Did the Constitution Mean to Early Americans?* edited by Edward Countryman. Boston: Bedford.

Labunski, Richard. 2006. *James Madison and the Struggle for the Bill of Rights*. New York: Oxford University Press.

Lash, Kurt T. 1998. Power and the Subject of Religion. *Ohio State Law Journal* 59:1069.

Laycock, Douglas. 1986. "Nonpreferential" Aid to Religion: A False Claim about Original Intent. *William and Mary Law Review* 27:875.

Leibiger, Stuart. 1993. James Madison and Amendments to the Constitution, 1787–1789: "Parchment Barriers." *Journal of Southern History* 59:441.

Levy, Leonard W. 1963. *Legacy of Suppression: Freedom of Speech and Press in Early American History*. New York: Harper Torchbooks.

———. 1985. The Legacy Reexamined. *Stanford Law Review* 37:767.

———. 1987. Bill of Rights. In *Essays on the Making of the Constitution*, edited by Leonard W. Levy. New York: Oxford University Press.

———. 1999. *Origins of the Bill of Rights*. New Haven: Yale University Press.

Lindquist, Stefanie A., and Rorie Spill Solberg. 2007. Judicial Review by the Burger and Rehnquist Courts: Explaining Justices' Responses to Constitutional Challenges. *Political Research Quarterly* 60:71.

Lindsay, Thomas. 1991. James Madison on Religion and Politics: Rhetoric and Reality. *American Political Science Review* 85:1321.

Locke, John. 1980. *Second Treatise of Government*, edited by C. B. Macpherson. Indianapolis: Hackett.

Long, Nash E. 1998. The "Constitutional Remand": Judicial Review of Constitutionally Dubious Statutes. *Journal of Law and Politics* 14:667.

McAllister, Marc Chase. 2004. Human Dignity and Individual Liberty in Germany and the United States as Examined through Each Country's Leading Abortion Cases. *Tulsa Journal of Comparative and International Law* 11:491.

McConnell, Michael. 1990. The Origins and Historical Understandings of Free Exercise of Religion. *Harvard Law Review* 103:1409.

McCoy, Drew R. 1980. *The Elusive Republic: Political Economy in Jeffersonian America*. Chapel Hill: University of North Carolina Press.

McDonald, Forrest. 1985. *Novus Ordo Seclorum: The Intellectual Origins of the Constitution*. Lawrence: University Press of Kansas.

McGinnis, John O. 1996. The Once and Future Property-Based Vision of the First Amendment. *University of Chicago Law Review* 63:49.

Maclin, Tracey. 1993. The Central Meaning of the Fourth Amendment. *William and Mary Law Review* 35:197.

Maddigan, Michael M. 1993. The Establishment Clause, Civil Religion, and the Public Church. *California Law Review* 81:293.

Madison, James. 1865. *Letters and Other Writings of James Madison*. 4 volumes. Philadelphia: Lippincott.

———. 1910. *The Writings of James Madison*, edited by Galliard Hunt. 9 volumes. New York: Putnam.

———. 1962-1991. *The Papers of James Madison, Congressional Series, 1751–1801*. 17 volumes. Chicago and Charlottesville: University of Chicago Press and University Press of Virginia.

———. 1966. *Notes of Debates in the Federal Convention of 1787 Reported by James Madison*, edited by James Madison. New York: Norton.

———. 1973. *The Mind of the Founder: Sources of the Political Thought of James Madison*, edited by Marvin Myers. Indianapolis: Bobbs-Merrill.

———. 1984-2008. *The Papers of James Madison, Presidential Series, 1809–1817*. 6 volumes. Charlottesville: University of Virginia Press.

———. 1999. *James Madison: Writings*, edited by Jack N. Rakove. New York: Library of America.

Matthews, Richard K. 1995. *If Men Were Angels: James Madison & the Heartless Empire of Reason*. Lawrence: University Press of Kansas.

Morgan, Robert J. 1988. *James Madison on the Constitution and the Bill of Rights*. New York: Greenwood Press.

Muñoz, Vincent Phillip. 2003. James Madison's Principle of Religious Liberty. *American Political Science Review* 97:17.

Nedelsky, Jennifer. 1990. *Private Property and the Limits of American Constitutionalism: The Madisonian Framework and Its Legacy*. Chicago: University of Chicago Press.

Neuborne, Burt. 1999. Toward a Democracy-Centered Reading of the First Amendment. *Northwestern University Law Review* 93:1055.

———. 2004. The House Was Quiet and the World Was Calm: The Reader Became the Book. *Vanderbilt Law Review* 57:2007.

Olken, Samuel R. 2002. The Business of Expression: Economic Liberty, Political Factions, and the Forgotten First Amendment Legacy of Justice George Sutherland. *William and Mary Bill of Rights Journal* 10:249.

O'Neill, Michael Edmund. 2002. The Fifth Amendment in Congress: Revisiting the Privilege against Compelled Self-Incrimination. *Georgetown Law Journal* 90:2445.

Padula, Guy. 2001. *Madison v. Marshall: Popular Sovereignty, Natural Law, and the United States Constitution*. Lanham, Md.: Lexington Books.

Pilon, Roger. 2002. Madison's Constitutional Vision: The Legacy of Enumerated Powers. In *James Madison and the Future of Limited Government*, edited by John Samples. Washington, D.C.: Cato Institute.

Pocock, J. G. A. 1975. *The Machiavellian Moment: Florentine Political Thought and the*

Atlantic Republican Tradition. Princeton, N.J.: Princeton University Press.

Rakove, Jack N. 1990. The Madisonian Theory of Rights. *William and Mary Law Review* 31:245.

———. 1996. *Original Meanings: Politics and Ideas in the Making of the Constitution.* New York: Knopf.

———. 2002. *James Madison and the Creation of the American Republic.* New York: Longman.

Read, James H. 1995. "Our Complicated System": James Madison on Power and Liberty. *Political Theory* 23:452.

Reid, Charles J., Jr. 1999. The Fundamental Freedom: Judge John T. Noonan Jr.'s Historiography of Religious Liberty. *Marquette Law Review* 83:367.

Reiss, David. 2002. Jefferson and Madison as Icons in Judicial History: A Study of Religion Clause Jurisprudence. *Maryland Law Review* 61:94.

Riemer, Neal. 1958. Two Conceptions of the Genius of American Politics. *Journal of Politics* 20:695.

———. 1986. *James Madison: Creating the American Constitution.* Washington, D.C.: Congressional Quarterly.

Riggs, Robert E. 1990. Substantive Due Process in 1791. *Wisconsin Law Review* 1990:941.

Rosen, Gary. 1999. *American Compact: James Madison and the Problem of Founding.* Lawrence: University Press of Kansas.

Rossum, Ralph. 1991. "Self-Incrimination": The Original Intent. In *The Bill of Rights: Original Meaning and Current Understanding*, edited by Eugene W. Hickok, Jr. Charlottesville: University Press of Virginia.

Rutland, Robert Allen. 1962. *The Birth of the Bill of Rights, 1776–1791.* New York: Collier.

———. 1987. *James Madison: The Founding Father.* Columbia: University of Missouri Press.

———. 1990. The Trivialization of the Bill of Rights: One Historian's View of How the Purposes of the First Ten Amendments Have Been Defiled. *William and Mary Law Review* 31:287.

Schwartz, Bernard. 1971. *The Bill of Rights: A Documentary History.* 2 volumes. New York: Chelsea House.

———. 1992. *The Great Rights of Mankind: A History of the American Bill of Rights.* Madison, Wisc.: Madison House.

Sheehan, Colleen A. 1992. The Politics of Public Opinion: James Madison's "Notes on Government." *William and Mary Quarterly* 49:609.

———. 2009. *James Madison and the Spirit of Republican Self-Government.* New York: Cambridge University Press.

Sheldon, Garrett Ward. 2001. *The Political Philosophy of James Madison.* Baltimore: The Johns Hopkins University Press.

Singleton, Solveig. 1999. Reviving a First Amendment Absolutism for the Internet. *Texas Review of Law and Politics* 3:279.

Smith, Adam. 1994. *An Inquiry into the Nature and Causes of the Wealth of Nations.* New York: The Modern Library.

———. 2000. *The Theory of Moral Sentiments.* Amherst, N.Y.: Prometheus Books.

Smith, Norman B. 1986. "Shall Make No Law Abridging...": An Analysis of the

Neglected, but Nearly Absolute, Right of Petition. *University of Cincinnati Law Review* 54:1153.

Smith, Rodney K. 2003. James Madison, John Witherspoon, and Oliver Cowdery: The First Amendment and the 134th Section of the Doctrine and Covenants. *Brigham Young University Law Review* 2003:891.

Smith, Ron. 1996. Compelled Cost Disclosure of Grass Roots Lobbying Expenses: Necessary Government Voyeurism or Chilled Political Speech? *Kansas Journal of Law and Public Policy* 6:115.

Smith, Steven D. 2000. Blooming Confusion: Madison's Mixed Legacy. *Indiana Law Journal* 75:61.

Sorenson, Leonard R. 1995. *Madison on the "General Welfare" of America: His Consistent Constitutional Vision.* Lanham, Md.: Rowman & Littlefield.

Steinberg, David E. 2004. The Original Understanding of Unreasonable Searches and Seizures. *Florida Law Review* 56:1051.

Storing, Herbert J., editor. 1981. *The Complete Anti-Federalist.* 7 volumes. Chicago: University of Chicago Press.

Sunstein, Cass R. 1995. *Democracy and the Problem of Free Speech.* New York: Free Press.

Thomas, George C., III. 2005. Time Travel, Hovercrafts, and the Framers: James Madison Sees the Future and Rewrites the Fourth Amendment. *Notre Dame Law Review* 80:1451.

Thompson, Dennis F. 1976. The Education of a Founding Father: The Reading List for John Witherspoon's Course in Political Theory, as Taken by James Madison. *Political Theory* 4:523.

Troy, Daniel E. 1999. Advertising: Not "Low Value" Speech. *Yale Journal on Regulation* 16:85.

Underkuffler, Laura S. 1990. On Property: An Essay. *Yale Law Journal.* 100:127.

Veit, Helen E., et al., editors. 1991. *Creating the Bill of Rights: The Documentary Record from the First Federal Congress.* Baltimore: The Johns Hopkins University Press.

U.S. Congress. *Annals of the Congress of the United States, 1789–1824.* 42 volumes. Washington, D.C., 1834–1856.

———. *Congressional Globe.* 46 volumes. Washington, D.C., 1834–1873.

———. *Senate Journal.* 1789. 1st Cong., 1st sess., 25 August–9 September.

Vile, John R. 2008. James Madison's *Report of 1800.* In *James Madison: Philosopher, Founder, and Statesman,* edited by John R. Vile, et al. Athens: Ohio University Press.

Viteritti, Joseph P., and Gerald J. Russello. 1997. Community and American Federalism: Images Romantic and Real. *Virginia Journal of Social Policy and Law* 4:683.

Weisberger, Bernard A. 2000. *America Afire: Jefferson, Adams, and the First Contested Election.* New York: Perennial.

Werner, John M. 1972. David Hume and America. *Journal of the History of Ideas* 33:439.

Wills, Garry. 1981. *Explaining America: The Federalist.* Garden City, N.Y.: Doubleday.

Wildenthal, Bryan H. 2007. Nationalizing the Bill of Rights: Revisiting the Original Understanding of the Fourteenth Amendment in 1866–67. *Ohio State Law Journal* 68:1509.

Wilson, James Q. 1990. Interests and Deliberation in the American Republic; or, Why James Madison Would Never Have Won the James Madison Award. *PS: Political*

Science and Politics 23:558.

Witherspoon, John. 1990. *The Selected Writings of John Witherspoon*, edited by Thomas Miller. Carbondale: Southern Illinois University Press.

Wolin, Sheldon S. 2004. *Politics and Vision: Continuity and Innovation in Western Political Thought*. Princeton, N.J.: Princeton University Press.

Wood, Gordon S. 1969. *The Creation of the American Republic 1776–1787*. Chapel Hill: University of North Carolina Press.

Yarbrough, Tinsley E. 2000. *The Rehnquist Court and the Constitution*. Oxford: Oxford UniversityPress.

INDEX